"When You Read This, They Will Have Killed Me"

The Life and Redemption of
Caryl Chessman,
Whose Execution Shook America

ALAN BISBORT

CARROLL & GRAF PUBLISHERS
NEW YORK

"WHEN YOU READ THIS, THEY WILL HAVE KILLED ME"
The Life and Redemption of Caryl Chessman,
Whose Execution Shook America

Carroll & Graf Publishers
An Imprint of Avalon Publishing Group, Inc.
245 West 17th Street
11th Floor
New York, NY 10011

AVALON
publishing group incorporated

The title of this book is derived from a final statement prepared by Caryl Chessman to be publicly read after his execution.

"When you read this," his statement read, "they will have killed me. I will have exchanged oblivion for an unprecedented twelve-year nightmare. And you will have witnessed the final, lethal, ritualistic act. It is my hope and my belief that you will be able to report that I died with dignity, without animal fear and without bravado. I owe that much to myself."

ISBN-13: 978-0-78671-627-2
ISBN-10: 0-78671-627-4

9 8 7 6 5 4 3 2 1

Designed by India Amos, Neuwirth & Associates, Inc.
Printed in the United States of America
Distributed by Publishers Group West

This book is dedicated to the memory of
Joseph E. Longstreth (1920–2003),
without whom the world would never have
known the name or work of Caryl Chessman.

CONTENTS

Introduction ▪ *xi*

PART I ▪ THE BOY BANDIT

1 "Death Row Was the Best Thing Ever to Happen to Me" ▪ 1
2 "Which Way to Hell?" ▪ 15
3 A San Quentin Appetizer: Chessman's First Two Visits ▪ 41
4 The Red Light Bandit ▪ 69
5 San Quentin's Least Wanted (1948–1952) ▪ 107

PART II ▪ THE TRANSFORMATION

6 The Coming of Uncle Joe ▪ 139
7 An Important Visit ▪ 161
8 Down to the Wire ▪ 189
9 Trial by Ordeal: 1955 and Still Alive ▪ 223
10 "King of Death Row" (1956–1957) ▪ 249
11 A Faith Worse Than Death (1958) ▪ 281
12 The Coming of Governor Brown (1959) ▪ 303
13 The Green Room Beckons ▪ 325
14 "I'll See You in the Morning" ▪ 341

Chessman's Legacy: An Afterword ▪ 375

Appendix: "And What If I Failed?" ▪ 379

Notes ▪ 385

Bibliography ▪ 391

Acknowledgments ▪ 397

Index ▪ 401

To find the true path to Paradise one must know the
way to Hell and then avoid it.
                    —NICOLO MACHIAVELLI

There's none so far astray,
Detached, abandoned, as might seem,
As to exclude the hope, the dream
Of fair redemption.
                    —HERMAN MELVILLE, "CLAREL"

INTRODUCTION

*A cat, I am told, has nine lives. If that is true, I know
how a cat feels when, under the most hair-raising conditions, it has been obliged to expend the first eight of
those lives in a chamber-of-horrors battle for survival,
and the Grim Reaper gets it into his head that it will
be great sport to try to bag the ninth. All pussy can
do is spit. Homo sapiens can write books.*
—CARYL CHESSMAN, *The Face of Justice*
(1957)

ON MAY 2, 1960, at 10:03:25 A.M., in the gas chamber at San
Quentin Prison, the State of California began its ninth, and
final, attempt to end the life of Caryl Whittier Chessman. At 10:12
A.M.—despite a stay of execution having been granted only seconds
earlier—Chessman was pronounced dead by the attending physician. The State of California had finally bagged the ninth life of
this remarkable cat. For more than a decade, Chessman had been a
thorn in the state's collective side, as well as a pinprick at America's
conscience and an international cause célèbre. His case drew support
from all corners of the globe and all areas of human endeavor, from
the sacred (Pope John, Albert Schweitzer, Episcopal Bishop James A.

Pike) to the profane (Steve Allen, Shirley MacLaine, Marlon Brando), from the cerebral (Aldous Huxley, Christopher Isherwood, William F. Buckley Jr.) to the mundane—correspondence and petitions of millions of people around the world who'd been touched by his case and his writings. Belgium's Queen Mother, and Eleanor Roosevelt—who by 1960 was, effectively, America's Queen Mother—made pleas to

When *Time* magazine depicted Chessman on the cover of the March 21, 1960, issue, Chessman was at the peak of his fame, both as writer and embodiment of capital punishment's cruel and capricious nature. The story, however, was cranky and unsympathetic, depicting Chessman as "arrogant, self-centered and pathologically egotistical," an unrepentant con who'd "dragged" his case through the courts for twelve years. Nonetheless, his presence on the magazine's cover cemented his nearly iconic status as a figure of note. *Author's collection*

spare his life. People went on hunger strikes, organized "auto caravans" and one rodeo veteran, calling himself a "minuteman," rode his mount from San Francisco to Sacramento, getting signatures for his "Save Chessman" petition along the way. From Brazil alone, a plea for Chessman's life sent to Governor Edmund "Pat" Brown in March 1960 contained 2.6 million signatures, as well as offers from forty Brazilians, many of them women, to die in his place.

Caryl Chessman had even made the cover of *Time* magazine—the ultimate perch of a Cold War–era icon—and was the subject of profiles and commentaries in nearly every major periodical in the United States, Europe, and South America. Hollywood adapted his life story for the screen. He was Topic A on radio and TV talk shows, and fodder for gossip columns. If you are an American of a certain age—born before, say, 1950—you recall the name of Caryl Chessman the way you recall the names Mickey Mantle, Marilyn Monroe, Lenny Bruce, and Bob Dylan.

Since his death in 1960, echoes of Chessman have been heard in every death penalty case and at the scene of every execution in America. If Chessman's death was not the very embodiment of arbitrary, cruel, and/or unusual punishment, then that claim can't convincingly be made for any American subsequently exterminated in the name of justice. His death was as unjustified as it was predictable in the political climate of his times. An only child who died without publicly acknowledged heirs, Chessman has been kept alive over the decades through the memory of those who lived through his last days, through book collectors (his books fetch high prices on used-book Web sites), and through death penalty abolitionists. Now, thanks largely to two troves of letters and unpublished manuscripts preserved by his agent, Joseph Longstreth, and lawyer, Rosalie Asher, Chessman can emerge as a fully fleshed-out human being. His books, too, are making their way back into print, and his voice echoes across the medium of the new millennium—the Internet. One group of especially tireless Chessmaniacs—for lack of a better word—is even committed to proving his innocence of the crimes for which he was executed. All will be revealed, they say, in the middle of the year 2007. That's when, they believe, the identity of the real "red-light bandit" will be released "50 years to the day after California rejected a moratorium on the death penalty." All of this is a half century after the fact of his still inexplicable execution.

■

SO, WHO WAS Caryl Chessman?

In his day, he was the condemned man's Job, languishing on California's Death Row for twelve years. Though such periods of limbo are now routine, Chessman's was at the time the longest tenure in any death house in American history. His nine stays of execution were also an American record. As Chessman himself observed in *The Face of Justice*, the third of four books he wrote and published from his death cell, "I won the dubious distinction of having existed longer under death sentence than any other condemned man in the nation's then 179-year history. Day after day, I would go on breaking my own record."

But Caryl Chessman was many things besides a statistical curiosity. In the twelve years between his sentencing and execution, Chessman lived and tirelessly labored on San Quentin's Death Row, shaping one of the most remarkable bodies of work in American legal history: three wide-selling memoirs: *Cell 2455, Death Row* (1954), *Trial by Ordeal* (1955), *The Face of Justice* (1957), and one novel: *The Kid Was a Killer* (1960), articles for respected journals (*Psychology Today, American Bar Association Journal*), as well as randy men's magazines (*Saga, Argosy*), and the aforementioned trove of unpublished letters, short stories, novels, and plays. This in addition to a nearly unrivaled expertise in American law gleaned from, by his own estimation, "reading or skimming 10,000 legal books." His autodidactic training prompted the celebrity lawyer Melvin Belli—who'd offered Chessman his services pro bono—to call him "one of the sharpest and best-trained lawyers I've ever met." It also prompted George T. Davis—Chessman's famed defense attorney after 1955—to admit to the journalist Irwin Moskowitz, "There have been instances in which Chessman has diplomatically informed me that he knew more about many points of law than I, and the humiliating truth was that he did."

Perhaps Elizabeth Hardwick, in a *Partisan Review* essay published at the time of Chessman's trip to the gas chamber, captured the full flavor of his achievement: "With extraordinary energy, Chessman made, on the very edge of extinction, one of those startling efforts of personal rehabilitation, salvation of the self."

Chessman's personal salvation on Death Row, his transformation

In April 1955, Columbia Pictures released a feature film adaptation of *Cell 2455, Death Row,* playing up its "rebel without a cause" angle, replete with hot cars, hot broads, hot guns, and cold prison bars. Columbia reissued the film again in early 1960, to take advantage of Chessman's by then worldwide notoriety. *Author's collection*

from career criminal to contributing member of society, resembled that of another prisoner who gained fame around the same time— Robert Stroud, the so-called "Birdman of Alcatraz." Stroud was given a death sentence for murdering a prison guard in 1916 (commuted to life imprisonment by President Woodrow Wilson in 1920). He lived for years in solitary confinement; his only companions were the 300 canaries he raised, studied, and chronicled in two books of enduring scientific value. From 1948 to 1959, Chessman and Stroud—arguably the two most famous prisoners of their time—sat in cells less than ten miles apart, reinventing themselves and, to some extent, reshaping the public's perception of the criminal personality. Like Chessman, Stroud drew Hollywood's attention; Burt Lancaster portrayed him in John Frankenheimer's 1962 film *Birdman of Alcatraz*, though Stroud himself was not allowed by prison authorities to view the results.

Chessman's bestselling book *Cell 2455, Death Row* was also adapted into a (less successful) 1955 film, which Chessman also never saw. It was also, posthumously, adapted for a 1977 television film, *Kill Me If You Can*, with Alan Alda as Chessman and Talia Shire as Rosalie Asher. In addition, Chessman's books were translated into twelve languages; journalists from around the world regularly visited him; and popular songs, like Ronnie Hawkins's "The Ballad of Caryl Chessman (Let Him Live, Let Him Live)" and the Dutch hit single, "The Death Song of Chessman," were released to help ward off the death that would eventually claim him. His influence extended even to then unknown songwriters, like the young Merle Haggard, who met Chessman while he was in San Quentin in 1959 serving time for armed robbery; and Neil Diamond, who would include Chessman (along with Edgar Allan Poe, Gunga Din, and Albert Camus) in his litany of those who were "Done Too Soon" (from Diamond's 1970 album, *Tap Root Manuscript*).

Due to his notoriety and the lingering questions surrounding the 1948 trial that brought him to Death Row, Chessman's fate came to embody the very concept of cruel and unusual punishment. He earned this distinction for the excessive sentence he received after a tainted trial in a hostile court presided over by a judge renowned for the severity of his sentences; for the State of California's prolonged and costly

When the Arkansas-bred rockabilly star Ronnie Hawkins recorded "The Ballad of Caryl Chessman (Let Him Live, Let Him Live)" in February 1960, he was the first popular musician to take a stand on the case. At the time, Hawkins was a young journeyman who'd been in the backup band of Conway Twitty and Carl Perkins; this, one of his early solo singles for Roulette was a risky move for him and his label. No stranger to political causes, Hawkins later worked with John Lennon and Yoko Ono on a Toronto Peace Festival and played on a Plastic Ono Band tour. *Author's collection*

effort to thwart every one of his myriad attempts to get a retrial or a proper hearing over the next twelve years; and for the fact that he was paying with his life for crimes in which no life was taken.

What had Caryl Chessman done that would make the State of California so adamant that he die?

The facts of the case, on their face, *seem* simple enough:

Chessman's arrest and sentencing stemmed from a string of robberies in the Los Angeles area over a number of days in January 1948, in which the perpetrator (or perpetrators) used a red spotlight attached to their car, to suggest to victims that they were police. The crimes took place in or around what were known to be popular "lover's lanes," where young people parked to neck and to stare at the lights of the City of Angels. In two of these robberies, a woman was removed from a car and taken to that of the perpetrator(s), where some sort of sexual assault occurred; though testimony conflicted and the graphic details were blurred for propriety's sake in the courtroom, it involved an unsuccessful rape attempt after which the perpetrator(s) forced the victim to perform fellatio. A blow job.

Thus, the perpetrator(s), descriptions of whom varied widely enough to suggest more than one person may have been involved, garnered the nickname "The Red Light Bandit." Caryl Chessman, then twenty-seven, already had an extensive criminal record involving robbery and car theft (but none for sexual assault) dating back to his teenage years. He was spotted in a car matching the one the "bandit" allegedly used. When confronted, he led the police on a wild chase—he was on parole for a previous crime and any arrest would have returned him to Folsom Prison—at the end of which he and an accomplice, a convicted burglar also out on parole, were arrested. The car contained stolen merchandise, a gun and pin-type flashlight matching the ones supposedly used by the Red Light Bandit.

But the physical descriptions of their attackers by the victims did not resemble Chessman. He was never identified by the assaulted women in a proper lineup. After being taken into custody, he was questioned nonstop for seventy-two hours and emerged a physically and mentally beaten man, by his own account losing twelve pounds during the three days he was in police custody. Photographs of him taken after his interrogation reveal a huge gash along his scalp line. Like many a suspect before him in those pre-Miranda ruling days, Chessman had been broken down into a confession. Essentially clearing their books of unsolved crimes, the Los Angeles police charged Chessman with eighteen felonies, including robbery, kidnapping, attempted rape, and "unnatural sex."

Given the climate of corruption within the Los Angeles Police Department at that time—documented by former members of the force Sergeant Charles Stocker and homicide detective Steve Hodel, among others—it is conceivable that the cops were waiting for a marked con like Chessman upon whom to dump a load of unsolved cases. Further, after Chessman's arrest, crimes using the same Red

Light Bandit methods continued to be committed in the Los Angeles area. Thus, it's within the realm of possibility that Chessman was framed, was served—as they said at San Quentin—"bum beef."

In an interview for this book, Hodel, now a private investigator and bestselling author, said, "It happened all the time during those years. Corrupt cops, corrupt judges, all on the take. All were in the employ and or 'doing favors' for those in power. Even 'straight' witnesses were easily corrupted or influenced. All the detectives had to do was tell the witness that 'we have a strong case with lots of other evidence connecting him, we just need the back-up of your ID in court to keep him off the streets.' Most witnesses 'just want to help' and once convinced that the right man is in custody, they are more than willing to stretch things to make a 'maybe it's him' into a 'it's him.'"

It is also conceivable, of course, that Chessman committed all, or some of, the crimes for which he was prosecuted in 1948. But regardless of his guilt or innocence, Chessman's "confession" was beaten out of him, and the travesty of his trial for the Red Light Bandit crimes is on the public record, for anyone to examine.

■

LET'S MAKE ONE thing clear: Caryl Chessman was no innocent or naïf, no martyr or angel. On the contrary, his memoirs, and his decade-long criminal record prior to his fateful arrest, suggest he was an inveterate sociopath on a collision course with prison, a one-man crime wave, a confirmed criminal. Some would insist he was a pathological liar. Even he admitted that his modus operandi as a young "bandit" was to "never tell a policeman or anyone in authority the right time." First arrested at age sixteen, he spent all but fifteen months of the remainder of his twenty-four years behind bars, the last twelve years on Death Row in San Quentin State Prison.

Though he no doubt had a hand in some of the eighteen crimes for which he was tried, Chessman repeatedly and persuasively argued his innocence of the specific crimes that brought him his death sentence.

"I wasn't a rapist who skulked and prowled around lovers' lanes," he adamantly and repeatedly said.

Chessman's iron will may have been his fatal flaw. Brilliant, quick-witted, arrogant, and blunt, Chessman alienated even those who wanted to help him. Maddeningly hard-headed and quixotic in his methods of fighting what he called "nickel-in-the-slot justice," Chessman paid the ultimate price for one singular act of hubris: he defended himself at his 1948 trial. Though he hired lawyers to help prepare his case and petitions for appeal, he personally argued his own case in a courtroom. This, because he'd "developed the habit of doing [his] own fighting" and "was cursed with a mind that would not yield."

"My soul," he famously announced, "is not for sale."

Such chutzpah may be admirable in a stage character or in one of Chessman's short stories, but in the very real life of a Los Angeles courtroom presided over by Judge Charles W. Fricke, it cast him immediately in the role of the hopeless, if not hapless, underdog. It led, inevitably, to conviction. And that conviction, Judge Fricke determined, warranted two death sentences.

The death sentences derived not from the attempted rapes but from a seldom used "Little Lindbergh Law" (Section 209 of the California Penal Code), which made it a capital crime to kidnap a person for the purpose of inflicting physical harm. Between 1942 and 1956, 180 persons were given death sentences in California; only one other person besides Chessman was sentenced to death for crimes in which no one was killed, and that person's sentence was later commuted to life in prison by Governor Edmund G. "Pat" Brown, who refused to intercede in Chessman's case.

Two death sentences for crimes that took no life? Why?

Why indeed? The more one investigates the curious case of Caryl Chessman the more this question stings the mind and challenges what one might have otherwise taken for granted as impossible in a free society. In the end, one is hard-pressed not to admit a disturbing truth: Chessman didn't die because the law demanded it; he died because a loophole in the law demanded it, a freakish whim of the law demanded it. He is the human asterisk, the man who died for something that no American since has had to face.

From the very start, the media depicted Chessman as a "psycho-pathic wild beast in a cage," a first impression Chessman was never able to fully alter no matter how well known he became. He realized, much later, that "caricature replaced reality . . . and I emerged as an ego-swollen, swaggering character, patently guilty, intellectually pretentious, unregenerate, cunning, slippery, vicious . . . which explains in large measure why I have spent nearly twelve years in a death cell."

Regardless of what the world at large thought of Chessman, the State of California came to see him as a threat to its existence, if not to the entire American way of life. Chessman was convicted not just for his crimes but by the times during which he lived, times that are not that different from our own in 2006, when the U.S. Congress can seriously debate whether to suspend habeas corpus and justify torture of prisoners. And he could not have had a less sympathetic representative of American justice than the judge who sentenced him, Charles W. Fricke, dubbed "San Quentin Fricke" for having sentenced more than twice as many men to death than any other judge in California's history.

"In one sense, to criticize Judge Fricke is to criticize America in 1948," wrote the legal scholar Frank J. Parker. "He was a highly representative specimen. America was passing through a period of moral absolutism, both righteous and frightened. These were the years of pride in American power which had triumphed in World War II, of frustration with postwar difficulties, and fear of nuclear holocaust. Also frightening to some in those years was the rapidity with which American life seemed to be changing and they responded by trying to freeze norms of conduct, whether for political power, dissent, race relations, or sexual activities. Regardless of whether Chessman did or did not commit the crimes with which he was charged, one can guess that to many Americans he seemed to typify all that was wrong in America, the way moral values were being trampled on by the young. In a word, he had no respect."

The trial and ensuing appeals, stays, and hearings have been covered, in detail, by many previous books and accounts, including one published in 1961 by a young lawyer named William M. Kunstler

(*Beyond A Reasonable Doubt?*), who went on to defend Abbie Hoffman, Jerry Rubin, Tom Hayden, and other radicals at the Chicago Seven trial in 1969. In the wake of Chessman's 1960 execution, several other books appeared that rehashed in detail the issues that were at stake and the legal minefield through which the system had been dragged. One in particular even posthumously unearthed new evidence—suppressed by the Los Angeles Police Department—that seemed to exonerate Chessman and bring belated shame upon the State of California. So many questions were raised by the original court proceedings that a new trial would, today, be demanded. And it's probable that, with a lawyer as skilled and media savvy as George T. Davis, whom Chessman belatedly hired in 1955—not to mention the availability of DNA evidence (one of the victim's coats was dotted with semen)—Chessman would have gotten one and perhaps been acquitted. Stranger things have happened in contemporary courtrooms in Los Angeles.

Some prominent people tried to launch careers via the case, most notably California's Governor Edmund G. "Pat" Brown, whose waffling on Chessman's fate was a source of regret for the rest of his life and may have crippled his dream of higher political office. Many others—among them journalists, commentators and lawyers—sustained careers via the Chessman case. Some wrote best-selling accounts of the case. Chessman, it seemed, was more valuable to the system alive than dead. He was articulate, charismatic, unrepentant, unafraid. He sold newspapers, he ate up radio programming, he gave television news something significant to chew upon during the first decade of its existence.

■

CARYL CHESSMAN DID not go gentle into that gas chamber. Using the proceeds from his best-selling first book, *Cell 2455, Death Row*—which the *Los Angeles Daily News* called "one of the best books of its kind ever written" and the respected scholar Harry Elmer Barnes called "the most remarkable portrait of a criminal career and personality ever produced"—he hired his own group of private investigators to follow every lead in the original case to clear his name. He also was able to call on the services and advice of such courtroom wizards as Melvin Belli, Erle Stanley Gardner, Rosalie Asher, and Davis.

Besides shedding light on the cruel and unusual punishment meted out to him in his specific case, Caryl Chessman also put a face on the then fledgling battle to abolish capital punishment in America. The light he shined on American society, and its wholescale embrace of the death penalty (forty-two of the then forty-eight states had capital punishment on the books when Chessman was sentenced in 1948), shone also around the world, then and now. America's embrace of capital punishment was roundly excoriated throughout the world.

Chessman's case stirred up enough outrage beyond America's borders that European and Latin American commentators regularly referred to it as "America's Dreyfus Affair." In at least one instance, the case posed a demonstrable threat to the president. That is, in February 1960, Chessman received his eighth stay of execution, largely through the intercession of the State Department, which feared that his death would trigger riots in Uruguay and Brazil during a visit there by President Eisenhower, whose life was thought to be in peril.

The State Department's fears were borne out when Chessman was executed for real that May. Within minutes of his death, riots broke out in Ecuador and Uruguay. In Lisbon, Portugal, a crowd hurled rocks at the American Embassy, breaking nearly every window in the building; in Rio de Janeiro, crowds assailed America as a "miserable country"; and in normally placid Sweden, the U.S. Embassy in Stockholm had to be surrounded by police to protect it from angry protesters.

Malcolm Braly, a San Quentin inmate at the time of the execution, was emboldened as a writer and inspired as a human being by Chessman's example. Years later, Braly wrote of Chessman, "He acted out the drama of the individual vs. the state, played his role without compromise and died bravely. . . . He taught them the power of the written word when he came to prominence with his first book. He had shouted from his cell and the world was listening."

■

NOWADAYS, THE MERE mention of the 1960s seems to conjure only images from its second half: the riots, Vietnam War protests, Black Panthers, hippies, Yippies, pop festivals, gurus, and psychedelia. But the cracks in the complacent We-Like-Ike era were already beginning to show in that very first year, one that would culminate in November with the election of the youngest man, at age forty-three, ever to serve as President of the United States, Senator John Fitzgerald Kennedy. Kennedy may

On April 30, 1960, about 125 men and women walked from Columbus Circle to Washington Square Park in New York City to protest Chessman's scheduled May 2 execution. *New York World-Telegram & Sun Collection, Library of Congress*

have received his party's nomination simply because the front-runner, Governor Edmund Brown of California, was perceived as having suffered grievous political wounds due to the Chessman case.

One could, then, do worse than cite the execution of thirty-eight-year-old Caryl Chessman on May 3, 1960, as the event that signaled the start of the sixties.

Author Frank J. Parker certainly felt this way. In 1975, he wrote, "In many ways, Chessman was the forerunner of Abbie Hoffman, Bobby Seale, George Jackson, the defendant who refuses to play by the rules."

After studying the case from stem to stern, Parker—a Jesuit priest—concluded that Chessman's trial constituted "a legal lynching."

The critic Denis Dutton recalled, "I can tell you exactly where I was in nineteen-sixty when the pellets dropped and the judge's secretary was redialing the number. I was in Mr. McLaren's tenth-grade chemistry class at North Hollywood High School. There was nervous tittering and laughter that went around the class when the clock showed ten A.M. I remember the angry Mr. McLaren telling the class to be quiet, that a man was dying and it was not funny. It's forty-one years ago, but it's a moment as clearly etched on my mind as news of the assassination of Kennedy or the World Trade Center attack. I was young, but I do recall the widespread sense from all over the political spectrum that there had been a miscarriage of justice. It is hard for me to understand why the sad story of Caryl Chessman has been so forgotten."

Whatever anyone thought of Chessman then, or thinks of him now, one can't help but be impressed with his will to live. He refused to let the walls and bars crush him. On eight separate occasions, like a character in a Dostoevski novel, Chessman stood in the shadows of the gas chamber, housed six floors below the condemned's cell block. A lesser man would have been broken by this continuous ordeal—especially a man who had compelling evidence of his innocence and a reason to live—and Chessman willed himself not to give in to the darkness.

"Death Row is always a place of horrors even for those able to hold the horror at arm's length," he wrote in 1956. "For death itself always is your mocking, obscene companion. . . . The price I have personally paid for these extra Sisyphean years has been prohibitive. My once bright dreams of a decent, creative future are maggot-infested. . . . My mirror tells me I am old and aged beyond my 35 years; the fatigue I feel is bone deep. I have an ulcer, and tonight it feels as though a hungry rat is gnawing at my duodenum. I fear for my continuing sanity."

A week before his death, Chessman wrote his agent, Joseph Long-streth to say good-bye to arguably his best friend in the world. He said, in part, "As you know, for the last 12 years, mine has been a harsh world where, if you failed, you didn't live to get a commendation for a good try and a pat on the back. It has been a world without next-times, and so perhaps the iron disciplines I had to impose on myself to survive against almost impossible odds on occasion gave the impression that I was a brusque, unfeeling guy who gave no thought to the sensibilities of others in his drive toward a goal. I am certain, however, you know how far from the truth this is. Time, circumstance and a complex of other difficulties, though, have combined to make it impossible for me always to communicate with a nice regard for diplomacy. Too often, to phrase it with a wry humor, the crises and need for virtually snap decisions have piled one atop the other until those old silent movie perils of Pauline appeared a form of casual relaxation by contrast.

"Happily, I have survived this long ordeal with my mental pro-cesses reasonably intact. Moreover, I feel I am a better man and a more mature one as a consequence of the experience, although I pray earnestly no other person ever has to go through what I have. I say that with no trace of self-pity. For now the world has been made acutely aware of Death Rows and execution chambers, and thus I feel what has happened to me—and what promises to happen Monday next—has not been and will not be in vain or without larger social significance. I think now the issue—whether the death penalty has a defensible place in a civilized community or whether it is not an ugly and demeaning anachronism that confounds social progress and confounds solution of the problem of what rational social man can do realistically and humanely to control the violence that lurks in all of us—is joined . . . I can die knowing I have done all I can. Yet much remains to be done and I am confident it will be done—by such men as yourself, Joe. . . . .Now, Joe, I must say good-bye. That is not easy, I admit, but it must be done. Good luck.

As ever, Caryl."

The *Los Angeles Herald Express* was the city's largest afternoon daily newspaper. Because Chessman's execution took place at 10 A.M., the staff was able to produce a special edition devoted almost entirely to the execution, protests, and reactions from around the world on that same day. It quickly sold out. *Author's collection*

PART ONE

The Boy Bandit

"Death Row Was the Best Thing Ever to Happen to Me"

ON **JANUARY 6,** 1955, Caryl Chessman—facing a January 14 execution date—wrote Joseph Longstreth: "It appears I shall never fully understand the workings—or machinations?—of Fate. In one sense, Death Row was the best thing ever to happen to me, for, resist and hate it as I might, it brought maturity, many friends and the chance to write and, in some small way, to accomplish something worthwhile with my writing. Naturally, the hard thing to face is not death itself, but its futility. The paradox is that just when I find I can be an asset both to myself and others death must intervene. Well, if it comes, so be it. I'm ready again, and thankful at least for what I've been able to do, the friends I've made, the meaningful things these last several months have held. I'm sure you understand."

Despite this letter's serenity—a stoic front Chessman was able to sustain to the end of his life in May 1960—few characters from Charles Dickens's novels could rival the real-life Caryl Chessman for miserable beginnings. He was Pip, Tiny Tim, Sissy Jupe, Oliver Twist, and the Artful Dodger rolled into one. His bleak house, hard times, and stolen childhood could have, were he inclined to blame them, provided a mother lode of possible explanations for his drift toward the criminal life. In *Cell 2455, Death Row*, he tried mightily to paint a picture of a brief idyll, that of his earliest days of childhood, before it was overwhelmed by illness and tragedy.

"In the evenings, after supper," he wrote, "Whit* would curl himself up in his mother's lap, and listen with rapt delight to the adventures of Peter Pan or Alice or Jack who had climbed the beanstalk. There were stories from the Bible too. Weekends and vacation time the three [he, mother Hallie and father Serl] had great fun together. There were trips to the ocean where, with tiny pail and shovel, Whit* discovered the wonders in the sand. Then the happy boy would stand and listen to the booming roar of the surf. . . ." These scenes, remembered from a death cell three decades later, seem almost too sweet, too good to be true, too removed from reality. And, soon enough, the brightness they reflected would be removed from his life, swallowed by the darkness that descended for keeps.

The truth of the matter is that Caryl Chessman had no childhood to speak of—and certainly not one worth recalling fondly. He had no brothers or sisters. He never mentioned cousins in his books or letters and only briefly, and unpleasantly, described his mother's adoptive parents. His only aunt, Victoria, of whom he was fond, died in the same car wreck that permanently crippled his mother when he was ten years old. He never shot the breeze about baseball, football, Tom Mix, Swift, or Sawyer. His sole cultural hero as a youngster was James Cagney, whose swagger he borrowed to ward off the fear that would otherwise, he said, "master" him.

Chessman spent most of the years normally allotted to childhood battling physical illnesses and chronic conditions while his mother reclined in a paraplegic's pulley-operated bed in the next room and his father scrounged for a health-ruining wage by pumping gas or repairing Venetian blinds. After 1928, when each of his father's string of odd jobs inevitably ended, the family depended on public assistance, a social stigma even during the Great Depression in the middle-class suburbs of Los Angeles where Chessman came of age. For much of his childhood, Chessman himself was housebound, if not bedridden, physically separated from others his age. When he did

---

* Chessman referred to himself in the third person, as "Whit," in the book.

attend school, he was made to feel different, but not in a special way. Weird was more like it.

As one girl who knew him then told the authors Milton Machlin and William Read Woodfield in 1961, "He wasn't a very presentable boy. He usually wore a green sweater with holes in both elbows and Keds with brown laces. His hair wasn't cut most of the time and it seemed to grow down his neck. He just gave the appearance that nobody at home took care of him very well."

Odd as this may sound, the best and arguably the most contented and productive years of Caryl Chessman's life were spent in prison. Like many young offenders before and since, he did his growing up and maturing, and made his greatest leaps in learning, behind bars. Prior to the convictions that led to Death Row, Chessman had already served 113 months in California penal institutions. When he was arrested and charged with the Red Light Bandit crimes, he had only been out of prison for forty-six days. He had spent, all told, all but two of the previous ten years behind bars. It was only after he was warming a bunk on Death Row that he realized his true potential.

■

EVEN BEFORE CARYL Chessman entered the world, dark shadows loomed over the two souls, Hallie Cottle and Serl Whittier Chessman, fated to be parents of America's best-known criminal.

Chessman's mother, Hallie, was an orphan from Chicago. She wasn't given up for adoption or rescued by the state from a broken and abusive home; in 1900, as a newborn, she was wrapped in a blanket and left on the steps of the West Side Baptist Church. A discard. A foundling. She never knew her mother and father, never learned who they were. She was adopted by Charles and Abigail Cottle, members of the church, who had also adopted a blind child. The Cottles, pious and hardworking, raised Hallie by the dictates of the Good Book. Despite her artistic inclinations—a love of poetry, music, and art that she would try to transfer to her son—the Cottles sent Hallie at eighteen to learn a trade at Gregg Business College, located in the

Loop, Chicago's business district. Upon graduating, she became, according to Chessman—who out of love may have pumped up his mother's résumé—"a competent and skilled private secretary to a man who had forged a multimillion-dollar business empire."

While at Gregg, she met Serl Chessman. He was from St. Joseph, Michigan, a small harbor town ninety miles northeast of Chicago on the southern shore of Lake Michigan. He was a likeable if somewhat directionless young man one year her senior who was attending business classes. His one claim to fame was his alleged lineage to John Greenleaf Whittier (1807–1892), the Massachusetts-born poet, editor, and abolitionist who was at one time a household name in America for his often memorized and recited ballads; he was, in fact, well known enough to provide the punch line for a popular schoolboy retort ("That was witty, but the man who wrote 'Snowbound' was Whittier.") Perhaps wanting to confer the lone mark of distinction he owned to a progeny that would honor it by future acts of greatness, Serl passed "Whittier" on to his son, as his middle name. (Caryl would "honor" it by using its shortened form, "Whit," for *Cell 2455, Death Row*'s protagonist).

After a short engagement, Hallie and Serl were married and moved to St. Joseph. In a pattern that was to define his life, Serl left the bustling city of Chicago for a snowbound, backwater village because he wanted to put his newly refined business skills to work, and Hallie, who already had a good job, ditched it to dutifully follow him. Machlin and Woodfield wrote that Serl "had many skills—was good with animals, handy with tools, and reputed to have a green thumb—but there seemed to be no place for these small talents in St. Joseph."

Serl and Hallie's only child, a seemingly healthy eight-pound baby boy, was delivered at home on May 27, 1921; he was christened Carol Whittier Chessman. That name, Carol, on a boy was unusual but not unheard of in the 1920s (the actor Carroll O'Connor, was born in 1924). Serl, whose own unusual name was Danish, chose the Danish "Carol" (alternately spelled "Karol") for his son. Like the male names Evelyn (as in Waugh) or Joyce (as in Kilmer), Carol seems odd to us now, just as names like Shaquille and Britney may baffle future generations. Surely, however, Hallie and Serl should have known that some sense of compromised masculinity would eventually accrue to a name like Carol.*

If they didn't grasp this, their son did. As a schoolboy in California, already the object of ridicule from other kids, "Carol" would begin to spell his name "Caryl" and that formation stuck (though, as far as can be ascertained, the name was never legally changed to "Caryl").

In some ways, Caryl was an even more peculiar name; it begged to be misspelled, mispronounced (as Carl), and misunderstood.†

Hallie's health was severely compromised by Carol's birth. She was warned by her obstetrician that she'd face grave risks if she had another child. Lacking any job prospects in Michigan and worried about his wife's health, Serl decided after the winter of 1921–22 to move his family to the warmer, more promising Canaan of southern California. In May 1922, the three Chessmans headed west in a 1918 Model T Ford.

The Chessmans were not alone. Between the years 1900 and 1940, the nation, it seemed, tilted toward the sunset, and anything not bolted down rolled west. In the 1920s, two million Americans migrated to California, and the population of Los Angeles tripled, as an exodus of dreamers filled the spreading metropolis to take advantage of the movie industry's expanding operations, the home construction boom, and the dry, sunny climate. By 1924, soon after the Chessmans arrived, there were 310,000 cars on the roads of Los Angeles every day. In addition to the new residents, a tourist industry brought millions more to play beside the Pacific Ocean, stare at the palm and orange trees, drive along the wide Wilshire Boulevard and,

---

* Johnny Cash touched on this theme in his 1969 hit single, "A Boy Named Sue." The song, written for Cash by Shel Silverstein, reached #2 on the *Billboard* Top 40, by far the highest charting any song by Johnny Cash would ever achieve. Perhaps fittingly, the hit version was recorded live at San Quentin Prison.

† Even after Caryl Chessman became a household name, people still gave the name a double take; those who knew nothing about the case assumed he was a notorious woman, like San Francisco's legendary 1950s stripper, Carol Doda, or perhaps even a transvestite. To this day, some people, when they learn of the case—with its overtone of "sex crimes"—assume Caryl was either a hermaphrodite or a man who had had a sex change operation. Even in 1960, on the verge of Chessman's execution, one in three people polled by a Los Angeles newspaper, identified him as a "convicted killer."

as a 1927 *New Republic* put it, to bask in the "easy optimism and lazy prosperity" of Southern California.

A decade later, during the Great Depression of the 1930s, the exodus to California continued apace, but the easy optimism and lazy prosperity were gone. This exodus had a more desperate edge to it, as depicted in the fictional but truthful novel *The Grapes of Wrath* by the California writer John Steinbeck. Southern California continued to be a mirage of sorts, not just a land of opportunity but, for the dirt-poor Okies who hit the road during the Great Depression, the last chance at the end of America's new highway system. This second wave would compete with the Serl Chessmans, who were already there for whatever menial jobs were available.

With all their darkest clouds in the future, the Chessmans arrived in an optimistic frame of mind and settled in a rented cottage at 3410 Greensward Road in Glendale, a fast-growing suburb next to Pasadena. In 1920, Glendale's population was 13,756; by 1930, it was 62,736, a fivefold increase in ten years. (Today, Glendale's population tops 205,000.) Though the Hollywood studios and hills were just a few minutes' drive to the southwest, Glendale may as well have been on another planet.

Dan Ziferstein, whose father Isidore would become associated with the "Save Chessman" movement of the late 1950s, has lived near Glendale for many years and was familiar with it as far back as the 1940s: "Some towns are one way or another and Glendale always had a reputation as a redneck community," he said. "Nowadays it's largely Armenian, though I don't know when that changed."

Glendale's most famous resident, before Chessman, was Marion Morrison, who attended Glendale High School from 1921 to 1924 and later, as John Wayne, became one of Hollywood's enduring icons. The city's reputation was cemented in 1936, when Glendale High School's football team played Pasadena High for the league championship; Pasadena's team was led by Jackie Robinson, who later gained fame by breaking Major League Baseball's "color line" as a member of the Brooklyn Dodgers. In that 1936 championship game, however, he was just another black face to the Glendale racists. Early in the game, in fact, Robinson was brutally injured after being piled on by Glendale tacklers; his injuries were serious enough that he had to be taken to the hospital, and his demoralized team was beaten.

In Arnold Rampersad's biography of Robinson, he portrays the racial atmosphere of Glendale as bristling with ill will: "Pasadena whites looked with envy on nearby communities such as Eagle Rock, South Pasadena, and San Marino—but especially on Glendale, which had the foresight not to employ blacks as domestics and now boasted that not a single Negro lived within the city limits." As late as 1962, Glendale's Brand Boulevard was the site of a huge procession of robed Ku Klux Klansmen, who marched with a burning cross, horse brigade, and marching band. In 1964, George Lincoln Rockwell—smitten with Glendale's reputation—chose the city as the logical place for the national headquarters of his American Nazi Party, where it stayed until the 1980s.

■

DURING THEIR FIRST four years in Glendale, the Chessmans were blissfully unaware of any of this. Serl was able to secure regular, well-paying work on the movie sets in Hollywood. In 1922, Serl got what must have seemed like his big break when he landed a lucrative construction job with the United Artists' production crew for *Robin Hood*, a romantic-action extravaganza starring Douglas Fairbanks. The elaborate and expensive sets, which included a drawbridge, castle, convent, and banquet room, required many hands to build and even by today's special effects standards seem remarkably authentic. Proving himself reliable and adept, Serl was hired to work on another Fairbanks/United Artists' vehicle, *The Thief of Baghdad* (1924), one of the most elaborate silent films ever made. He helped build an entire imaginary city filled with domes, minarets, archways, and other exotic frippery that looked "Arabian," not to mention the wooden frame suspended by piano wire on which sat the "flying carpet."

The pinnacle of Serl's Hollywood career, however, was his work on the set of *The Son of the Sheik* (1926), starring the silent film era's most bankable star, Rudolph Valentino. *The Son of the Sheik* was the sequel to *The Sheik* (1921), which the film historian Jeanine

Basinger called "an anomalous occurrence in movie history—a really bad movie that was so popular with the public that its star achieved legendary status from it." *The Son of the Sheik*, wrote Basinger, "was a rip-roaring story of rape and action in the Arabian desert." Its July 1926 world premiere at Grauman's Million Dollar Theatre was, said Basinger, "one of Hollywood's most glamorous affairs. Valentino arrived with his latest flame, Pola Negri, on his arm, and she rose to the occasion by wearing a tight silver gown and a diamond tiara. Everything indicated not only that Valentino was on top but that he had a long and fruitful career ahead of him."

According to an interview Caryl Chessman gave *Newsweek* in 1954, Valentino during these few halcyon weeks or months paid friendly visits to the Chessman home where he "bounced me on his knee." Serl, for all his later misery, did have the unusual experience of working in close quarters with the two leading men of silent film, Fairbanks and Valentino, who could not have been more different. "The primary appeal of Fairbanks lay in his quintessentially American, and therefore unthreatening, presence," writes Basinger. "He was closer to imaginary male heroes like Jack Armstrong, the All-American Boy, the lads of Horatio Alger, or even the Lone Ranger, than he was to someone like Valentino, who was erotic, foreign, and sexually ambivalent." Film critics of the time, most of whom were men, loved Fairbanks and hated Valentino.

Serl Chessman, flush from his brushes with Hollywood glamour, entertained dreams of producing silent films himself. This would be in keeping with Serl's business "vision"—investing in silent films on the verge of their obsolescence.*

The fragile but optimistic Hallie was content to stay home to raise her gifted son. She believed, according to her son, "there was a

---

* *The Son of the Sheik*, as it happened, was Valentino's last film. At the peak of his fame, he died on August 23, 1926. His death, at age thirty-four, is thought to have been the result of either a burst appendix or a bleeding ulcer, and his funeral procession in New York was, to many a heartbroken fan, one of the darkest days of the decade. Be that as it may, Warner Brothers was already experimenting with sound technology in 1926, and the following year released its first feature-length "talkie," *The Jazz Singer*; the silent film genre soon died as suddenly as its leading heartthrob.

meaning and a beauty to be found, to be set to words or to music or on a canvas, and from the day of his birth, Hallie had never wavered in her conviction that her son would one day find and express in his chosen way this meaning and beauty." To facilitate these hidden gifts, Hallie read to her son constantly, and he seemed to take in an astonishing amount of what she said. From the age of four, Serl took to calling the boy "the little professor" for his ability to recite verse after just one reading and his precocious observations about the world ("The ocean's talking to me").

The first portent of her son's physical fragility arrived when he was five years old, while Serl was laboring six days a week on film sets for Valentino. A common cold lingered, and turned into pneumonia. Only the intercession of a doctor with a hypodermic needle—a shot of pure adrenaline directly into the heart—saved Carol's life. Months later, he was able to return to kindergarten, but his lungs, compromised by the pneumonia, were now afflicted with bronchial asthma, which would curtail any normal boyhood activity for the next several years. Each time an asthmatic attack came, Carol was sent to his bed, which was encased in a tent into which healing vapors were pumped. He would lie there for weeks at a time, the spell would pass, and he would cautiously resume his childhood.

At this time, Southern California was something of an idyll—as long as one didn't look too hard at the land deals, water battles, increasing crime, Mob presence and corrupt Los Angeles Police Department. Priming the tourist pump were the chambers of commerce, hotel owners, the *Los Angeles Times* and something called the All-Year Club of Southern California, which spent $5 million in the 1920s to promote the area as a year-round tourist Canaan. By 1927, annual tourist visits exceeded 250,000, competing for space on the roads with the millions who had already moved there. The Automobile Club of Southern California set the tone for automotive tourism, with its popular promotional magazine *Touring Topics*. The center of its universe was Sunday—set aside as "Motor Car Touring Day"—when its 124,000 members would take pleasure drives around the area.

Serl took note of all these cars and the traffic-choked roads. Saving enough from his Hollywood jobs—and having gone nowhere with his idea of producing silent films—he opened his own gas station, the first of a series of businesses that would briefly flourish and then fail.

■

DURING THESE EARLY years of their California existence, the Chessmans moved constantly, always within the Glendale-Pasadena area. When Chessman was seven, his family settled in his favorite of all their homes, a rented cottage in Pasadena across from the Flintridge Hills, behind which loomed the Sierra Madre Mountains.

The drier air and open vistas of the setting seemed to revive Carol's health. He was able to return to school, where he did well and, by his own account, "made friends with all his schoolmates." He received private tutoring in French (Hallie's doing) and befriended a rich family down the road with whom he precociously listened for hours on end to their recordings of classical music. Inspired by the "colors" the music produced in him, he claimed to have spontaneously learned to play the piano. When he told his mother this, she arranged for piano lessons, which he enthusiastically embraced. At this point, his mother may have been living out her own thwarted dreams through Carol. As she took closer charge of his life, Carol was presented with what would become a recurring motif, even at this young age. That is, he was a person apart, he didn't fit in, and he possessed talents that longed to be nurtured. The name, the fragile health, the artistic inclinations, the mother's constant attention . . . he was well on his way to becoming a Mama's boy, a sissy.

To counter this, he wandered with the other boys in the neighborhood among the Flintridge Hills. During one session of play at a nearby creek, Carol was bitten several times by mosquitoes. He soon ran a fever and felt drowsy. What was at first thought to be influenza—and treated as such—turned out to be even worse: encephalitis, an inflammation of the brain caused by a virus. While today, encephalitis is known to accompany common childhood illnesses like measles, mumps, and chicken pox, and is treatable, when Chessman contracted the disease in 1927 the world was awash in a double pandemic of influenza and encephalitis, the latter having only recently (in 1918) been isolated and identified as a unique disease.*

One of the possible after effects of encephalitis—including Chessman's case—is a semipermanent "brain injury" that can cause learning disabilities, speech problems, memory loss, or lack of muscle control. To the young Chessman, the long recuperation from this episode made him feel that his life had been "shattered." The disease, he later wrote, "destroyed, literally ate away, that portion of the brain which gave him his tonal sense. He was left tone deaf. . . . Gone were the beautiful colors, the lively, wonderful colors, the friendly colors; left behind was a murky residue, gray, inanimate, dead."

The illness, according to Machlin and Woodfield, also transformed Chessman's personality. "He became moody and temperamental. If he was scolded in school or at home, he would either begin a temper tantrum or burst into tears. The previously good-natured youngster also seemed to develop a cruel streak during those difficult months of his eighth year, often directing it at those dearest to him." This included his dog Tippy, whom he kicked in a rage and then, he later recalled, harangued himself, saying, "Something's wrong with me! I do things I don't want to do, but I can't keep from doing them!"

One unsettling, unintentionally revealing event that Chessman later recounted from this time involved a bullwhip. Sufficiently recovered from the encephalitis to play outdoors again, he borrowed a bullwhip from one of the neighborhood kids. He was playing absentmindedly, and with increasing menace, beside his house with the whip, when his mother came outside to check on him. Chessman, claiming not to have known she was home (but how does a boy of eight not know his parents are home?), struck her with the whip with such force that she was knocked to the ground. He claimed this was "unwitting," an accident, but he was a sickly eight-year-old and she was thirty-year-old healthy woman and

---

* Oliver Sacks worked extensively with post-encephalitic patients, documenting their conditions in his best-known work, *Awakenings*. Sacks described a "worldwide pandemic" of encephalitis that began in 1916–17 and "in the ten years that it raged, this pandemic took or ravaged the lives of nearly five million people before it disappeared, as mysteriously and suddenly as it had arrived in 1927."

she was struck hard enough to be knocked to the ground. Serl, alerted to the bullwhipping by Hallie's cries, came running outside. Sizing up the situation, he grabbed the whip from his son and began beating him with it.

After the whipping, Carol ran away, "ashamed" and "confused," and stayed hidden in the hills until midnight. Despite his parents' assurances that they "knew he had not struck her purposely," he felt that the world was now a "strange and sinister" place and that he was capable of terrible, destructive acts. His interest in music and art waned. He also lost interest in normal boyhood friendships, preferring the company of his mother. After school each day, he recalled, the two of them went for long walks together, writing that he "became a mother's boy, shy, obedient and, on the surface, altogether lacking the normal, healthy aggressions of lads his age."*

■

AFTER CARYL'S BOUT with encephalitis, the Chessmans' Southern California pleasure drive was all downhill. Literally. One day in

---

* Only after Chessman was executed were the profound aftereffects of encephalitis fully understood. Indeed, by then, it had come to light that post-encephalitis seems to have played a part in a large number of what were called "sex offenses," including rape. Herbert A. Bloch and Gilbert Geis, in their widely acclaimed textbook *Man, Crime, and Society: The Forms of Criminal Behavior* (1966), wrote: "The case for post-encephalitis as a causative factor relies upon a considerable number of histories of individuals who prior to the onset of the encephalitis syndrome were apparently extremely well-adjusted and law-abiding and then subsequent to the attack erupted into a wide range of uninhibited and criminal behaviors. Caryl Chessman, executed in California after a notorious delay, claimed to have suffered as a child from encephalitis. Levy has reported on one hundred delinquents, all post-encephalitis cases, whom he describes as 'overactive, restless, with short attention and concentration spans, unpredictable, acting before thinking, destructive, and usually not showing any remorse and not learning by experience.' Lewis, discussing arson, maintains that 'encephalitis assumes the foremost place as a precipitating factor with the juvenile and post-adolescent incendiaries and their largest number are dangerous pyro-maniacs,' while Abrahamsen insists that in a small number of cases, including among them persons who have acquired a disease such as encephalitis, the label 'born criminal' is of validity." Of course, for Chessman to have claimed post-encephalitis as a cause of his criminal pathology, would essentially be admitting to something he'd long insisted he couldn't possibly have done: the Red Light Bandit crimes, which were "sex crimes."

1931, Hallie, her sister-in-law Victoria, and Carol were invited on a pleasure drive in a new Ford owned by a Pasadena neighbor. Tooling down Colorado Avenue, their Ford, a small open roadster, was hit broadside by a much larger Cadillac touring car. In the accident, Aunt Victoria sustained a fractured skull and died the next day. Caryl broke his jaw and mangled his nose, injuries that would later earn him the derisive nickname "Hooknose" and give him the look of a pug boxer that he carried to the gas chamber. Hallie was thrown through the windshield, crushing two vertebrae and rendering her permanently paralyzed from the waist down. Though she could get around to some extent in a wheelchair, Hallie would spend most of the remainder of her eighteen years of life in a bed at home.

The house of cards continued to collapse. Serl, already strapped by his failing gas station, now went broke trying to pay medical bills. The Chessmans could no longer afford to live in Pasadena; they found a house in a rundown Glendale neighborhood, at 3280 Larga Avenue, near Glendale High School. Serl's gas station went bankrupt, and he eked out an existence doing a series of odd jobs as a carpenter, handyman, Venetian blind installer and repairman, butcher. In 1933, when Caryl was twelve, the Chessmans went on public assistance.

But their medical woes were not over. In 1936, at age fifteen, Caryl contracted diphtheria, an acute infectious disease that clogs lung passages with a tough membrane. He was treated at the county hospital, after which he was required to spend six months in bed. This was rock bottom for the Chessmans: an unemployed father; a paraplegic, bedridden mother; a sickly, bedridden son; the only money coming into the household a charity handout. All the promise of the gifted son was now a bitter pipe dream, a cruel joke. The "bottoming out" event: Caryl having to crawl from his sickbed to pull his father's head out of the gas oven, thus foiling a suicide attempt. Serl had taken out a life insurance policy and claimed that he thought he could better provide for his family dead than alive. It's hard to imagine—no matter how large an insurance payout may have been provided—how a paraplegic mother was going to raise a troubled and chronically ill son alone.

Thus, it is not surprising that when Caryl regained a semblance of his own health, he looked for some way to redeem himself and help his family. Like many a young teenager, he got a paper route. Then, he began stealing groceries off the front porches of the houses along his route. His crime career had begun.

"Which Way to Hell?"

ALTHOUGH CARYL'S RUSE of an early morning paper route could only fool his parents for so long, they must have wanted to be deceived for as long as possible. Common sense demanded that someone leave the house each day and return with provisions or a paycheck. And common sense would have told them that Caryl's "take home" was considerably more pay than a paper boy was capable of earning. Still, that Caryl, the so recently ill son, showed such enterprise may have been the single bright spot in their existence.

His desire to make money was inspired by more than filial devotion. After his father's suicide attempt and his own recovery from diphtheria, he was looking for any excuse to leave that grim Glendale rental, his devotion to Hallie notwithstanding. Once he regained enough strength to dress himself and walk a straight line, that's what he did.

Chessman recalled this period as having "been in bed so long that learning to walk was a slow and painful process. . . . Within a week he had regained a shaky use of his legs; within two weeks, he was helping around the house."

This sweet image soon soured when two friends dropped in for a visit, just before Serl returned from his rounds of the Glendale charity agencies, his parcels clearly labeled: NOT FOR SALE. While Caryl was humiliated by the pitiful Cratchit-like proof of his family's impoverishment, one of his friends couldn't suppress the obvious: "Gosh, you sure must be awful poor to have to eat that stuff. I feel sorry for you."

While one cringes at the thought of the young Chessman's shame—at least this is how he reported what happened—one wonders at the friend's cluelessness. In late summer 1936, the nation was deeply mired in the Great Depression. Most Americans had grown accustomed to the drabness of everyday life and, with Franklin Delano Roosevelt at the helm, were comfortable with the idea that the patrician in the wheelchair had the best interest of the miserable many, as opposed to the wealthy few, at heart. Rich businessmen loathed FDR, calling him "a traitor to his class," but "the people" spoke loudly and clearly in November 1936, returning him to office by one of the largest landslides in American history. Alfred Landon, the Republican, won only two states.

Everything in America was scarce, with the possible exception of despair, and Serl Chessman had every reason for despairing: his wife a paraplegic, his son chronically sick and undernourished, his job prospects hanging by a thread, his family on public assistance.

Caryl, for some reason, did not inherit a propensity for despair, or even depression, from his father. Rather, Caryl's despair expressed itself differently—in anger and arrogance, rather than self-pity. The obstacles tossed in his path had already been prodigious. He'd survived near fatal bouts with encephalitis, pneumonia, and diphtheria. The residual effects of the diphtheria had "seriously overtaxed" his heart, and he suffered from chronic, recurring asthma that he would never shake. He had a permanently mangled face and a defective septum from the car wreck that had paralyzed his mother and killed his aunt. The doctor who'd most recently treated him at the county hospital warned him that, without bed rest, "he might not live another six months."

Hallie, meanwhile, insisted that all their troubles were "God's will."

Caryl had bought that line to soothe his mother. The God he'd purchased was the simplest imaginable, as depicted in *Cell 2455, Death Row*: "From Hallie, Whit came to know God. God was the wise and good Father; they were all God's children. God looked down upon them and protected those who sought and needed His protection. God expected them to help one another, to be kind and good to one another, and to find and pass on, in the way in which each was best qualified, the beauty and meaning of life."

Despite her years of suffering, Hallie had rarely complained or assigned blame, even as the medical bills that accrued from her paralysis stripped every ounce of energy from Serl's body, warping her husband into a stoop-shouldered, pitiful old man by his midforties. Harold Doty, whose mother was a close friend of Hallie Chessman's, said that he recalls Serl as a "small, birdlike man" who seemed to keep his suffering to himself. Doty said his mother had nicknamed Hallie "Happy Chessman" because "despite her severe health problems, her intense pain in her back and bed sores the size of fists, she always kept an optimistic outlook on life."

Regardless, Caryl was troubled by the thought: If this was God's will, why would He inflict such punishment on one family?

With precious few life experiences to fall back on, Caryl had simply accepted that such a question would never be answered; that, indeed, it might not be answerable. He tried prayer, to no avail. He visited Hallie's minister, telling him, "Mom told me it was God's will that she was paralyzed and I used to pray to Him every night to let me take her place, to paralyze me and let her walk again. Then when I went to my dad he told me God probably wouldn't do that because He must have had some reason for letting Mom get her back broken."

Though Chessman doesn't name this man of the cloth in his account, he was the Reverend Herbert H. Richardson of the North Redondo Chapel in Redondo Beach, where the Chessmans had been worshiping since their arrival in the Los Angeles area. Reverend Richardson had grown close to Hallie and Serl Chessman over the years, and he was no doubt impressed by their troubled son's level of maturity about their dire situation. But Caryl didn't stop there. According to his version of events in *Cell 2455, Death Row*, he told the minister, "Dad spent all his money on doctors trying to help Mom. Finally he went broke and pretty soon we didn't even have enough to eat. Then, like I told you, I caught diphtheria and we went on relief and I just couldn't stand living like we were after my dad turned on the gas and after the day Joey saw we were on relief and said what he did. I figured then God wouldn't be too mad at me if I took something for us to eat. I just had to help my folks. I couldn't stop myself. Besides, I thought I only had six months to live."

This account of a fledgling Jean Valjean put Reverend Richardson in a theological bind. Caryl detailed his crimes, some of which went beyond the parameters of taking "something for us to eat." The minister asked for a few days to think over a response worthy of Solomon, one that would cover his backside legally while offering the empathy the teenager seemed to expect from a man of the cloth.

"I think God made a mistake when He didn't let me die like the doctors said I would," Caryl offered in parting.

Chessman the writer never shared the minister's advice to the young Caryl. Instead, perhaps embellishing for dramatic effect—for, surely, no man of the cloth would let such a problem go unaddressed— he said he sought out the minister one final time, several weeks later. On that occasion he told—not asked or suggested, but told—the minister to forget all of the crimes to which he had confessed, to forget that he had even come to him for guidance. Caryl had decided he no longer needed guidance from above.

But Richardson did not forget. Years later, when Chessman was on Death Row fighting for a new trial, the old family minister would join other members of the cloth, psychiatrists, sociologists and activists to form a coalition dedicated to sparing Chessman's life. At that time, at great risk to his reputation—since Chessman was such a public pariah—Richardson shared with the media his fond remembrances of the precocious young man he had known.

■

INSTEAD OF SOME Biblical ideal about being one of God's beloved flock, Chessman admitted to holding a brutal self-image: "scrawny fifteen-year-old boy, barely five feet tall and weighing not more than one hundred ten pounds. An asthmatic, puny, wheezing machine. A poor anonymous nothing who wanted to be a something. A neurotically anxious nothing. And he saw himself for what he wanted to be: a man. Tall and strong. A man who couldn't be hurt. A man who knew and made his way without doubt. A man who couldn't be scared."

After Caryl Chessman's death, his agent and friend Joseph Long-streth reflected on the early influence of the Cottle family on Hallie and, in turn, her influence on Caryl.

"The Cottles' early influence was powerful, and not good," he said. "As very religious people, they influenced and directed Hallie, and it was her almost fanatical belief in the goodness of God which Caryl could not comprehend—never learned to—and which pained him. The ambivalence of his emotional attachment to his mother and yet his intellectual rejection of her, to him, untenable and intolerable blind beliefs may well have been more decisive in his psychological make up than has ever been recognized, admitted, or analyzed. Caryl had a healthy (and I think, personally, justified) dislike of the Cottles."

So, perhaps, in order to become that man he longed to be—oddly enough, Chessman did grow to be more than six feet tall and weigh 180 pounds—Caryl put himself through one more painful regimen, to "conquer the fear inside."

But there was one rite of passage on which Caryl had not reckoned. That is, he fell in love and had his heart broken, this traumatic psychosurgery administered by a "nice" girl named Barbara. Barbara was from a strict middle-class family, not unlike the humorless Cottle clan who'd adopted his mother in Chicago. Barbara's family lived in a more moneyed part of Glendale; the only time her parents let her out of sight was on Saturday afternoons when they dropped her at the local movie theatre for the matinee. As it happened, a taller, stronger guy had designs on Barbara, a guy unburdened by doubt or intellect, a guy straight out of Caryl's fantasized self-image.

The guy was called Sonny: a toddler's name on a fully grown manchild. According to Chessman, their encounter was a true-life Charles Atlas advertisement. Beefy Sonny saw Chessman talking with Barbara and approached him. Sonny informed Caryl that Barbara was his girl, though this was news to her. Rather than ignore Sonny or defend Barbara's honor, Chessman was paralyzed by fear. The scene that followed was more humiliating than a Charles Atlas ad. There, the girl leaves her puny date to swoon in the arms of the muscle-freak. Here, Barbara stood by her guy even when he started sobbing. This inflamed his asthma, turning the sobs to bleats. Sonny called him a comical litany of names straight off the matinee screen: "scrawny little runt," "yellowbelly," "gutless wonder," "jellyfish."

Barbara took the matter into her own hands, raking her fingernails across Sonny's simian mug. Only then did Chessman rise to the occasion, to be throttled by Sonny in three "solid, sickening blows." Chessman fled, bleeding like a wounded jackrabbit. When he got home, he packed and continued running. Leaving a note to his parents, Chessman headed east, toward the hills and desert. On his way out of his rundown neighborhood, he ran into Barbara, hiding in the shrubbery. She'd come to warn him that her parents were going to have him arrested. Sonny had told them that Chessman and she had been "doing something bad" and that Chessman had been bragging about it to his friends. Her father had already beaten her for this alleged fall from grace; another beating was in the offing for defying them by sneaking out of the house to warn him.

Barbara saw only one solution: they must get married. Though they were both only sixteen, Chessman didn't run from the idea of marriage, crazy as it would have been. But he rejected the idea as impossible. He knew she was a "good" girl, a bit like Hallie, perhaps, in that regard, and he knew that he felt something not unlike love for her. But he could not get that image of himself from this afternoon out of his head . . . a pitiful wretch, wheezing at Sonny's feet, his girl watching in pity.

Chessman found a pay phone and called Barbara's parents. He made her father promise not to beat Barbara, and he told him that what Sonny said was a pack of lies, that their daughter's virtue was intact. After walking Barbara home, he told her to leave a note in the hollow of a palm tree nearby. He then, as he recounted, "hid himself in the nearby hills of his childhood, away from all of his kind."

What followed was something of a rite of passage. His three-day self-imposed banishment led to an old cabin he'd remembered from his carefree Pasadena boyhood. He had no food and drank water from a nearby reservoir. He sat sleepless in his soiled clothing, blanking his mind of all things but loneliness, anger, and humiliation. Though he writes about this episode with convincing earnestness, one has to wonder what was he trying to prove in that decrepit cabin, not to mention what state of panic his parents might have been in. Was this his version of an Indian sweat lodge? Were his ritualistic scars the hacking of phlegm from the asthma, his visions the dementia caused by shivering through sleepless nights whipped by breezes from the desert?

"Then, late the third evening, he came down from the hills on hunger-weakened legs," he wrote in *Cell 2455, Death Row*, as if reciting Scripture. "He found Barbara's promised note in the hole in the palm tree near her house."

The news was bad: Barbara had been beaten; she and her family had moved away. Though this was a wholly unbelievable scenario—what family would pull up stakes and move to another town simply to avoid a scrawny teen suitor?—Chessman later dated his decision to embrace a life of crime to this event. More than likely, the situation was as simple as this: the scrawny, impoverished boy couldn't have the good girl from the respectable family. His bitterness and self-pity caused him to lash out at society.

Chessman wrote, "It was then that Hate and Rebellion took off their masks and introduced themselves. They had been hiding within for a long time, playing a waiting game—for sickness, frustration, resentment, hostility, fear, confusion to build into an intolerable tension—for anxiety to generate a pressure that could not be withstood."

The next day, Caryl sought out Tim, "a member in good standing of a gang composed of would-be young toughs and their girl friends." Tim "had made several unsuccessful efforts in the past" to recruit Caryl. This time, Chessman joined Tim's gang, as 1936 turned into 1937.

■

FROM THE PILFERING of groceries through the open windows of parked cars, Caryl graduated to sneak thefts from cash registers. He would create a diversion and, when the store clerk was occupied by it, reach behind the counter, grab, and run. He stole the cars of sunny Californians who'd left their keys in the ignition, then began stealing them the time-honored way: jimmying open door locks, hotwiring ignitions, taking them out for high-speed joyrides into the wide open hills beyond Glendale and Pasadena. When he had had his fill of them, Caryl simply ditched the cars—often, literally, leaving them in a ditch—and went home to his parents' house as if returning from his paper route.

Chessman later described the exhilaration of these driving adventures: "He stole—'expropriated,' he would say—car after car, mostly fast, sleek, new ones. With the same studied passion with which he had played the piano years earlier, he practiced driving or 'tooling' these hot heaps. He learned to corner, to broadside, to speed and snap-shift them. He purposely rolled and crashed them. He sent them hurtling through traffic at high speeds. He sought out patrol cars and motorcycle cops and taunted them into chasing him, just for the thrill of ditching them, just for the hell of it, and for practice."

Driving, he wrote, "was a joyous form of creative expression. Driving made him free. Driving was his personal, triumphant accomplishment. His coordination, his timing was uncanny, and nature had given him perfect depth perception. With these assets, plus an open contempt for his own safety, he had learned to drive with such astonishing skill that his exploits behind the wheel soon multiplied and became legend. An exhilarating feeling of amoral triumph swept over him. Good and bad, right and wrong, were only blurred, unheeded abstract concepts, without real meaning. He had failed at being good, at fitting in, being a contributor. Now it was different. Now he couldn't be ignored. He was only sixteen, but he was a factor."

When he was inevitably caught, rifling through a butcher's cash register, Chessman crossed into new territory: he was arrested. Taken to Glendale Police Station, he crossed further into new territory: he escaped. In *Cell 2455, Death Row*, Chessman re-created the scene: "He eagerly answered all questions put to him, and the dick beamed, much pleased with himself. 'Now we're getting somewhere,' he said, and the questioning continued. [He] obligingly told the dick everything he wanted to know. Except for the fact that it was unabashed hokum, the cop would have gotten himself a promotion on the strength of it. Instead, he ended up with a fairy tale and no prisoner."

When the "dick" turned his back to get the fingerprint kit, Chessman leaped out a second-floor window, onto the top of a truck, drove the truck up to the wall surrounding the police station and scrambled over the wall to freedom. He was undoubtedly pleased to have outwitted a police force with such a fearsome reputation.

"The Glendale Police to this day have a hardcore, tough way about them, like Los Angeles police," said Dan Ziferstein, whose father later tried to save Chessman's life. "You did not want to get caught doing anything wrong in Glendale. Chessman probably saw the local constabulary as a challenge, a source of authority to not just beat but to make fun of."

Indeed, he did, as he admitted: "The game of cops and robbers was the most competitive game in the world. Whit liked the rewards of that game and he gave not a damn for the penalties, but that didn't erase the fact that he was contemptuous of those rewards. Those who preached, 'You can't win; you can't outsmart the law!' were nothing more than talking parrots or provocateurs; the most they could accomplish was to excite him and his kind to anger, greater defiance. To act out the disproof."

■

CHESSMAN'S SEXUAL RITE of passage could not have occurred with a "good" girl like Barbara. Such things require "bad" girls. Tim's gang had a bad-girl-in-residence named Virginia. Chessman met her after his hiatus in the cabin. She tempted him with a cigarette. Though he didn't smoke, Chessman "puffed on it experimentally." Then out came the fifth of Scotch—liberated from Tim's parents' liquor cabinet—and the gang began to drink. Not wanting to appear square, Chessman "wanted to gag but managed not to. After that the mixture went down easier and he began to feel pleasantly lightheaded."

Chased from the house by Tim's livid mother, who arrived unexpectedly, the group headed to downtown Glendale. They came upon a car parked outside a drugstore, its door unlocked, engine running. On a whim, they piled inside and Chessman took the wheel. Compounding his car theft, he honked the horn, bringing the car owner running from the store just in time to see them gleefully pull from the curb in a rubbery screech.

Chessman had lost the "good" girl, his ticket to the straight and narrow, and he'd spent three days in torment over it. He'd molted that skin. And now here he was—hot car beneath him, steamy babe beside him, and the hounds of Hell egging him on.

"Let's go for a ride to Hell," Chessman said. "I'll do the driving."

Virginia nestled her leg beside his on the seat, tuned the radio to some suitably wild sounds, and asked, "Which way is Hell?"

He wrote, "Having the powerful car under his control wrought a change in him. It opened up, with alcohol's help, a new world, a world a man could conquer and do with what he pleased."

A traffic cop, mounted on a motorcycle, came into view. Chessman tensed up. Noticing his hesitation, Virginia waved theatrically at the cop, as if to announce, "I am sexy and I am young and this is America!" The cop simply smiled and waved back. Virginia said, "Did the big bad policeman scare you, little man?"

The gauntlet was tossed when the light turned green.

"The car leaped ahead, around a corner, onto the open highway. The speedometer needle climbed. The windows were open and the wind roared in their ears. He shot through a stop sign and Virginia wasn't relaxed any more."

Chessman heard a police siren and sped up, whipping the stolen car through a series of insanely tight curves. Even so, two motorcycle cops were gaining ground. He hit 80, then 85 miles per hour, even as they approached a congested intersection. Everyone in the car was screaming, except the driver. They were flailing at him, cursing him, begging him to slow down or stop and let them out. But he sped up and "Somehow a space opened up for him at the intersection and he got through, not expertly, perhaps even miraculously, but he got through. He turned onto a side street, then another. He had ditched the bulls."

From this suicidal exercise in bravado, Chessman concluded, "If you used your head and your guts, you could do what you wanted and get away with it. The premise lit up in his mind like a neon sign, and suddenly Hell took on a special allure of its own."

Virginia feigned contempt, saying he was "lucky" and "a half-pint show-off." She told him to meet her at the malt shop the next day after school and "I'll make you run back home to mama, yelling for help."

That same night, perhaps as an outlet for his newfound sexual hunger, Chessman went on a binge of thievery. In one manic seven-hour rampage, he stole two cars, committed three burglaries, and stashed the loot (cigarettes, booze) in the cabin where he had recently taken sanctuary. Tim went along for the ride, and at the end of the night he warned Chessman about Virginia. "That broad is dynamite. And she's hotter than a two-dollar pistol."

The next morning, having been awake all night and gone for four days, he walked into a completely changed Chessman home. Though Serl and Hallie had been worried sick about their runaway son, they now knew everything about his chosen path. The cops had been by looking for him.

Serl's attempts to admonish him only angered his wayward son.

"Serl was a shell of his former self; life had beaten him down," he wrote in *Cell 2455, Death Row*. "The rebellion flared in [Caryl's] mind and it hardened him. His dad had taught him that honesty is the best policy. His mother had taught him that they were God's children. They, his parents, were good and decent and honest beyond dispute, and yet look at them. Oh, God, look at his parents! At that moment [Caryl] would have battered and smashed anyone who might have suggested to him his mother and father would be rewarded in the next world. After this, the very idea of it seemed the vilest cruelty imaginable. Why, why had they been so wantonly treated for being good and decent and honest?"

When Serl asked for an explanation, his son said, "Maybe it's just because I am fed up with poverty. Maybe I just feel like having some fun for a change."

Caryl walked out of the house, found Virginia holding court with a table full of desperately horny young men at the malt shop. Though she was a slut, none of these "little men" would get past first base with her, even as they stood expectantly in the on-deck circle. Caryl saw her and hesitated. He grabbed a soda at the counter and drained it, like John Wayne in a shoot-'em-up Western. He stepped forward. Virginia obliged by addressing him, "Well, if it isn't the little boy!"

Future prison psychiatrists might have made some hay out of the following, included in Chessman's *Cell 2455, Death Row*: "His face felt hot. His eyes took in every detail of the sinuous girl: the hair, the white, strong teeth, the cat's eyes, the full, red mouth, the ivory column of neck, the casually worn sweater. Too, the knowing look, worn as off-handedly as the pancake makeup, and the animal animation. A blatant advertisement of an available commodity, and a psychological cannibalism. Perhaps the male spider suspects that the female intends to eat him as soon as she has mated with him. But at least Mr. Spider has an excuse for what he does."

He and Virginia left and got in the car that Chessman had stolen for the occasion, an immaculate tan 1934 Ford coupe.

"Drive fast," Virginia commanded. "Drive crazy fast."

He did as she beckoned and they headed for the hills above Los Angeles, parking near his cabin. Virginia wanted a cigarette and a drink. He disappeared and returned with three cartons of cigarettes and a bottle of expensive champagne, loot from the previous night's thievery. Virginia slugged down the champagne and continued to belittle him.

"You think Barbara was a nice girl, don't you, little boy?" she prodded.

"I know she was," Chessman insisted, angrily.

"How do you know? Did you get her cherry?" Virginia asked.

"Shut your dirty mouth!" he shouted. Again, psychiatrists would have noted: He wanted to kill Virginia with his bare hands.

Chessman gunned the Ford to life and, suddenly filled with moral rectitude—after a 36-hour spree of drunkenness, burglary and stolen cars—he intended to drive Virginia home. The truth is he could not do the one thing they'd both known this was all leading to. The one thing that, in 1937, had no suitably flippant word to describe it, but awkward, almost creepy expressions like "get her cherry." Sex was something that was just done, a quick, nasty, brutish physical act that would solder the two of them together in their "badness." Even the crimes for which Chessman later received his death sentences—two blow jobs—were never explicitly described in court or in the papers. America did not *do* sex.

How could Chessman not know that Virginia was about to render him the ultimate favor, taking from him the oppressive weight of his sexual inexperience? All men should be so lucky to have a Virginia enter their lives at this auspicious time, a "broad" who knew the score. But Chessman, so precociously smart in many ways, was dim on this score. Virginia pulled her skirt above her knees. She pulled it higher.

"He looked because he didn't know what else to do," he later recounted. "He looked because Virginia had told him she knew a shortcut to Hell. He looked, and he told himself that being an animal was enough; because that is what we all are, nothing but animals. He looked, and the animal part of him was excited by Virginia's legs."

She slapped him, then hit him with the empty champagne bottle. He grabbed her angrily, "his hand accidentally fell on her bare thigh."

"Do I have to draw you a picture?" Virginia screamed. "You're either scared or else you're a pansy."

Sex and violence and hints of perversion all mixed together. The sum total of their sexual encounter was, Chessman wrote, "He made love to her, not expertly. Virginia was like an alley cat. She scratched and bit and cursed, but wouldn't let him go."

It had to be one of the strangest sexual encounters anyone has ever included in a purported work of autobiography. When they were done, with predictable swiftness, Virginia unleashed a drunken monologue about her life as a "slut." Chessman claimed to have started sobbing at this point, begging her to stop, wailing, "It's all wrong!"

The sixteen-year-old Chessman was visited by an adult-sized epiphany: "Until that instant they both had been inexperienced actors clumsily playing a scene from a badly written play, not even knowing why or how it had happened that they had been cast in their respective roles. . . . She had known a shortcut to Hell and had shown it to him. Not Hell, a place; but hell, a state of mind. The worst hell of all. And probably the only one. This mental hell was . . . wanting to believe in what was good and right and decent yet being obliged to question the goodness, the rightness and the decency of all things."

Caryl vowed to "start by believing in Virginia, by believing in her even when she refused to believe in herself. He could take her hate for his own. He could fight for her and himself too." He begged her, "Don't let them make you throw your life away. . . . Give your hate to me. Let me have it. I need it. I'll use it against them. I'll get even for both of us. . . . Let me do the fighting. Let me take your place in this dirty jungle."

He claimed that, at this point, Virginia swore eternal friendship to him. But her name, or a description of anyone like her, never appeared in any of his future writing.

■

THE TRANSFORMATION WAS complete when Chessman acquired a gun. This evened the playing field against those, like the simian Sonny, who would try to push him around or, like the Glendale Police, try to tell him what to do.

In fact, he got even with Sonny soon thereafter, running into him one afternoon at the community swimming pool. Sonny was with "two stooges" and a "tall blond girl in a two-piece bathing suit." Sonny "looked brutishly huge and tanned. He was smoking a cigarette and he held it through the fence so the blonde could take a drag. She did and puffed the smoke out foolishly, in a cloud, without first having inhaled it. Then she said, addressing Sonny with her eyes as well as her voice, 'You wait right here. I'll be out in a jiffy.' She disappeared into the girls' dressing room with a suggestive twitch of her ample derriere. Sonny whistled appreciatively."

Sonny, the two goons, and Chessman must have, for the next few moments—each in his own private sanctum—fantasized the blonde in the dressing room, slithering out of her two-piece. See her suggestively pulling the bottom half of her garment down her luscious gams, jiggling the top half over her head, her pale white—almost pink from their twin existences in these perfumed, pungent nether regions beyond the reach of air, sun and sweaty hands of horny, pre–Sexual

Revolution boys—jugs wobbling proudly. One can practically smell the ozone of spent testosterone.

When the blonde rejoined Sonny, the pack of reprobates moved out in unison down the sidewalk. Chessman sprang forward, blocking their path and brandishing his loaded revolver. He told Sonny, "Take that step and I'll blow you to Hell." Sonny did not move. The brutishly huge Sonny was scared. A wave of revulsion filled Chessman.

"Anger amounting almost to blood lust had taken hold of him," he wrote. "It was goading him. Sibilant words of hate were pouring from his lips without his being more than partially aware of what he was saying: that those who arbitrarily took advantage of others who were smaller were unspeakably vile. That he would happily kill all the Sonnys in the world. That he'd like to squash them as bugs are squashed."

He gave Sonny a tongue-lashing in front of his goons and his blonde: "You caused me to lose Barbara, Sonny. Your filthy mouth caused that. You trampled on something I thought was sacred and your rotten mind soiled it. So now I'm getting even, Sonny. I'm taking the blonde here. She's going with me. And if you or your two stooges don't like it, or if you tell anybody about it, I'll kill all three of you. That's not a threat, that's a promise. Now scram. All of you."

Chessman "took" the blonde, just as it had been laid out in the Charles Atlas ad.

■

Chessman continued to attend classes at Glendale High School, though his schoolwork suffered from his extracurricular activities. Despite his lack of preparation for the lessons, Chessman tried to dominate class discussions. A schoolmate from this period told *Time* magazine in 1960, "He always talked way over people's heads, and he had a superior attitude toward other students. A lot of them disliked him. Caryl never seemed to make friends with nice boys, and he finally took up with the some bad ones."

Thus, it was no surprise to his classmates when, during the summer of 1937—just after his sixteenth birthday—Chessman was arrested for car theft and sent to a forestry camp run by Los Angeles County. Twice he escaped from the minimum-security camp, and twice he was returned. By September it was determined that Chessman was not just in need of penitent labor, he was in need of "reform." He was sent to Preston State Industrial School in Ione, a town twenty-five miles southeast of Sacramento. This grim institution—Chessman called it "a reformation factory"—stood near Sutter Creek, where gold had been found in 1848.

He behaved himself for the next six months at Preston State Industrial School, the hard knocks having instilled in him a new credo: "Don't be a wise guy. Be tough, be 'right,' but not wise in the sense of thinking you know all the answers and running off at the mouth all the time. And never tell a policeman or anyone else in authority the right time."

In other words, put on a good show for the white hats and cultivate your contacts among the black hats. Not for nothing did inmates refer to Preston as "crime school."

Preston held seven hundred inmates, ranging in age from fifteen to twenty-one, a group of future criminals and car hops and day laborers that Chessman characterized as "young rebels and young savages and young fools." His kind of people. The friends he made during this six-month stint later formed the nucleus of his "Boy Bandit Gang," which spread the name of Caryl Chessman far and wide in Los Angeles County.

Chessman put on such a good show for the guys in the white hats that he gained his release from Preston unconditionally in April 1938. Within a month, he was back, deeper than ever, into a life of crime and trouble. He had stolen the Pasadena postmaster's Ford V8 sedan. Actually, he'd expropriated it, since the postmaster's wife had left the key in the ignition.

He assembled a group of reform-school graduates and went on a month-long crime spree. He told himself he was amassing money to spend on his mother, for an operation that would restore the use of her legs and for a private detective who could find out for her the names of her real parents.

Meanwhile, he spent his early evenings—until Hallie fell asleep—

in a rocking chair at his mother's bedside. "This was an old habit they had, softly talking the night away, for sleep was a luxury the pain-ridden Hallie seldom enjoyed without the aid of drugs and she far preferred the company of her son to a drugged sleep. They talked happily of everything bright and warm under the sun—of writers and artists and poets and books and paintings and poetry and happenings both new and old and other people and other times—and yet they did not once mention their dark and unhappy personal world." He also didn't tell his mother about hiring the private detective or about his one-man crime wave, or even that he had confiscated the Pasadena postmaster's car.

The Ford V8 sedan was used in a series of robberies of bordellos in the Hollywood Hills. Here, pimps and madames discreetly serviced their sometimes famous clientele. Theirs was no small-time operation. In his book *The Dream Endures: California Enters the 1940s*, Kevin Starr cited a probe of the Los Angeles Police Department that led to "the Purge" of 1939, when twenty-three high-ranking officers were forced to resign and forty-five others were weeded out in the next six months. Why? As Starr writes, "Los Angeles was supporting an intricate network of brothels, gambling houses, and clip joints, all of it run by well-organized syndicates. . . . A number of police were on the take for so many operations—an estimated six hundred brothels, three hundred gambling houses, eighteen hundred bookie joints, twenty-three thousand slot machines—to be flourishing."

Before the so-called Purge, the bordellos and bookie joints flourished, and, as later became obvious to Chessman, the police department was full of bad apples who were lining their pockets with the proceeds. Like the hirelings of the Mob they essentially were, these police simply slid into the positions vacated by any of their colleagues who were caught. The system of corruption was intact when Chessman and his associates made their raids on the brothels.

Chessman felt an equal lack of remorse for his gang's robberies of bookies, the front men for the lucrative illegal gambling operations that predated the rise of Las Vegas. Chessman's justification was simple: he was "hijacking the hijackers." In his retrospective view, these acts were not criminal. He was, like Robin Hood, stealing from the devil and using it to help the angels. He would use the stolen money obtained from illicit sex to free his invalid—and sexless—mother from the mystery of her past.

Chessman and his pals were playing with fire. Benjamin Hymen "Bugsy" Siegel, a transplanted New York associate of the national crime syndicate bosses Meyer Lansky and Lucky Luciano, would not have been amused by their antics, if his crimes had been as prodigious as Chessman claimed. Siegel, a murderous borderline psychopath, had been sent to California by Lansky in the late 1930s to oversee the West Coast operations of "the Syndicate." Since his arrival, Siegel had run the rackets, including prostitution and bookmaking, the golden geese Chessman was raiding. Had Chessman not been caught by police during this spree, he would in all likelihood have ended up a bullet-riddled cadaver, tossed into a ditch, another Mob hit, another unsolved murder.

Chessman played the part, though. His driving expertise was put to good use during these stick ups, some of which led to high-speed chases along the serpentine roads north of Los Angeles. On these jobs, he was accompanied by cohorts with nicknames right out of Raymond Chandler: Moose and Red. The car chases often featured a liberal exchange of gunfire, car to car, like a scene in a real-life tough guy movie.

All of these robberies bore the unique stamp of a single perpetrator, a skinny teenager who talked tough and assumed a superior air. No longer the anonymous nothing of Glendale High, he was now a renowned bandit living by his wits and his own peculiar code. He was a "somebody," as Edward G. Robinson's Rico Bandello proclaimed in *Little Caesar*, the seminal 1930 film. In less than two years, Caryl had left his paper route far behind. He attended "tea parties" where he "blasted" his first "stick" of marijuana.

Chessman later described the sensation: "He got so high he had to get down on his hands and knees to get off the curbs. Everything was hilariously funny and when he started coming off the kick he was ravenously hungry."

Deciding he didn't like marijuana, Chessman went to the dealer who'd supplied his gang. Herein lies one of the enigmas of Caryl

Chessman: he disapproved of drugs and drunkenness and wanton behavior and yet he was a confirmed criminal, with a violent streak he barely kept under wraps. Among the crimes for which he was later arrested, for example, was the 3:00 A.M. looting of a drug store, during which he took all of the cigars in stock and piled them on the floor and then smashed bottles of liquor over them.

As for this pot dealer, Chessman coyly described a violent argument that "was resolved suddenly and decisively." He wrote, "He then buried his snub-nosed gun where it would never be found." When someone later asked him what happened to the pot dealer, Chessman snapped, "Don't go jumping to the conclusion that I murdered the sonofabitch, because I didn't."

His star turn as a famous hoodlum faded on his seventeenth birthday. His gift from the state was a return to Preston State Industrial School. It was indeed a gift. With his extensive record, Chessman could have easily been given "hard time" at the state prison. Instead, he was being offered one more chance to get it together before adulthood.

As bitter and nightmarish as his later dealings with the authorities were from Death Row at San Quentin, Chessman never said that the State of California did not offer him every break in the book as a young man.

■

HE SPENT THE next year at Preston, cementing the relationships that would later prove fruitful and fateful. He learned new skills, some of which were legal (typing, printing, mechanical engineering). He put on yet another good show of attending classes and taking advantage of the school's library facilities.

"He read voraciously, particularly the work of the philosophers," Chessman wrote of this time. "He read of the gentle Nazarene and of the cat-faced Florentine, Niccolo Machiavelli. He read and studied and thought. He enrolled in typing class . . . he taught himself to type, and won a job in the assistant superintendent's office as an inmate clerk."

He seemed, to those in authority, a cheerful, diligent young man, someone who'd put away childish things. He was released in June 1939. He was eighteen, legally an adult.

The change was all on the exterior. He later wrote, "Because, seeking, he found too much, cynicism formed an essential ingredient of his philosophy—not an affected, surface cynicism, but a cynicism that lay deep and hidden inside him. . . . When you least expected it, it rose and smote you between the eyes. One Sunday, he attended the service conducted by the Protestant chaplain, who meant well and undoubtedly did good. Holy Joe, most inmates called him. As a thundering condemnation of sin was being delivered from the pulpit, a homosexual in the back row slid down and committed an act of sex perversion on four boys, one after the other. Practically every inmate in the church knew what was going on; the chaplain and the supervisor present didn't."

His parents, in the meantime, had moved to a nicer rental home on Larga Avenue in Glendale, and they welcomed their wayward son back. Chessman later wrote about his return with unusual fondness. Even so, his account sounds as if it were written to fool a parole officer or to convince himself that what he was walking into wasn't the fate that would inevitably reclaim him: a life sentence as a confirmed criminal.

"Here was a healthy, happy, loving atmosphere, not cloying or smothering, not calculating or possessive. Life had treated my mother and father ruthlessly and I had been anything but a model son. Yet they still retained a quiet, unaggressive courage and a pervasive faith in me."

Serl had found a rewarding job. Converting the garage into a workshop, he was now a manufacturer of Venetian blinds. Just as everybody had wanted a car in the 1920s, everyone now wanted Venetian blinds. Serl tried to convince his son to follow in his footsteps, to make this Venetian blind thing a father-son partnership.

At Caryl's request and Hallie's encouragement, Serl fixed up a room and office on the back porch for their prodigal son. He preferred a corner of the garage, though, and repaired there at night, to pursue what he had always dreamed of becoming: a writer.

Years later, Chessman recalled his conversations with his mother in an almost enviably serene light:

"We talked cheerful small talk for a while and then my mother said, 'My portable typewriter is in the closet and I had Dad buy some typing paper, which you will find with it. I want you to take the portable out with you, Hon. I think you may want to use it.'

"'Mom,' I said, 'I'm convinced you're a mind reader.'

"'Then you do want to write?'

"'More than anything in the world. But I'm afraid I want to do something I cannot do.'

"'But you can. You should and you must.'"

His writerly ambitions were put off for ten years. He only picked up the pen in earnest in 1948. Unfortunately, by then he was San Quentin Prisoner #66565, resident of Cell 2455, and owner of two death sentences.

Machlin and Woodfield, in their book *Ninth Life*, indicate that Chessman at this time married a woman who had been a girlfriend from high school. They don't name her, and no record of this marriage exists. However, they said that she "spent most of her time in a futile effort to make Chessman try to 'go straight.'" She decided to marry him, they wrote, in order to "change the self-destructive pattern into which his life was falling." The marriage was brief, ending as prematurely as his writerly ambitions. Within two weeks of returning home, Caryl was arrested for stealing—pathetically—a gas cap and (in violation of an earlier parole) possessing a handgun. He spent ten days in the Los Angeles County Jail, in Glendale. His was beginning to become a familiar face to the Los Angeles Police Department. This was not a good thing. As his fellow Californian Philip K. Dick would observe in his novel, *Flow My Tears, the Policeman Said*, "Once they notice you, they never completely close the file."

Sure enough, on October 13, 1938, Chessman was arrested in a stolen car, and at this point, according to Machlin and Woodfield, Chessman's "wife" filed for and obtained an annulment. For the car theft, he was sent to Road Camp No. 7, a county-run facility located in the Santa Monica Mountains overlooking the Pacific Ocean and

Malibu. Paroled on June 30, 1940, now nineteen years of age and running out of second chances, he came home to work with his father.

Serl had ditched the Venetian blinds. He was a florist now, though
he barely eked out a living from his Glendale shop. By now, his son
couldn't even pretend to be buckling down. He was constitution-
ally unable to pantomime going into business with his father. Who
would believe him anyway, other than the preternaturally optimistic
Hallie?

Serl was at a loss for what to tell Caryl, the son who had long
since lapped the old man in intelligence, wit, and drive. Here he
and Hallie were in the most wide-open, optimistic, sunniest place
in America—the worst of the Great Depression was over—and they
were living like bottom feeders. Barely into their forties, Hallie and
Serl were already decrepit shut-ins. Hallie at least had the excuse of
medical trauma, which was ameliorated somewhat by her unques-
tioning religious faith.

But what could sad, suicidal Serl have to offer? A future as a Venetian blind manufacturer? A peddler of daisies and black-eyed Susans?
A role model as a breadwinner?

The pretense of a stable family life ended when Caryl began keeping the company of a sixteen-year-old girl, identified as "Judy" in
Cell 2455, Death Row, but whose real name was Lucy Ann Gaylord.
He'd known Lucy Ann since childhood; she, like "Barbara" and his
alleged first wife, had seen something good in Chessman, and had
hovered around the fringes of his circle of acquaintances, hoping that
he would either be scared straight or outgrow this perverse need to act
out his neuroses through crime. Here, again, was another one of the
paradoxes of Caryl Chessman: "Nice" girls liked him. His life, even
on Death Row, would be touched by the affections of "respectable"
women like his lawyer Rosalie Asher and the journalists Bernice
Freeman and Eleanor Garner Black.

According to FBI files, Lucy Ann and Caryl eloped and were married in Las Vegas on August 8, 1940. Mr. and Mrs. Chessman moved
to an apartment in Glendale provided by Lucy Ann's father, a respectable businessman. Caryl tried to reenroll in Glendale High School,

to earn the final credits for a diploma, but school officials banished him from the property after uncovering his criminal record.

Lucy Ann described for Machlin and Woodfield their courtship as, for her, a teen romance replete with "malted milks, movies, and the beach," and their married life as not unpleasant. "Chessman was always good to me," said Lucy Ann. "Even when we were going together as high school kids he always respected 'no.' He was never one to use force." She continued to nurse the idea that he'd pull his life together "despite the fact that his dresser drawers were loaded with artillery" and that he seemed to have a lot of ready cash on hand for someone without a steady job.

Chessman called in his chips from his days at Preston. Just after New Year's 1941, his assembled crew set to work helping Chessman realize his dreams of becoming a latter-day François Villon. He and his "coquillards" came to be known by the press as the "Boy Bandit Gang" and "Los Angeles' Dead End Kids." The youthful gang engaged in liquor store and gas station robberies and car thefts. They wandered back to the brothels and bookie joints, hitting those in lightning-style raids. The highlight of their career—and an incident that would be thrown in Chessman's face in 1948 by still bitter Los Angeles police officers—was the theft of a police patrol car from two humiliated highway patrol officers from Montrose whose weapons had also been liberated.

Chessman could no longer avoid trouble. A transformation like that of Paul on the road to Damascus was his only hope, which really meant he was beyond hope, his fate sealed. On February 3, 1941, Chessman's gang was "rounded up" at their hideout on Orchid Street in Glendale. In the ensuing exchange of gunfire, two policemen were wounded, as were two of Chessman's gang members, one critically. Four others (Robert Tollack, William Taylor, Donald Abbott, and Andrew Rutledge) were arrested and charged with thirty-nine counts of criminal activity; Chessman was portrayed as the "leader," which pleased his ego immensely. He and Tollack were charged with assault ("slugging and robbing" him) on a highway patrolman, Phil Parslow, when the latter allegedly tried to apprehend them after a gas station robbery. Taylor faced the most severe charge of attempted murder, of Fred Bovier, a Glendale police officer.

Chessman obliged the newspapers by behaving arrogantly, laughing and mocking the proceedings. Photographs of him at this time show an anorexically thin, pallid, pimply, adenoidal punk. He was now smartly dressed, in the manner of a hipster. His clothes were overlarge, exaggerated, as if taken from a film noir wardrobe. He looked like the sort of amoral grifter who'd extend his hand, then kick you in the nuts or toss hot ashes in your eyes and run, laughing hysterically, with your wallet in his hands. A cock of the walk with nowhere to go but down.

After his arrest in February 1941, Chessman claimed to have struck a deal with the police. He managed to obtain immunity for one young woman who was arrested with his gang and got some charges reduced for others who participated in the crime spree. He alone stood trial for eleven felony charges (nine robberies, one assault, one attempted murder). These charges were reduced to four robberies and one assault with a deadly weapon. Chessman's sentence was sixteen years to life. To serve it, he was sent to San Quentin State Prison, across the bay from San Francisco.

His friend-to-be Bill Sands would write, in *The Seventh Step*, pondering how he'd managed to stay out of prison once freed and why others, like Chessman, had not:

"Why do men go back to prison, time after time, until they die or are too feeble to commit any more crimes? What I saw was resentment. All cons resent the treatment they got as children—an unfair teacher, an insincere father, a bitch of a mother, or a myriad of other grievances—so they commit an act of defiance. This brings them into conflict with the law—and they resent the treatment they get at the hands of cops, social workers, juvenile authorities. So then they are started on the endless carousel called recidivism, which is defined as 'sinking back into crime.' From first offenders, they become second offenders, multiple offenders, eventually habitual criminals, and every sentence they serve in hatred and resentment. Some are restless to get out, so they can prove again that they are still rebels against a system that is unfair. Others are willing to try to make it honestly—and yet they fail."

Malcolm Braly, who served time in San Quentin in the 1950s and 1960s, also pondered the mystery of recidivism, after he too got out of prison for good. In *False Starts: A Memoir of San Quentin and Other Prisons*, his assessment of his own uncontrollable criminal urges would have struck a chord with Chessman: "I don't believe we're born with an instinctive sense of property, we're trained to this, and at a certain age most boys steal. Most boys also stop. I didn't. I've logged months of anxious introspection as to why I didn't, and it is only now, some forty years later, that I begin to see how stealing cast me in my first successful role. I was more driven, hence less fearful, than my friends, and this was sweet to a boy who had often been the butt. I would take reckless and large chances and when my buddies, figuring the odds, refused to follow, I mocked them as yellow and went on alone."

3

A San Quentin Appetizer:
Chessman's First Two Visits

SAN **QUENTIN PRISON** was built in 1852, two years after California was admitted to the United States and four years after gold
was found at Sutter's Mill. These events are not unconnected.

On January 24, 1848, at the junction of the American and Sacramento rivers, sixty miles northeast of San Quentin, gold was discovered on an agricultural estate owned by John Augustus Sutter. Sutter
was a Swiss-born adventurer who came to the United States in 1834
and made his way to San Francisco in 1839. He hoped to start a Mexican colony in the frontier north of the city. To that end, he petitioned
the Mexican governor in Monterey for a land grant, which he, amazingly, received. Sutter's "colony"—actually a baronial estate he named
Nueva Helvetia—consisted of orchards, vineyards, and a mill. It was
near that mill that the first nuggets of gold were found, the magnet
that started the "rush" that would transform North America.

By January 1848, when gold was found at Sutter's mill, California
was nominally an American territory (that status was finalized by the
February 2, 1848 signing of the Treaty of Guadalupe Hidalgo, ending
the war with Mexico). And Sutter himself would be a delegate to the
state constitutional convention in Monterey the following year. The
"gold rush" was not just an impetus to speed up the statehood process,
it was unstoppable. Before gold was found, the state population of
non-Indians was 14,000. By 1852, it was 250,000, Nueva Helvetia was
in ruins and Sutter was bankrupt, like thousands of others. Though

Sutter resettled in Pennsylvania, most of the failed prospectors went broke and stayed in the Bay Area. Out of desperation and emboldened by a lack of law enforcement, many turned to crime.

Actually, the dramatic change in population occurred in an even more compressed time period. The first steamer filled with prospective "gold diggers" did not arrive from back East until February 1849. By the end of the year, 50,000 more arrived from all points of the compass: South and Central America, Europe (some escaping the revolutions of 1848), and Australia, among them many of the convicts who had been sent earlier by Great Britain to Van Diemen's Land (now Tasmania).

Thousands of young women arrived as well. Many came to work as domestics but turned to prostitution. Because little effort was made to suitably house this influx, much less offer them humane services, teeming slums and desolate shantytowns rose all over the San Francisco Bay Area.

Regardless of how they arrived, people in the Bay Area, rich and poor, were in the service of a speculative gold-fueled economy that rivaled past manias in world history, like the South Sea Bubble of the 1720s and the Tulipmania of Holland in the 1630s. In the 1850s, they came—unchecked by anything but disease, murder, or Indian attacks—to try their luck panning for gold in the river basins north of San Francisco—the American and Sacramento rivers, as well as the Feather, Yuba, Cosumnes and Mokelumne.

Criminal activity reached epidemic proportion. In San Francisco alone, it is estimated that 1,200 homicides were committed between 1850 and 1854 (with, tellingly, only one conviction), and 4,000 people were murdered in all of California between 1849 and 1855. In the summer of 1849, for example, a group of fifty white thugs raided a Hispanic section of the city called Little Chile. What began as an attempt to collect on a debt ended in a full-scale rampage befitting ruthless pirates: looting, pillaging, raping, beatings. The ringleaders were caught, tried, and sentenced to hard labor, but only a few weeks later, they were released by city officials, as there was no jail large enough to hold them all.

Even if justice barely existed in San Francisco—many of the city's officials were criminals themselves, including the keeper of the county jail—it was meted out in a summary fashion among the men in the field. Vigilante hangings and floggings were common.

In 1849, buckling to public pressure, the city of San Francisco bought a decommissioned two-masted square-rigger, the *Euphemia*, to be used as a county jail. Other counties, like San Jose, Monterey, Santa Barbara, Los Angeles, and San Diego, also had jails. However, there was no state prison. In April 1850, the new state government bestowed state prison status on all county jails, which allowed inmates to be used as unpaid (read: slave) labor. The first official state prisoner was Charles Currier, a twenty-two-year-old from Massachusetts convicted of grand larceny in Sacramento; he began his term on January 25, 1851. The need for a place to house Currier and his like was suddenly an urgent topic among state leaders.

An arrangement was made by a former Mexican general, Mariano Guadalupe Vallejo, and a San Francisco politician of dubious moral fiber, James M. Estell. This duo offered the cash-strapped state legislature (then housed in San Jose) $137,000 and 20 acres of land as the site of a state prison if they agreed to move the state capital to a city Vallejo and Estell were planning to build on the northern shore of San Francisco Bay.

A deal was struck on April 25, 1851, allowing Vallejo and Estell a "lease" on the bodies and labor of all state prisoners for ten years. There were only five prisoners then, Currier included. Governor John McDougal then ordered all county sheriffs to turn over their state prisoners to Colonel John C. Hays, the sheriff of San Francisco. Hays and Major John Caperton had gained custody of the convicts via a deal with Vallejo and Estell, whereby the prisoners—now up to forty men—were to be used to build a state prison, among other profit-making jobs (so Hays and Caperton hoped). Another old ship, the *Wabau*, was pressed into service as a floating prison and towed to Angel Island, the largest piece of land in San Francisco Bay. The prisoners were made to work at a quarry on Angel Island or, in chains, to repair San Francisco streets.

The conditions were so appalling, even by mid-nineteenth-century Wild West prison standards, that in early 1852, seventeen prisoners overpowered their captors, took their weapons and escaped by boat. Hays and Caperton, who were losing money, begged out of the deal with Estell (Vallejo had sold his rights to prison labor) and lobbied to get the state legislature to pass a bill authorizing funds to build a state prison on their land. The new California Governor John Bigler took over the lease of the state convicts.

The three major islands in San Francisco Bay were examined as likely sites—Angel, Alcatraz, and Goat (now called Yerba Buena). All were ruled out for various reasons.* The site chosen was Punta de Quentín, which just happened to belong to another local politician and profiteer named Benjamin Buckalew. He sold twenty acres of land to the state. On July 14, 1852, the *Wabau* was towed across the bay and moored in the protective crook of the peninsula, just off the shore from where the new prison was to be built.

Punta de Quentín (Point Quentin), the smallest of the bay peninsulas along the Marin County shoreline, was the next best thing to an island. It was surrounded on three sides by the water of the San Francisco Bay and the San Pablo Strait, forming a protective and sheltered cove. It was conveniently located three miles south of San Rafael, the Marin County seat, and twelve miles north of San Francisco, accessible by steamboats. Just inland from the point, hills rose to a height of 2,600 feet (at Mount Tamalpais), in effect surrounding the peninsula on all sides by impenetrable natural obstacles.

The name Punta de Quentín allegedly derives from a Licatuit Indian warrior called Quentin who fought fiercely against Mexican troops and led a final stand in 1824 on this peninsula. The Indians were defeated and Quentin taken prisoner. The addition of "San" to the name derives from the Catholic presence and the habit of naming all towns or villages San or Santa, in order to curry favor with the Spanish colonials. A less substantiated story, presumably spread by the Catholic Church, has it that San Quentin was named for a third-century Roman beheaded by the Gauls, from whose body it is said sprang a white dove that flew to heaven.

---

* The federal government would not be so picky in 1934 when they needed a place to put their most hardened criminals, and "the Rock," the most legendary of America's prisons, was opened on Alcatraz Island.

During the prison's construction, inmates slept nights on the *Wabau* and labored to build the new prison during the day.

Kenneth Lamott, in *Chronicles of San Quentin*, wrote, "On fair days the able-bodied men worked ashore preparing the site for the first building; at night they were locked below, four or five men to each eight-foot-square compartment. During the warm summer days they stewed in their own juices, while in the rainy winter they stayed below day after dreary day. In the mornings the effluvia of feces and sweat and general decay was so strong that the guards refused to go below until the lower decks were aired out."

Criminality was the watchword from the prison's inception. Estell somehow finagled a building contract with the state via his San Francisco Manufacturing Company. He proposed a facility that would seemingly rival the hanging gardens of Babylon, replete with Doric columns, Roman towers, minarets, and a bell tower. Estell's relentless publicity campaign failed to convince the legislature that this was anything but another of his scams, and they canceled the contract in May 1853.

Still, Estell threatened to seize the property and state officials relented, allowing Estell to oversee the construction of a much less ostentatious facility. The first building completed was called the Old Prison or the Stone Building (or "the Stones" by prisoners) or the Old Spanish Prison, for its Spanish colonial architecture. This not unattractive structure was built on two levels, with an upper floor housing forty-eight cells, two rows of twenty-four each, placed back to back. Each cell was 10.5 feet by 6 feet and designed for two prisoners. The first floor was divided into a 160-foot-long dormitory (called the Long Room) and the turnkey's office.

By the time the Old Spanish Prison was completed in January 1854, there were two hundred fifty convicts living on the *Wabau*. By January 1855, each cell of "the Stones" held four men, and San Quentin was already overcrowded. More than half of the prisoners were from thirty-one different foreign countries; a disproportionate number were "the heathen Chinee," as the San Francisco journalist Bret Harte called the poorest of the poor Chinese laborers. San Quentin's earliest register, according to Lamott, contains the following woebegone names: A Hing, A Mor, Ah Hoy, Ah Lum, Wang You Fou, Ah Wah, Ah You, Me Sing and Ah Fuck, the latter summarizing the collective feelings of the inmates.

The Old Spanish Prison, which lacked running water and electricity, was razed in October 1945, to be replaced by a roomier but less attractive building that still stands today. Before then, however, Chessman moved into this quaint structure in 1941, the first of many different San Quentin cages in which he would reside for the rest of his life.

San Quentin is seen from atop one of Marin County's numerous picturesque hills. From this bird's eye view, taken on April 20, 1910, by prison guard Richard M. Smith, one can see the prison farm, San Quentin village, the prison, and the surrounding expanse of water of San Francisco Bay. *Courtesy Anne T. Kent California Room, Marin County Free Library*

■

DESPITE THESE DUBIOUS beginnings, San Quentin had by 1940 become a model prison, thanks to one man, Clinton T. Duffy, a devotee of "modern penology." In his twenty-three years of service to the prison, he is credited with transforming the sprawling, rusty San Quentin Prison from what was widely regarded as an antiquated hellhole and powder keg into an efficient, relatively habitable place. He is still spoken of in hushed tones of veneration.

During his prolonged residency at San Quentin—off and on from 1941 to 1960—Chessman lived through the reigns of three different head wardens: Clinton Duffy, Harley O. Teets, and Fred Dickson. His most persistent critic was Duffy. The story of how these two came to be such bitter enemies has the whiff of Greek tragedy.

Warden Duffy was the son of William Duffy, a farmer and justice of the peace from across the bay who, in 1894, was hired as a guard at the prison. The "guard" title back then had no formalized job description as it does today; one was more a jack of all trades. Mr. Duffy, in fact, was best known as a cook, and, according to Lieutenant Vernell Crittendon, the present-day San Quentin historian, he revolutionized the serving of the meals to the inmates. Clinton Duffy, born in 1898 within eyeshot of the guard tower, grew up in the village of San Quentin, where his father had moved his family. As the son of a San Quentin employee, Duffy was raised in housing provided by the state on the grounds of the prison complex. His boyhood was filled with tales of the tough customers on the other side of the prison walls within whose shadows he played.

Close proximity to the world's largest prison was not as grim as it might sound. The natural setting is still among the most breathtaking in the Bay Area, with Tiburon, the San Francisco–Oakland Bay Bridge, and a panorama of Marin County hills as backdrop (real estate developers, in fact, are eagerly awaiting the day when and if the prison is ever closed). The Duffys lived in the part of San Quentin Village located inside the front gates of the prison. Here, one can still find eighty-six homes built expressly for prison staff and families. The modest, tidily-kept homes are laid out in a quaintly nostalgic pattern, like an old-fashioned Main Street, and even today recall an era of small-town America that has disappeared everywhere else in the San Francisco/Oakland area. Though the roar of traffic from the interstate hovers within a few hundred feet of the prison's front gate, San Quentin still retains this placid, cut-off-from-the-world atmosphere.

Growing up there was anything but a prison sentence for

Clinton Duffy. There was plenty of room for kids to roam in relative safety; the original twenty acres had expanded to four hundred forty acres, much of it farmland, meadow and hills. The prison itself was architecturally interesting, with its sun-baked brown bricks and red roofs, the castle-like front entrance and the five-story guard tower that resembled the rook from a chess set. Add to this the effect of the two towering Star of Norfolk pines (from Norfolk Island off Australia) and the palm trees along the water in front of the wall, and, if one didn't know otherwise, one might have mistaken San Quentin upon first glance for a Mediterranean resort facility. Of course, very little of the area's natural beauty, besides the skies and tops of Marin hills, were visible to inmates from their cells or from the main prison yard.

Clinton Duffy's most vivid childhood memory was of the day after the 1906 San Francisco earthquake and fire when the prison had to be evacuated and all the inmates moved onto a boat. The boat was anchored offshore from the Duffy house; young Clinton recalled his father standing in the front yard with a rifle, guarding the domicile, in case of an offshore mutiny. From this early, intimate exposure, Duffy developed one odd but all-consuming ambition: to become San Quentin's warden.

Duffy's childhood sweetheart, Gladys, was also the child of a San Quentin prison guard and grew up in the same village. When she and Clinton were engaged in 1920, she was teaching at the prison school and Duffy was committed to a tour of duty in the U.S. Marines. Upon his return in 1921—the year of Chessman's birth—he and Gladys were married and found lodging in the San Quentin community. Duffy seemed poised to pick up where his father left off, but he had no interest in becoming a San Quentin guard or cook; the promotional possibilities were nil (wardens generally did not rise from within the rank and file). While Gladys continued to teach prisoners, Duffy secured a job as a notary public and became friendly with the San Quentin warden, James B. Holohan. Through this association—he did notary work for the prison—Duffy earned Holohan's trust and was hired as assistant warden in 1929.

A decade later, on July 13, 1940, Duffy was named acting warden, when Warden Court Smith faced an investigation by the State Department of Corrections for a litany of alleged wrongdoing. Smith's tenure as warden was arguably the most troubled in the prison's history. He and his notorious Captain of the Yard, Ralph New (a Holohan holdover), were widely loathed by the prisoners. Beatings were commonplace, and insubordination was rewarded with a stint in "the Dungeon"—solitary underground cells with no running water, electricity, or heat, and in which inmates were fed only bread and water—or with even longer stretches in "Siberia," isolation cells where inmates routinely suffered mental breakdowns from the deprivations. In the two years before Smith's ousting, odd things began to happen. One inmate, for example, climbed a thirty-five-foot searchlight tower and stayed up there for twenty hours, demanding to be "taken to an island." Another lifer who worked in the prison barber shop stabbed four inmates with scissors before he could be subdued. Three prison riots occurred in the two weeks after a guard shot "a Negro convict" in an attempt, according to a newspaper story, to stop "a savage fight" in the yard between two black inmates. Because the two inmates were said to be fighting "over ownership of a fountain pen," the "savagery" of their fight may have been dubious; what wasn't dubious was the pervasive sense of unrest under Court Smith.

It grew so pervasive that in February 1939, thousands of inmates went on a hunger strike, refusing to eat "corned willie" (corn beef hash). Concessions were made and then just as quickly ignored, so the prisoners went on an even more ominous strike a month later. What the prisoners were really striking about was not the food, but the entire Warden Smith regime. Duffy, as associate warden, was seen in an opposite light. When on September 1, 1940, at the age of forty-two, Duffy finally got his official dream posting, as head warden of San Quentin prison, the headline in the *San Francisco Chronicle* read, "There's Joy in San Quentin as Shakeup Takes Effect."

Duffy wasted no time. On his first day as the cock of the San Quentin walk, he fired the cruel overseer Ralph New and he got rid of the Dungeon. On the next day, Duffy disposed of the medieval assortment of whips and straps regularly used on the inmates, and ordered that dumplings be added to the gravy in the mess hall. Three days a week, he sat in the mess hall and took dinner alongside the prisoners.

Soon thereafter, fresh water, rather than the readily available salt water offshore, was pumped into the prison shower rooms. And, the following year, a Duffy-sponsored bill was passed by the state legislature that underwrote the cost of educational, recreational, and even some leisure activities at the prison. Inmates were able to acquire basic reading skills and high school equivalency diplomas. Radio broadcasts were allowed in the cells—accessible via headsets only—and a radio program called "San Quentin on the Air," created by prison talent (including Chessman) was aired outside prison walls every Sunday evening at seven on the Mutual Network. A weekly prison newspaper was started, and within four months the *San Quentin News* was sold to the public by subscription. Each week, the *News* featured a column by Warden Duffy. In his first column, Duffy wrote, "We want to present Mr. Average Inmate to our friends in the free world just as he is—a human being who has made a mistake and who is paying, according to society's law, the price." He revived the minstrel (glee club) and variety company and encouraged the staging of an annual Christmas production. Food improved above and beyond the adding of dumplings to the gravy. The Christmas dinner menu in 1941 was "chilled California celery, roast young pig, chef's gravy, sage dressing, creamed peas, candied yams, raisin bread, pineapple pie, apples, oranges and fruit cake."

At Duffy's request, Artie Shaw brought his orchestra to perform in the mess hall and Leo Durocher, manager of the Brooklyn Dodgers, conducted practice with the prison baseball team. Duffy screened motion pictures for the first time in the prison's history; he even held a separate screening for the men on Death Row. He invited guest lecturers and inspirational speakers, including the First Lady, Eleanor Roosevelt, and Paul Robeson, as well as Hollywood stars Joe E. Brown, Glenn Ford, Caesar Romero, and the inmates' favorite, Edward G. Robinson. San Quentin was so important to him that Duffy wrote one of the first and best histories of the place, *The San Quentin Story* (1950), much of it serialized earlier in the popular *Saturday Evening Post.*

■

DUFFY'S GREATEST LEGACY, he felt, was the Inmate Representative Committee, an unsupervised board made up of elected prisoners who discussed grievances and policies. Duffy himself was not allowed to attend their meetings, except by special invitation.

For all these reasons, then, it can be argued that Warden Duffy was more than just an overseer; he had San Quentin in his blood, and its operation, as well as the fate of its inmates, was a personal matter to him. Though he was a no-nonsense, straight-talking leader, Duffy took paternal interest in many young inmates, singling out those he felt showed promise and interceding with what today might be called "tough love." "Modern penology" to Duffy was simple: "Not all these men were vicious criminals, not all incorrigible, not all lost souls."

One of his greatest success stories was inmate No. 66836, a rich boy gone bad named Wilber Power Sewell, who later changed his name to Bill Sands and became a respected member of the rehabilitative community. Young Sewell/Sands was the son of a Superior Court judge, of all things, but his parents divorced and the boy grew up, as Duffy described it in the introduction to Sands's best-selling *My Shadow Ran Fast* (1964), "in a home evidently lacking in love, understanding, direction, religion and discipline."

More specifically, Sands wrote that he was "the only child of a wealthy and politically powerful man and his beautiful cultivated wife. . . . We lived in the biggest house at the peak of the highest hill in Whittier, California."

Sands was no dabbler in crime. He, like Chessman, went at it full bore from his teenage years. Sewell/Sands was, in fact, facing a possible incarceration of ninety-nine years in San Quentin for three separate counts of robbery and assault, after many successful robberies and violent scrapes dating back to his juvenile years. His trajectory of crime, youth and intelligence were almost mirror images of Chessman's.

Duffy watched Sands "grow up" in San Quentin and "change from a Big Yard Hoodlum Possibility to a young man with a purpose and direction." Duffy's wife Gladys became involved in the rehabilitation of this young man too. Sands even took to calling her "Mom."* Sands's "purpose and direction" was to become, by the 1960s, a counselor for young prisoners preparing for release or an early parole. Duffy took understandable pride and personal interest in Sands' career.

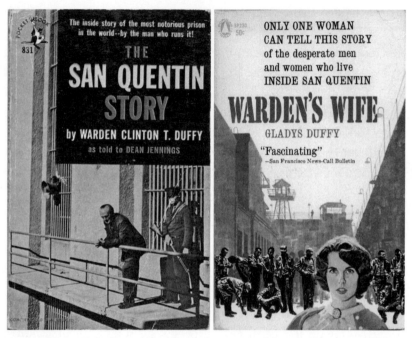

Warden Clinton T. Duffy and his wife Gladys were both born to San Quentin prison employees, both grew up in the village within eyeshot of the prison walls and both devoted their professional lives to the prison. Clinton was associate warden and then warden and Gladys was a teacher in the prison educational program and mentor to many convicts, who affectionately knew her as "Mother Duffy." Both Duffys were impressed by, and took parental interest in Chessman during his first stay at the prison. Duffy wrote a multi-part love letter to the prison for *Saturday Evening Post*, which was adapted for *The San Quentin Story* in 1950, and Gladys wrote her love letter to her husband, and the prison, in 1959. *Author's collection*

And yet, Duffy's clear-headed conservatism, where right versus wrong were the only players, faced an Olympian battle. The recidivism rate in the United States in the 1940s, when he was mentoring

---

* Over the years many prisoners fondly referred to Gladys as "Mother Duffy." She also caught the writing bug, penning *Warden's Wife* (1959), a valentine to both the prison and her husband.

Sands, was a shocking 80 percent for men and as high as 90 percent in some states. The system was, as Sands put it, an "almost total failure." Some prison inmates were mentally ill, but in those days few distinctions or provisions were made for them. They were tossed in with the general prison population. Sands describes one inmate, brilliant in mathematics, who "spent all his time hanging around the urinal trough, occasionally dipping his fingers into the liquid and rubbing it through his hair."

Though steadfastness and discipline like Duffy's were noble, they weren't getting the job done. Still, the warden persisted, telling the tough, unrepentant Sands upon his arrival, "My job, as I see it, is not to be just a keeper. My job is to help men rehabilitate themselves and return to society—as contributors, not as liabilities. But to those men who want to fight, all I can do is point out that I am the man you're fighting, and I have too much on my side for you to win. Right and all the might of the State of California."

Sands responded favorably to this treatment, as did many other inmates. Such was the power of, and respect for, Warden Duffy that he could walk, unescorted, across a prison yard filled with inmates, some of whom were convicted murderers with (as Sands put it) "enough knives hidden among them to stock a cutlery warehouse," and be greeted with a nearly mystical reverence.

Sands became convinced that the "impossible" was possible when he saw Duffy walk across a packed prison yard by himself on a hot summer day, during a time when the prison was gripped by a restless violence that "rang an alarm bell in the minds of the con-wise." Into this pit of ornery vipers strolled the implacable Duffy. Sands recounted, "As the men pressed about him, cheering, applauding, calling his name, the crush overwhelmed him to the point where he was beyond any hope of help from watchful eyes and guns above or from any other human source."

The prison's festering mood under Warden Smith seemed to break at the sight of the unarmed, good-hearted Duffy walking among society's detritus. Duffy recalled: "It never occurred to me that it should be any different this day; this was my home, this was my yard, too. . . . I saw them not as strangers or criminals or even numbers on a file card, but as human beings whose virtues and faults I knew better than anyone else, whose case histories I had studied for the parole board, whose wives and mothers and children I had known from many a tearful visit over the years. . . . My mind might be mistaken, but my heart tells me I am safer in San Quentin than most other men are on the streets of their home towns."

During that first walk, Duffy stopped every few steps to listen to an urgent plea, then another, then another, asking only that the various requests be jotted down on scraps of paper, matchbook covers, cigarette papers so that he, on his word of honor, could "take care of it." Amazingly, Duffy later pawed through the wad of paper and set about helping those with legitimate beefs.

"It had been impossible in all the years of San Quentin's existence for a warden to walk unescorted into that Main Yard when it was occupied," wrote Sands. "At the very least, what we witnessed and were a part of daily, was, by definition, a miracle. . . . It was happening beyond man's understanding of natural laws. . . . His credo was that punishment alone was not enough; it must be accompanied by enlightenment and rehabilitation."

Sands, describing Duffy, wrote, "I was looking into the eyes of the toughest man alive, tougher than any con, tougher than all of the cons put together. This was toughness, the quality I had come to admire most, in its most positive sense, reflecting true inner strength and real durability. Not mean, not shrewd, not violent—just simply the toughest man I'd ever encountered."

■

JUST AS HE had with Sands, Duffy took an interest in Chessman when the young man arrived for his first stint in San Quentin in 1941. This was six months after Sands arrived for his first and only stretch. His conviction, like Chessman's, was for armed robbery. While Sands had had a difficult time adjusting to San Quentin—he was sent to solitary confinement for persistent fighting with other inmates and given six months' hard labor—Chessman made an immediate positive impression on Duffy.

Being singled out by Duffy was a big deal at San Quentin, and the warden took an immediate shine to the well-spoken twenty-year-old Chessman. He asked him to join his office staff. This plum assignment was the antithesis of working in the antiquated jute mill, where most other inmates toiled for eight-hour shifts weaving burlap bags and gunny sacks from a tough fiber of the jute plant. The jute mill, built in 1882, was San Quentin's largest industry. In 1942, a prison reform association called it "the worst industry in any prison in the United States." No tears were shed by the inmates when a fire razed the old structure in 1952—the largest fire ever battled by Marin County fire departments—and it was never rebuilt.

Chessman took full advantage of Duffy's work assignment.

"I had just organized a secretarial school," Duffy later recalled in *88 Men and 2 Women*. "And I suggested [Chessman] attend it. In an incredibly short time he could take dictation at 120 words a minute and was an expert typist. Before long he was teaching these courses."

"Warden Duffy told me that Chessman was one of the most patient, understanding instructors he had ever seen," wrote Bernice Freeman in her memoir *The Desperate and the Damned*, about her time on the San Quentin beat. "He had a genius for handling illiterates. There were a great many at San Quentin, mostly of Mexican descent. Chessman taught dozens of them to read and write. The fact that he was a fellow inmate was a great source of pride to them. A young convict named Manuel Chavez once traced out his own name for me, then said, 'Caryl Chessman taught me this. He is a prisoner here like me, but is not at all like a prisoner. He is maybe my age, but I think of him as a father. He has made a way for me to learn to write my name and to read books. I never went to school before, but now Mr. Chessman teaches me in the prison school.'"

Chessman became so adept at teaching others to read that he codified his technique in a number of mimeographed pages that, taken all together, comprised a sort of textbook. He also taught English, typing, shorthand, and bookkeeping. He was fast becoming one of Duffy's pet reclamation projects.

Once Sands saw the light, after six months of weaving jute, he too was sent to the Clerk of the Parole Board. This was two days after Chessman arrived at the same office. Sands was assigned a typewriter and a desk next to "a young convict who was typing at a tremendous rate of speed." The prison guard who escorted Sands to his desk told him that this young convict would show him the ropes.

"Although I did not recognize the other cons doing desk work," Sands wrote. "I knew the man next to me to be a member of the 'tough and solid' clique of the yard. He was called 'Hook,' presumably because of his overly large, broken nose. After the bull left, Hook stopped typing."

"Hook" was Chessman. His way of introducing himself to Sands was in character, though it also revealed a less calculating side. Chessman wanted Sands to be his friend.

"So you have the second-highest I.Q. in the joint!" Chessman told Sands, sticking his hand out in greeting. "Meet number one . . . We're only two points apart."

Chessman had, after only two days in the typing pool, been given the task of training new recruits. He and Sands were brought even closer together when they both found themselves transferred from their claustrophobic two-man cells in the newer section of the prison to the Old Spanish Cellblock, where inmates were boarded dormitory-style, sixteen men to a suite. Sands and Chessman chose bunks next to one another. The nickname "Hook" was soon exchanged for "Chess," a prison moniker Chessman would own until he died.

Chessman and Sands bunked and worked side by side for the next year and a half. They were fast friends, loyal to one another until the end—and even beyond that point, in Sands's case. Chessman was able to complete his assigned weekly typing chores by Wednesday, which gave him the option of taking two days off to use at his leisure. Instead, he assisted Sands so that the two of them could take off by Thursday afternoon. With their free time, they cofounded the prison debating team, and coauthored scripts for the prison radio playhouse, and performed skits. Chessman continued to impress the prison officials. Gladys Duffy noted, "He volunteered for extra duties; he organized a debating team. He was a model inmate."

An autodidact in the jailhouse is, of course, not an uncommon phenomenon. Indeed, what else does a self-respecting inmate have to do to occupy his or her time, besides mutely watching television and counting the passing hours and days of a sentence? But

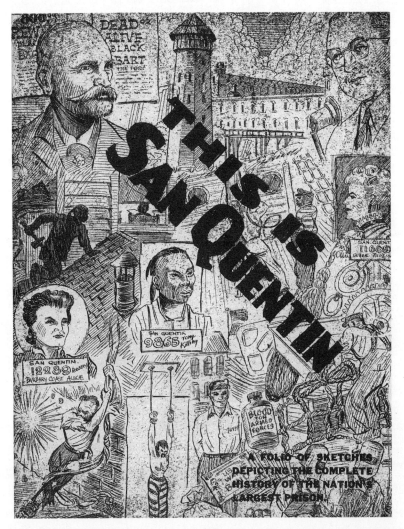

Warden Duffy strived to treat San Quentin inmates like human beings. Among the many programs he initiated was this quirky prison history produced entirely by inmates. The main contributor was "Peek," the name by which the book's illustrator chose to be known. Each page offers a slice of prison history and daily life, circa 1944, when it was published. The San Quentin Museum Association sells a reprint of this publication today. *The San Quentin Museum Association*

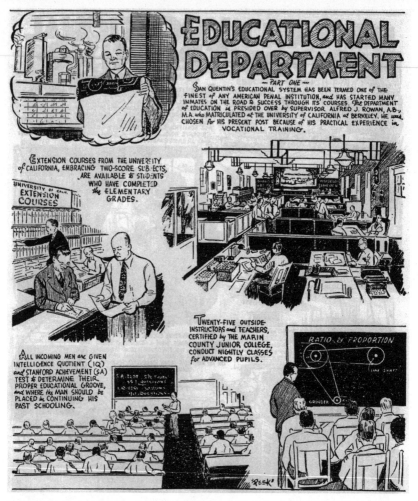

These scenes were familiar to Chessman, who took full advantage of all educational aspects of San Quentin during his first visit there. He even taught some of the classes. *The San Quentin Museum Association*

Chessman was clearly in a league of his own, charting new territory in prison house self-education. Varying reports of his high IQ can be found, ranging over the years from 136 to 178. The latter, reported by *Newsweek* in 1959, was called the "highest in San Quentin history."*

---

* The matter of Chessman's IQ came up after his execution, in a letter from Negley Teeters, a professor of criminology at Temple University, to Joseph Longstreth, Chessman's agent. Teeters had used the 178 figure in a book about criminology but was challenged by some "contending that his intelligence was much overrated."

The San Quentin Museum Association

So, how brilliant was he? Consider this, from Freeman's memoir:
"He was as brilliant a speaker as a teacher, and San Quentin rarely lost a match when he was on its debating team. With him and Red Tully leading the way, the prisoners defeated Stanford University and chalked up an impressive record against other schools, colleges, and clubs in the San Francisco Bay area."

Longstreth confessed to never having seen the 178 figure in any medical or prison file, that the number "may well be another of those enthusiastic press things, the result of the imagination of some reporter who needed desperately to make the wire services to help with his own advancement."

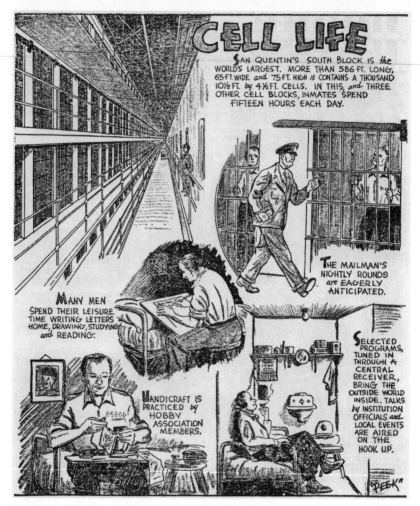

For most of the time during his first visit to San Quentin, Chessman was cellmates with Wilber Power Sewell (prisoner #66836), who later changed his name to Bill Sands and became one of America's foremost advocates for prisoners. *The San Quentin Museum Association*

■

FOR THE NEXT two years, he and Sands were nearly inseparable.

Most important, Chessman had in Sands a confidant whose intelligence and stability he respected and to whom he could explain his self-styled outlaw credo. He pulled no punches with Sands, never feigned remorse for his crimes or even pretended that, given another chance, he would get in lockstep on the straight and narrow. Rather, he tried to convince Sands of the "excitement" of operating successfully outside the law, as a philosophical activity. While Sartre and his clique would sit around Parisian cafes chainsmoking and chinwagging about existentialism, Chessman was living the life of the pure existentialist. He could have been a stand-in for Norman Mailer's "White Negro," the "psychic outlaw" the novelist marveled at in his infamous 1957 essay.

To Chessman—who was, and remained until his death, an agnostic—it was a test of wits: his intelligence against the police, against others in the Los Angeles crime underworld, against all forms of authority, including Warden Duffy's. As he was fond of pointing out in his books, Chessman insisted that crime *did* pay, and that it paid rather handsomely if done properly, and that money itself was not its strongest lure.

Chessman thrived during this time, developing his mind and his body. He lifted weights, swam, boxed, played baseball and football, and spent time helping around the Garden Beautiful, the prison's showpiece. This verdant haven in the center of the yard, which was started in the 1880s, had become the pride and joy of Dr. Leo Leonidas Stanley, the prison's surgeon and chief medical officer from 1913 to 1940. Dr. Stanley was as renowned for his dahlias and roses in the old Garden Beautiful as he was for his nasal reconstruction surgery—nose jobs. He felt that a man's perception of his own physical ugliness would lead to crime; thus he wanted to help remake their faces. He had some other unusual theories about criminal pathology, insisting that syphilis, tuberculosis, cancer, and port-wine stains (large, reddish-purple birthmarks) caused crime. He conducted his experiments at the prison hospital, an impressive structure that, when built in 1885, was the first of its kind in an American prison. He also set up a TB ward, which had unfortunate consequences for Stanley personally; his first wife contracted TB at the prison compound and died there.

Dr. Stanley gained his greatest notoriety for his research in "glandular rejuvenation." He was one of the leading proponents and practitioners of "testicular implantation," which consisted of surgically implanting and, later, hypodermically injecting prisoners with ground up testicles. This was purported by an earlier medical researcher,

Dr. George Frank Lydston of Chicago, to negate criminal urges. Between 1918 and 1940, Dr. Stanley and his staff performed 10,000 testicular implantations at San Quentin prison, claiming that inmates benefited greatly from the treatments, sleeping and eating better, becoming 'toned up' and 'more active and energetic.'" Partly as a consequence, many inmates experienced a rejuvenated interest in and capacity for sexual relations, not that it did them much good inside San Quentin.

Joseph T. Hallinan described the procedure in *Going Up the River: Travels in a Prison Nation*: "The exact procedure varied over time. In the early days testicles were removed from the scrotums of men who had just been executed—some of them so recently executed that their bodies were still warm. The testicles were then ground into a substance the consistency of toothpaste and injected with a syringe beneath the skin of the abdomen. . . . Demand for the testicular treatments at San Quentin soon outstripped supply. Typically, no more

San Quentin Prison's Garden Beautiful, the rare Norfolk pines and "The Porch" are seen in this 1915 photograph taken by prison guard Richard M. Smith. The Porch was the Captain of the Yard's office, where prisoners filed complaints and picked up work orders. Though the garden and the Porch are gone now, the towering Norfolk pines are still the prison's most stunning visual element from afar. *Courtesy Anne T. Kent California Room, Marin County Free Library*

Dr. Leo L. Stanley, Chief Surgeon at California State Prison, San Quentin. *Courtesy Anne T. Kent California Room, Marin County Free Library*

than five or six inmates a year were executed at the prison, yielding, on average, a testicle a month. Owing to this shortage of human material, Dr. Stanley began using the testes of rams, and later those of goats, boars, and even deer. Like the human testicles, these were shredded and injected into the abdomen wall of inmates."

Largely ridiculed at the time, the work Dr. Stanley and others blazed the trail for Viagra, the potency drug that, until reports in 2005 of its possible side effect of blindness, was the fastest selling pharmaceutical in the world. By 1942, partly due to reforms set in motion by Duffy, this practice was stopped. Thus, Chessman missed by mere months his chance to become a human guinea pig.*

■

WHILE CHESSMAN WAS in San Quentin, the nation had been lured into war by the Japanese attack on Pearl Harbor on December 7, 1941.

---

* Dr. Stanley donated his personal papers to the California Room at the Marin County Civic Center, where voluminous and graphic files of his medical experiments can be found.

Warden Duffy was determined to use his captive work force to aid the war effort. To that end, San Quentin became the most productive prison in America. Among the projects begun while Chessman was there was the manufacture of huge (75 by 225 feet) steel submarine nets, placed in coastal harbors, including the entrance to San Francisco Bay near the Golden Gate Bridge—where they remain today—to keep enemy submarines from entering. Cargo nets, braided rope "ship fenders," air raid sirens (many still in use), assault boats, ration books, and transport bunks were manufactured by the thousands for both the Allied armed forces and the home front. Another hugely successful project begun while Chessman was at the prison was a salvage and reclamation effort of battle-damaged warships. From the Pearl Harbor wreckage alone, San Quentin inmates reclaimed one million pounds of copper, lead, and rubber, bundled it and shipped it off to be used for more war matériel. They donated gallons of blood, increased burlap production at the jute mill, and grew their own vegetables on the prison grounds.

For the rest of 1942 and 1943, Chessman immersed himself intensely in every conceivable intellectual and physical pursuit the setting offered. He was a fixture at the prison library, reading at a graduate student's level in literature, history, philosophy, and mathematics. He wrote for (and then helped edit) the prison newspaper, wrote scripts for the prison radio station, earned his high school equivalency diploma, and took college correspondence courses. He told the prison administration that he planned to become a psychiatrist when he got out of prison.

His intellectual and extracurricular efforts were rewarded in May 1943, when his sentence was reduced and he was transferred from the maximum security San Quentin to the minimum security California Institution for Men, at Chino. Warden Duffy had personally interceded to get his protégé the new assignment. Only those for whom some hope for accelerated rehabilitation existed were sent to Chino. At Chino, there were no armed guards, towers, or even walls, per se. Visiting privileges were liberal, as were the educational opportunities.*

---

* The institution at Chino is still in operation today, housing more than six thousand "minimum through medium custody inmates."

Despite Chessman's long criminal record, they bent the rules a bit so that he could be sent there to develop his skills into some form that was marketable in the real world beyond the pipedreams of isolation cells, iron bars, barbed wire, and thick prison walls.

While at Chino, Chessman concocted an elaborate, if delusional, plan to assist the war effort. Never one to think small, he claimed that he wanted out of prison so that he could use his connections in the criminal underworld to travel to Germany, in order to kill Adolf Hitler.* At the time of Chessman's transfer to Chino, West Coast residents were wary of air attacks by the Japanese. Chessman volunteered for duty as an aircraft spotter; his request was approved. On August 13, 1943, Chessman walked away from his secluded, offsite observation tower and made his way back to his old stomping grounds in Los Angeles.

One can easily imagine how Chessman's escape must have been a source of embarrassment to Warden Duffy, perhaps tarnishing his reputation as a canny judge of character. It was also, no doubt, a slap in the face from an unrehabilitated street punk in whom he'd placed his trust. Duffy was forced to swallow the bitter truth that he'd been outsmarted by someone thirty years his junior, conned by the swaggering Chessman's good manners, his "yes sir, no sir" charade. But the warden was no Pollyanna. He knew the risks involved in granting special privileges. And he had escapes of his own at San Quentin to worry about. On November 1, 1943, two inmates sawed through their bars, raced down the hill toward the outer walls, heaved a homemade incendiary bomb at one of the guard towers, and in the ensuing mayhem were able to escape. On December 26, 1943, four more inmates escaped, and Duffy fired six guards for "laxity."

In her memoir, Mrs. Duffy wrote about Chessman: "This was not the first time that a prisoner for whom we had high hopes had let us down. . . . His behavior might not have been so inexplicable to us had he been less intelligent. But he was smart enough to know that the odds were all against his remaining free for more than just a short time."

---

* During World War II, many San Quentin inmates applied for parole in order to serve in the military; the inmate population, as a consequence, dropped from 5,200 in 1940 to a low of 3,700 in 1942.

Chessman's explanation for his escape—that he wanted to assassinate Hitler—was laughable. "It was fantastic," wrote Mrs. Duffy. "Yet it did sound like Caryl Chessman. He wanted so much to amount to something, and what surer way was there of attaining immortal fame than by ridding the world of the Fuhrer."

During his three weeks of freedom, Chessman spent most of the time hidden out with another obliging lady; he called her "Gabriella" in *Cell 2455, Death Row,* but her real identity isn't known. "Gabriella" nicknamed him "François" (for Villon). Though he'd hoped to collect some debts from a former associate, Chessman soon reverted to the typical trajectory of career criminals. He stole another car. He pulled off some robberies. He hung out with willing ladies. Besides "Gabriella," he shacked up with "Gina" (another mystery woman) and Lucy Ann, who apparently bore no grudge and who was, legally, still his wife. It was during this time that Lucy Ann got pregnant, presumably with Chessman's child. Chessman refers in some of his unpublished letters and journal entries to a daughter born in May 1944, which would make this his only window of paternity. A letter written from one of his lawyers to his literary agent after his death, however, refers to a woman named Genelle as being the mother of his daughter (perhaps she is the mystery woman named "Gina" from his book). It is not out of the realm of possibility that Chessman could have gotten two women pregnant during his few weeks of freedom, Lucy Ann and Genelle. Chessman was unquestionably a compulsive thief, but he was also something of a lady's man. Why none of these women testified at his eventual trial for the Red Light Bandit crimes is an enduring mystery. If nothing else, they could have attested that he was not a "sex deviant."

Predictably, he was recaptured in Los Angeles on September 5, 1943, and charged with escape, car theft, three robberies, and one attempted robbery. He was sentenced to five years, to be added to his earlier sentence of sixteen years to life.

In January 1944, he began the second of three residencies at San Quentin State Prison. Despite Warden Duffy's frustration with his former protégé, Chessman readjusted to prison life. The lack of manpower and the sheer amount of war preparation work to be done may have contributed to his less than hostile reception. He secured a front office secretarial job for Associate Warden Fred Dickson, who later became San Quentin's head warden. Though it's a cliché to suggest that prison life provided the discipline Chessman lacked in the "real" world, he did remarkably well for himself. Indeed, he impressed enough members of the powers that be—Duffy had essentially washed his hands of Chessman—that when the Adult Authority met to determine his ultimate sentence, he was told he might be paroled again in a year.

Lucy Ann, however, wasn't willing to wait. She visited Chessman at San Quentin. He agreed to give her a divorce, which came through in 1947. Lucy Ann disappeared from Chessman's life, though she would resurface again years later, once Chessman became world famous as a Death Row author. By then, she was remarried, bearing the name Lucy Ann Short, and a daughter—presumably by Chessman—was raised as her new husband's own.*

In August 1945, Chessman was transferred to Folsom State Prison, where recidivists, or "two-time losers," were sent. Addressing the parole board, he said, "Gentlemen: my mother is dying of cancer, my father is also in poor health. I am needed at home, and I've had my fill of prison. You can believe me when I say that I don't intend to do any more time."

For whatever reasons, the parole board believed he had been rehabilitated. He served, without incident, two more years and was paroled on December 8, 1947.

Less than two months later, he was arrested as the infamous Red Light Bandit.

∎

PUTTING ASIDE CHESSMAN'S guilt or innocence of the Red Light Bandit crimes, Mrs. Duffy in her memoir found other, more "thought provoking aspects to the Chessman case."

She wrote, "One question which cannot be brushed aside is: Why did the rehabilitation programs at both San Quentin and Chino fail so

---

* Several efforts by this author to contact Lucy Ann, still alive as late as 2004, were not successful.

completely with him? Why did he continually revert to a life of crime? He isn't a weakling, mentally or physically. He isn't a moral cretin. Perhaps, the answer is that a specific means of nullifying a criminal education is yet to be discovered. . . . Of Chessman, the prosecuting attorney said, 'This young man is completely worthless.' Similar comments were made about Thatcher, and about Nathan Leopold* who was given the chance to prove that he could make worthwhile contributions to society. So many wrecks are worth salvaging."*

---

* "Thatcher" was Phil Thatcher, a career criminal who spent time in San Quentin and Folsom Prisons. At Folsom at age thirty-six, he had a religious conversion, after which he organized the New Life Youth Camps, which had an impact on the lives of many troubled young men and was pardoned by Governor Earl Warren in 1953. Nathan Leopold (1904–1971) was one half of the notorious Leopold and Loeb, Chicago teenagers who killed a young boy for "thrills" in 1924. A plea for mercy by the famed lawyer Clarence Darrow got them life in prison rather than death sentences. Loeb was stabbed to death in his cell in 1936. Leopold spent his time learning languages (he was fluent in more than twenty-five), raising canaries, and organizing the prison education system. His good works earned him parole in 1958; he married in 1961 and moved to Puerto Rico where he lived quietly and by all accounts happily until his death.

4

The Red Light Bandit

BESIDES BEING A hotbed of organized crime, law enforcement on the take, shoddy land deals, and shoddier housing developments, Los Angeles in the 1940s was a petri dish of sexual excess. In addition to the usual nocturnal element found in any big city, Los Angeles was, from 1941 to 1945, the playground of choice for men in uniform on weekend furlough or shore leave looking for some action on the home front before possibly being killed in action overseas. Though the Los Angeles streets were wide open, the city's mouthpieces were politically conservative, even close-minded. There were six daily newspapers in Los Angeles at this time, two owned by the conservative William Randolph Hearst (*Los Angeles Examiner, Evening Herald and Express*) and two by the conservative Chandler family (*Los Angeles Times, Los Angeles Mirror*).

The tension between the conservative, superpatriotic and (after 1945) virulently anti-Communist ruling class and the no-holds-barred social scene gave the city something of a split personality, the pathology for which was found daily in the scandal sheets and on the police blotter. Some extremely gruesome and salacious things went down on a regular basis. This criminal milieu made for exceptionally good newspaper copy, especially when celebrities or fat-cat city fathers were discovered succumbing to the temptations of the spirit and the flesh. Almost daily, the papers were filled with titillating details of celebrity affairs, serial adultery, rape, mayhem and crimes of passion which inspired a cottage industry of true-crime magazines and added fuel to the tanks of the Hollywood gossip columnists Louella O. Parsons and Hedda Hopper.

Like the never-ending migration of people, crime flowed into Los Angeles in one long wave. The Los Angeles Police Department's statistics for 1948 indicate that 2,876 robberies, 530 rapes, 107 kidnappings, and 39 violations of Section 288a of the California Penal Code were reported.*

These, of course, don't include "victimless" crimes like prostitution, numbers running, illegal gambling and drug trafficking, all of which had mushroomed since the 1930s. The city's population in 1940 was 1,504,277 (the county's was 2,785,643), which skyrocketed to 1,970,358 in 1950 (4,151,687 in the county). Perhaps the statistical backdrop to Chessman's criminal career is most graphically conveyed by this figure: Los Angeles County accounted for 40 percent of California's population in 1950. Such density of population, having mushroomed in so short a time, would inevitably breed a criminal underworld.

Like all cultures based on puritanical ideas of sin and damnation, Los Angeles thrived on this Sodom and Gomorrah, alternately fascinated and repulsed by it. And, according to a contemporaneous account by Police Officer Charles Stoker, Los Angeles' version of Frank Serpico, the city's police force aided and abetted the crime and covered up for the criminals. Stoker, who wrote of his fight with the police establishment in *Thicker 'n Thieves* (1951), uncovered a pattern of corruption that was so rife and widespread, especially in the Gangster and Vice squads, that he, being an honest cop, was an odd man out. When another corruption scandal and purge hit the department in 1950, Stoker's early warnings were ignored, and he was forced out of his job. He died of a heart attack in 1975; he was working for the railroad when he should have been collecting a police pension and polishing his medals of commendation.

---

* The code reads: "Any person who willfully and lewdly commits any lewd or lascivious act, including any of the acts constituting other crimes provided for in Part 1, upon or with the body, or any part or member thereof, of a child who is under the age of 14 years, with the intent of arousing, appealing to, or gratifying the lust, passions, or sexual desires of that person or the child, is guilty of a felony. . . ."

In *Black Dahlia Avenger* (2004), Steve Hodel, a retired Los Angeles homicide detective, looked back on the same period of time documented by Stoker. As much as it pained Hodel to admit it about the department he loved and served with distinction for twenty-four years, he came to realize that the Los Angeles Police Department, the Los Angeles Sheriff's Department, and the District Attorney's office in the 1940s were no better than paid hirelings of Bugsy Siegel and Mickey Cohen. They "not only tolerated corruption, they fostered it," said Hodel.

While the police and sheriff's departments tolerated some criminal activity, they were shocked by a series of grisly rape-murders of women in the mid- to late-1940s. Not just any women, but young and aspiring actresses, heiresses, socially prominent divorcees—"classy dames," as it were. Between July 1943 and October 1949, there were as many as twenty cases of, as Hodel put it, "lone women found savagely murdered in the streets of Hollywood and downtown L.A."

The most famous and arguably most horrifying of such sex-soaked crimes was the Black Dahlia murder, which took place exactly one year before Chessman was arrested for the string of sex-soaked crimes that would briefly supplant it in the crime ledgers and scandal rags.

Elizabeth Short was a twenty-two-year-old aspiring actress who grew up in Medford, Massachusetts. Her parents separated when she was six; her father, Cleo Short, walked away from his family in 1930. Elizabeth grew up to be a popular and attractive teenager, but she was hounded by restless impulses. After dropping out of high school at seventeen, she went to Miami Beach, where she worked as a waitress. She met a World War II fighter pilot, fell in love and had her heart set on marrying him. In early 1943, while he was stationed overseas, she moved to Santa Barbara, 100 miles north of Los Angeles, and got a job at the Camp Cooke post exchange. She soon learned that her wayward father was living nearby in Vallejo, but their reunion was acrimonious and short-lived; he wanted nothing to do with his former family. She moved back to Santa Barbara and, though still considered a "minor" at nineteen, frequented clubs where military men gathered; she, by all accounts, loved men in uniform. She was arrested in September 1943, for being in a place that served liquor and sent back to Medford. She drifted back to Florida and then California by war's end.

Her beloved pilot was killed in a crash in April 1945, and her itinerant cycle began again. She moved again to Miami Beach; by 1946 she'd drifted back to California with a vague idea of trying her luck in Hollywood. Her big Hollywood break never arrived. During the year she lived in Los Angeles, she retained no fixed address and lived in boarding houses and apartments with groups of other aspiring models and actresses. She dressed with sophistication and favored black clothes. She became a fixture at Los Angeles nightclubs and dated a number of men simultaneously—she slept around, but she was not turning tricks. She was not a nymphomaniac—perhaps she was, in fact, a typical aspiring actress, desperate for a break if not affirmation of her beauty—but she wasn't a drunk or a druggie (by all accounts, she sipped soft drinks during her nocturnal rambles). She just seemed driven by fear and danger.

Her fall from grace ended on the night of January 14, 1947, when her body was found, in two large pieces, in a vacant lot at South Norton Avenue near Thirty-ninth Street in Leimart Park. Short's body had been cut cleanly in half at the waist. Her legs were found spread apart. It was determined that she'd been ritualistically tortured for hours, sodomized, and cigarettes snuffed out on her back. She was made to eat feces and then beaten to death. After she died, her killer(s) cut her open and removed chunks of her body, which were then crammed into her vagina (pubic hair trimmed by the killer) and rectum. The final signature of the killer's, or killers', handiwork: the corners of Elizabeth Short's mouth had been surgically extended into a large "smile."

The twisted crime transfixed Los Angeles. For twelve weeks straight, the newspapers were filled with the lurid details of "Black Dahlia" (the name bestowed on Short by the press, presumably taken from the 1946 film *The Blue Dahlia*, the screenplay for which was written by L.A.'s king of noir, Raymond Chandler), her allegedly sinful life, and sordid death. Every conceivable theory was propounded for her demise, including lesbianism, pornography (she, like many aspiring actresses, posed in the nude), alcohol, drugs, psychosis—all but incipient communism. She was referred to in nearly every story as a "playgirl" or "party girl"—code words for "slut." The implication was she had it coming, that it was just desserts. The killer, who was never apprehended, got lost in translation; perhaps readers saw him as their stand-in, poking, prodding, examining what made the Black Dahlia tick, and ultimately finding her, just as right-thinking citizens did, repulsive.

James Ellroy suggested that this might be the case. Ellroy, a novelist who grew up in the neighborhood where Short's body was found and whose mother had been brutally murdered in Los Angeles, wrote in his memoir *My Dark Places*, "The case was a huge news event. Jack Webb steeped his twelve-page summary* in the ethos of the time: Femme fatales die hard and are complicitous in attracting death by vivisection. He didn't understand the killer's intention or know that his gynecological tampering defined the crime. He didn't know that the killer was horribly afraid of women. He didn't know that he cut the Dahlia open to see what made women different from men."* The Dahlia case, Ellroy, said, "defined [Short's] time and place."

Indeed it did, yet what has been called the "most shocking murder in the twentieth century" would remain unsolved until 2003. It appears that the Los Angeles Police Department did not want the case to be solved. It took the retired Hodel to plumb the depths of this crime in his astonishing book *Black Dahlia Avenger* (with a foreword by Ellroy). Hodel not only discovered a deep personal connection to Short's murder, he learned that his own police department had, in 1947, hidden, buried, and destroyed evidence in the

---

* Jack Webb, actor and shill for the LAPD, published a book called *The Badge* (1958), in which he summarized the Dahlia murder along with other crimes. The book was an offshoot of his radio and TV series, *Dragnet*, which ran in various incarnations from 1949 to 1970. Ellroy called *Dragnet* "the saga of dead-end lives up against authority. Suppressive police methods insured a virtuous L.A. . . . It was the epic of isolated men in an isolating profession, deprived of conventional illusions and traumatized by their daily contact with scum. It was '50s-style male angst—alienation as a public service announcement." Criminals were often compared to Communists on *Dragnet*.

Dahlia case in order to protect prominent citizens. It was, Hodel wrote, "an organized conspiracy within the Los Angeles Police Department . . . one of the biggest corruption scandals in the history of the department," and its coverup stayed intact for fifty-five years. Even now, they refuse to acknowledge that this cold case has finally been solved.

Nonetheless, the pressure on the police department after the Black Dahlia, and the other murders of lone women that were to follow, was intense. As Hodel wrote, "The stigma of the nation's most horrific and sadistic murder, the Black Dahlia, had been burned into the collective psyche of the Los Angeles public and the case remained an open wound that would not heal."

Three weeks after Short's death, in February 1947, the wound widened when another brutally mutilated female corpse was found. This was Jeanne French, who had been "stomped to death" and whose naked body was covered with a message, inscribed in red lipstick, "Fuck You, B.D." This became known to the six competing Los Angeles dailies as "The Red Lipstick Murder," and like the Black Dahlia remained unsolved, the coldest of cold cases. But, as Hodel learned, evidence related to this crime was also tampered with inside the police department. Again, it was part of an "organized conspiracy."

This chain of brutal rapes and murders of lone young women continued throughout the rest of the year: Ica M'Grew on February 12; Evalyn Winters on March 11; Dorothy Montgomery on May 2; Laura Trelstad on May 11; Anna Diresio on May 12; Rosenda Mondragon on July 8; Marian Newton, in San Diego, on July 17.

In the wake of the Black Dahlia, Red Lipstick, and other murders, Los Angeles police used the pretext of searching for the killers to set up roadblocks and indiscriminately search stopped cars. On March 15, 1947, seventy-two suspects were arrested as part of this "Crime Crusher" effort, and on March 26, another fifty-five were rounded up. It was, it turned out, a publicity stunt to make it look as though they took the murders seriously. Hodel has suggested they already knew who committed the murders but were sitting on the evidence.

∎

INTO THIS HYSTERIA-TINGED atmosphere marched the would-be poet laureate of banditry, Caryl Chessman. He could not have picked a worse climate in which to reembark on a life of crime in Los Angeles. Since his incarceration in Folsom Prison, Chessman had served six years for armed robbery and again seemed to pull himself together within the discipline of the prison system, so much so that he was paroled in December 1947, with several years cut from his original sentence. He moved back in with his parents, at Larga Avenue in Glendale. The façade of normalcy was gone, and familial relations were strained to the breaking point. Nevertheless, Serl Chessman hired his son to be a handyman at his florist shop. Chessman was twenty-six and was not likely to get another chance. He was to enjoy only forty more days of life outside the walls of a prison.

In the interim since Chessman's last imprisonment, seismic shifts had occurred in the Los Angeles criminal underworld, indicating a power struggle from within the Mob's own ranks. The biggest crime news of the year occurred just six months before Chessman walked out of Folsom Prison. Bugsy Siegel, who'd run the rackets, including prostitution and bookmaking, since his arrival in Los Angeles in 1939, was executed "gangland style" on June 20, 1947, at the Hollywood bungalow of the actress Virginia Hill. He had purchased the bungalow, at 810 North Linden Drive, for Hill; when she was out of town, as she was this June day (having, some suspect, been tipped off to the "hit"), he liked to repair there to decompress. The hit man or men (some speculate that two were involved) waited for him in the bushes outside. Nine shots were fired; six hit Siegel in the face. Like the Dahlia and Lipstick murderers, the killer(s) were never apprehended, though their identities were probably known to the police.

According to Sgt. Stoker, the Hollywood prostitution ring that Chessman had regularly preyed upon in his "boy bandit" days was a Siegel enterprise. Brenda Allen, the Heidi Fleiss of her day and owner of the nicknames "Hollywood Madame" and "Queen of Hearts," oversaw a prostitution ring that had as many as 114 prostitutes under her bordello's roof; Allen took in $1,200 per day, a chunk of it going to the police for protection. Sgt. Stoker had, with a grand jury's support, arrested Allen in 1948, at which point his days on the police force were numbered. He was indicted on a trumped-up burglary charge, was acquitted, but was fired from the police force for "conduct unbecoming a police officer" for operating "without the approval of his superior officers on the vice squad."

After Siegel's murder, the syndicate was taken over by Mickey Cohen, a less flamboyant, more buttoned-down but equally murderous Brooklyn-born mobster. While Siegel had accepted police graft as part of the price of doing business in L.A., Cohen was less willing to share the loot. This guaranteed a less hospitable reception from the segment of the police force who were on the take, many of whom were on the same vice squad that would hang Sgt. Stoker out to dry.

How corrupt were the Los Angeles law enforcement agencies in the 1940s? It could be argued, based on Sgt. Stoker's revelations and the findings of a 1949 grand jury, that a large segment of them were more corrupt than the criminals they were hired to stop. For example, a rogue group of police illegally wiretapped Cohen's home while it was being built. During the first year of his residence, in response to his unwillingness to spread the wealth, they built up a large file of damning intelligence on Cohen. They had no interest, however, in arresting him for the nefarious doings they uncovered, nor were they interested in ending his reign as a crime lord. They simply wanted to extort money from Cohen, using the tapes and transcripts as collateral. Another time, when Cohen indicated that he would testify to the 1949 grand jury about widespread corruption among the police and the D.A.'s office, rogue cops were suspected in an attempted hit on his entourage outside a Sunset Boulevard cocktail lounge. They killed a state attorney general's investigator but only wounded Cohen. Presumably recalling those six bullets that hit Siegel, Cohen reconsidered his decision to testify.

Los Angeles law enforcement officers, corrupt and honest ones alike, had long memories. If they were capable of carrying out a hit on a big fish like Mickey Cohen—and even murder a state investigator in the process—they would certainly not hesitate to squash any of the small fries who got in their way. Indeed, it is likely that ill will from Chessman's earlier incarnation as the Boy Bandit Gang leader—his cutting into their profits by robbing pimps, madames, and bookies—still lingered.

"The Los Angeles Police Department would be on notice that Chessman was back in town, no question about that," said Hodel in an interview with this author. "The jungle drums between the Big Houses and cops through their snitch/informant network were always active. Very little of a criminal nature came and went without most cops knowing about it. Chessman would have bigger problems if he invaded or crossed into the cops' gambling and vice operations, than those of any organized crime. If he hit bordellos, such as Brenda Allen's, or others, that could be a major problem for him."

Chessman obliged his nemeses on the police force by returning almost immediately to a life of crime. According to Machlin and Woodfield, he also took up with a prostitute who worked out of a house near the Hollywood police station and whose boyfriend was a police detective there. This was in addition to reconnecting with an old girlfriend who, by then, was married to a gangster, who routinely beat her. Chessman swore revenge on the man, who did likewise on him.

In short, within days of his December 1947 return to Los Angeles, Chessman had both arms elbow deep in hornets' nests. His rearrest for something, anything, was inevitable. And when that arrest occurred, it seemed that the cops wanted to pin everything they could think of on him. Among the eighteen crimes with which Chessman was originally charged were the following: robbery (taking checks and money from Donald E. McCullough on January 3, 1948); grand theft (stealing Rose K. Howell's car on Jan. 13, 1948); burglary (entering Mary Tarro's house on January 17, 1948); and robbery (taking clothes worth $500 and $214 in cash from Melvin Waisler on January 23, 1948). These were just the crimes with which he was charged. Undoubtedly, the police thought, if he were capable of such manic criminal activity, he'd committed others in that short span of time. He admitted as much at his trial for the Red Light Bandit crimes later that year, confessing to having assisted in the robbery of an illegal bookmaker.

■

CHESSMAN'S LIFE AS a free man ended on the night of Friday, January 23, 1948. He and an accomplice named David H. Knowles pulled a robbery at a Redondo Beach clothing store at 6:30. While Chessman guarded the door, Knowles—a convicted burglar out on parole from the California Institution for Men at Chino—forced the proprietor and a clerk into the back room at gunpoint; then, the two men stole $300 from the till and some clothing off the racks. Chessman and Knowles were later identified by the victims as the robbers.

Within an hour of this robbery, an All Points Bulletin was issued by the Los Angeles police. It read, verbatim:

> Male Cauc, possibly Italian, swarthy complexion, 23–25 years, 5'6" to 5'10", 150–170 lbs, thin to medium build, dk brn wavy hair—close cut, dk brn eyes, crooked teeth, narrow nose with slight hump on bridge of nose, sharp chin, possible scar over eyebrow. Armed with .45 old looking blk automatic. Puts on white handkerchief covering lower part of face when talking to victims. Uses small pen type flashlight. Believed to be driving early model 1947 or late 1946 light gray or beige club coupe, back of front seat is split to facilitate getting into back seat, dash board has red and white numerals on speedometer & clock which reflects a red cast on dash board when lighted (possible all of dash board is painted red), 4" beneath each front headlight there is a circle parking light. On body in rear above license holder is a plain chrome bar with "Ford" in center of bar. A red spot light has been seen on left and right side of car—believe this to be a portable spot light with red lens; possible radio underneath dash board, no antenna on car. Believe suspect when operating keeps license plate in baggage compartment in rear of car and after leaving

scene of crime replaces license on auto. Clothes worn by suspect vary from brown or black slacks with tweed coats, brn, leather jacket, gray checked overcoat, light gray hat. Interrogate any and all occupants using above described vehicle, check rear compartment for spot light and license plates. Use caution as suspect armed. Any info notify this dept. (Forbes & Hubka-HWD-DR 426758. C B Horrall). Cop ck. At end of 19th line delete last two words "in baggage" make it read "license plate and spot light in baggage."

Officers Robert J. May and John D. Reardon received this APB and had already pulled over two cars bearing a resemblance to the one described in the report. They spotted the car that Chessman was driving, a gray Ford coupe, at 7:40 P.M. Chessman was headed north on Vermont Avenue near the intersection of Hollywood Boulevard in Hollywood; Knowles and another, unnamed man were his passengers. The police patrol car began its pursuit, with Officer Reardon driving. Noticing the police car in his mirror, Chessman pulled into and through a Richland gas station and then proceeded south onto Vermont Avenue. Chessman later claimed that they had gone to the gas station to use the rest room and, upon noticing the police, he pulled away with Knowles in the car, leaving the third man behind. While the latter was completing his business in the rest room, Chessman and Knowles continued on. Though tantalizing as a potential witness to Chessman's role in the Red Light Bandit crimes—or perhaps even the Red Light Bandit himself—this third accomplice was not named on the night of the arrest, and only later came up during the trial, when Officer Reardon testified that he did not see anyone exit Chessman's car at the gas station. (The mystery this third party added to Chessman's case has still not been resolved.)

Reardon turned on his red light and his siren, and Chessman sped up, crossing Sunset Boulevard at 50 miles per hour. It is presumed by those who came to loathe Chessman that he was fleeing because he was guilty of the Red Light Bandit crimes. It could more persuasively be argued, however, that he was fleeing because he was driving a stolen car, one that had presumably been used in a robbery; he did not have a valid driver's license; and any violation of his parole would send him back to state prison for a long time. Whatever Chessman's motive for fleeing, he ran a red light at Santa Monica Boulevard, nearly broadsiding a car in the process. As he and the police sped past Los Angeles City College at upward of eighty miles per hour, Officer May leaned out the passenger window and began, like someone in an Edward G. Robinson movie, firing his revolver at Chessman's car. Having emptied his own revolver, May secured Officer Reardon's revolver and recommenced firing at Chessman's car. Knowles was, according to Chessman's later testimony, in a panic in the front seat throughout this gunfire, trying to crawl over Chessman and out of the speeding vehicle.

It seems, in hindsight, inconceivable that such a scene would take place on a busy city thoroughfare just after dinnertime—bullets ricocheting wildly, cars being broadsided or grazed, pedestrians scattering, glass flying—but there it was. Contrast this chase scene with the 1994 pursuit of O. J. Simpson in his white Ford Bronco through the same streets of Los Angeles at the same time of day. Simpson, the prime (sole) suspect in a ghastly double murder of his wife and her companion, and arguably at that moment the most wanted man in city history, was allowed to dictate the terms of surrender with the Los Angeles police. Chessman and Knowles, wanted for questioning in connection to some robberies, could easily have been shot to death, not to mention innocent bystanders wounded or killed, before a single question was asked or charge filed. So it went in 1948 when Los Angeles was still, in many ways, living out the myth of the Wild West and the legacy of Capone's Chicago.*

Somehow, amid this fusillade, four of Officer May's bullets hit their target, one shattering the rear window of the stolen Ford. Nevertheless, the cars continued past Melrose Avenue and Beverly Boulevard, at which point an approaching police car pulled into Chessman's path. Chessman veered the Ford up on to the sidewalk, turned left

---

* The U.S. Senate's Kefauver Committee, charged with investigating the rising crime wave in America, concluded in 1947 that Southern California was the "new Chicago" for organized crime syndicates.

on Sixth Street, and came to a crashing halt, colliding with a squad car at Shatto Place.

David Knowles surrendered as soon as the car stopped, but Chessman ran down Shatto Place, with Officer May in hot pursuit, continuing to fire his revolver. Officer Reardon and another officer, E. D. Phillips, joined the chase and all three cornered Chessman against a fence. They beat him with a flashlight. He was unarmed.

His Ford bore the stolen license plate number 8Y1280; there were two more stolen license plates on the back seat. The car was registered under license plate number 7P5618. In the car were some of the stolen merchandise from the Redondo Beach clothier: a topcoat, leather jacket, three suits, some pants and hats. Other items confiscated included a red ribbon, pair of gloves and a "hair rat,"—a hair-shaping device used mostly by women—as well as a .45 caliber automatic, a toy pistol, and a pen-type flashlight.

Chessman was dressed in a tan gabardine topcoat, brown tweed sport coat, and dark slacks. He wore brown leather gloves.

Three officers, including May, accompanied Chessman on the drive to the Hollywood police station on North Wilcox. Officer May reportedly asked him, "Why didn't you shoot back?" but Chessman did not respond.

He was officially booked as Caryl W. Chessman, of 3280 Larga Avenue, Glendale. He was searched and in his pocket was found a small nut with a piece of wire attached, $150 in currency, an "Eversharp pen and pencil set," a wallet, and some papers.

Among these papers, curiously enough, was a tantalizing glimpse of the life Chessman might have led, had he turned his hand to literature rather than to crime when he left prison in December 1947. He had a hand-drawn map of several houses in Malibu, an exclusive enclave near Topanga Beach. One of the houses was labeled "Walter Wanger" and thus was presumed to belong to the film director of that name. Later, at Chessman's trial, the house in question, at 18708 Old Malibu Road, was identified as actually belonging to Ludwig Bemelmans,* an author Chessman admired and claimed to have wanted to meet. Other houses depicted belonged to the actor Sterling Hayden (who later became an acclaimed novelist) and the actress Doris Dudley. In his testimony at Chessman's trial, Wanger (rhymes with "stranger") memorably said, "I've never owned a house at Malibu. I know some people who live there, however. They're lucky."*

The map was drawn by René (a.k.a. Robert) Salembier, whom Chessman had earlier befriended in Folsom Prison and with whom he'd reconnected on the street. Salembier had been a factotum for Bemelmans, claiming not only to work as his chauffeur but also as his secretary. Salembier was impressed by a satiric story Chessman had written in and shown him in prison, purported to be the introduction to a satiric novel about Hollywood he wanted to complete.†

According to testimony at Chessman's trial, Salembier "thought the story was as good as his former boss's stuff" and, further, told Chessman that "Bemelmans himself would be a fine character to satirize" ("This man I worked for was, as we say in the street, a poser"). After Salembier's testimony, the prosecution gave up the attempt to portray the map as part of a plot to burglarize Bemelmans. It is still a mystery why the house was labeled "Walter Wanger" on the map.‡

■

THE POLICE DID, in fact, remember Chessman well from his earlier incarnation as the boy bandit ringleader. As soon as he arrived at the Hollywood station, he was reminded by officers on duty about an incident

---

* Ludwig Bemelmans (1898–1962) was an artist, writer, and bon vivant best known for his books about Madeline, the precocious lass trapped inside a Parisian convent school, which he'd begun to publish in 1939. His was a rags-to-riches story, having emigrated from the Austrian Tirol to the United States in 1914, working as a busboy and banquet official at the Ritz-Carlton for many years before turning his hand to full-time writing and art. He lived in Hollywood during the war years, working as a screenwriter for MGM; though the work was frustrating—only one of his screenplays, *Yolanda and the Thief* (1945), was made into a film—he enjoyed the leisurely pace of Southern California. By the late 1940s, Bemelmans had moved his home base back to Manhattan. It is easy, given Chessman's later taste in literature, to see how he'd be fond of Bemelmans's writings.

† The story was "Dust Thou Art," which was found among Chessman's unpublished manuscripts.

‡ Wanger himself faced serious criminal charges two years later, when he shot an agent named Jennings Lang on December 13, 1951, for "unwarranted attentions" to his wife, the actress Joan Bennett; he eventually served a three-month sentence for assault with a deadly weapon.

in 1941 in which he'd humiliated two fellow cops by stealing their guns and their squad car. Rather than deny it, Chessman had, according to a detective at his trial, swelled with pride over the incident.

After being booked, Chessman spent almost three days in police custody—from Friday night until Monday afternoon—before charges were filed; that is, before a "confession" was extracted from him. During those roughly seventy-two hours without a visit from a family member, friend, or lawyer, Chessman was questioned, cajoled, beaten, and "tortured" (his word) by a series of Los Angeles police officers that included homicide detectives Arnold Hubka, Colin Forbes, and Elliott Goosen (homicide was not included among the charges), as well as Sgt. Donald W. Grant. Such elaborate "third degrees" were par for the course in the days before the 1966 *Miranda* decision.* Coerced confessions, whether by beating, sleep deprivation, torture, or isolation were the norm. As long as they were done out of sight of the district attorney, they were ignored, if not tacitly tolerated. David Goewey, in his book about Sing Sing Prison in the 1940s, writes, "As long as the D.A. didn't see anyone getting hit or kicked, he could plausibly deny being witness to any brutality. And as long as the transcripts contained suspects' assurances that their statements were voluntary, the law was satisfied."

This is what happened to Chessman and Knowles following their arrests on January 23, 1948. Both suspects testified that they were beaten by Sgt. Grant soon after they arrived at the station. Knowles told the court that he could hear Chessman being beaten severely in the next room just prior to Knowles himself being beaten unconscious by Grant. Grant did not appear as a witness at the trial of either Knowles or Chessman. Among the detectives who did appear at Knowles's and Chessman's trials was Forbes, who had taken over the interrogation from Sgt. Grant on Saturday morning, January 24. Off and on for the rest of the day, Forbes interrogated Chessman.

---

* In *Miranda v. Arizona*, the U.S. Supreme Court guaranteed that an arrested suspect had the right to remain silent and the right to have an attorney present during questioning. The decision would not have been necessary had law enforcement officers not routinely beaten confessions out of suspects for decades; the Los Angeles Police Department was renowned for excesses in this regard.

According to his later testimony, he got Chessman to admit his guilt for the clothing store robbery. At one point, he took Chessman to a steak house across the street from the Hollywood station. The offer of a meal did not sway Chessman, who continued to deny the sex crimes. A police psychiatrist named Paul J. De River also interviewed Chessman but could get nothing out of him about sex crimes.

By Monday, January 26, on Chessman's third day of custody, Forbes said that he had gotten the suspect to admit guilt to the sex crimes. No signed or taped confession was presented in court, however, and no other record exists, other than Chessman's testimony, of what took place in the final day and a half of custody before this alleged confession was made.

At his son's subsequent trial, Serl Chessman testified that he wasn't allowed to visit his son at the police station until late Monday afternoon, January 26. He said that he noticed then that there were extensive bruises on his son's body.

■

KNOWLES WENT ON trial one month before Chessman. Because he had "pistol-whipped" one of the clothing store employees with his gun while Chessman was in the front room standing guard, Knowles was found guilty of a California Penal Code Section 209 kidnapping. Though, as Chessman would learn, this violation carried a potential death sentence, Knowles was given two consecutive life terms, one without possibility of parole, and two other terms of five years to life.*

Chessman was transferred on January 27 to Cell Block 10A2 of the county jail. There, two other men in custody, Manuel Fox and Howard Gibson, later said that they had noticed that Chessman's cheekbones were swollen, one thumb was dislocated or fractured, his shins were

---

* Giving compelling ammunition to those who later insisted Chessman's two death sentences constituted cruel and unusual punishment, Knowles never served the bulk of his sentence. Once Chessman was sent to Death Row, Knowles won an appeal hearing in the State Supreme Court, which voted 4 to 3 to reverse the robbery counts, and was eligible for parole; by the time of Chessman's execution, Knowles was back out on the street.

bloody and raw from the knees to the ankles, and his chest was completely discolored from bruises. Fox said that he'd noticed also that Chessman was retching from having been "kicked in the groin." He pissed blood for days thereafter. According to medical records, he lost twelve pounds in the two and a half days in custody.

The police medical report, however, claimed "inspection reveals no marks, scars or bruises," according to Machlin and Woodfield.

The only officers who later testified at Chessman's trial were those who had not beaten him.

"There are only two kinds of police officers," Chessman would tell the prosecuting attorney in court, "the kind that beat you after they catch you and the kind that testify in court after you have been beaten."

Given the climate of corruption within the Los Angeles Police Department at this time—documented by both Sgt. Stocker and Steve Hodel—it is conceivable that the police could have been waiting for a marked former con like Chessman upon whom to dump a load of unsolved cases. That he also had a history of stealing from police-protected rackets—and taking delight in it—gave them added motivation for payback.

As noted earlier, it is conceivable that Chessman committed all, or some of, the crimes with which he was charged on January 23, 1948. Regardless of his guilt or innocence, however, Chessman's "confession" was partially beaten out of him and he was subjected to treatment that would not be tolerated today. Although most of the LAPD's old records, including Chessman's, have been destroyed, the travesty of his trial for the "Red Light Bandit" crimes is on the public record, for anyone to examine, either via William J. Kunstler's 1961 detailed deconstruction of Chessman's original trial, *Beyond a Reasonable Doubt?* or Frank J. Parker's 1974 book *Caryl Chessman: Red Light Bandit.*

■

THE BEATING OF Chessman was an attempt to get him to confess to a series of crimes in the Los Angeles area that, as long as they remained unsolved, would result in a nonstop stream of bad publicity for a law enforcement community already facing pressure from the public and the state's attorney general's office. Chessman, in their eyes, had a close enough resemblance to witnesses' descriptions to make his "interrogation" seem worthwhile, and he was that same arrogant punk who'd been ripping them off since 1940.

According to the police blotter, five incidents of "red light banditry" had taken place in the Los Angeles area between four thirty A.M., Sunday, January 18, 1948, and two A.M., Thursday, January 22, 1948. A late-model Ford was cited by victims in four of the five incidents. The incidents were, as follows:

> 1) In Malibu, on the Pacific Coast Highway, Dr. Thomas B. Bartle was robbed at 4:35 A.M. The assailant was described to the police as "stocky, 5'6", 150 lbs." The assailant wore no mask, and had crooked front teeth. Though none of these features matched Chessman (who stood over 6 feet tall and had straight teeth), the assailant was said to identify him at the police station.
>
> 2) Thirteen hours later, at five P.M. on an isolated road overlooking the Rose Bowl in Pasadena, an assailant was said to have robbed Floyd E. Ballew and Elaine Bushaw, who were parked here. The assailant, who allegedly slapped the woman and robbed the man, was not wearing a mask and was described as 5'7" tall and weighing approximately 150 pounds. Though, again, this physical description did not match Chessman, he was allegedly identified by the couple at the police station.
>
> 3) Twenty-six hours later, on January 19, at 7:30 P.M., a couple was parked in Flintridge Hills in Pasadena— Chessman's revered boyhood stomping grounds—overlooking the lights of Los Angeles. The assailant was masked this time and allegedly forced Mrs. Regina E. Johnson, parked in the car with Jarnigan Lea (not her husband), at gunpoint out of the car and led her to his car twenty-two feet away. The assailant allegedly told Mrs. Johnson to

remove her underpants. She informed him that she was menstruating, so he exposed himself and forced her to perform fellatio, an "unnatural sexual act" under Section 288a of the California penal code. Mrs. Johnson claimed to have glimpsed the assailant's face behind the mask. It was her adamant testimony that was credited with getting Chessman one of his death sentences. The assailant's semen was said to have been on the victim's coat, but no tests were run on it.

4) On the same day (January 19) on Mulholland Drive in Laurel Canyon, Gerald Stone and Esther Panasuk were robbed at gunpoint. Stone testified that the car was not the same one (or same make and model) as the others identified. There was no physical or sexual assault; the couple was robbed and left alone.

5) On January 22, at one thirty A.M. seventeen-year-old Mary Alice Meza and twenty-one-year-old Frank Hurlbut were sitting in a parked car on Mulholland Drive after having attended a church dance. A masked assailant parked behind the car, flashed a red light and approached the victims. He was said to have forced Mary Alice Meza out of Hurlbut's car and into his, demanding that Hurlbut pull forward a few yards and wait for him. Instead, Hurlbut drove away; the assailant pursued briefly and then gave up. He kept Meza for two hours, during which he forced her to undress and lie down on the back seat, at which point he attempted rape, which was verified later by bruises. Meza, a virgin, was menstruating, and the assailant allegedly forced her to perform fellatio, after which he dropped her off within a few blocks of her home. After a rash of red light banditry, an APB was put out for a late-model Ford.

■

MUCH SPECULATION HAS been made over the years about who might have been the real Red Light Bandit if indeed Chessman was innocent of the kidnapping charges. Two editors from *Saga* magazine, Milton Machlin and William Read Woodfield, published a book-length exposé the year after Chessman's execution in which they proposed that the real bandit was one Saverio Terranova (aka Thud Carson, Charles E. Downey, Frank Felice, Thomas A. Ganser, Charles Kelso, Fred Larson, Leroy Reece, Louis Reece, Charles S. Tarranova, Charles Saverine Terranova, Charles Sevrine Terranova, Henry A. Terranova, and Saverin Terranova). The speculation was fueled in part by Chessman, who claimed in court that "Joe Terranova" was the man he and Knowles had let out of the car at the Richland gas station on January 23, the same man who'd supplied the Ford coupe that Chessman was driving upon his arrest, a car later determined to have been stolen from Rose K. Howell of Pasadena on January 13.

Chessman spent some time with the two *Saga* editors toward the end of his life when they were putting together a magazine feature on his case. Chessman told them that he had met Terranova in Folsom Prison, where the latter was known as "The General." They had run in some of the same circles, inside and outside of prison, and they bore a passing physical resemblance to one another. They were never friends; as Machlin and Woodfield said, "they did not particularly care for each other personally . . . [Chessman's] principal value to the gang was as a getaway chauffeur."

He and Terranova were the same age, both born in 1921, but Terranova, if one believed the FBI's physical descriptions, more fully fit the initial descriptions given by the assault victims on the nights of the crimes in January 1948. He was, according to the FBI wanted poster, 5'9", weighed 170 pounds, and had a scar on his forehead from a knife fight, just as some victims described. His criminal record included armed robbery, burglary, car theft, and passing bad checks. He was deemed armed and dangerous and, according to the FBI poster, capable of just about any crime.

After leaving Folsom in December 1947, Chessman testified that he'd met with Terranova in Los Angeles "five or six times" prior to his arrest for the Red Light Bandit crimes. He had, he said, helped Terranova get a stolen car repaired. He'd also participated in the robbery of a bookmaker with Terranova; they split the $2,300 take.

According to Machlin and Woodfield, Terranova had ties with a mob competing with Mickey Cohen's syndicate for control of Los Angeles bookmaking. Terranova, the reporters claimed, "was looking for help on an assignment . . . to harass Cohen's bookies." Their modus operandi was to shake down a Cohen bookie while he still had the "juice"—the protection money paid to the police—thus engendering the wrath of both the cops and the syndicate.

Machlin and Woodfield's case for Terranova's guilt seemed sensational and compelling at the time but is, in hindsight, inconclusive. The real Terranova was sent back to Folsom, from which he was released in 1955, and he was later arrested for other crimes in Texas. His criminal impulses burned themselves out by the time he left prison in Texas in 1961, at which point he married, moved back to Los Angeles, and raised a family.

His son, Ricci Terranova, was born in 1963 in Texas, and the family moved to Venice, California, in 1967. Ricci, now in the music business in Los Angeles, told this author that, though he was born after the Chessman case had run its course, he spoke regularly with his father about his criminal past and about Chessman. Ricci is adamant that his father was never an accomplice, or even a friend, of Chessman's.

"The only time my father told me he actually met Chessman was when they were incarcerated in Folsom Prison," he said. "There was an incident that took place between them at Folsom. Chessman was quite the loud talker, my dad said, he liked to 'shoot his mouth off,' and my father punched him out. It was not really a fight. My father threw one punch and that ended it."

Charles Terranova told his son that the district attorney tried to cut a deal with him regarding the Red Light Bandit crimes.

"They wanted my dad to admit to being associated with these crimes," he said. "They told him they would reduce his sentence if he admitted to being an accomplice. But my dad wouldn't do that."

Ricci Terranova also takes exception to the physical description of his father provided by the FBI.

"My father was not a small man," he said. "He stood close to 6 feet 1 inch and was strong. I'm five foot ten, and he towered over me. He was a proud Sicilian. If you asked him 'Are you Italian?' he'd say 'No, I'm Sicilian!' I always knew him to be honest and ethical in his dealings with other people. He was a painting foreman with the school district. He painted all the structures on Fourth Street in Santa Monica. He owned a cleaners with my mother and he also owned a landscaping business. He worked hard and adored my mother. These crimes . . . were heinous; my father was not that sort of man. When a person has a violent tendency, that they strike out at people and cause physical harm, I don't think that that just disappears. My mother wouldn't tolerate being with a violent person. Something would have certainly indicated to me and my mother that he had this violent impulse, but he was not a violent man. My father got wrapped up in something when he was young and then got to a point in his life when he realized he was not the only one who matters."

Others picked up on Machlin and Woodfield's thesis over the years, doggedly following up every possible lead in an effort to prove Chessman's innocence of the Red Light Bandit crimes.

Harold Doty, a friend of the Chessman family, said that he knew, even back then, who the real Red Light Bandit was. As he would testify at Chessman's trial, Doty was at the Chessman's house twice, for extended visits, during the week that some of the so-called Red Light Bandit crimes were being committed in January 1948. He did not know Caryl Chessman well, having met him only after he had gotten out of prison in December 1947. His connection with the family was through his mother, who was good friends with Hallie Chessman. An amateur radio buff, Doty had volunteered as a friendly gesture to fix Hallie Chessman's radio, and he had been in and out of the Chessman house that week doing so. Doty told this author in 2006, "Caryl Chessman was in custody when the last Red Light Bandit crime took place. They arrested the man who did it, and he confessed to being the Red Light Bandit. But the Los Angeles Police Department hushed it up. They already had their man."

The real Red Light Bandit, Doty said, was Alex Greco.

"There was a vacant lot between the Greco house and the Chessman house," said Doty. "I do know that Alex Greco and Caryl knew each other because I saw them in a car together."

Mr. Doty said that he never saw any mention of Greco in the

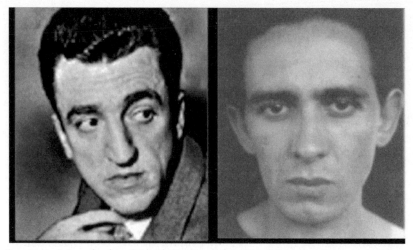

Former Los Angeles homicide detective and author (*Black Dahlia Avenger*) Steve Hodel has examined evidence regarding the criminal career of Fred Sexton. He believes that Sexton committed sex assaults on women, including murder/ mutilations, during the time that Chessman was out of prison in the Los Angeles area and that he bears some physical resemblance to Chessman and had a scar under his right eye that some victims noted about their assailant. *Author's collection*

newspapers after his initial arrest. Chessman, he believes, took the rap for him.*

"Serl and Hallie Chessman never discussed Caryl's problems with me after he went to prison," said Doty.

Steve Hodel thinks it is possible that the Red Light Bandit crimes for which Chessman was convicted may have been committed by one of the two perpetrators of the Black Dahlia murder, Fred Sexton, an artist friend of Man Ray who, like Ray, dabbled in surrealism.

"I did have some concern over the possibility that there could be a mix-up of identities/crimes between George Hodel and Fred Sexton and Chessman," he said. "Primarily because George and Fred were abduct- ing women off the street and raping, releasing, and or killing them at the same time, in the same area. . . . In the little research I did on Chessman, I discovered that he and Fred Sexton were very close in physical description, and even more troubling was that Sexton had a scar on his face, which was a major ID problem with one or several of Chessman's victims. Part of Chessman's defense was 'see no scar.' I

---

* The only record this author could find for a "Greco" between 1948 and 1951 was for a "Joe Greco," arrested for bookmaking in Burbank in 1949.

wondered, could Sexton have committed crimes that Chessman was convicted of? But I didn't follow that path. With no witnesses, it was just a huge can of worms and I dropped it."

Further muddying the Red Light Bandit waters, crimes continued to be committed after Chessman's arrest that bore at least some of the trademarks of the Red Light Bandit. On January 25, 1948, for example, a gunman approached a car in a lover's lane at the end of Doheny Drive in the Hollywood hills. A *Los Angeles Times* news item said that he ordered, at gunpoint, three teenage girls to get out of the car and accompany him, presumably to perform sexual favors. The two teen boys in the car offered the assailant fifty dollars not to harm the girls. The man took the money and left, and the quintet fled to the nearby Hollywood police station, to report the crime. Ironically, Chessman was being held at the same station, was in fact in day two of his nonstop interrogation at the time

Willliam Woodfield's examination of Los Angeles Police Department files in late 1960, just months after Chessman was dead, found several crime reports from as late as April and June 1948 that utilized the same "Red Light" methods to rob motorists and sexually assault passengers. There's even a Web site, www.carylchessman.com, that holds out the hope that secret documents will ultimately prove Chessman's innocence. Chessman himself fueled these hopes with some of his public pronouncements from Death Row. The Web site states, "Chessman claims that he arranged for proof of the identity of the real Red Light Bandit to be released 50 years to the day after California rejected a moratorium on the death penalty. We estimate that date to be sometime in the middle of 2007." If this proof exists, it stretches credulity that someone has remained silent for half a century and, if they have, that they would still be alive to release the alleged documents.

■

CHESSMAN'S TRIAL TOOK place between April 29 and May 21, 1948, in Department 43, on the eighth floor of the Hall of Justice, at the corner of Broadway and Temple Street in downtown Los Angeles.

The newspapers played it up as a victory for a police department that since the Dahlia, Lipstick, and other assorted unsolved murders and gangland slayings had been widely seen by the public as inept and corrupt. Thus, they were eager to see Chessman sent away to San Quentin, carrying with him the stigma of an entire department, as well as clearing eighteen crimes from the books. To that end, their prodigious power, backed by the D.A.'s office and the judge, was arrayed against one man, who further obliged them by defending himself.

Since Chessman's death, these proceedings have been pored over by legal scholars and journalists and have convincingly been shown to constitute, in the words of Frank J. Parker, "a legal lynching." Rather than rehash the events of the trial—which have been covered in two exhaustive and excellent books*—the bottom line of Chessman's life is that, no matter how miserable the justice meted out to him, he was never able to get a new trial. This trial was his one and only shot, and he was at the time either unaware of the enormity of the case and the formidable forces arrayed against him, or he simply ignored them. Perhaps genuinely feeling that he was innocent of at least the kidnapping charges, Chessman was prepared to go down on his own terms. He was twenty-seven years old and full of piss and vinegar. They'd never make these charges stick. He'd do his time for the robberies and be back out in a few years.

Only they did make them stick, and Chessman provided some of the adhesive. He seemed to be working in league with the prosecution. That is, he could not have a) picked a worse legal counsel (himself) or b) had a worse jury (eleven of the twelve were white suburban women, exactly like the two kidnap victims). And, perhaps more daunting, he could not have been assigned a worse judge (Judge Charles Fricke, nicknamed "San Quentin Fricke" for having sent more people to the gas chamber than any judge in state history) or a worse legal opponent (J. Miller Leavy, one of the sharpest and most successful attorneys in Los Angeles).

---

* William J. Kunstler's *Beyond a Reasonable Doubt? The Original Trial of Caryl Chessman* (1961) and Frank J. Parker's *Caryl Chessman: The Red Light Bandit* (1975).

All in all, the outcome of Chessman's trial was preordained—if not obvious to everyone but himself—before the first witness was called.

Therefore, the trial's proceedings only bear revisiting in this narrative as they relate to the pivotal moments, the appearances of the two witnesses that doomed Chessman, Regina Johnson and Mary Alice Meza. The two charges of kidnapping (counts IV and X) of Johnson and Meza—not the attempted rape or the forced "copulation of his penis with their mouths"—were what got Chessman his death sentences. Under California law, kidnapping—even if it was moving victims a few feet from one car to another—was subject to the death penalty. This was entirely due to Section 209 of the California Penal Code, also known as the "Little Lindbergh Law."

■

SECTION 209 COVERED kidnapping for the purpose of robbery, ransom, or extortion. If in the course of the kidnapping the victim suffered "bodily harm," the kidnapper was subject to death, or to life in prison without parole. The choice was the presiding judge's.

Section 209 was a legal anomaly, a fluke that ended up on California's books in 1934. Even as it was designed to prevent harm to crime victims, it may have led to some untimely deaths, as well. As Chessman later noted in *Trial by Ordeal*, "Bodily harm, by court definition, can mean a slap across the face, a tweak on the nose, a binding of the victim's wrists. Since the kidnapper can be given no more for killing his victim than for tweaking him on the nose or binding his wrists, and since a dead victim reduces appreciably the chances of being identified and apprehended, the kidnapper is virtually invited to commit murder."

He goes on, eerily noting, "I personally know of two cases where the 'invitation' was accepted." In one case, two kidnapper/murderers were tried and acquitted because there was not enough evidence to link them to the crime (not to mention a dead eyewitness). In the second case, the kidnapper got a second-degree murder conviction, with a sentence that might have been as short as five years. Chessman's point, then, was that if the victim had not been murdered, and had lived to prove the kidnapper's guilt, the kidnapper would have been facing the gas chamber at San Quentin, as Chessman was.

Chessman wrote, "The state hadn't even known about the kidnapping, until the defendant, a professional criminal, told a plausible story of having had an argument with the deceased. (That was true as far as it went. Actually, the argument was over the location of the victim's money and was rather one-sided.)"

But the Little Lindbergh Law could theoretically apply to purse-snatching. If, for example, the woman doesn't relinquish her hold on the purse, she can be dragged a number of feet (technically kidnapping) and if she falls and breaks her arm or even twists an ankle this is "bodily harm." The purse-snatcher could, theoretically, have gone to the gas chamber in California in 1948 thanks to Section 209. The awful irony of the Little Lindbergh Law was that rape didn't constitute bodily harm in itself. Every aspect of Section 209 was subject to abuse, subjective interpretation, and misapplication.

The law came about as a result of the March 1, 1932, kidnapping of Charles A. Lindbergh Jr., the twenty-month-old son of Charles and Anne Morrow Lindbergh. The crime took place in Hopewell, New Jersey, then a rural town southwest of New York City. Whoever took the baby from his crib had climbed, via ladder, through the second-floor window of his nursery, then back out again. The baby was driven five miles away and believed by many to have been beaten to death, stripped, and buried in a shallow grave in the woods.

The heinousness of the crime shocked the community, and the celebrity of the parents riveted the nation as had few cases in American history. The kidnapper then misled the distraught parents into thinking the baby was alive and extracted $50,000 ransom from them. A nationwide manhunt ensued, one of the most intense in American history. Even Al Capone, from his cell in Atlanta's federal penitentiary, offered his assistance. A murderous thug like Capone looked good beside a baby killer.

Even while this was going on, the U.S. Congress, always sensitive to tidal waves of public sentiment, passed what became known as the Lindbergh Law on May 18, 1934, which made kidnapping across state lines a federal and capital offense. It was this law, tweaked and modified by the state of California the same year—when Chessman was thirteen years old and trying fruitlessly to find his niche in Glendale—that doomed the Red Light Bandit in 1948.

No arrest was made in the Lindbergh kidnapping until September 1934, when one of the gold certificate bills from the ransom money turned up at a service station in the Bronx. The attendant, having noted the license plate in case there was trouble with the bank in depositing the customer's bill, passed the information on to the police. Five days later, they arrested Bruno Richard Hauptmann, a German carpenter who lived with his wife and child at 1379 East 222nd Street, in the Bronx.

The murder and kidnap trial, held in Flemington, New Jersey, was one of the most press-blanketed in U.S. history, rivaling the Scopes Monkey Trial in 1927 and O. J. Simpson's murder trial in 1994. It was "trial by newspaper," as Chessman described his own situation. Though the scene at the courthouse was a media circus, the evidence against Hauptmann was insurmountably huge. He had a stash of the gold certificate bills that were used for ransom money and had made a $25,000 deposit with a brokerage firm. He was convicted of first-degree murder on Valentine's Day, 1935, and executed in the electric chair on April 3, 1936, at New Jersey's state prison.

■

THE FIRST KIDNAPPING victim to testify was Regina Johnson, described by William Kunstler as "an attractive honey-blonde in her middle thirties" and by Al Matthews, a court-appointed lawyer who assisted Chessman but did not argue the case, as "a suburban matron who had managed to keep her shape." She was married to Harry Johnson, a man twenty years her senior. In 1945, she had contracted infantile paralysis but bore no outward signs of the disease. She was, Kunstler said, "sturdy" and "a comely witness." She was also more coherent in her narrative than Mary Alice Meza, more believable and formidable to Chessman's defense.

And yet, at the heart of her testimony, is this curious fact: when she was assaulted, Mrs. Johnson was parked in a car in a lover's lane at night with a man who was not her husband. This was, of course, no reason to condemn her, nor to suggest that she'd invited sexual aggression, but it was odd enough to warrant some pause on the part of the jury. Because Chessman, acting as his own attorney, couldn't touch such a hot button, it's surprising that Leavy, the prosecuting attorney, did. Perhaps sensing that the situation gave the appearance of dubious morals, Leavy asked Mrs. Johnson on the witness stand about her relationship with Jarnigan Lea, the man with whom she was parked. Mr. Lea, it was learned, lived across the street from the Johnsons. In his late forties, Lea was a former Navy submariner who was now a woodworker. After his wife died, he had moved in with his elderly parents. The Johnsons and Leas had been friendly for years; Mr. Lea's sister was close friends with Regina Johnson.

The couple parked in front of the Sacred Heart Academy, switched off the headlights, and watched the night descend on downtown Los Angeles. According to Johnson, a car pulled up behind them, flashing a red light. The driver of that car got out and approached their vehicle, asking Lea for identification. She quoted the assailant as saying, "This is a stickup." Lea handed the assailant his wallet and she handed him her purse.

Then, she said, he forced her to get out of the car and walk "twenty-two" feet to his car. He threatened to kill both her and Lea if she didn't give him a blow job. Johnson said, "He told me we would both be taken away in a casket, the both of us, unless I did what he wanted." After the assailant ejaculated, she said, he gave her a handkerchief to wipe the semen from her face. (The official charge for this act was "Violation of Section 288a of the California Penal Code for forcing Regina Johnson to copulate his penis with her mouth on January 19, 1948.") Both she and Lea identified Chessman at the Hollywood Police Station on January 24, five days later, as their assailant.*

Chessman, sporting a double-breasted pinstripe suit his father had provided, was cautious at first when he cross-examined Mrs. Johnson.

---

* This ID did not come from a proper police lineup. Rather, the couple pointed at Chessman, sitting alone, from across a crowded room.

However, perhaps sensing his life hung in the balance, he pressed her more aggressively, asking her whether Lea tried to intercede to stop "this person" from forcing her into his car. She angrily told Chessman, "He told you to have mercy, that I had been ill. You told him to shut up or you would let him have it, he would be taken away in a casket, and you said, 'She is going with me,'" Johnson continued to insist throughout her testimony that Chessman was her assailant. This frustrated Chessman greatly and may have been the turning point in his trial. The transcripts indicate the following exchange:

> CHESSMAN: Did this person, at the time he took you out of this car, state what his intention in taking you back to the other car was?
> MRS. JOHNSON: No, you didn't tell me until after I had gotten in your car.
> CHESSMAN: How long were you in this Ford?
> MRS. JOHNSON: In your car?
> CHESSMAN: How long were you in the Ford?
> MRS. JOHNSON: In the car with you? Is that what you mean?
>
> Chessman objected to Judge Fricke that Johnson was "not responsive to his question." He also insisted that "the defense maintains its innocence."
>
> Judge Fricke angrily said, "I don't care what the defense maintains. The objection is overruled." He then browbeat Chessman: "You would get along very much better if you respect the court's rulings."

Chessman seemed to lose heart at this point, asking only a few more desultory, inconsequential questions before finishing. After her testimony was over, Johnson returned to her seat at the back of the courtroom, next to her husband. As Kunstler wrote, "She was smiling broadly. Perhaps she had expected her inquisitor to ask some probing questions as to why a married woman was parked with a male friend in one of Los Angeles' favorite trysting spots."

It was learned some time later that Johnson's brother had, at the time of this trial, been arrested for burglary. Soon after her testimony, he was released, uncharged. (A few years later, Regina Johnson divorced her husband and remarried, becoming Regina Brennan.)

Jarnigan Lea, for his part, stuck to the story he'd told police initially. According to Kunstler, Lea "relished his moment in the sun." The most curious aspect of his testimony was his insistence that Harry Johnson was the one to suggest that he and Regina go for a ride. "He told me to get Regina out of the house, that she was tired, cross and nervous, she had been working all day, and he wanted to read," Lea testified.

The most damaging part of Lea's testimony was his narrative of the kidnapping, which he related directly to the jury, whose members, said Kunstler, "were eating up every word." Lea related that Johnson had said, "I am going to faint. Will you please give me a drink of water" and that the assailant had said, "I haven't any water . . . get going." "I didn't turn around; I had been told not to turn around, and I was very much afraid for her life, because she was under the point of a cocked gun and I was positive it was loaded. So I could hear her get in the car, or a door slam, rather, and I heard another door slam, and I could hear him say, from where I sat in the car, 'Well, you know what I want.' She said, 'No, I don't.' She was crying; she was rather hysterical, naturally. And so, then, there was some low talk, and I could hear her pleading, 'Please don't do this, don't do that.' I could hear her pleading with him; I could hear him say that he would kill her. It seems like he just repeated, repeated and repeated, I will kill you! I will kill you! I will kill you! They will carry you away in a casket; they will carry you away in a coffin.' I just sat there. I never felt so helpless in my life."

The coup de "disgrace" was Lea's testimony that, "I heard him make one statement, rather loud. He said, 'Suck it.'" When Mrs. Johnson got back in his car, Lea noticed that her coat was soiled. "It was semen, of course," he told Leavy.

■

THE FINAL NAIL in Chessman's legal coffin, the one he would tirelessly try to extricate for the next twelve years, was provided by Mary Alice Meza. Before her appearance on the stand, police and medical witnesses were called to comment on her physical condition right after the attack. Dr. Kearney Sauer, a police surgeon for the City of Los Angeles, was a professed expert on women who'd claimed to be sexually assaulted. Dr. Sauer had examined Mary Alice Meza the morning after her attack. Typical of the testimony was this exchange:

> **LEAVY:** State what kind of examination you made of Mary Alice Meza.
>
> **SAUER:** An examination was made of the vulva and the entrance to the vagina for damage, in that she stated that she had been attacked.
>
> **LEAVY:** Assuming, doctor, that some sexual attack on this young lady that you examined here, but after the sexual attack and the emission of semen, male discharge, in the region of her private parts—assuming that the young lady after the attack and the emission of semen in the region of her private parts had gone home and wiped her private parts, in your opinion, could it be unlikely you would find any semen or spermatozoa at the time of your examination?

Chessman, in his cross examination, asked Sauer if he'd looked for any evidence of semen on Mary Alice Meza's clothes (no). He asked if the doctor had "found any conclusive evidence of penetration?" ("There was apparently a penetration of some firm object past the labia majora and minora, yes.") Chessman wanted to know if this could have been caused by a finger (yes). Chessman presumably wanted to show that there was at least a reasonable chance that Frank Hurlbut, the young man in whose car Meza was parked, had been fondling her; why else would they be parked in lover's lane? Hurlbut himself said, on the stand, that they had been parked on Mulholland Drive for an hour, from midnight until 1:00 A.M., before the Red Light Bandit appeared. What were they doing up there for an hour?

Had this "bandit" followed his previous methodology, he would have taken Meza to his car, had his way with her and returned her to the car Hurlbut was driving. But Hurlbut sped off, leaving Meza behind with the assailant. This explains why the "bandit" kept Meza for three hours, then drove her home after he was done with her. Her protector had flown the coop.

Meza's appearance was eagerly anticipated by the media and the courtroom spectators. She was perfect press fodder, a teenage virgin and raven-haired beauty ravaged by a skulking pervert. She was the complete obverse of the Black Dahlia, in their collective mind. She was, so to speak, the White Rose.

Meza showed remarkable poise on the witness stand, especially for someone who, two years later, was committed to Camarillo State Mental Hospital, where she spent most of the rest of her life in the throes of intractable schizophrenia. However, six months after being attacked by the Red Light Bandit, Meza was strong enough to withstand being cross-examined by the man she claimed had raped her.

Meza testified that after the church dance Hurlbut suggested they go park "for a while" on Mulholland Drive. She estimated this "while" to be twenty minutes, though Hurlbut had said it was closer to one hour. She said that she was taken at gunpoint into the assailant's car and that her assailant began chasing Hurlbut when the latter sped away rather than wait for her. After giving up the chase, the assailant drove to a secluded area with Meza. She asked him what he wanted, and he said, "You know." She told him she was having her period. She testified that he said, "Show me," and that she lifted her skirt to reveal a "sanitary belt." She got hysterical. Instead, she said he exposed his penis and "made me put my mouth down on it. He told me he would kill me, strangle me, if I didn't, so I did." He then made her undress and get on the back seat, face down with her legs spread. She felt him climb on top and "there there was an emission . . . through my legs, between my legs." He then drove her home, she said, around 4:00 A.M.

She positively identified Chessman in the courtroom as her assailant.

Thus, it was with a great anticipatory hush, that Chessman approached the witness stand to cross-examine Meza. She admitted that she'd initially testified to the police that her attacker was no taller than she was, "5 foot 4 or 5." She also admitted to having said the attacker had a scar over his right eyebrow, near his ear.

It was also during this cross examination that Chessman put on the record how she first came to identify him as her alleged assailant. That is, late on January 24, two days after the attack, Chessman was taken in handcuffs by Detective Forbes to the sidewalk outside Meza's house, where she had positively identified him from the second floor, from more than fifty feet away, and with her eyes nearly swollen shut from an allergic reaction.

She also admitted upon cross-examination that her assailant had told her he was Italian. She said he told her he was from New York and was unfamiliar with Los Angeles. And that he'd done this to her because his wife had been unfaithful to him while he was away in the navy. This, of course, could have been a ruse on the bandit's part to confuse her, but her physical description of her assailant was so far from Chessman's physical appearance as to throw into doubt other parts of her testimony.

And yet, Chessman's trial, for all intents and purposes, was over at this point. The eleven women in the jury had seen and heard all they cared to see and hear. In their minds, the sex criminal defending himself had shown no remorse.

■

ONE FINAL PIECE of testimony from Chessman's trial needs recounting. For sheer pathos, it has seldom been matched in a Los Angeles courtroom. This was the arrival of Hallie Chessman, pleading for the life of her only child. It was May 10, 1948, the day after Mother's Day.

Though Hallie's court appearance was ultimately not enough to sway the jury, it can be said, in hindsight, to be Exhibit A for the limitless love of a mother for her child. She was in pitiful and pitiable shape by May 1948. Barely fifty years of age, she had already dwindled to an atrophied shell after nearly two decades of paralysis. On top of this, she had also recently been diagnosed with inoperable cancer. The cancer was too widespread to give it the usual sorts of limiting diagnoses that would offer even fleeting hope to a patient—breast cancer, lung cancer, etc. Instead, the cancer was pervasive, indiscriminately devouring the few remaining living morsels of Hallie's being, while she subsisted on a steady diet of painkillers and sleep medication.

Since Hallie could no longer be moved into a wheelchair, she was rolled into the courtroom in a hospital bed. And her testimony was offered to the ceiling rather than to the juror's faces because she could neither sit up nor turn her head to the side. All that Hallie had left in the world was her religious faith, and even that was under assault at the thought of her son deflowering some menstruating virgin and a polio-stricken housewife, above and beyond all these other assorted charges of thievery and mayhem. Her son was innocent of these terrible charges, she said. He had to be. It was God's will that he was innocent. It was God's will.

Imagine the gasps of pity from the gallery, and the brief wave of softening toward the defendant. Could someone this loved by his mother be as evil as the prosecutor insisted he was? Even Leavy must have briefly been moved by the sight, all the while cursing the defendant's potentially winning strategy. How could he compete with a dying mother's love for her son?

Caryl Chessman soon squandered the goodwill he had accrued at the arrival of his mother, though he did at least have the good sense to defer to his court-appointed legal adviser, Al Matthews. This was not a calculated move, a means by which Caryl could demonstrate his humanity. He'd conducted his own defense up until this point, and, in keeping with his hardheaded personality, he would have gladly conducted the interview with his mother, to go down with his own listing ship, as it were. However, emotionally, he realized he could not handle the job. One shudders at the possibilities, had he gone through with his initial strategy. One can see him with his professorial pointer, striding to the blackboard, gesticulating, asking the witness to speak up, speak up, the jury can't hear you and are you sure, absolutely sure of this, because earlier in a statement given to the court you said such and such, and this and so. A cool, lawyerly attitude by a son to his dying mother would have appalled a jury filled with suburban housewives, and mothers.

Matthews got the call, and he handled the situation as well as it could be handled. However, at this point, Chessman's defense was like a basketball team that had dug itself a huge hole in the first half, and despite regrouping and chipping away at the lead, watched as the clock ran out.

In what must have been one of the most agonizing moments of the trial, or any trial that year in Los Angeles, Mrs. Chessman, staring at the ceiling, did her best to supply her son with an alibi. Matthews later described her, to Kunstler, as "looking like a very sick Whistler's Mother." Matthews got Hallie to recount the events in her household prior to the outbreak of the Red Light Bandit crimes. She recalled that on the date of her adoptive mother's funeral, January 3, 1948, Caryl was with her the whole day. Pathetically, she said, "I had requested particularly that he stay with me during the time of the funeral. I had quite a number of others who had dropped out there, but I particularly wanted him to stay with me the day of the funeral."

On January 17, 1948, she said, her son had been "laying the Congoleum rug that we had gotten that day." When asked by Matthews if Caryl was there that same evening, she said, "Yes, he was there very definitely all day and all evening because I—he did not leave me at all that day."

On the night of January 21, 1948, she recalled that Caryl had been home because she'd suffered a terrible attack of pain requiring a visit from her doctor, J. Mark Lacey. Dr. Lacey shot her up with a sedative. She said Caryl was home, "because I had been so dreadfully ill that he wanted to be sure—have me to be sure that I was all right after I would have to take a hypodermic. They gave me a hypodermic, so I could sleep all afternoon." It was later that night, past midnight (thus, technically, on January 22), that Mary Alice Meza was kidnapped.

As for January 23—another important date in the crime sequence for which her son was being tried—Mrs. Chessman recalled asking Caryl to, according to the trial transcripts, "go over to Gerda Adair's . . . to see her for me, and he had gone over there and had called me up and told me that he had been over and was starting home, and he would be home within an hour or an hour and a half." This was between six and six thirty.

Leavy then cross-examined the pitiable Hallie. One can only imagine Caryl seethed at the sight of this. Leavy, in a rare lapse from his bulldog demeanor, gently went over the testimony Hallie had just given. As Kunstler noted, "Leavy was getting nowhere with Mrs. Chessman . . . called it quits and the exhausted witness was quickly wheeled out of the courtroom."

5

San Quentin's Least Wanted
(1948–1952)

WHATEVER RESENTMENT **W**ARDEN Duffy harbored for Caryl Chessman seemed justified when his former protégé arrived at San Quentin State Prison on Saturday, July 3, 1948, after Judge Fricke pronounced his death sentences. In the years since Chessman's last visit, Duffy had transformed San Quentin into a model of progressive penology, and the warden had no time to waste on prisoners headed down the cul de sac of Death Row. His prime concern for those unfortunate souls was to make their stay as painless as possible and to follow the dictates of the law in regard to their extermination, as unpleasant as that duty was to him.

Upon arrival at San Quentin, Chessman was given a shower, after which his body cavities were searched. He was fingerprinted and photographed at the Identification Department. At the Distribution Department, he was given jeans, a denim work shirt and jacket, and a pair of soft slippers—what Chessman called "the distinguishing mark of the condemned man." He was issued the prison identification number 66565 and escorted across the prison yard to North Block, or North Seg as it was known to prison staff, where he was delivered to his assigned cell on the top (fifth) floor. The cell—a concrete and steel cage 4.5 feet wide, 10.5 feet long and 7.5 feet high—had a steel door with impenetrable bars on the window to the corridor. It was double-locked once Chessman was inside, the second lock a steel slat at the top of the door that, with Kafkaesque finality, kept the door from being opened even when the traditional lock was disengaged. The room was furnished with a metal cot, wooden table, a stool, a shelf above the cot, a commode and sink bolted to the back wall. There was no window in the wall of the cell; the only view Chessman would have for the next twelve years was past the steel bars on his door which looked out on an electric government-issue office clock affixed to the bars across the corridor. To a doomed man, the clock was a reminder of how time ceaselessly passed and yet also stood still.

While no photograph exists (or was allowed) of Chessman in his cell—all photographs of him after this point were either taken in an administrative office or outside a courtroom—the San Quentin museum has on exhibit a photograph of the cell block where Chessman lived for twelve years. It looks like the very maw of Purgatory, an anonymous blur of metal bars running down a long, gray corridor fifteen–feet wide, with no distinguishing characteristics other than pure institutional misery. It was, as Chessman put it, "as far in prison as it is possible to get." Seeing this photograph makes Chessman's eventual achievements all the more remarkable, starting with the fact that he put one of these otherwise anonymous cells briefly on the world's map: Cell 2455.*

Among the first things Chessman acquired was the latest issue of *The San Quentin News*, the in-house publication written and edited by prisoners for prisoners (the editor was listed as "Jack W." and the associate editor as "J.O."). By 1948, this paper was distributed to prisons in all 48 states and to some in foreign countries and had the largest paid circulation of any American prison-generated publication. Each of the 4,709 San Quentin inmates, including Chessman, received a free copy, delivered to his cell door. Each week, this paper was filled with book reviews, upbeat, newsy reports on various prison work programs, sports roundups—San Quentin had excellent gymnastics, boxing, and baseball teams—feature stories about noteworthy visits from celebrities like Paul Robeson, Eleanor Roosevelt, and Art Linkletter, and Warden Duffy's front-page column, "Facts, Not Rumors."

---

* The cell-numbering system at San Quentin is different today; there is no indication, plaque or notice attached to what was formerly No. 2455 to indicate it was the home for twelve years of a famous author.

Death Row cells. *Leo L. Stanley Collection, Anne T. Kent California Room, Marin County Free Library*

In the issue for July 9, 1948—the first one Chessman received—Duffy's column was about his vacation in Hawaii. In it, the warden gushed about the South Pacific scenery with his "prison family," though it's not clear how a free man's exotic journey would improve morale of the men then trapped in San Quentin. Also included were stories that, given Chessman's predicament, must have cut like a knife, grim proof of a world fully prepared to move on without him. One story was about the large number of parole cases the Adult Authority ruled on in May, and the "all time parole peak" reached by San Quentin inmates in June (freedom!), another about the progress of a prison construction project, another about the forestry program, still another about the record amount of burlap churned out by the prison jute mill.

The story that must really have cut Chessman to the quick was headlined "Budding Authors Are in Abundance." In it, Herman K. Spector, the senior librarian, announced that he'd received 285 original manuscripts from inmates that he was submitting to magazine editors and book publishers. Only nine of this number were rejected by prison authorities as inappropriate and forty-seven others deemed appropriate, with revisions.

Though Chessman missed becoming a guinea pig for Dr. Stanley's scientific experiments by just a few months on his first San Quentin visit, he was the beneficiary in 1948 of a new, seemingly more benign development in prison treatment: bibliotherapy. In any other setting, Spector, San Quentin's librarian from 1947 to 1967, would have been considered a cultural prophet, anticipating the advent of book clubs and reading circles by at least three decades. He held "Great Books" classes, conducting group discussions about authors from Homer to Thomas Hardy. He also greatly expanded the prison library, which prior to his arrival had been housed in a Quonset hut. He called his library "a hospital for the mind," and his inventory of books reached 33,420 by 1956. Prisoners were allowed to visit the library once a week and check out as many as five books per visit. Under Spector's gentle tutelage, prison readership rose to an average of two books per week per inmate. While Chessman, as a Death Row inmate, could not participate in the reading circles, he did have access to Spector's library, and he took full advantage of this privilege.

The most voraciously read titles in the prison library were, of course, the law books. This created ill will within the administration of the Department of Corrections, especially after the habeas corpus petitions rose from 814 in 1957 (some of which were prepared for other inmates by Chessman) to 4,845 by 1965. To the bureaucrats in Sacramento, it seemed that Spector and Chessman had, between them, created a prison population of self-made lawyers and wannabe Hemingways.

Spector also directed a series of creative writing classes that according to the author and journalist Joseph Hallinan turned San Quentin into "a writer's colony, a criminal version of Yaddo." In 1947, for example, his classes produced 395 manuscript submissions for publication. By 1961, the number was 1,989. The studious atmosphere created by Spector may account for San Quentin's amazing legacy of prison authors. In 1953, he published a booklet called "San Quentiniana," an annotated list of "books published by officials and inmates of San Quentin." The roster of inmate authors predating Chessman was impressive, including Jack Black, whose *You Can't Win* (1926) is still in print; Ernest G. Booth, best known for his novel

With Sirens Screaming (1945); Richard J. Krebs, who wrote under the pen name Jan Valtin, and whose *Out of the Night* (1951) remains one of the strangest memoirs of World War II; David Lamson, whose *We Who Are About to Die* (1935) details his year on Death Row at San Quentin, before his conviction for the murder of his wife was overturned; Ed Morrell, best known for inspiring a Jack London hero; and Robert J. Tasker, whose account of prison life in *Grimhaven* (1928) has few rivals for authenticity.

Those San Quentin writers who came after this list was compiled, including Chessman, Bill Sands, Eldridge Cleaver, Malcolm Braly, and George Jackson, would have undoubtedly been included in any future booklet Spector might have compiled.*

Perhaps Chessman, who fancied himself more than a "budding" author, was motivated by the *News* story about Spector's writing program. He soon acquired a typewriter and began keeping a single-spaced diary, the first entry for which was August 15, 1948. Among the bitter observations were, "A fool, incontrovertibly, is a fool is a fool. Well, so be it. But, then, there are all kinds, sizes and variety of fools. The species and specie (acceptable in illiterate use, thus acceptable here) we are concerned with is he who, generally, acts as his own attorney, and, specifically, is a currently defunct (civilly) individual 'languishing' in Cell 2455 on the Condemned Row at California State Prison at San Quentin. To wit, Comrade (without being pink) Caryl W. Chessman."

■

WARDEN DUFFY WAS nearing the end of a long, distinguished career at San Quentin when Chessman returned in 1948, and he had

---

* Spector's legacy, unfortunately, was not preserved by the prison or the Department of Corrections. California did not want to be known as America's finishing school for convict authors, so when Spector retired in 1967, the prison destroyed the crowning achievement of his stellar career, the files on his reading and writing programs. Replacing Spector's emphasis on mental and intellectual rehabilitation was a more effective method of prisoner control: television. As Hallinan noted, the prison library's collection of 36,000 books in 1974 dwindled to 8,902 by 1990. Today, each prisoner at San Quentin can have his own television set in his cell.

little patience for backsliding inmates, especially the wayward Chessman, who was still stewing in his sense of injustice, stumbling over his own ego. He and Duffy clashed constantly over the next three years. In late October 1950, Chessman got deeper on Duffy's shit list after he was accused of being a "ringleader" of a "riot" on Death Row, for which he was sent to an isolation cell in "the hole." He did not go quietly into "the hole." In fact, he managed to sneak a handwritten writ of habeas corpus out to the Marin County Superior Court and, after a court appearance in San Rafael at which he pleaded his case with sufficient earnestness, he was released back to Cell 2455. Soon thereafter, he got in a shouting match with a couple of other Death Row inmates. Because he'd already embarrassed the prison that week, he was sent back to "the hole," for "loud talking."

Filled with righteous indignation, he continued to create havoc on the Row, with constant petitions to the courts and requests for more legal material. He was, in short, a pain in the neck for Warden Duffy who, finally, in early 1952, took a position as a member of the Adult Authority, the state agency that makes decisions about parole. Duffy was replaced as warden by Harley O. Teets, who the historian Kenneth Lamott said was "a better administrator and tighter disciplinarian than Duffy" and for whom Chessman gained a measure of grudging respect.

Duffy's impressions of Chessman—or at least the ones that dominated his 1962 memoir, *88 Men and 2 Women*—were based on the existential outlaw image that the twenty-seven-year-old still retained at the beginning of his San Quentin encore in July 1948. In his diary, Chessman noted on September 14, 1948, "I have been victimized far more than any of my alleged victims. The incidental fact I just don't happen to be the guy who committed these crimes is no longer the issue, it seems. Well, so be it . . . Caryl Chessman needs more than a trained nurse now; he needs a skilled surgeon with the courage to diagnose and then remove the cancerous growth, not from him, but that is clinging to him and can so easily attack other, unwary men." This unwavering pride and lack of humility created the impressions that lingered with Duffy, coloring and distorting his memoir, at least insofar as it touches Chessman, negating the favorable earlier impression he'd had of him. Duffy's account reads more like an attempt to settle an old score, perhaps salve an old sore as well, whenever it addresses Chessman.

"I knew Caryl Chessman," the retired warden wrote. "And if he is ever recognized as a martyr it will be a travesty."

Among the warden's criticisms of Chessman were that he spent his time preparing legal writs to delay the executions of other Death Row inmates. Even if Chessman derived some pleasure from thwarting the gassing of one of his condemned peers, it is hard to find fault with this.

"I don't recall that he actually saved anyone permanently, but he certainly prolonged the lives of scores of fellow prisoners by composing legal documents which they were incapable of writing themselves," wrote Duffy, as if delaying someone's death, or rather, prolonging their life, were nothing but a minor achievement.

Some of Duffy's other criticisms seem disingenuous, given that Chessman was facing the gas chamber for crimes he insisted he didn't commit. Anyone in Chessman's position would have done everything he could to avoid meeting that fate. If one believes he is innocent of the crimes for which he faces death, how can he be expected to be a model, or docile, prisoner? How can he not be filled with bitterness?

Another criticism—"most of the other prisoners hated him"—was wrong on two levels. First, the phrase "the other prisoners" embraced a wide population. San Quentin's population capacity was 6,000 and, during the twelve years Chessman was on Death Row, wavered between four thousand and six thousand, including many psychopaths and murderers (neither of which Chessman was), and the idea of gaining the respect, much less the love, of most of this number would seem to be a badge of dishonor. Second, Duffy might have been an extraordinary warden, but he presumed more than he could possibly know when he said he spoke for "the other prisoners." Research into this topic has shown that the opposite was true. That is, Chessman may have initially been seen by many inmates as a showboat, but his prolonged fight to avoid the gas chamber and his achievements as a writer eventually earned their deep respect. In a sense, his fight became their fight.

Some of Duffy's reminiscences in his book about Chessman are not even accurate. For example, in coming to the conclusion that Chessman should have been spared a date with the gas chamber, Duffy cited the case of Edward W. Brown, sentenced to death in 1946 under the same Little Lindbergh Law that doomed Chessman two years later. Brown was black, and his death sentence was commuted to life in prison without the possibility of parole by Governor Earl Warren (later Chief Justice of the United States).

Governor Warren did not doubt Edward W. Brown's guilt for the crime for which he was given a death sentence. He just was "unable to agree that an offense of this nature merits the extreme penalty." Warren also wrote, "I am afraid that the fact that the defendant is colored and the victim is white may have had much to do with this penalty."

Duffy wrote, "I suppose I don't blame Chessman for fuming that day in May of 1947 when Edward Brown was led out of Death Row. And I could understand when he commented bitterly, 'I guess I'm just the wrong color.'"

Someone may have fumed and bitterly said this, but it wasn't Chessman, who did not arrive on San Quentin's Death Row until July 3, 1948. By then, Brown was off the Row. Furthermore, nowhere in either Chessman's writings or accounts of his life in prison is there any mention of racial animosity on his part. Chessman was, of course, no saint in this or any other regard, and he may even have harbored the same level of race hostility as any white man in the 1940s. However, in his writing and in all accounts of his life, he seems to have steered clear of any of the usual race-baiting of his day. Not only that, he worked on writs for black Death Row inmates and had a rapport with the Latino prisoners, even setting up a successful literacy and reading program for them.

Such an error casts doubt on some of Duffy's other, more inflammatory descriptions of Chessman, such as, "In Death Row he was a tough prisoner to handle, mean, demanding, contemptuous, arrogant, and defiant. Nearly always either in the middle or the cause of an argument, he made life so miserable for the guards that they almost welcomed the occasional fights on the row because they gave them a chance to lock him up for a few days. Chessman treated them like lackeys . . . He was the worst griper in the row's history . . . He pounced on every excuse to make a demand, for demands harassed the guards and harassing guards was one of the few things that gave Chessman pleasure."

Duffy's recollections contradict, among many other witnesses, the recollections of his own friend and greatest success story, Bill Sands.

Though Sands never lost respect for his friend, he eventually realized that "Chess was headed one way and I another."

Years later—four years after Chessman's death—Sands still harbored a deep respect for his late friend, and his 1964 memoir, *My Shadow Ran Fast*, served as a corrective to the harsh public persona of the "vicious beast" who'd inhabited Cell 2455 all those years. On one point Sands was most adamant and certain: he believed Chessman could not have committed the Red Light Bandit crimes.

He wrote, "It would be less than accurate for me to tell this without stating, unequivocally, that the Caryl Chessman I knew so well from 1941 until he was transferred out of San Quentin in 1943, convicted of armed robbery, was a man physically, mentally and emotionally incapable of committing the sex crimes for which he was eventually tried and executed."

He continued, "Members of an all-male society do talk about sex, you know. Exhaustively. Chess's ideas, experiences and aspirations were on a par with those of the other solid cons who form the backbone of any prison population—normal, healthy and not overly imaginative. When you live with a man twenty-four hours a day for almost two years in the close confinement of a prison, you get to know him far better than most men know their brothers. And if someone tells you your brother is a sex deviant, you damn well know whether he is or not. Caryl Chessman was no sex deviant. Not then. Not ever. He shared not only with me but with the vast majority of the men in prison, the contempt and disgust for rapos, punks and jockers." (The latter two terms were 1940s prison jargon for effeminate homosexuals and their macho prison "husbands").

Chessman, Sands insisted, was the opposite of a sex deviant or a "rapo."

"He had a strong personality and a brilliant mind," he wrote. "His resourcefulness and persuasion are now a matter of worldwide knowledge and perhaps a specific and stinging memory to the individuals who finally accomplished his execution."

Duffy's assessment would also be countermanded by that of Bernice Freeman, the reporter for the *San Francisco Chronicle* who covered the San Quentin beat. Freeman was a favorite of Chessman, who was able to get messages to her, and to other reporters, through sympathetic San Quentin guards and other prison staff. Freeman had, many times, been phoned by the same unidentified tipster who passed along messages from Chessman to her. Just before his death, she got a call from an "anonymous" source, which she wrote about in her 1961 book, *The Desperate and the Damned.*

> "Chessman is sure this is it," a man said in a quiet, familiar voice. "He wants to thank you again for your fairness to him and the other men on the Row. I know how good you've been to those fellows. You and Miss Asher are the only real ladies some of them have ever met."
>
> After I thanked him, the man said, "I've been calling you for a long time, Mrs. Freeman. I guess you won't be hearing from me anymore."
>
> "I suppose not," I said. Then, after a pause, I remarked, "You've called me so often for Chessman. You see him all the time, so you must be a guard. Weren't you ever afraid this might cost you your job? What made you take the chance?"
>
> "Because I feel sorry for all those poor devils," he replied. "And for Chessman especially. He's put up a great fight. I kept hoping he'd win it."

Dr. William Graves, the San Quentin physician from 1951 to 1953, testified on Chessman's behalf at a hearing to commute his death sentence. Among his recommendations were, "If he were released, I have little fear that he would commit violence. . . . He was the best-behaved man on Death Row during the two years I was at San Quentin, without question."

Duffy also contended that, "Most of the other prisoners hated him. They couldn't stand his egotism and his arrogance. 'Chessman held everybody in contempt,' an inmate who had once been on the row told me not long ago. He didn't care whether other men lived or died. All he wanted was the satisfaction of beating the law. . . . I never heard one man, in Death Row or on the main line, express the slightest doubt that Chessman was guilty of the charges against him."

Not one man? Caryl Chessman had built up an elaborate system of collaborators, that included representatives from every stratum of the prison, from other inmates on Death Row to those on the "main line," and even extending to the guard staff. It was via this system that he was able to smuggle an entire manuscript—*The Face of Justice* (1957)—out of San Quentin. All of these people gladly helped him, and risked severe punishments for doing so, in his legal fights and in smuggling messages out to the public. There were many men at San Quentin, inmates and staff, who doubted his guilt.

Again, from Dr. Graves, contradicting Warden Duffy: "Chessman has made enormous strides forward in understanding himself since I met him. That's why I am so sure he is not a psychopath. You don't see this sort of progress with a psychopath. Tremendous stress will break most of us, but some individuals will rise above it and be stronger for the experience. Beyond that, he has a very real interest in other people. Psychopaths are completely selfish. They are not interested in others. . . ."

In 1958, Associate Warden W. D. Achuff told a journalist, Irwin Moskowitz, "The fights that Chessman has been in over the years have been very minor things that were overplayed by the press. Chessman's role in these fights often has been that of a peacemaker. I wouldn't say Chessman has been any more of a disciplinary problem than any normal person would be if you cooped him up in a tiny death cell for 22 hours a day. I guess you could say the only real problems we've had with Mr. Chessman have been literary."

Still, despite his later condemnation of Chessman and to his enduring credit, Duffy swallowed his pride and appeared at hearings in March 1960, two months before Chessman's execution. The revered warden risked further tarnishing his reputation in a state that widely favored capital punishment, by testifying in front of the state senate's Judiciary Committee, asking that the Legislature abolish the death penalty and, thus, spare Chessman's life. Duffy, unlike Governor Brown, had the courage of his convictions, telling the committee, "I do not believe in the death penalty, because its inequality is apparent. . . . You have yet to find anyone executed who was wealthy."

In his memoir, Duffy reiterated this point, writing, "[Chessman] shouldn't have died . . . he shouldn't have been sentenced to the gas chamber in the first place."

Duffy claimed to "hate the death penalty because of its inhumanity. Doomed men rot in a private hell while their cases are being appealed, and they continue to rot after a death date is set. They live in the company of misery, not only their own but their neighbors'. . . . One night on Death Row is too long, and the length of time spent there by the Chessmans . . . constitutes cruelty that defies the imagination. It has always been a source of wonder to me that they didn't all go stark, raving mad."

Even as late as the 1970s, Bill Sands was standing up for his old friend. By then, Sands had started the Seventh Step Foundation, a groundbreaking and successful organization—based loosely on the "step" method perfected by Alcoholics Anonymous—that hired ex-convicts to counsel and rehabilitate other convicts. The seventh of "the seven steps to freedom" was: "Maintaining our own freedom, we pledge ourselves to help others as we have been helped." In talks to prisoners and in his fund-raising speeches to community organizations, Sands often cited his old friend "Chess." Chessman was, by then, a legend behind America's prison walls as well as in the "squarejohn" world outside. Among the champions of Seventh Step was Dr. Graves, Chessman's Death Row physician.* Also, when Sands's fledgling foundation desperately needed a guiding hand, Clinton T. Duffy came out of retirement to work for the man who was once one of his

---

* Graves had resigned in protest over Chessman's death sentence, and set up a private practice in San Gabriel, a Los Angeles suburb.

unrepentant San Quentin cons. Duffy told a rapt media, Seventh Step "may well be the greatest single advance that has ever been made in man's efforts to rehabilitate or remotivate men in prison."

Sands's rehabilitation was complete; at its heart, though, was a little piece of Caryl Chessman.

■

IN AUGUST OF 1948, Chessman was paid a visit by an attorney who became the most important woman to him during the last twelve years of his life. Her name was Rosalie Asher, and she had come to visit Chessman at the request of Al Matthews, his legal adviser in Los Angeles. Born and raised in Sacramento, Asher was one of the first women to graduate from Sacramento's University of the Pacific McGeorge School of Law. A practicing attorney as well as the Sacramento County law librarian, Asher was three years Chessman's senior (thirty to his twenty-seven), single, attractive, fond of the finer things in life—theater, cinema, cabaret, opera, fine dining, furs, stylish dresses, and martinis. She was a real lady, the sort of woman to which a prison guard or an inmate might say, "What's a classy dame like you doin' in a joint like this?"

Despite her cultivated appearance, Asher was no stranger to San Quentin's Death Row. Four years earlier, she had represented a condemned prisoner named Wilson de la Roi. De la Roi was originally sentenced to a life term at Folsom State Prison in 1939 for second-degree murder. While serving this sentence, he allegedly stabbed to death another inmate in the prison laundry over "20 sacks of weed," and was sentenced to the gas chamber on July 15, 1942. He was moved to Death Row at San Quentin to await his execution, at which point Asher interceded. Asher fought hard for her client, already a confirmed killer, and managed to gain eleven reprieves for him. Despite her best efforts—which were duly noted in the press—de la Roi was gassed in San Quentin's chamber on October 25, 1946.

Asher's relationship with Chessman was complex, complicated, mysterious, and ultimately indecipherable. He dedicated one of his books to her (*The Face of Justice*), and her name was on his lips when he died in the gas chamber in 1960. Clearly, Asher was intrigued and titillated by her client from the start; no other reason can explain why she agreed to advise him on legal matters beginning in August 1948. He was broke; therefore, she was either working pro bono or was running up a bill she didn't expect would be paid. She was, as early as September 1948, also acting as a sort of ad hoc, unpaid literary agent. From his cell, Chessman funneled short-story manuscripts to her; she took them to her office in Sacramento, where one of the law clerks made clean typescripts. At Chessman's direction, she submitted the stories. Not much sold until Joseph Longstreth walked into Chessman's life five years later.

Asher went to great lengths, geographically, to tend to Chessman's needs, too. In order to meet with him on a semiregular basis, she had to make the long journey down to Marin County from the state capital, often flying from Sacramento to San Francisco and "cabbing" (her word) out to San Quentin. This undoubtedly took valuable time away from other clients and burned up resources. Asher was as devoted to her profession as to her mother, with whom she lived in the same Sacramento house where she was raised. Helping Chessman took time away from tending to the elderly Mrs. Asher's needs.

And yet, there is no getting around the impact of the attention Chessman initially lavished on her. Found among her records was a ten-page, single-spaced letter/diary that Chessman wrote to/for her, covering the dates August 15, 1948, to December 30, 1948. Disguised as a newsy update on the workings of his mind and ego, it amounts to a wooing of Asher, one of the first verses of the siren song that lured Asher back to San Quentin time and again. Filled with flowery linguistic pyrotechnics—which would be largely absent from his later mature published works—it begins, "A rose, according to the late, quaint Gertrude Stein, is a rose is a rose; and telescope it ad infinitum though you may, providing you have the time, the inclination, and a certified commitment to Mendocino,* the damned thing remains just that—a rose." It featured throughout such tortured syntax as the following: "Being of obstinate and, yea, somewhat quaint nature;—Rather than

---

* Mendocino State Hospital was one of the state's asylums for the insane.

donning a false face on this Hallowed E'en, I think I shall remove mine and, in the argot of the unwashed, jump right into old man Cosmos' mouth, in a manner befitting the occasion, i.e., brashly."

Amid such sprinklings of poesy and jailhouse philosophy, Chessman tried to make the case of his innocence for this nice lady lawyer. "As I told you, Miss Asher, I am convicted of crimes I did not commit, and, if I felt it would be to my advantage, I would accompany this absolutely factual statement with a display of histrionics that would startle Shakespeare. . . . Naive lad that I was, I once thought that truth was binding on all men. Apparently, judging from what has happened to me, truth is apparently [sic] of no legal consequence. I know; the oh, so honorable Charles W. Fricke told me so." He did convince Asher that he had been given a raw deal in the courtroom of Charles W. Fricke, and her conversations with Matthews confirmed the truth of this.

To reassure her of his decency, if not innocence, Chessman wrote, "If you have gained the impression your client is something of a quaint, or even mentally unbalanced character, take a look out your window at the moon. Do you see three sets of bars in the way? I do . . . Yeah, your client is crazy, all right. He's crazy enough still to have faith in people like Al Matthews & Miss Rosalie Asher."

Chessman's ego was still so unblemished that, even with two death sentences hanging over his head—largely the result of his own hubristic courtroom antics—he still would not allow anyone else to take full charge of his case. (In late 1955, when matters stood hopelessly against him, that honor fell to George T. Davis, someone whose own ego may have dwarfed even Chessman's.) "I feel, Miss Asher," he pompously informed his lawyer, "my position is much like a boxer's. He has seconds in his corner to watch and advise during the heat of battle and, generally, tell him what to do. Yet he does his own fighting. When you start with innocence as an absolute this 'thing' necessarily reduces itself to nothing but a legal slug fest and I would prefer to do my own slugging. It is with full knowledge you doubtless could and would do a much better job."

This was not, at least he told Asher, due entirely to his own hardheadedness. It had more to do with—if one could believe Chessman's explanation—a sense of fair play and honor. He insisted to Asher that he'd been "framed" for the Red Light Bandit crimes and "what really hurts is the job wasn't even artistic." It has remained one of the enduring mysteries of the Chessman legend that the framing, and the identity of the framer(s), are not conclusively known even today. If anyone would have known Chessman's deepest secrets, it would have been Rosalie Asher. And she never indicated, one way or the other, whether she knew the ultimate truth.

On September 11, 1948, in his diary/letter to her, Chessman wrote, "Sometimes I used to wonder what the most pleasant feeling in the world was. Now I know. It is the feeling one gets from having the utmost confidence, faith and trust in another. . . . I suddenly felt a permeation of the utmost trust, confidence and faith in Miss Rosalie S. Asher."

Four days later, he was "taking another healthy swing at R.S. Asher's drum," lavishing praise on her for the legal "miracle" he felt she was performing. In the course of this entry, he would say something that, for sheer irony, should have supplied many hours of retrospective laughter from Asher. That is, Chessman said, "I realize your position . . . is not that of a nursemaid who must, every time her small charge begins to yowl, pat him on the head and say, 'There, there.' . . . I do not intend to take advantage of your efficiency and willingness to safeguard zealously the rights of a client. I will not willingly impose upon you with requests that are frivolous or without substance. I do not want to be indulged; I am not entitled to whimsy. I have no right to demand attention because I am, speaking figuratively, afraid of the dark."

And yet, out of necessity and because Asher willingly gave of her time, this is precisely what he did for the next twelve years.

■

MUCH OF CHESSMAN'S early defiance on the Row may have been an effort to dramatize his "innocence" for his mother's sake. Hallie Chessman was, by mid-1948, gravely ill. In his diary for September 15, 1948, Chessman wrote, "With my mother expected to live but a short period I do not want to sit idly by while still weighted with these convictions and under sentence of death. It would not be fair to her because I know the blow my present arrest and conviction was to her; it was very nearly a death blow. For her sake, I seek only a fair and impartial trial, because I know that such will mean an acquittal."

On December 1, 1948, he wrote, "My father also said my mother is critically ill and, from the way he wrote, expected to die momentarily. That, for me, is just about the last straw, because I know my mother is dying from a broken heart as much as from a malignant physical growth. I know what a bitter, humiliating experience this has been for her—to know that her son is going to his death for a crime committed while he was at home with her, talking far into the night with her because she had had a relapse and didn't want to be alone with that awful physical pain. Even then talking of and believing in a bright future. I was home and I was what she believed in. She didn't know then what a cruel, heartless thing was about to happen."

Hallie Chessman hung on longer than anyone expected, dying a year later, on December 2, 1949. She died, Chessman was told, "expressing her faith in me."

"After endless years of pain and poverty, she was dead," Chessman later wrote. "And her son was on Death Row waiting to die. And her husband was an old and broken man."

■

IF NOTHING ELSE, Death Row provided Chessman with uninterrupted time to write. It did not transform Chessman into a writer; he already thought of himself as a writer when he landed in Death Row, estimating that he'd pursued the muse for twenty years (meaning that he'd started, if one trusts his math, when he was 8). Furthermore, between crime sprees, he'd already written a number of stories and a full novel. Some of his short stories had been published, he claimed. He had what he called a "reasonably good batting average—not 1.000 but never less than .250, which at least gets me out of the sandlot league."

Soon after arriving on Death Row, Chessman wrote in his diary for October 3, 1948, "I am a writer. When I say this I do not mean that wishing to be a writer, in my wishfullness, I have applied the Guy Ballard* mystical 'I Am' technic, that thunder clapped . . . and that I thus became a writer. I mean that mixed up in my heredity was a clamorous little writing gene, an obnoxious little villain that forced the role upon me; I mean that with consciousness came the urge—and the sweat and tears and a voracious intellectual appetite fed the urge, nurtured it, until only at the expense of becoming a schizophrenic could I suppress it. I mean that for the last twenty years, by trial and error, I have been developing the technics of the 'slick' fiction writers; by slick I mean the slick paper mags, as the Post. Only trouble is that Caryl W. Chessman is also, in all things, a revolutionist; he is never content with the tried & true, the inane cliche; he wants new combinations, a new style—the results are at times amusing, at others, terrifying but rarely lucrative."

Despite the egotistical extravagance of this passage, it's clear that Chessman, had he avoided a life of crime, possessed the skills to have pursued a career in writing—journalism, screenplays, perhaps hard-boiled detective fiction. However, it's important to grasp just how these skills ripened and changed on Death Row. His writings that survive from before 1948 are, like the early passage from his Death Row diary, clever and cocky but, ultimately, facile and empty. They are interesting simply because they were written by the same man who wrote *Cell 2455, Death Row*. Had he spent the remaining years of his life cranking out stuff like that, he would be remembered only as a curiosity within California prison annals, if at all.

He learned, on Death Row, that writing was more than just an activity to fill time; it was the very elixir of life, the reason to get off his cot in the morning. And, after 1954, when his father died, it was literally all that he had left in the world. He had no religion, no hobby, no athletic inclinations.

Indeed, the act of writing under these conditions transformed Chessman as a person. As Rosalie Asher later told her "niece" Bonnie

---

* While hiking in Northern California in 1930, Ballard met "the Ascended Master Saint Germain" near Mount Shasta. His experiences, built around what he called "I AM" activity, spawned a worldwide mystical movement still in existence today.

Fovinci,* "He went into prison a criminal punk and ended up a real human being."

■

ANY GIVEN DAY on Death Row was like any other day. The mind-numbing, soul-deadening routine, some convicts have confessed, made the trip to the gas chamber seem like something of a relief. This may have also been true for Chessman in the first four years after his conviction in Judge Fricke's court , at least in his weaker moments.

Most of Chessman's energies during the early years of his Death Row residence were focused on appealing his original sentence and contesting the preparation of a transcript from his original trial. The latter legal maneuver was made necessary when, on June 23, 1948—a month after the jury found Chessman guilty of seventeen out of the eighteen counts—the court reporter, Ernest W. Perry, died after transcribing only one-third of the trial record. Though Perry's remaining shorthand notes were deemed "completely undecipherable" by the Executive Committee of the Los Angeles Superior Court Reporters' Association, the Los Angeles County Board of Supervisors hired Stanley Fraser to complete the transcription job that Perry had started. Chessman, rightfully, protested, to no avail. Fraser's garbled final transcriptions were sent to Judge Fricke in February 1949, who approved them on August 18, 1949. The next two years of Chessman's life were consumed by a high-stakes battle over the viability of Fraser's transcript, petitions for a rehearing with the State Supreme Court and the U.S. Supreme Court, and ultimately the decision by the State Supreme Court on December 18, 1951, that his original seventeen convictions stood. His first execution date was set for March 28, 1952.

During this time, Chessman's behavior continued to be unbendingly defiant, and unbearably so for the prison staff, the state justice department, and the conservatives, who tsked-tsked endlessly over the reports written about him.

---

* Bonnie Fovinci was not legally Asher's niece but was often referred to by her as such. Fovinci was a close enough family friend to serve as the executrix of Asher's will after her death in 2001.

All the while, the clock in the corridor outside his cell never stopped reminding Chessman of his impending fate. The only way he could submerge the fear and panic was to bury himself in his legal work and to fall into the Row's regimented daily schedule. The day began when the food cart made its round at eight A.M. Chessman often skipped breakfast; instead of the eggs and potatoes normally served, he got extra rations of milk for a troubled stomach that eventually became a severe ulcer. His morning meal, consumed in his cell, was a cup of hot black coffee and two cigarettes. At nine a prison guard brought a razor and blade and an inmate porter brought in a bowl of hot water—there was no hot running water in the cell. After Chessman shaved, the porter retrieved the razor and blade and the cell was locked and slatted behind him. If it were Wednesday or Sunday, Chessman followed the guard and porter to the shower room, where he was allowed a full bath, then marched back to his cell, where he was issued a clean set of clothes (his sheets and pajamas were laundered each Friday). For the next two hours, in his cell, Chessman typed letters or manuscripts, prepared legal documents, or read.

At eleven thirty, Chessman was allowed a two-hour recreation period, during which he could walk in the corridor in front of his cell or, at one end of the corridor, play checkers, chess, or cards with other Row inmates in the day room, which was large enough to accommodate Ping-Pong tables and even a volleyball court. Here, also, the inmates were shown a film each Thursday. Toward the end of Chessman's stay, the films were replaced by a television set. At one thirty, he returned to his cell. Within half an hour, the second and last meal of the day was served from a food cart. Chessman ate the meal, putting aside a snack and some milk for later in the evening. If the two meals weren't sufficient enough to sate his hunger, he had canteen privileges, which allowed him to purchase candy, cigarettes, and personal hygiene products, depending on how much credit he had on the books. He read or paced the cell for an hour, then napped until six, bringing the total number of hours slept, by his own estimation, to between four and seven out of twenty-four.

At six, the floor guard delivered black coffee. Chessman allowed himself two more cigarettes while drinking the coffee. Then he pulled out his typewriter and wrote until eight. He "read, talked, studied and, for a half hour at least, did some more pacing of the cell floor," until ten. If he were deep into a manuscript, Chessman would write by shorthand sitting on his bunk, a writing board across his lap, well into the night, typing up the resultant text the next day. On those nights, he did not fall asleep until four A.M., or later.

All told, Chessman spent twenty-two hours a day locked in Cell 2455; the general population spent fifteen hours a day locked in theirs. During his first five years on Death Row, he watched as forty-eight men walked past his cell on their way to the gas chamber. Three of these men he knew from his days of crime in Los Angeles. He had only one goal, and it kept him sane: "to leave the Row alive."

Following these rules, Chessman was able to pass four years until there was a discernible change in his prospects.

■

OUTSIDE THE WALLS of San Quentin during the first third of Caryl Chessman's residence on Death Row (1948–1952), the American landscape was changing dramatically. Freed from the yoke of a victorious world war and living off the newly enacted G.I. Bill of Rights (a.k.a. the Servicemen's Readjustment Act of 1944), Americans moved away from the cities and began procreating like there was no tomorrow. In 1946, 3.4 million American babies were born, an increase of more than half a million from 1945, and the birthrates continued to soar, peaking at 4.3 million in 1957. This was the first wave of the "Baby Boom" that is generally said to have ended in 1964. Much of this prodigious American progeny was raised in newly minted suburbs, which had taken their architectural cue from William J. Levitt's experiment in uniformity, Levittown, the first of which opened on Long Island, New York, in 1949.

The bible for this boom belt was Dr. Benjamin Spock's hugely influential *Baby and Child Care*—one in three American mothers eventually used it—the first edition of which was published in 1946. Spock's revolutionary impact was due to his shifting the baby-rearing paradigm from the rigid fundamentalism upon which the nation was

founded (and under which Serl and Hallie Chessman were reared)
to a more commonsensical, pragmatic approach that included such
outlandish ideas as displays of affection, parental flexibility, duty-
sharing, and breast-feeding. Spock encouraged mothers to nurture
their children's individuality, which was at odds with the bland but
benign setting in which they were being raised. Fathers were, meanwhile, the family breadwinners; "the man in the gray flannel suit"
(the title of Sloan Wilson's 1955 novel) left the house at dawn to join
the "rat race" and returned at night, smelling of guzzled booze and
secretarial perfume.

Piercing this suburban bubble now and again were the chilly
winds of a Cold War. In 1949, China became "Red China" when Mao's
Communist Revolution officially established a government, and the
Soviet Union acquired the atomic bomb. America's economic boom
times were dazzled by new fads like TV and "going steady" but also
disturbed by threats posed by an escalating "arms race" and Communist witch hunts. These latter inquisitions had actually begun in
1938, when a congressman from Texas, Martin Dies Jr., became the
head of the newly formed House Un-American Activities Committee
(HUAC); from this bully pulpit, Dies labeled anything he didn't like,
including his President's own New Deal programs, "un-American."
Dies spent more time attacking "liberals" and "Communists" than
he did investigating the genuine threats to wartime national security
such as the Nazi American Bund, Knights of the White Camellia,
and the Ku Klux Klan, inspiring Vice President Henry A. Wallace
to observe, "The effect on the morale of the country would be less
damaging if Mr. Dies were on the Hitler payroll."

Thanks to Dies, "un-American" became the new political epithet,
and after the war it was thawed out and used to batter anyone who
stepped out of line. HUAC itself grew out of control, focusing its seemingly unlimited powers and budget on Hollywood, publishers, and
labor unions. At its 1946 labor convention, the Congress of Industrial
Organizations (CIO) passed a resolution that said, among other things,
"This committee [HUAC] has indicated that every democratic and
progressive movement in American life is subject to its vicious smears.
On the other hand, it ignores and even encourages the activities of

native fascists."* In 1947, HUAC investigated the film industry, which resulted in prison sentences for the so-called Hollywood Ten (among whom were Herbert Biberman and Dalton Trumbo). In 1948, Whittaker Chambers accused former State Department official Alger Hiss of spying for the Soviet Union, which emboldened HUAC and brought a young California congressman named Richard Nixon to national prominence.

The 1950 conviction of Alger Hiss for spying, while not connected to Chessman, created shock waves that splashed into all corners of America, including San Quentin. As cited, one of Chessman's diary entries, for August 15, 1948, signs off, "To wit, Comrade (without being pink) Caryl W. Chessman." With Hiss, America had the very embodiment of the cultured intellectual smarty pants, the know-it-all-who talked over the average Joe's heads—an accusation, with implied hints of suspicious motives, leveled at Chessman for his 1948 courtroom demeanor. During this HUAC hysteria, which ran for the entirety of the 1950s, blacklists were drawn up, resulting in the loss of jobs and careers for many talented people. Famous people were dragged into the spotlight to testify before the estimable committee (whose chairman in 1947–48, J. Parnell Thomas, was sent to prison in 1949, for taking salary kickbacks from fictitious office personnel). Anyone who used big words and/or championed progressive political causes came under suspicion from the media.†

Only five years after the end of the bloodiest war in world history, the United States found itself dragged by right-wing ideologues into yet another global conflict, in Korea, one that threatened to go global when Communist China got involved. That war lasted until 1953 and resulted in the deaths of more than fifty-four thousand American troops—almost as many as were later killed in the Vietnam War—but back home, in the safe, secure suburban bubble, Americans

---

* The CIO, sensing the need for solidarity in this emerging right-wing climate, merged with the American Federation of Labor in 1955, to form the AF of L (later AFL)–CIO.

† Because of the negative connotations that accrued to its name, HUAC was renamed the House Internal Security Committee in 1969, then abolished in 1975.

seemed blissfully unaware of the carnage. Even today it seems as if the United States suffers from a collective amnesia about the Korean War, something that cannot be said for the Vietnam War.

■

CHESSMAN'S ROAD-TO-DAMASCUS, LIFE-CHANGING moment took place on June 25, 1952. It was a Wednesday, he noted in *Cell 2455, Death Row*, a few minutes past one in the morning. He had, the previous day, been handed an envelope by Warden Teets containing a stay of execution by Judge Albert Lee Stephens of the United States Court of Appeals for the Ninth Circuit, pending a decision on his appeal of his original conviction. Teets stood outside the bars of Chessman's cell as he read the typed legal brief. Chessman had been certain that the stay would be denied and that he would die that Friday. He had been fully prepared to die, he told Teets.

Teets wondered out loud whether Chessman even wanted another chance. He seemed to imply that Chessman really longed for the state to help him commit suicide.

Harley O. Teets was measurably less hostile toward Chessman than Duffy was at the end of his tenure. Teets had been an associate warden under Duffy before the latter's retirement in 1952, so he was already familiar with Chessman's case. Even as late as 1952, Chessman still described himself as a "hating, rebellious, young-old prisoner." He was still living and reacting completely on his own terms, "aggressively fighting for my life," he wrote in *Cell 2455, Death Row*, "and yet paradoxically giving the impression I did not give a damn about it or anything. From all surface indications, I appeared determined to go to Hell, but equally determined to get there in my own way, on my own terms and at my own good time."

It took this June 1952 stay of execution—one Chessman did not think he would get—to shatter the existential crust that had formed on his personality. The stay was hand-delivered by Warden Teets, who stayed, after Chessman opened it to learn of its contents, to talk to his prisoner. Teets was baffled by what he saw as Chessman's "carrying defiance to its absolute extreme," of his using "every last ounce of brain power, cunning and cleverness" to "beat the system or belittle it." Teets knew that Chessman had a sharp mind and demonstrable talents, that he was the smartest guy on Death Row, if not in all of San Quentin. Though he said he "didn't enjoy putting men to death," Teets leveled with Chessman on the day he handed him Judge Stephens's stay, telling his prisoner that, in effect, it was no skin off his nose if the state killed him in the gas chamber. Speaking like an avid proponent of the "new penology"—which Duffy had sworn by but Teets had only partly embraced—the warden said he was more concerned about the implications to society if Chessman, or, rather, the "Chessmans of the world," died without changing.

"I don't believe I had ever felt more wide awake or more strangely calm in my whole life than I felt at that moment," Chessman wrote of this encounter.

Perhaps it was Teets's more cerebral approach to Chessman that turned the tide, because the new warden hadn't said anything that Duffy hadn't earlier repeated ad nauseam. Or, maybe it was the warden's challenge combined with the hopelessness of Chessman's situation that did the trick. Either way, when writing about this, Chessman sounds like an alcoholic who has finally "bottomed out" and discovered the path to sobriety. Once this line has been crossed, anything is possible and anything that comes is appreciated.

It seems improbable that anyone would be grateful for a death sentence, but Chessman later wrote, "Death Row is doubtless the best thing that ever could have happened to me. Since I was sixteen, it was a race between Death Row and the morgue as to which would claim me first. Luckily for me, Death Row won . . . I know it's nothing less than a miracle that I'm alive and out of the self-destructive psychological jungle in which I was trapped for so many years. It took the kill-or-cure medicine of Death Row to bring me to my senses and give me a future."

He further elaborated on why, or how, he changed, in *Trial by Ordeal*: "The impossible occurred. Virtually overnight I changed radically—and there was nothing phony about the change. It was real. What had brought it about? I got a stay that I didn't expect. And with it came a challenge from the Warden, whose words made me think, made me see myself for what I really was—an angry, hating, fighting failure."

His conclusion: "Long after I should have been dead, I wrote myself back to sanity."

■

IT'S CLEAR THAT the management at San Quentin could not bring themselves to admit the State of California made a mistake with Chessman. Too much was riding on his being executed. Complicating an already complicated situation—and adding to Chessman's bitterness—the California legislature passed a law in 1951 modifying the Little Lindbergh Law so that, in most cases, it did not come with a death sentence and those convicted under this loophole would be eligible for parole. Had the Red Light Bandit committed the crimes in 1951, he would more than likely not have been looking at the inside of a San Quentin death cell.

At that point, it must have seemed to the State of California that Chessman was like the rogue elephant in George Orwell's 1936 essay, "Shooting an Elephant." Orwell, a member of the British Imperial Police stationed in Burma at the time, did not want to shoot the rogue elephant who had stomped a villager to death; the elephant had returned to passivity, he was a valuable asset to the village, and Orwell himself was opposed to killing animals on general principles. And yet, the natives expected it of him; the most important consideration, then, was that no member of the imperial government be allowed to lose face. As Orwell writes, "I had got to shoot the elephant. I had committed myself to doing it when I sent for the rifle. A sahib has got to act like a sahib; he has got to appear resolute, to know his own mind and do definite things. To come all that way, rifle in hand, with two thousand people marching at my heels, and then to trail feebly away, having done nothing—no that was impossible. The crowd would laugh at me. And my whole life, every white man's life in the East, was one long struggle not to be laughed at."

California's "sahibs" had to gas Chessman. Not to would be to lose face, to be laughed at. Chessman knew this, writing of himself, in the first person in 1954: "Bullheadedly, I had virtually placed the state in the position where it must destroy me."

Nonetheless, Chessman's life had been ruled by his own iron will and failure to bend, even when doing so would have made his situation better. What baffled Teets most of all was this pragmatic observation: What did Chessman think he'd gained for all his defiance?

Rather than lay down the law, so to speak—and what good would that do, anyway, since Chessman was likely to die regardless—Teets suggested, "If you have the guts, Caryl, now you can make some sense out of your life and do something with it to repay Judge Stephens for the chance he's given for you."

In the past, Chessman had been more likely to scoff at such paternalism, to view it as an invitation to grovel in gratitude for crumbs at the feet of the judge. He recalled the preacher who'd come to the Los Angeles County jail after his 1948 conviction and hectored him from outside his cell: "It's too late to save your life, so get down on your knees and beg God for forgiveness for this wicked life you've led!"

When Chessman asked Teets, four years later, what he had in mind, the warden said, "Figure it out for yourself" and walked away.[*]

Warden Teets, of course, had his own ulterior motive for challenging Chessman on this score; his life and the institutional life of the prison would be so much easier if Chessman "settled down" and "stopped making trouble." As Chessman later wrote in an unpublished, third-person account of his case, "Chessman had been a rebellious, hard-to-handle prisoner, found to be more tractable when writing. Accordingly, he was encouraged to write, some say, simply because it was felt this was the easiest way to keep him quiet and in

---

[*] Warden Teets did not leave a written record of his time at San Quentin, so it would be hard to verify the full accuracy of Chessman's depiction of this event. However, in his 1961 memoir, *Death Row Chaplain*, Byron E. Eshelman, one of San Quentin's religious leaders, indicates Chessman changed around this time, as does Bernice Freeman's *The Desperate and the Damned* (1961). Further, Teets never contested any of the material in *Cell 2455, Death Row* related to Chessman's San Quentin years. Thus, it's not clear if Warden Teets later regretted the gauntlet he'd hurled at Chessman's feet in 1952; after all, because of it, and the opportunity he made of it, Chessman soon became one of the most famous prisoners in the world, which further complicated Warden Teets's life and disrupted the routine of Death Row for the next half decade.

line. . . . His prison keepers did not vaguely suspect the autobiographical book he began when given the green light would be completed before he kept his appointment with the executioner and that, in any case, it would be no more than an amateurish effort at which no publisher would take a second look."

Of course, it might simply be that the governor and the court system were putting pressure on Teets to quell this one-man rebellion. Chessman may have been personally defiant but he'd also become an effective and tireless jailhouse lawyer for others on the Row and was admired and looked up to by some as a natural leader. Though not as well known then as he later became for his writing, Chessman had already begun to attract notice outside the prison for his legal work which had earned stays and rehearings for some of the other Row residents. The "rogue elephant" Chessman was slowing down the judicial process in the State of California.

Regardless of his motives, Teets's challenge pacified Chessman. The night after his encounter with Teets Chessman could not sleep thinking about the warden's words. As he paced in his tiny cell, he calculated that it was his "1,453rd night on Death Row. More than 35,000 hours. Almost one-eighth of my life." Friday, his scheduled date with the gas chamber, would be "just another day, not the end of the world." Despite what he calculated to be 200 to 1 odds, Chessman was determined to "win in the courts." But the warden's words ate at him. So what, he seemed to say, what have you gained by another stay, another court date, another filing, if you've lost your own soul in the process?

Chessman detailed the self-inventory he began making in the wee hours of the morning inside his cell on Death Row. It's unlikely that these realizations came full-blown overnight, that they'd been simmering below that surface of his defiance. Chessman was simply too eloquent about these matters for a reader to believe he'd had an instant religious conversion, and was speaking in the tongue of one who'd seen the light. Few people grappling with demons have moments like that; wisdom often comes from acknowledging something you knew all along.

Chessman finally got this, writing, "Slowly I found it possible to

see my condemnation in terms larger than my own predicament . . .
I had been brought to the Row and then had spent four rugged, ugly
years here, aggressively fighting for my life, and yet paradoxically
giving the impression I did not give a damn about it or anything.
From all surface indications, I appeared determined to go to Hell, but
equally determined to get there in my own way, on my own terms
and at my own good time. I have told here the story of my life for
the first time, and my purpose in telling it is not to try to justify or
to excuse what I have done. Perhaps my actions cannot be justified.
They perhaps cannot be excused. But surely they can be understood,
and a large social significance derived from them."

Chessman estimated that in the first five years of his stay on
Death Row he wrote 450,000 words just in legal filings, for which he
spent three thousand hours preparing; he wrote two thousand letters and read two thousand legal books and journals. His prodigious
legal work became so unwieldy that he outgrew his cell. The newly
impressed Warden Teets allowed Chessman to convert the empty
Cell 2439 into an office—the only time in the history of Death Row
that anyone was ever accorded such a privilege.

Chessman's writer muse found another outlet. He began working
on "the story of my life" for real. The result, two years later, made
his name famous in all parts of the world.

PART TWO

The Transformation

6

The Coming of Uncle Joe

And now, thanks be to the unknown power which
rules us, my past has buried its dead. More than that;
I can accept with sober cheerfulness the necessity
of all I lived through. So it was to be; so it was. For
this did nature shape me; with what purpose, I shall
never know; but, in the sequence of things eternal,
this was my place.

—GEORGE GISSING,
The Private Papers of Henry Ryecroft

CHESSMAN'S FORTUNES CHANGED in so many ways after he met
Joseph E. Longstreth that it is tempting to say the friendship that
formed between these two men allowed him to bury the past. More
realistically, though, Longstreth represented to Chessman a break
with, and from, the more sordid manifestations of his criminal history,
allowing him to harbor some tangible hopes for the future—insofar
as someone on Death Row could be said to have a future or, for that
matter, much in the way of hopes. Before Longstreth entered it in
October 1953, Chessman's life had, for the previous five years, been
an unbroken chain of clanging boredom, manic legal research, case
preparation, floating despair, and sudden violence inherent in a maximum security prison existence. The only relief was the occasional
visit from Rosalie Asher and letter from his father. And, prior to his
life there in San Quentin, he'd spent another decade in Los Angeles

among hoodlums, cheap punks and molls who accompanied him on his various criminal escapades, broken only by trips to reform school or prison.

Although a rap sheet was all he had to show for his life up until then, Chessman had always harbored a dream of being a writer. More accurately, he envisioned himself as a literary outlaw in the mold of François Villon, the fifteenth-century French poet, vagabond, and thief who himself survived three trips to Death Row and was, ultimately, banished from Paris for killing a priest.* For a person of Chessman's gifts and genius-level I.Q., his cohorts in and out of prison could not have provided much in the way of intellectual stimulation other than serving as the props for his fantasy of being a twentieth-century Villon. These were his pawns, his own pack of homegrown *coquillards*.†

Though Hallie Chessman had tried to nurture her son's literary gifts—convincing Serl to let Caryl convert the garage into a studio— she herself was intellectually limited. The only book about which she could claim any authority was her bedside Bible. And, although Caryl later said in his own books that he had regular, long discussions with his bedridden mother about the meaning of life, these heart-to-hearts did not straighten him out. Soon after she fell asleep, he admitted, he slipped out of the house to prowl the streets with his *coquillards*. The beleaguered and suicidal Serl, scraping out a paltry existence performing odd jobs, thought Caryl's writing was a luxury but was careful about voicing his opinion on this score.

And yet, it is clear from the papers he left behind that Chessman had made several attempts to become that heroic writer. Between the nocturnal prowling and the lockups, he had somehow managed to fill hundreds of pages with his thoughts by age twenty-six. He had even

---

* François Villon was, like Chessman, precociously smart, receiving his degree from the Sorbonne at twenty-one and then spending most of the rest of his life either on the run or in prison. He was best known for *Grand testament* (1461), his reflections on life as beggar and thief, and *Ballad des pendus*, or "Ballad of the Hanged Man," written for his own epitaph while facing a death sentence. His poetry, according to Ioan Davies, "has become, over time, the clarion cry of the incarcerated intellectual."

† *Coquillards* were the gang of thieves that tormented France after the Hundred Years War and with whom François Villon consorted.

drafted a few mature, if unpublishable, short stories, and a novel of satire with the strange working title *Nov Smoz Kapop?* which, even as late as 1960, he had hopes, of dusting off and knocking into shape.

However, the chance of actually realizing that dream—a life as a writer—was remote, if not impossible, before he met Joseph E. Longstreth. This invaluable connection came about through a flukish correspondence that Chessman initiated. In an interview conducted in 2002, Longstreth recounted how Chessman had gotten in touch with him.

"I was in New York and I had established a literary agency with a couple of friends, called Critics Associated," he said. "That existed because I was doing a great deal of freelance work for editors, publishers and agents and so forth. And I thought, 'why in the hell should I be doing all this work for X number of dollars (I forget the amount now) when I can be doing it for myself and getting 100 percent?' We [he and fellow writer-editors Alan Honour and Kathryn Hitte, who also worked as assistant juvenile editor at David McKay, and graphic designer Al Miglio] all felt the same way."

Meanwhile, a total stranger sat on Death Row 3,500 miles away, daydreaming about cracking the proverbial safe of the publishing industry.

"Caryl had sent a manuscript about his life to Simon & Schuster and asked them to send him a list of accredited agents," said Longstreth. "And my name was on the list. Caryl was interested in music, an aspect of his life and personality no one has commented on in all the accounts then or since. At the same time this was going on, I had translated and arranged a libretto for an opera which was being produced and was running in New York, Mozart's *Don Pedro*, as staged by the Lemonade Opera. (The opera consisted of an amalgam of Mozart's music, with an original libretto.) It was very well reviewed by the press and my work was singled out by name in most of the reviews. Caryl loved music, and he was reading all these reviews in the New York papers and my name was in the reviews."

Meanwhile, Caryl's father would unwittingly provide the link between his condemned son and Longstreth. Serl Chessman was still living in Glendale, and with his health on the skids, he'd secured the services of a housekeeper, a divorcee named Frances Ann Couturier. She had been his regular waitress at a corner restaurant, where they had traded confidences for many months. Frances, who was twenty-five when Hallie died, was pregnant with her second child when her husband, a navy man stationed in Los Angeles, abandoned the family. After the second child was born, a daughter named Cheryl, Serl suggested that Frances, Cheryl, and her two-year-old son, David, move in with him. With this move, he found a cure for his loneliness and she found a haven for her family. In exchange for room and board, Frances cleaned house, prepared meals, and kept Serl company, while the kids crawled underfoot. Photographs of Frances at this time show her to be a fresh-faced, wholesome, and buxom young woman, with wavy brown hair, full lips, even white teeth, and a penchant for flowered dresses. To someone like Serl, her smile must have cast a klieglike beacon into the far corners of his existence. It's worth noting that Serl, though he was a nearly broken man, was still in his fifties, and he had not had a woman in his bed, if one dates this from Hallie's car wreck, in twenty-five years. Surely, that wholly human thought entered his head when Frances cast her smile his way.

She met Caryl Chessman by proxy. That is, Serl wrote to his son regularly and had entrusted Frances with carrying on that fatherly duty. He dictated parts of the letters to her and, with each mailing, she added little tidbits about their daily lives to this condemned but kind stranger in San Quentin. Caryl's responses were warm and personal; he was grateful that someone was looking after his father.

"Frances was one of three or four people who had the warden's permission to write Caryl," said Longstreth. "What do you write to a man on Death Row? Well, since she was reading books to her two children, she wrote about what she was doing. Among other things, she mentioned the books that she was reading. One of her children's favorites was a book I had written [*Tiger Tizzy*]. She told Caryl the author was Joseph Longstreth. And that was the only name that meant anything to him on Simon and Schuster's list of agents. So he thought, 'This guy writes, has been published, and is reviewed.' So he simply addressed a letter to me in New York, put it in the mail, and that's how I got involved with Caryl Chessman. I had never heard of him before then."

That letter, dated October 26, 1953, was a four-page, single-spaced missive, both business-like ("I am positive the sales potential of the book will be greatly enhanced if it is illustrated and indexed") and honest ("I'm a three time loser, now 32 years of age"), and yet containing the undisguisable traces of intact ego that had kept death house despair at bay for the five previous years. The letter opened, "While I realize my manuscript must speak for itself, so too should its author. I'm a condemned man. I've spent the last five and one half years here on Death Row at California's historic San Quentin Prison waging a really rugged legal battle for survival. . . ."

In four paragraphs, Chessman had detailed most of his legal maneuvers, his criminal past, his previous incarcerations, and his media notoriety, just in case Longstreth had missed the minor media storm that accompanied the Red Light Bandit episode. He also mentioned that he had already won two stays of execution, one from California Supreme Court Justice Jesse W. Carter (on February 29, 1952) and one from U.S. District Court Judge Albert Lee Stephens (on June 23, 1952) and was awaiting the setting of a new execution date.

"I have known every kind of criminal, from the petty and obscure to nationally known killers and 'public enemies.' I have been accused of almost every kind of crime. Long psychiatrically diagnosed an 'aggressive psychopathic personality' or plain 'dangerous criminal psychopath,' the press in its enthusiasm has tagged me everything from 'fiend' to 'criminal genius.' . . . Please be assured I don't mention all the above because I am in the least proud of it, but solely to point out introductorily the considerable extent of my experience with crime, criminals, courts, the law, penal institutions, penologists—and capital punishment. I might add that since being brought to Death Row I have come uncomfortably close to being executed more than once and have watched nearly fifty men take that last grim walk past my cell."

Anticipating hesitance on Longstreth's part, Chessman laid out a case for the book's need and ease of publication. His letter had all the earmarks of a seamlessly professional book proposal, and yet, it should be added, *he had already written the book!* Sitting in his death cell, pecking away on a battered Underwood typewriter, he had completed the massive nonfiction manuscript that would bring him worldwide fame. The impetus for writing the manuscript, Chessman said, had begun seventeen months earlier, "after winning a stay of execution that literally jerked me back from the grave and psychologically from beyond the grave." He credited Warden Harley O. Teets, whom he characterized as a "modern, progressive penologist," with offering encouragement and "making it possible for me to do so."

The manuscript, Chessman assured Longstreth, had already been cleared by both Warden Teets and the Director for Corrections at the state level, a tough cookie named Richard A. McGee. Chessman said he'd begun securing permissions to quote from other sources in his book and even estimated that the book would "run just slightly more than 500 pages and should sell well at $5." (*Cell 2455, Death Row* ran to three hundred sixty-one pages and sold in hardcover for $3.95.)

Finally, he addressed the potential personal interaction that such an undertaking would require. "It may be that initially you will feel hesitant or chary about dealing with a doomed man. You needn't. I'm not a sinister or devious character. My reputation is as a gunman not a con man. I can guarantee you, for my end, that our author-publisher relationship will be pleasant, reasonable, entirely satisfactory."

In response to Chessman's initial letter, Longstreth expressed interest in seeing his writing. Soon thereafter he received a package in the mail. In it was the seven-hundred-fifty-page, forty-three-chapter manuscript for what would eventually be published as *Cell 2455, Death Row*, a book that would make Chessman's long-harbored dreams come true: he would become a best-selling author, an international cause célèbre.

"When I got the manuscript, there was a two-page, single-spaced cover letter, which addressed his own situation," recalled Longstreth. "I've forgotten the exact words, but toward the end he said something to the effect of 'Incidentally, we should hurry, because I'm due to be executed in two months.' As though the usual book gets done in six weeks. Let's go to press. That's how it all began."

Longstreth was as impressed by Chessman's writing as by his

beguiling honesty. And the very first publisher Longstreth approached, Prentice-Hall, Inc., bought the manuscript from him on the spot, after, Longstreth admitted to Chessman in a letter, "a six martini lunch." Longstreth would go on to be the agent, and guiding hand, for the three other books Chessman published during his lifetime and the guardian of his writings long after Chessman's death. More than that, he may have been Chessman's most loyal male friend, as well as the lifeline that allowed Chessman to dream of one day being free.

■

JOE LONGSTRETH WAS the antithesis of every person with whom Chessman had been intimate in his life—civilized, well bred, multitalented, endlessly patient and optimistic, and yet, having served in the military, seen combat, and lived on his own in the Big Apple, he was no Pollyanna or prude. In short, he seemed the perfect foil for Chessman, the magnet that could draw out all the good and valuable while shoving back all the bad that Chessman had done and all the darker facets of his genius.

Upon examining the voluminous correspondence between these two men during the next seven years and the tirelessness, patience and all-around good humor of Longstreth, it's safe to say that Chessman would have remained an obscure footnote in San Quentin history without him. And, without Longstreth to keep watch over Chessman's legacy, his unpublished manuscripts would have been burned along with his own gassed cadaver, rather than cared for, preserved, and neatly organized in watertight cases up until Longstreth's death on April 15, 2003.

Longstreth's unassailable decency and trustworthiness were not lost on Caryl Chessman. Despite his seen-it-all swagger, Chessman was amazed that he'd found someone like Longstreth. On November 27, 1953, he wrote his new agent a letter, attaching it to his signed Critics Associates contract. He was sufficiently jazzed up, at this premature date, to be discussing the possibility of a film version of *Cell 2455, Death Row,* one that he foresaw as best handled by a heavyweight like the man he was once accused of planning to burgle, the director Walter Wanger. Besides being familiar with Chessman from having to appear as a witness at his 1948 Red Light Bandit trial, Wanger (1894–1968) was a leading producer from Hollywood's golden days. Prior to 1954, he had worked with every major studio and introduced stars like the Marx Brothers, Greta Garbo (in *Queen Christina*), John Wayne (in John Ford's classic Western, *Stagecoach*) and had, of late, worked with a British director, Alfred Hitchcock. By Hollywood standards, he was socially aware. Well read, well informed and willing to take risks, Wanger would go on to make the classic Cold War cautionary tale, *Invasion of the Body Snatchers*. It is not surprising, or out of the realm of possibility, that he would be interested in Chessman's plight or his tale.

Still, such premature enthusiasm was typical of Chessman's manic intensity. His book was not even in galleys—it had, in fact, not even been officially accepted by Prentice-Hall—and he was already picturing it as a Hollywood blockbuster. After expressing these grand dreams, Chessman turned personal, reaching out to this cultured stranger in New York City.

He wrote, "I was wondering, 'What sort of person is Joseph Longstreth? A stiff old fogey or a real guy, a human being?' Well, now I know. He's the latter. He's human enough, perceptive and sensitive enough, to realize that the traditional concept of a doomed man is more often than not a spurious one. I like to believe that my situation hasn't brutalized me to the extent where I am unable or unwilling keenly to appreciate the help of friends, new or old."

■

INDEED, WHAT SORT of person was Joseph E. Longstreth?

Born in 1921 in Richmond, Indiana, Longstreth hailed from a middle-class, politically moderate Hoosier family. As a young man, he exhibited artistic talents that the Midwest at that time could not possibly fulfill. Longstreth did not shun the area, nor did he adhere to the Wolfean dictum that he could not go home again. In fact, after he had his globe-trotting adventures and served his time in Manhattan, Longstreth moved back to Richmond in 1957, running Critics

Associated with his companion Alan Honour from the farm they purchased together. Also, soon after moving back home, he started a radio and television career, for nearly five years hosting a popular daytime variety show ("The Joe Longstreth Show") broadcast out of Akron, Ohio. A world-class musician to boot, Longstreth played and taught piano and cut short his TV career to become one half of the preeminent classical harpist duo, Longstreth and Escosa, which toured the world for eighteen years. Joseph Longstreth was, just as Chessman had pegged him, a true renaissance man.

At the outbreak of World War II, Longstreth joined the Army Air Corps, and spent the first four years of the war training pilots to fly B-29s, after which he flew missions of his own over Europe toward the end of the war. During his service, he earned medals for valor as well as the rank of major. Longstreth stayed in Europe after the war, graduating from the Royal Academy of Dramatic Arts in London, then studied in Paris with Louis Jouvet. (Jouvet [1887–1951] was one of the leading actors and directors of the French stage.) Blessed with gentle good looks, Longstreth appeared as an actor in films made in France and Italy. He settled in Rome for two years, to study piano at the Santa Cecilia Conservatory.

He came to New York City in both 1950 and 1951, as part of the company for two Broadway shows. When he met Chessman in late 1953, he had been living in Manhattan for little more than two years, working as a freelance writer, actor, librettist and musician. He achieved some attenton for his translation of a libretto written for a "new" Mozart opera, *Don Pedro* for the Lemonade Opera, a review of which, in *The New Yorker*, Chessman had seen. He worked on plays and musicals for children, and wrote children's books. Besides the aforementioned *Tiger Tizzy*, Longstreth later wrote four other children's books. As an agent, he was then handling, besides Chessman's book, a "book on dog care for 5 to 8 year olds."

He formed Critics Associated (its original office was at 16 East 8th Street) with Alan Honour, whom he'd met at the Royal Academy in London. Honour had himself been a fighter pilot during World War II, a seven-year RAF veteran who'd spent enough time in the Middle East to be fluent in Arabic. He moved to the United States in 1948 and eventually hooked up with his old friend Longstreth in New York.

Longstreth related all of this to Chessman in response to his question about what sort of person he was. He, however, warned Chessman that they should not grow any closer than this cordial professionalism. "To be truthful," he wrote, "we have to keep check on ourselves here not to get too involved in your situation. We feel that we will be of more value and greater service to you 'cold' than if we allow ourselves to be moved too often by our feelings."

Nonetheless, he provided amusing descriptions of the three people with whom he worked, which seemed to leave the door to closer friendship slightly ajar. Honour was, for example, described as "a stocky, shrewd, tough little Englishman who is a grand guy to work with, a real friend, and a fiend on fairness and fair-play. He's been in the USA for about five years now and likes it very much though its basic materialism troubles him. He's concerned about the future of the country and the youth. Alan is a person of very high standards and he worries about society and civilization which seems to be losing whatever grasp it may have once had on real standards of value."

The group (Longstreth, Honour, Kathryn Hitte, Al Miglio) formed the company to make a living while working on the less lucrative projects that they individually wanted to do. "We all live in Greenwich Village which is not, I assure you, as decadent and bohemian as movies and some books would lead one to believe. Our world isn't a very pleasant one in many respects. We're constantly badgered on every side by utter commercialism and crass misrepresentation, but we try to remain above it, understand it, and do our little bits about it. We're neither saints nor sinners (though my father has always said there are only two classes of people—the caught and the uncaught!)."

This sort of casual exchange with intelligent people was something Chessman had likely never encountered. He wanted badly, one can tell from his correspondence, to speak on the same intellectual and cultivated level with his new associates and to taste this sweet life, if only by proxy, outside the prison walls. This occasionally engendered awkward locutions from Chessman, such as (from a letter dated December 9, 1953), "I share with you the view that you shouldn't put yourself in the position where you are obliged to act unwisely for haste's sake. We don't owe haste that much fealty."

It was clear, from the correspondence, that Chessman envied Long-streth greatly. Perhaps he saw the agent's uncaged and cosmopolitan life as one that he himself would have had had he not succumbed to his own sociopathic impulses or to what must have seemed like the Chessmans' genetic predisposition for failure.

Chessman's agent and loyal friend Joseph Longstreth relaxing at his home in Richmond, Indiana, in 1958 with his dachshund, Deeb. Longstreth always held out the possibility that Chessman, were he ever to gain his freedom, could find a safe haven on his farm. *Courtesy Peg Longstreth*

■

AT THE TIME that Chessman put out the feelers that brought his writing to the attention of Joe Longstreth, he also took his legal case to "the Court of Last Resort," an advisory board of legal professionals (lawyers, forensics technicians, writers) who were devoted to helping the wrongly accused and convicted. This "court" was created in 1946 by Erle Stanley Gardner, who, though best known as the author of the Perry Mason novels, was an attorney and prosecutor with an affinity for those denied justice by the legal system. Based in Temecula, California, fifteen miles east of San Clemente, Gardner was egalitarian in his outlook, helping anyone who gave him a compelling reason to do so.

Chessman was, no doubt, inspired to contact Gardner by his former legal counsel, Al Matthews, who had worked with the "Court" to overturn the death sentence of William Marvin Lindley, who'd been convicted of the sexual assault and murder of a woman in 1943. With Matthews's help, new evidence had been found to clear Lindley of the crime. Lindley was eventually acquitted in a new trial and released.

Chessman made his pitch to this famous legal giant, sending a brief summation of his case to his Temecula address. Gardner expressed interest in his case and asked for a more lengthy description. On December 15, 1953, Chessman sent him a four-page, single-spaced history of his case which, for mind-numbing detail, could not be topped. In answer to Gardner's surprised query about the death sentences, Chessman wrote, "Yes, I am sentenced twice to death not for murder but for kidnapping—and kidnapping of a highly technical variety. While the State Supreme Court, I think wrongly, didn't agree with me (*People v. Chessman 1951, 38 Cal. 2d 166, 190–192, 193*), I am convinced I am now in the unique position of being twice sentenced to death for the commission of acts (regardless of by whom committed) no longer punishable at all under statute 209 of the California Penal Code."

Furthermore, he insisted, "This is not the only unique thing about this case. The court reporter died and what I claim and have consistently offered to prove is a prejudicially incomplete and inaccurate Reporter's Transcript of the trial proceedings was accepted and used as a basis for hearing the appeal on the merits and affirming the death and other judgments . . . You'll note I have never once been given any chance to prove my contentions. Every last one of them, including those dealing with the record, remain untried after five and one half years here on Death Row."

Gardner, as Longstreth would point out to Chessman soon enough, wanted to know why he didn't bring forward the evidence that would prove his innocence of the Red Light Bandit crimes. Chessman responded, "You are doubtless correct that my petition for writ of certiorari would have been immensely strengthened if there appeared in it a brief statement of my contentions as to innocence. Such a statement, be assured, will be given a prominent place in the petition for rehearing. I shan't endeavor to rationalize or justify my failure to have that statement in the petition for certiorari. Still I believe my reasons for omitting it are pertinent. This claim of innocence has become a sore subject with me. Every time I've tried to tell someone I'm innocent I've been rewarded with a knowing look and I've been repeatedly told that courts don't concern themselves with the question of innocence, as such. So I've grown bullheaded; for the most part I've hammered away on the illegality of the conviction and offered the claim of innocence on a take-it-or-leave-it basis.

"After all, situated as I am, all I can do is 'say' I'm innocent. And anyone can do that. You know and I know that even the most patently guilty can and often do blandly claim their innocence. Well, I don't like to be laughed at. I don't like to see innocence treated as an impertinence. Moreover, I've been determined to prove my own innocence and not another's guilt—or accept the obvious alternative: execution. I've looked at death too long to give a hoot about it. Sure, I'd like to live, but that doesn't prevent me from appraising my situation realistically and from insisting on retaining what I define as integrity."

Later in the letter he resorted to the third person: "And let's face it: Chessman is a three time loser, and the public is not quick to sympathize with three time losers, be they guilty or innocent. Too, there's a segment of the public and law enforcement who believe that, whether he's guilty or innocent of these particular crimes, Chessman is a dangerous, sinister character. Thus the question of guilt or innocence can become irrelevant. This is a heaven sent opportunity to send me on my way; the courts have said I was 'legally convicted'; they have given me no chance to prove otherwise. Their word is law. Now, that's not paranoia speaking; it's hardheaded objectivity. I don't regard myself as a persecuted man. I'm just a plain damn fool in a jam who found himself too late and who, ironically, just doesn't happen this time to be guilty, a fact that has small importance to anyone but myself.

"The cause of Chessman is of importance only to Chessman; the cause of justice is (or should be) every man's concern. I felt, whether I lived or died, I could contribute something." Chessman closed by offering to cooperate fully with Gardner, accept whatever published conclusions he might come to, good or bad, about his case and to submit to "a twenty-four or forty-eight hour polygraph examination."

In closing, Chessman wrote, "You can toss them into the nearest fireplace and know that Chessman still will think as highly of you and the Court and the invaluable work you are doing as before."

Gardner did not take Chessman up on this latter offier. Instead, the famous attorney and author showed abiding interest in Chessman's case. Three days before an execution date the following year, Gardner sent a telegram to Governor Goodwin Knight, saying "I believe that the best interests of law enforcement will be served by letting Inspector Riedel of the Berkeley Police give Caryl Chessman a lie detector test to determine his guilt or innocence." Further, Gardner suggested that "public confidence in justice may well be undermined unless further careful consideration is given to Chessman's claims of innocence." In a follow up letter to the governor, after Chessman was granted a stay, Gardner wrote, "The case has given me a lot of uneasy moments. I have had enough experience with mistaken identification to realize how terribly easy it is in a case of this sort for people to make a mistake."

■

IN RESPONSE TO Longstreth's newsy observations about life in Manhattan, Chessman wrote, on January 10, 1954: "In spite of the unpleasant and intrusive quality of the crass commercialism, which I'm positive all of you are quite capable of giving the back of your hand to, I'm sure you love the work you're doing, the life you're living. And if this letter glows faintly green, well, it's only a reflection of the envy of its bemused writer. But be assured it's a healthy and a stimulating envy. Moreover, happily, the distance from the cloistered place called Death Row to the magic, skyscraper land of New York has been traversed. And I'm still marvelling that it has. Because the bars and the walls have lost their capacity to mock. Now I'm laughing at them, heartily. Death may still be just as near—even nearer—but as far as I am concerned life has assumed a far greater and more intimate importance."

The letter's fleeting glimpse of Chessman's immediate surroundings stand in stark contrast to Longstreth's existence: "I can hear the rain and the sound of a curious, not an angry, wind. Other than that, and the clacking of the Underwood [his typewriter], the Row has grown pensively quiet this Sunday afternoon. Some of us have turned inward and look to the past to sustain us. Miraculously, the man at this typewriter is filled with hope for the future, and he is inexpressibly glad to have found it possible to plead the 'cause of the criminally damned and doomed.' Even the most disciplined stoic finds pause here and the need to contribute in some way to showing a mistaken society that Death Rows are a terrible mistake."

Perhaps it was this neediness, the desperation behind the mask of self-confidence and iron discipline that touched Longstreth more deeply than any other quality about Chessman. Obviously, he knew Chessman was prodigiously talented, that he possessed a superhuman stamina and will, not to mention enough strength of character to forge a unique literary vision against all conceivable odds. But something else spurred Longstreth. Maybe it was just his Midwestern decency, the impulse to help the guy lower down the rung than he was, the Christian ethic that was instilled in him by his parents.

It can't go unrecorded, however, that Longstreth had a secret of his own that, in 1954, was viewed by the world at large as shameful, unnatural, and in every place other than bohemian enclaves like Greenwich Village and San Francisco, illegal. In that sense, he had a connection with Chessman that he may have only subconsciously realized. Longstreth was, at that time, a homosexual, living quietly and perhaps platonically with another homosexual (Honour). It could be argued that, in the 1950s, being gay was tantamount to living the life of a criminal, or at the very least the life of an ex-convict terrified that coworkers, bosses and friends would discover a damning secret.

While none of this was overtly expressed in the correspondence between these two men, it could not have gone unrecognized by either. Longstreth, clearly, was titillated by Chessman as a man, and Chessman had lived in institutions where only men—all of whom had normal physical urges and many of whom suffered from mental illness—prowled. He would not have been naïve to homosexual impulses—no other sexual encounters were possible in a prison—though it's clear that Chessman was almost certainly an ascetic.

Whatever the ingredients that created their developing friendship, theirs would become a strong bond.

And it all began on this cheery note, as a sort of mutual admiration society.

■

BY JANUARY 13, 1954, Longstreth had already found a publisher for *Cell 2455, Death Row*. Not just any publisher, but Prentice-Hall, one of the most respected in New York. And, not only that, he had negotiated, by his reckoning, "one of the most liberal contracts for a first author that I've seen. Not, mind you, that I don't think my author is worth it!"

Flush with this success, Longstreth proposed to Chessman that he come out to San Quentin to meet his new client in person. And, on January 18, 1954, Chessman wrote Longstreth an ecstatic letter, attached to the signed and initialed book contract for *Cell 2455, Death Row*. "Chessman is one most fortunate young man. I can only repeat: Joe, you've worked wonders for me!"

Exhibiting the organizational skills that would have made him, on the outside, a successful businessman or impresario, Chessman was able from his Death Row cell to plan Longstreth's proposed trip to San Quentin. He not only outlined his itinerary, he suggested a motel (The Bermuda Palms on San Quentin Road, midway between San Rafael and the prison), which bus to catch from the airport, where the bus depot was located in San Rafael, and how to get from there to his motel and to the prison. He also suggested the proper flights to catch from New York to San Francisco. He arranged a time and place within the prison (the associate warden's office) for the two of them to meet and discuss at uninterrupted length their publishing plans. He did everything short of planning Longstreth's wardrobe.

In the meantime, at Chessman's request, Longstreth had sent a signed copy of his children's book, *Tiger Tizzy*, to Frances Couturier's son, David. Before passing it on to the boy, Chessman admired it in his cell on Death Row. The image of a caged, condemned man expressing such gushing admiration for a children's book is touching, and Chessman's emotions really did seem genuine: "If it's aimed at 5 to 8 year olds, then I'd better take another look at my birth certificate," he wrote Longstreth. "Because here is one 32-year-old who is fascinated with your book's bright cheeriness, its 'different' text, its intriguing tiger and all his friends, everything about it. . . . And I now speak for two tiny friends who think Uncle Joe is one swell guy."

In the same letter, Chessman introduced Longstreth to another one of his friends, Rosalie Asher. This brought the third person into the most important triangle of Chessman's life. Chessman described Asher to Longstreth as "a good friend our age who is an attorney and an extra competent one. She and I had a long talk yesterday. She drove over from Sacramento to see me and we discussed my situation, the book, everything. In the survival department, she is anxious to help in every possible way. Also, she's giving me a hand in gathering some of the photographs I want for illustration purposes. . . . Also I'm darned glad to know you'll be able to have a talk with Rosalie Asher. You'll find her an extremely intelligent and capable young woman and, in matters of law, I have the same complete faith in her that I have in you in all of our dealings. Don't hesitate to speak your mind with her about me or my book."

Chessman and Asher concluded that it "would be a very good

idea" if Longstreth met with her when he flew out to the West Coast. To arrange this, they discussed having her fly to the San Francisco airport from Sacramento, arriving at the same time that Longstreth was due to arrive from New York. "My friend's name and address is: (Miss) Rosalie S. Asher, Attorney at Law, County Law Library, County Court House, Sacramento 14, California."

■

THE PLANNING FOR Longstreth's trip to San Quentin went smoothly. The dates were confirmed for February 12–14, 1954, and Chessman had secured Warden Teets's permission to allow them uninterrupted time together in one of the administrative offices. Eager to take an active part in the book's promotion, Chessman even suggested a number of legal strategies that may otherwise have been overlooked by the experts in New York. Rather self-importantly, he told Longstreth, "I'd like the promotion department at Prentice-Hall to work in a little closer collaboration with me than it normally does with authors."

To this end, he had already arranged an interview with Bernice Freeman, a "crack newspaperwoman" with whom he was collaborating on a story for the *Los Angeles Mirror*. Freeman, who lived in nearby San Rafael, had covered the San Quentin prison beat for the *San Francisco Chronicle* for twenty years. In that time, she had developed a loyal readership in the Bay Area. She was writing a separate piece about Chessman and the book for the *Chronicle*, the wire services, and *Saturday Review*. She, too, had expressed an interest in meeting Longstreth on his visit. She had, in fact, volunteered to pick Longstreth up at the prison after his day of work with Chessman. The agent's dance card was getting filled before he got anywhere near the ballroom.

"I might add, I've known Mrs. Freeman for 13 years," said Chessman. "I'm certain she won't throw any bean balls our way. And she even has offered to help me get any pictures I may desire for use as illustrations that may be available in the files of any of the big LA or SF dailies."

■

ONE OF THE unlikeliest women to find redeeming value in Caryl Chessman, Bernice Freeman was a star at the *Chronicle*. One of two daily newspapers at the time in San Francisco (the other being the *News Call-Bulletin*), the *Chronicle* was a Hearst family newspaper with an ultraconservative editorial bent. A veteran crime reporter, Freeman had also been married to a guard at San Quentin and raised her four daughters within the shadow of the prison walls.

Freeman was, in other words, no shrinking violet around convicts. Though compassionate in her reportage—which is to say she was fair to both sides—she understood the pathology of the criminal mind as well as any prison psychologist and could tell when an inmate was playing games. And yet, during the eighteen years that she knew him, Chessman remained a pleasant enigma to her and, eventually, came to find a special personal connection to her.

Freeman ("Berni" to both the convicts and the prison staff) first met Chessman in 1942, on a visit to Warden Clinton T. Duffy's office. Only twenty years old, Chessman had already been "playing the angles" of the crime game for six years, and at the time was serving a sentence for armed robbery. Because of his intelligence and obvious promise, Chessman had been cleared to do secretarial work in the warden's office. It was a plum assignment, allowing Chessman to busy himself with work that required him to use his brain and allowed him to project an air of self-importance. Though it was this latter aspect of Chessman's personality that made a lasting impression on Freeman, she initially was taken aback by his physical appearance.

"When I walked into the warden's office one day in 1942, I was greeted by a tall slender convict with dark wavy hair, a soft, well-modulated voice, and the manner of a gentleman," she wrote in *The Desperate and the Damned* (1961). "His trousers were beautifully pressed, his black shoes well-shined, and his shirt immaculate. . . . Except for a vague hint of arrogance, he seemed no different from any other wholesome young man of twenty. He could have been a college sophomore."

The engaging presence soon gave way to the cool manner that Chessman used with any representative of the straight world. When, upon his demand, Freeman gave Chessman her name and occupation, he sardonically responded, "Oh? From the press, eh? Please sit down." He then made an officious production of going into the warden's office to announce the visitor's arrival, emerging moments later to say, as if to a pilgrim paying a call on the royal court, "The warden will see you."

From this less than promising start, a friendship of sorts emerged. Freeman, who was particularly close to Warden Duffy (he would eventually write a cloying and paternal foreword to her 1961 memoir), was a frequent visitor to the office. She doubly looked forward to her visits now, because of the intelligent repartee she could engage in with the precocious Chessman and his sidekick, another "engaging youth," named Red Tully.

"They were two of a kind," wrote Freeman. "Arrogant, decisive, full of self-importance, and possessed of remarkable native ability, channeled in a wrong direction. Each had a great respect for the other. Red Tully was the only man I knew Chessman to admire consistently. They were probably the only two in San Quentin who could argue each other to a standoff." (This was before Bill Sands entered Chessman's picture.)

The ultimate enigma to Freeman was the same one that stumped all those who got close to Chessman, even wardens Duffy and Teets, who came to resent his presence to the point of wishing his extermination. Duffy, for example, noted in his memoir, "Chessman was a very impressive young man. . . . He was extremely polite and delighted to work for me, since it got him out of the jute mill where most new convicts were assigned at that time."

"A young man of his intelligence could have been successful at almost anything he tried," echoed Freeman. "Why had he chosen a career of crime? Perhaps because he could not take full advantage of his capacities except under strict restraint. In prison he was brilliant, charming, and versatile and sought the company of others who could talk and think at his level. Out of prison he was a thug who sought the company of other thugs."

His biggest problem, in Freeman's opinion, "was his absolute lack of faith in anything." Her frustration about this spilled out in March 1954 in a letter to Joseph Longstreth, who was then Chessman's literary agent: "Seriously, Joe, why does he behave this way? We know how abnormal the man is. We recognize his vast conceit, his neurotic tendencies. The strain under which he lives. But I am at a loss to understand his total lack of humility. Perhaps it is because I would give so much to have his writing ability."

This was similar to something the attorney George T. Davis had noticed during his own relationship with Chessman. In frustration, after his last visit to Chessman in May 1960, just before his trip to the gas chamber, Davis said, "Perhaps his greatest flaw, his greatest lack of character, was his unrelenting unwillingness to believe in something greater and bigger than himself. He almost prided himself on the fact that he remained an agnostic to the end. You can't say 'God bless you' to a man like that, but I thought it anyway when I left him for the last time. His guilt, as far as I am concerned, is a moot question."

Though in hindsight it is sad to imagine what doors could have opened to Chessman were he to have pursued an acceptable path, imagine how it must have felt to Freeman as she watched his brilliance flower in prison, long before he became the notorious public pariah and conservatives' whipping boy known as the Red Light Bandit.

Freeman had lost track of Chessman back in 1943, when he was transferred to Chino. To her dismay and despair, she was reunited with him in 1948, after his two death sentences returned him to San Quentin. This time there would be no hope for secretarial duty in the warden's office and only flickering hopes for any future worth dreaming about. In the ensuing years, Freeman had continued to work the San Quentin beat. She had also had her share of problems following a divorce. Floundering in her personal life, she was beset by health problems by the time she met Longstreth in 1954.

■

WHEN FREEMAN WAS introduced to Longstreth, by means of her letter, the final details on clearances of people portrayed in *Cell*

2455, Death Row were trickling in. The advance notice was red-hot; Chessman had sold two short pieces, "A Voice from Death Row" to *American Weekly*, and "Crime Doesn't Pay" to *This Week*. Longstreth was also negotiating with *Life* and *Look* magazines and some of the New York daily newspapers for serial rights to the pending book. Even the venerable *Stanford Law Review* planned to reprint a chapter from the book in an upcoming issue. In short, things could not have gone better. Rather, only if Chessman were somehow sprung from his death cell and given a visiting professorship at the University of California at Berkeley could things be said to have gone better.

But then, all this changed by the time Longstreth arrived on, ironically, Valentine's Day weekend.

He wasn't prepared for the reception he received.

7

An Important Visit

I **WORKED IN** the prison with Caryl on the first book," said Longstreth in a 2002 interview. "I say I worked in the prison with him, that sounds like I was in the cell next door. I wasn't. But I'll never forget the first time I ever met him was in the assistant warden's office. I'd never been in a place before where there were guards in every corner with guns. It was quite an experience. I had cut the first three chapters of his manuscript and actually opened the book with his third chapter. And then put back in the other three chapters elsewhere in the narrative. They were good chapters, but they were not suitable for openers. And Caryl was just infuriated. He threw the manuscript on the floor and the guards were suddenly on alert."

While Longstreth was able to calm Chessman down and even go on to have a productive and, in hindsight, important author-editor weekend with him, the war over the manuscript had only just begun. Longstreth would learn this when he got back to New York. He was, however, jarred by the reception that Chessman had given him. Before they barely had time to say hello, after all the cordial back and forth letters, Chessman—taller, heavier, stronger, more desperate—was looming over him, shouting about the desecrations he had done to his precious manuscript. Longstreth had to have wondered, alone in a room with a possibly dangerous criminal with nothing to lose, whether he had made a terrible mistake by opening the door to this man.

This was, however, not the first inkling that something was bothering Critics Associated's newest client. Prior to Longstreth's visit,

Chessman had expressed concern to Honour over the editing job that Monroe Stearns, at Prentice-Hall, was doing on his manuscript—a job Chessman only knew about through Longstreth. Chessman had never actually seen edited pages, which fanned his paranoia that this total stranger was elbowing him out of the process.

Because of that concern, Longstreth had interceded and done some rather substantive tinkering of his own. The intent was to make the book open in a way that would set this unknown Death Row resident into some sort of context for readers, rather than—as Chessman had it in the original draft—hit them with a haymaker of raw ego from the opening bell.

When Chessman saw the results, he exploded. In that moment, he may have been releasing all the tension that had built up during the past five years in San Quentin, or all the tension from all the years stretching back to his first attempts to write in the converted garage of the Chessmans' house in Glendale. One can only guess that Chessman, too, must have been wondering if he had made a terrible mistake by opening the door to these strangers. Maybe he felt that, after all the notetaking, all the hours of typing and sleepless nights scribbling, his dream of publication was being yanked from his grasp, and that he would soon meet the dreaded fate of tip toeing in institutional slippers, bound tight with emasculating pink laces, to the gas chamber. Total anonymity and abject humiliation at the end of the road.

Whatever the cause of his meltdown that day in February 1954, the initial manic phase of ecstasy and celebration was over. Chessman was scheduled for execution on May 14, 1954, and he saw this book, should the state go through with their plans, as comprising the entirety of his literary legacy. It was a precious possession to him, not something to be tinkered with by a bunch of martini-lunching Manhattan know-it-alls.

To his credit, Longstreth spent the remaining six hours of their meeting deflecting the focus to the rest of the book, suggesting that he would take up his concerns with Prentice-Hall when he got back to New York—all the while knowing that the changes would remain in place. It was Chessman's book, yes, but it was Prentice-Hall's money, and, as the literary agent, Longstreth saw his role as trying to placate both parties. He knew Monroe Stearns would not bend and Chessman, in his precarious predicament, didn't have much of a leg to stand on. Forcing Chessman to concentrate on all the other, less controversial details of putting the manuscript to bed did the job of temporarily calming his client's inner demons.

Longstreth won further approval in Chessman's eyes by spending Sunday in Los Angeles, visiting Serl Chessman, Frances Couturier, and her two children. The kids, in awe of this suave, kindly stranger from the East, instantly dubbed him Uncle Joe, a name Longstreth seemed to enjoy. That important sidetrip happened only by a fluke. Longstreth had run into Frances Couturier at the San Rafael bus depot on Saturday afternoon, Valentine's Day. She was on her way to visit Chessman at San Quentin, and Longstreth was on his way back from visiting him. Longstreth, charmed by what he thought was a guileless Frances, told her he would extend his trip and come to Los Angeles the following day for a visit.

Longstreth recalled the visit pleasantly in a letter to Milt Machlin, an *Argosy* editor who was working on a posthumous book about Chessman. Machlin had asked Longstreth what he recalled about Serl, to which he responded, "He was a most fascinating man . . . an odd-jobs man, doing a little here, a little there, and a dabbler in various 'arts,'" such as photography, radio in its infancy, etc. He was a lover of nature, and thus did gardening work as well." While Frances cooked the dinner, Longstreth talked at length with Serl Chessman and played with the Couturier children. Chessman must have seen Longstreth's visit to his "family" as a validation of sorts. Here was living proof that Serl's only begotten son—the prodigal and the black sheep all rolled into one—was capable of having decent, law-abiding friends. It also provided some comfort, no doubt, to the financially shaky Serl that his son was on the verge of making it. Anywhere else but in the Chessman family, of course, Caryl's current plight would never be construed as "making it." A resident of Death Row, regularly referred to in his home state's press as a "monster," Chessman, if he was known at all beyond California's borders, was some vague pervert who did nasty, unmentionable things to young women.

In a letter that awaited Longstreth when he got back to his office in New York, Chessman said, "My Dad, Frances and her little kiddies have had a pretty rough time of it and I'm sure it'll be apparent to you why I'm so anxious to help them. The prospect of being able to do so soon makes me feel very good, and I'm not for an instant unaware that it is your concerned and sympathetic assistance that is making this possible."

Of his own explosion, Chessman only averred that, "On that first day, I got the impression you'd brought your New York weather with you." All in all, though, Chessman said, "I've pronounced our talk and our ironing out of all the kinks in the edited manuscript time most profitably and enjoyably spent."

■

BEFORE HIS CHARMED visit with Serl, Frances and the kids, Longstreth met Bernice Freeman in San Rafael for a few minutes late Saturday afternoon. Even in that brief encounter, they had time to establish a friendly rapport. Longstreth was impressed enough to suggest that Freeman write a book about her own distinguished career on the prison beat and offer himself as editor and agent. When he got back to New York, he also arranged for her to interview Chessman for NBC-TV news, a coup that would not only give the impending book a major push, but would, Longstreth was not afraid to admit, help his own literary career and hers as a journalist.

On February 26, 1954, he wrote Freeman a gushing note that began, "How can a gray-haired bachelor thank a stunning grandmother for her wonderful reception, her constant thoughtfulness and her real understanding?" He reported that NBC was interested in her conducting the interview with Chessman at San Quentin, pending permission from prison authorities, and that he had "already discussed you and your book with two editors, one of whom is interested, and the other of whom said, 'I want it.'"

She wrote in response on February 28, "It wasn't just a pleasant dream after all!" Being a pragmatist about prison authorities, Freeman cautioned Longstreth that "there is little hope" that Richard A.

McGee, the Director of Corrections, would permit NBC's filming at San Quentin. (In subsequent letters, she would refer to the powerful McGee as "The King" and "The Great White Father.") McGee held Chessman in low regard; he'd already told Longstreth he would not support his appeal for clemency (bad news that Longstreth chose not to share with Chessman), so granting permission to make a film celebrating the convicted Red Light Bandit was almost certainly out of the question. Freeman also saw little hope of Chessman getting a reprieve from his May 14 execution. (She was right about the former, wrong about the latter.)

The day before Longstreth's arrival, Freeman had spent two hours with Chessman at the prison interviewing him for a *Chronicle* profile. She said he was adamant about not exploiting the book for his own legal purposes, vis-à-vis a reprieve or stay. "Over and over again he stressed with deep sincerity, 'Chessman and the book must not be connected in any plea for leniency. . . . If I have to go, I'll go. But I will not use this book as a reason to keep on living.'" Freeman volunteered to meet personally with Governor Goodwin Knight (whom she referred to as "Goodie," his commonly known nickname) to present a petition for his stay of execution.

Freeman confessed to being "thrilled and awed" about the suggestion that she write a book. Since her meeting with Longstreth, she admitted to rereading two books related to her field, *Newspaperwoman* by Agnes Underwood and *Women in Crime* by Florence Monahan, because, she said, "I want to do much better than either." Still, she asked Longstreth for encouragement on how to get started, and in the very next letter, dated March 6, he proceeded to outline the approach she should take, as well as the writing tone, the way to divide experiences into the "most vital, the most dramatic, the ones with the profoundest influence on your career." In this letter and a follow up letter on April 13, Longstreth essentially outlined the book that Mrs. Freeman would eventually write; he even sent two pages of suggested copy, written off the top of his head, to "be used as a stimulant." Freeman's book, outlined in these two letters, was published by Thomas Y. Crowell in 1961 as *The Desperate and the Damned*, by Bernice Freeman Davis, with a foreword by the ubiquitous Clinton T.

Duffy). It remained one of the disappointments of Longstreth's career that, when it came time for her to find a publisher, Freeman sought out another agent. By then, their friendship had faded.

Longstreth was not able to meet Rosalie Asher on that February 1954 trip. They had tentative plans to meet at the airport, upon his arrival, and "find a nook and maybe even a drink" to discuss the legal aspects of publishing her client. Though they missed connections on that trip, they did become cordial, if not friendly, through correspondence in the coming months. They even discussed sharing responsibilities for Chessman's estate, as well as (at Chessman's strange insistence, since he really owed them nothing) setting up trust funds therefrom for Frances Couturier's two children, should he be killed as scheduled in May 14, 1954. Asher's forty-year friendship with Longstreth, unlike Freeman's, was built to last.

■

CHESSMAN'S METHODICAL PLANNING was thrown for a loop by news that reached him on March 2, 1954, two weeks after Longstreth had met and had dinner with his father. About ten minutes after learning the news, Chessman sat down and wrote Longstreth, "The prison chaplain brought some tragic news: my father died today. And the pain is all bottled up inside. I have immediately wired Frances: 'Just received word of Dad's passing and am inexpressibly saddened. Letter follows. Know you will find the courage to carry on and that you will make all arrangements for funeral. Wire if there is anything I can do to help.'"

He continued, "Oddly, Joe, I've relived my life in the last ten minutes; it came back with a cruel, vivid clarity—and there was the gentle Hallie and the equally gentle Serl. There was their toddler, Serl's 'little professor.' And now they're gone, both of them. And here I sit, on Death Row, somehow knowing they're still with me and always will be. In these moments the need to live is a cold and demanding thing. I'm thankful that I feel no sorrow for myself, no maudlin self-pity, but only a sense of inexpressible loss and yet a gladness still that I had such parents. And a feeling of guilt is here with me—guilt that

I haven't yet become the son I knew they wanted and deserved. As a memorial to them, I must. I must live and write and do everything possible to avert other parents from knowing the sadness and the harshness and the heartbreak Hallie and Serl knew. And I know you will help me, Joe. I know you will help me become the writer I must become and write what must be written."

What hurt Caryl the most, he told Longstreth, was that his father hadn't lived to see the publication of his book, or to share in the enjoyment of the financial windfall that the author was confident would soon arrive. "Just when I was able to help my Dad and make his life a little easier, Providence had to claim him," he wrote. "Moreover, as you doubtless know, he was planning to visit me within the next few weeks. It's a comfort to know you were able to meet him and have a talk with him. I'm glad and thankful for that; and I'm thankful, too, that Frances is there. I know how tough this will be for her, but I'm sure she is made of the stuff that will enable her to carry on and to see that my father gets a good burial."

It is hard to understand why Chessman thought Frances would be emotionally immobilized by the death of a man for whom she was little more than a caretaker, albeit an affectionate one. More to the point, why would she be any more broken up about someone not related to her, someone she'd known for one year, than his only child? And, given what transpired with Frances over the next three years, it would have been worth it then for someone to ask Chessman, while he was tossing his money so generously her way: How well do you really know this lady?

Chessman's letter to Longstreth, only minutes after learning of his only remaining blood relative's death, also contained a weird segue that revealed more accurately how he felt about his father's death. "I know that, above all else, my Dad would want me to carry on, so I'll finish this letter with a few things I wanted to write about before the arrival of the chaplain a few minutes ago."

Just like that, snap, Chessman turned to other business at hand, breezily recounting a recent talk with Bernice Freeman, who'd expressed a fondness for Longstreth, with whom she had exchanged some letters. He said that while he was meeting with Freeman in one of the assistant warden's office, former warden Clinton Duffy, his erstwhile nemesis, dropped by to say hello. "He, too, is most interested in it [*Cell 2455, Death Row*], and, as you know, his interest derives from the fact that he's known me since I entered prison at nineteen."

The next several days were filled with family duties and business concerns regarding estates or, in the case of Serl Chessman, outstanding bills. Serl had accrued almost five thousand dollars in debts, which Chessman eventually paid off with the subsidiary rights from the book. Agonizing over these hassles and pondering his own mortality, Chessman was unable to concentrate on business related to the book, though his frustration about the editing was simmering under the surface.

Frances came to San Quentin to visit him again on March 3. "I can't get over what a real champion she is, and her loyalty is unshakeable," he told Longstreth. "As you know, she loved my Dad like a father, and David and Cheryl too loved their kind 'Grandpa.' Now he's gone. I'm still more than a little numb over the loss. The end came so unexpectedly—of a heart attack. . . . These last years of his life were pretty tough for my father; to make ends meet, he drove himself more than he should have, for he knew his heart was bad. But he was one of those fine old guys who was determined to keep his head up and make a go of it. This is the price he paid to maintain his self-respect. I'm saddened but at the same time I'm proud of him. His life was one tragedy after another; yet he would never yell quits."

This reminiscence of his father seems forced, even insincere, sitting as it does in direct counterpoint to the feelings expressed in the book his father did not live to read, *Cell 2455, Death Row*, with its portrayal of the pitiable Serl. The treacly recollection reads like boilerplate remorse, as if Chessman was trying to say the sorts of things a normal son would say about a normal father. After all, when his family was at its most desperate and needed a guiding hand, Serl had tried to bail out on them, twice attempting suicide, and once having to be saved by a preteen Caryl who was bedridden at the time. The irony of Serl's debts also seemed lost on his son, whose earning power on Death Row was greater than everything his father had earned in a lifetime.

Chessman mentioned the "Judy problem" for the second time in his correspondence with Longstreth. "Judy" was the name given to the woman identified as Chessman's wife in *Cell 2455, Death Row*, who was Lucy Ann Gaylord in real life. Chessman had lived with "Judy" after he was released from San Quentin the first time, at age twenty-one. Now, eleven years later, at the instigation of a lawyer (referred to as "her representative"), she—now remarried, with three children, and taking the name Lucy Ann Short—wanted some cash outlay in return for permission to use the descriptions of her in the book's narrative. She made enough demands that Longstreth, against his better judgment, felt it best just to pay her off and get her out of their hair. This agreement cost a whopping seven thousand dollars (the book's advance was only one thousand). Even so—and lending credence to the rumors that he may have had a daughter with Gaylord—Chessman said, "I must comment that 'Judy' and her 'representative' sold themselves a little short. But it is they who have chosen to call the turn. Yes, Joe, I know you will keep your word to her, and naturally I want you to do so, the sooner the better."

About this situation, which had caused a major delay in the book's production process, Chessman commended his agent, "You handled our 'Judy' problem with infinite tact and mastery! Frances had written to me only that you had decided to attend to it."

The "tact" was twofold—getting the money to "Judy" without alerting the media and keeping from Frances the identity of this mysterious "Judy." By this point, it was clear to Longstreth that Frances was putting on a pretty good show of being in love with Caryl Chessman.

■

By mid-March, however, Chessman went back on the war path about the editing that had been done on his book. He became nearly impossible to deal with, exhibiting the entire arsenal of pathologies that defined his life before Longstreth. Here again was the know-it-all punk who insisted on representing himself in court in 1947, the hubristic hardhead who brought his own death sentences upon himself, who insulted witnesses in the courtroom, lectured the judge, and hectored the police.

He told Longstreth and Honour that the editing of the last two chapters of the book was a "travesty." In a misguided bout of navel gazing, he told Honour: "According to the Bible, 'We brought nothing into this world . . . we can carry nothing out.' To my way of thinking, not even the essence of ourselves. But we can leave something behind. Those who feel they have infinity at their disposal enjoy an advantage—and a disadvantage—over one who believes he must do his work now, under the pressure of time and circumstance.

"'Nothing happens in life without reason,' you say, and I agree without reservation. But I must add my opinion that reason and reasons are not the same. Events can fit themselves into a meaningful mosaic even though the reasons for their occurrence have been dictated by chance. 'The Moving Finger writes; and having writ, moves on.' I make my case swiftly, at times strangely. And I seek, not so much reasons as reason. Once again a sudden end is near. And when I look within this transient entity called Self, and then beyond, I find nothing worth eternalizing. The philosophical or metaphysical projection of soul (or call it what you will) beyond the barrier of death is a dream I find too bold, too presumptuous. These few short years are enough. Let others who will follow after me have their chance at life. Let them build and destroy; let them love and hate; let them dream and dare to dream. To what avail? I know and I don't know. It's a question each of us must answer for ourself."

Though he was close to pouring gasoline on a fire of his own making, Chessman had not yet burned his bridge, telling Honour, "I would like to live a while longer, to write another book or two, to look at the sky and the sun and the stars again. But my desires and the probability of their non-fulfillment don't distress me. I'm thankful for having met Joe, to be able to call him agent and friend, to call all of you at CA friend, to be able to exchange a thought with you. And don't consider yourself an outsider, Alan; you're not. Your letters are a big help. Perhaps someday, if the gods are kind, I shall have the chance to come to New York and meet you personally. You see, I still find it possible to hope."

After Honour played the bad cop routine with Chessman by dressing him down in no uncertain terms, Longstreth stepped back into the room, all sweetness and light, on March 18, 1954. He assessed what they had all accomplished to date. He defended Prentice-Hall's handling of the book, reminding Chessman to accept his good fortune.

"You've acquired many new friends, some of whom you are totally unaware, and we all wish you well. And we're doing everything in our power to swing things your way," he said. It was a diplomatic letter, kindly yet firm.

Longstreth described Warden Teets as "a remarkable man. . . . His understanding of the numerous and intricate problems involved in each and every individual situation cannot come from study and experience alone—it must come from within. He's a good man, Caryl, and for what it's worth, I think you should avail yourself of every opportunity to be as frank, honest, and straightforward with this man as it is possible for a human being to be."

Though he had no real reason to do so, Longstreth closed his letter with an apology, presumably a figurative olive branch: "To err is human and I'm so human."

Longstreth's letter reached Chessman only after he'd mailed his most incendiary letter yet. The can of gasoline was out and the book of matches was about to be struck. And it could not be taken back. That is, Chessman was threatening a lawsuit against Critics Associated and Prentice-Hall to stop publication of *Cell 2455, Death Row* unless his changes were put back into the last two chapters. He had, without consulting his agents, written a letter to Monroe Stearns at Prentice-Hall to that effect.

"This is bitter to take, Joe," he wrote, then petulantly signed off with "So long."

Patient as Job, Longstreth reminded Chessman that Prentice-Hall was spending thirty thousand dollars on an ad campaign for the book. "Caryl, you and I are young men. We are in our early thirties, and it's ridiculous for us to suppose that we know everything. . . ." He suggested to Chessman that he had chosen to see only the bad and ignore the good. And he finally put it on the line to his client and friend: "Caryl, if you say that Chessman's way is the best, way, that Chessman *knows*, I submit a very flat statement which I know you'll understand for exactly what it is. You're wrong. You stand in your own way too frequently, and our most genuine efforts have gone into helping you in every conceivable manner to express yourself in the best, most advantageous light possible. Believe me, Caryl. Please believe the naked honesty of this."

Honour followed up Longstreth's letter a week later, proving himself to be, as Longstreth had warned Chessman, "a tough little Englishman." Honour might have been smarting at the attacks on his friend, or he might even have been jealous of the attention Chessman was getting from Longstreth. Regardless, he warned Chessman that Monroe Stearns, a senior editor, was a thoroughgoing professional, one of the most respected men in the publishing business.

"I would back his judgment before yours every time," wrote Honour, sticking the Manhattan-Know-It-All shiv into his side and twisting it. "And I say this knowing full well how much I feel for you and understand you. . . . It is not only undiplomatic, it is in very bad taste. Caryl, I feel that I am your friend. I have no compunction or hesitation at all in writing and telling you off in this way. You deserved it. . . . The brilliance of your intellect doesn't blind me to the undeveloped aspects of your personality. These undeveloped aspects are the ones which cause the trouble."

Nobody outside of the legal establishment had ever spoken to Chessman this way. It was not unlike the dressing down he had received from Warden Teets that, as he related in *Cell 2455, Death Row*, had been the gauntlet that led him to put aside his rage at the system and write down his own life story. If Chessman had had early friends like Longstreth and Honour (or, for that matter, Teets) outside of San Quentin, he would never have seen the inside of a prison cell.

■

LONGSTRETH, AS WAS his natural inclination, took a more gentle approach to Chessman over this breach, but it was clear that his still relatively unknown client had nearly railroaded his own writing career. Only Longstreth's diplomacy saved Chessman's ass, as he related in a letter of March 23, 1954: "Yesterday was one of the most exhausting days I've ever spent in a publishing office: I pray that it is never repeated, anywhere, anyhow, with anyone, for anyone. For several hours, the actual publication of your book hung in the balance: and that is not to say by Prentice-Hall: by anyone ever! Why? Not just because an author had taken exception to editing, and because an author had threatened suit—but for many, many other reasons which are too numerous and complex to list and explore."

It still was not certain, at this point, if the book would even be published. Under such circumstances, Longstreth's was an amazingly generous letter. "You may not agree with compromise. I do, and experience has taught me its value. . . . Now for the calm before the storm . . . the storm of a great publication success. *Cell 2455, Death Row*, by Caryl Chessman. Am I angry? No. Am I hurt? Perhaps. Does it matter? Definitely. Enough is enough is enough is enough. Indeed, what else could enough be?"

Writing to Asher, Longstreth reiterated the storm that had blown through New York courtesy of her legal client. The situation was worse than he'd intimated to Chessman. On the day the presses were set to roll, Prentice-Hall had weighed the possibility of killing the project. "Caryl Chessman came dangerously close, Monday, to being the best un-published author in history," Longstreth wrote. "And I can say, in all modesty, that the chances are he isn't [unpublished] because of my work." This is why Chessman's accusations of "letting him down" were particularly hurtful to Longstreth. He had his agent so bollixed up that he seriously wondered if Chessman's plans to tie the book up in litigation might somehow be tied up with his petition for a stay of execution. "Is he getting desperate?" he wondered. "Not that I'd blame him, understand; but surely he can see the foolhardiness of many of his statements," which he characterized as "childish gibberish."

Asher assured Longstreth that he had done everything he could have for his client and that his performance "truly calls for superlatives." She had known Chessman since 1948 and had witnessed from the beginning his penchant for self-sabotage. "Many people felt that in insisting on representing himself at his trial, Caryl was his own worst enemy. It seems that's still true. And he is so completely stubborn. . . . While he professes a willingness to discuss a given situation, I find that seldom is his predetermined decision changed by any such discussion."

She also, in this same reply to Longstreth, put the lie to a myth that has lingered over the years—that she was somehow romantically interested in Chessman. "For a long time, as you know . . . I have done (and will continue to do) everything I can for Caryl—but not really from the heart. It is a job to be done, but not a cause to embrace. . . . I've wondered more than once whether Caryl's unwillingness completely to trust anyone is genuine, or just an alibi for retaining control of his actions. So I'd wonder, too, if his feeling, expressed to you, that anyone had misled him, is genuine. Another of the imponderables! How horrible a thing it is, though, to be confronted with a human being with absolutely nothing real about him. Or consistent." In a follow-up letter, on April 5, she said, "You need do no soul searching. If anyone signed Chessman's death warrant, it was Chessman himself; and it's important that none of us allow that basic truth to be beclouded either by pangs of sympathy or by accusatory haranguing on his part. . . . If I had one scintilla of sense, I would have stayed out of this mess when I had the chance."

Of course, some might argue, Asher's tireless and as yet unpaid work on Caryl's behalf surely went well beyond the dictates of "pangs of sympathy." And, it's worth noting, her name was Chessman's last utterance before he died

■

HEARING NOTHING FROM Chessman, Longstreth followed that up three days later. "I was very concerned that you might harm the book and yourself thereby, by the lack of diplomacy displayed." In the meantime, Chessman had sent Prentice-Hall a personal letter that Longstreth had sent him. And though he had every reason to be angry at Chessman for this breach of confidentiality, Longstreth reminded him again that the book would be a great success and all this would be forgotten in time. The material that had been excised from the book was some of the more tedious legal minutiae. Chessman, perhaps because he had lived with it for years and developed a reputation as an extraordinarily gifted "jailhouse lawyer," could not understand why the material would not captivate his readers.

"We must, as honorable people and friends, say what we think. We cannot run the risk of letting you stand in your way and defeat the very purpose which caused you to write this book," Longstreth said. "And, if all goes well, and you achieved the desire to complete the trilogy, how much more attention will you not command if this first one has the success it bids fair to having?"

Though he was still miffed—and everything Longstreth said eventually did come to pass—Chessman adopted a self-pitying tone on March 29. "Oh sure, Joe, I know it had to be this way," he said. "And things like this only disturb me because I'm a no-good so-and-so. I'm just an ungrateful character who is too stubborn and blind to appreciate all that has been done to my book. I'm all wrong, I have to be, because you all say so."

After all this, "This is not to accuse you of bad faith. . . . Maybe I hadn't written a book that nicely fit 'trade' book specifications . . . but maybe, too, I wrote the kind of book I wanted to write."

He most vociferously objected to the substantial trimming of material related to psychopathic personality and capital punishment. "For better or worse, the meaning of my book *has* changed. I don't like to be told that it hasn't," he said, grandiosely adding, "However, I've decided to go along with what has been done. . . ."

But not without one final thrust: "Tell me, Joe: were you ever even so much as inside a prison until you came to see me? And do you think Stearns ever has been? Do either of you know anything about them? My point is only that the next time, if that time ever comes, you want to help and befriend a guy in my situation that you don't adopt a 'father knows best' attitude. Try to keep in mind the iceberg—how much appears on the surface, how much beneath."

To be fair to Chessman, he was facing a death date on May 14. He had no way of knowing that he would get a stay of execution, and cheat death for another six years besides. As far as he knew, he was going to die in little more than a month's time, and his book—the only thing that really mattered to him in the world—was, as he perceived it at least, being hijacked from him. Though he saw a compelling reason to want to fight for his life, he would not beg for mercy. Should he be granted a stay of execution, he told Longstreth that he had in mind to write two more books, tentatively titled *Death Row Diary* and *These Places Called Prison*. And, after they were done, he wanted enough time to revise his novel *Nov Smoz Kapop!*

To Honour, two days later, he defended his anger and accused him of arguing dishonestly by doing what he accused Chessman of doing, using language guaranteed to provoke: " . . . and then took Olympian refuge in the might and exalted fortress of the righteousness of everyone but Chessman."

"It might interest you to know, Alan, that at one crucial point in my fight for survival two courses were open to me," he said. "They were diametrically opposed and only one could be right. My life hinged on the decision. Good friends, among them some of the best attorneys in the business, strongly urged the one course. They were absolutely acting in good faith; they had in mind only my best interests. I knew they were wrong; I took the other course. It was the right one. I survived, but I lost many good friends for failing to follow their advice. That proved I was ungrateful, untrustworthy, 'wrong,' etc.

"In fact, almost all my life my friends have been ever-ready to tell me what to do, to think for me, to insist I do things their way. And they're always quick to yowl and criticize and condemn when I don't listen to them even before they trouble to look at the roots of what motivates me to act as I do sometimes. You, too, Alan, didn't once so much as try to find out what was behind my objections to the book. You were content to believe that whatever it might be was wholly irrelevant—because all of you knew best anyway. . . . Perhaps the whole difficulty is that we define friendship differently."

Chessman at this point was acting like a jilted lover. He had let his guard down and been hammered, or so he fantasized, by people he thought were his friends. He was also angry that Longstreth had written directly to Frances, without clearing it through him, because the agent's letter about the editing squabble misled her into thinking myself alive another two to four years. In time, I might even get the convictions thrown out and secure an acquittal at a new trial. But to do that I would have to spend almost full time with the law, relentlessly. I'd have no time to write; the demands on my time would be too great. So I don't think I'll return to the courts."

And yet, the ninety-one-day reprieve would be used to, among other things, prepare an application for executive clemency. This would ask that his death sentences be commuted to life in prison, which—against every instinct in his being—would be an admission of "defeat" but it would also save his life and free his time for writing—the only thing that mattered to Chessman now.

"So you see, Alan, I've learned something of the virtues of compromise too," he said. "I've rolled the dice. What will it be: life and a chance to write or a visit to the gas chamber on May 14? If the decision goes against me, I'm quite prepared to die."

Addressing his earlier explosions of anger, Chessman said, "The ways of the so-called psychopath (or ex-psychopath) are often seemingly baffling, senseless ways, but usually there is purpose in those ways and that purpose is rarely to be perceived by the use of the traditional tools of evaluation. I haven't ignored your constructive criticisms . . . but I learn empirically, Alan, and the psychological machinery I use is necessarily constructed of materials forged in a different furnace from most men's. Egocentricity doesn't direct it as often as you might suspect."

The rave reviews for *Cell 2455, Death Row* continued to roll in. Freeman's article and review appeared in the *Chronicle*, and both were lavish in their praise of his efforts at self-rehabilitation. The condemned man was becoming known beyond the borders of his state. Chessman told Longstreth, on April 20, "All I can do is shake my head in wonder. And, figuratively, shake your hand for being the best d——[*sic*] agent there is."

Longstreth was glad to hear that Chessman—who had received seven advance copies of *Cell 2455, Death Row* in his soon-to-be-famous cell—expressed how much he liked the book. "I think you've written a fine, fine book. It is a real contribution, and I feel so proud to have had such a hand in it. We all do."

the book was being withdrawn from publication. And she was highly upset by the news; fond as she may have been of Chessman the person, she had two small children to raise, and he was the closest thing that she had to being their provider.

With equal arrogance, Chessman had personally petitioned Governor Knight for executive clemency, without first consulting with Rosalie Asher or Bernice Freeman, both of whom had made plans to take a separate petition to Sacramento themselves. He had enclosed the galley proofs of *Cell 2455, Death Row*—which had already gone to the printers—and suggested that Knight forward any concerns or criticisms directly to the publisher. This, almost certainly, would have brought the entire project to a complete halt, which may have been what Chessman secretly desired. Nonetheless, the governor registered no complaints with Prentice-Hall about the book. More than likely, he didn't even look at the galleys.

But Longstreth was unflappable. On April 2, he wrote, "The single item which distresses me most (though there really is no single item, I guess) is the reference to the mysterious thing which we don't know about, can't know about, won't know about, which you can't tell us. . . . Another thing is you telling me how much you disliked my writing as I did to Frances. I like Frances and I understand her position and her troubles. I've even sent Frances money, not to mention trying always to write and cheer her up, without being dishonest in my attempts to do so. However, if my correspondence to Frances must be governed by other than my own feelings about right and wrong, good and bad, then it surely becomes a heartless, impersonal kind of thing which can have no value to her. I liked her and I liked her children. I also liked your father tremendously and thoroughly enjoyed knowing him.

"I'm not a professional 'do gooder' and maybe I'm a flop at even trying to be of a little assistance when I think my aid can be of service or my point of view and or experience can be of some value."

Nonetheless, Longstreth agreed to write Governor Goodwin Knight, to ask for a stay of execution (he actually wrote two different drafts of a letter, one asking for a stay, the other for a reprieve, and he sent both to Chessman for him to choose which to send). He also enclosed a gift intended to change the tone of their communications over the previous two months. It was a drawing by William Steig, called "I'm Only Human," and Chessman hung it on the wall of his cell where it stayed for the next six years of his life.

Longstreth wrote Bernice Freeman the next day, corroborating her observation about Chessman's stubbornness. In frustration, he wrote, "That man has had more attention than most any unpublished author I've ever known. And, he knows best! No one can tell him anything. Well, I shan't try again." He admitted that their friendship had suffered a wound, but his professional pride and "my obligations to another human being" won't allow him to toss in the towel on Chessman. "I shall go through the necessary motions," he said. To Asher, he was even more forthright, to the point of being "disgusted" with Chessman. He was angry enough to suggest that Chessman would never write or publish another book "dead or alive," and that his "better judgment has been swayed, successfully, by Mr. Chessman. I find myself in the horrifying position of having to write to the Governor and say things which I cannot find it in my heart to believe. . . . But will I be failing in a human obligation if I refuse at this point?"

■

PERHAPS IT WAS Longstreth's diplomatic letters that turned the tide, because Chessman was now immensely thankful for what his agent had done. He gave Longstreth's letter to Rosalie Asher to present to the governor. Somewhat pedantically, he also apprised Longstreth of the difference between reprieve and stay. Chessman just wanted a reprieve (a three-month extension), to get some legal work completed that had been hanging over his head from his father's death. Not surprisingly, Serl's will was nowhere to be found, and his estate, such as it was, was a mess. Frances, too, had her heart set on some of Chessman's money, and if it meant playing the damsel in distress and lady in waiting, she was willing to do so. Apparently, she pitched a fit about some of the correspondence that came her way.

"The last thing I want you to do is to stop writing to Frances,"

wrote Chessman to Longstreth. "Your letters and the help you h provided meant a great deal to her and to me. But there are some thir I don't believe you know that you should. Frances has been right the verge of a serious nervous breakdown. First she recently lost sister. Then my Dad died, and that really was a blow. Next someon who should know better frightened her by telling her I didn't have a chance; that May 14 would be it. Too, her little boy is at that difficult stage and he is sickly; another tough problem. So when she heard from you that the book might be held up or enjoined, it was almost one straw too many. I apologize for being so blunt. But right then I was furious. I don't know if she has told you or not but it was right at that time she had to get medical help. I of course want you to be honest with her; yet I also hope you don't have occasion to give her any more bad scares.

"Again I apologize for my bull-in-a-China-shop reaction," he said.

■

THOUGH THE BOOK was not to be officially released until May 4, advance copies of *Cell 2455, Death Row* went out in early April, and already by April 16, word had reached Critics Associated that *Saturday Review* was giving the book a rave notice. This was just the first of several early reviews that made Prentice-Hall feel they had a possible hit on their hands.

Perhaps in light of these reviews—which seemed to corroborate the instincts of his agent and publisher—Chessman wrote Honour a conciliatory letter on April 17. He told him he was at work on some short pieces and a "novelette." He felt he had compromised by asking Governor Knight for a reprieve.

"It was probably the toughest decision I've ever made, for I have been conditioned over the years to fight, to never give an inch no matter how formidable the odds," he explained. "I've decided to gamble my life against the chance to do something useful with it. And I don't mean to sound grand when I say that. I could go on slugging away in the courts. I could doubtless win another stay. I probably could keep

The reviews, he said, are "very true" and "accurate." "You've captured something, there's an emotional quality which you've successfully projected which I sincerely believe is going to leave an impact on the public which will not be forgotten."

Longstreth, in the meantime, was upset about the pending application for clemency. "One minute I feel full of pessimism, the next, I'm in the clouds with certainty," he said.

Honour likewise was glad (more likely relieved) to hear that Chessman liked the book; he expressed also how upset he was about the pending execution date. "I get sick to my stomach as I have not been since my service days at the thought of this futile taking away of lives. . . . You are very much in our thoughts and we have everything crossed," he said. "We have had our ups and downs in the comparatively brief period we have known you, but Joe and I have always, despite everything, believed that the worst times so far as getting along with people or situations which you might not particularly care for, were behind you. It is a terribly hard thing to believe and know, as we do, that just as you are on the verge of so much that is good and worthwhile and of value to the society we are part of, we are so helpless to do anything to assure its continuance.

"I am truly humbled in the face of such courage and clarity which comes from you at this time."

On April 24, Chessman wrote Longstreth, "I had a good visit with Frances Thursday. She asked all about you, and there's no doubt about it: she and I are charter members of the Uncle Joe Admiration Society."

Longstreth assured Chessman that Monroe Stearns harbored no ill will or hurt feelings over their battles on editing, nor did the publisher. (In fact, Prentice-Hall published Chessman's next two books, *Trial by Ordeal* and *The Face of Justice*.)He and Stearns even met for lunch to celebrate the success of the book.

"I know you'll be lunching with us in spirit," said Longstreth, then thought he might be overstepping. "Sometimes, Caryl, I don't think it's very nice of me to tell you about such plans, or such meetings, but it would be pretty unrealistic if I assumed that you didn't think about such and sundry at times, even now [facing a death sentence]."

Cell 2455, Death Row was published in 1954 to immediate media fanfare. It soon topped the bestseller lists in San Francisco and Los Angeles and reached the number three slot on the national bestseller list. Eventually it was published in twelve foreign language editions and sold half a million copies in the U.S. alone by 1960. *Author's collection*

■

WITH HIS EXECUTION two weeks away, Chessman had still not heard anything on his application to Governor Knight. He busied himself with writing to keep from obsessing over the wait. Also, with Rosalie Asher's assistance, he drew up a will. Prior to this, he had avoided doing so because he feared that the information would be leaked to the press and that, Asher told Longstreth, "executing a will would be too pessimistic a move."

Asher had been worried since March that Chessman's literary

success might be going to his head, making him uncharacteristically optimistic about his chances for commutation. She really began to worry when he was entertaining out loud ideas "as to how soon he could secure a parole." She enjoyed seeing him "so hopeful and full of plans," but her experience in the law told her his chances were slim, at best, for anything other than another stay of execution. She also recalled that, despite her tireless efforts extending over three years and eleven stays of execution, another of her San Quentin Death Row clients, Wilson de la Roi, had been sent to the gas chamber in 1946. Longstreth secretly felt Chessman could not make it on the outside. As he wrote Asher on March 18, "When he mentions parole, I don't like it. I do not believe, based upon my talks with him and upon his violent reactions in certain letters of late, that he is equipped to combat with the trials and tribulations of everyday living in the horrifying twentieth century." Asher was reserving judgment on that score. "I do agree with you that he could probably not cope with life on the outside," she responded. "Or he would not, if he could."

Soon enough, Chessman altered his optimistic view about parole, with the resolution of the legal case of Wesley Wells. Wells, like Chessman, had been given a death sentence for crimes that had resulted in no deaths. Wells had been in and out of prison since 1928, shuffled back and forth between San Quentin and Folsom for disciplinary reasons (he also killed another prisoner in a gang fight). He had been sent to solitary confinement on forty-five different occasions, racking up 1,738 days on "the Shelf." When asked about this statistic by Bernice Freeman of the *San Francisco Chronicle*, Wells explained, "I believe in standing up for my rights." Wells eventually caught a five-years-to-life sentence for robbery and, during the course of serving that at Folsom State Prison, Wells threw an ashtray at a guard who'd allegedly used racial epithets. Though the officer was unharmed, Wells was sent to Death Row in August 1947, under Section 4500 of the state penal code: "Any prisoner serving a life sentence who was guilty of an assault was a candidate for the gas chamber." Wells was African American and his cause was taken up by Charles Garry, at the suggestion of Cecil Poole, who would, ironically, one day, as Governor Brown's clemency secretary, stand so firmly against Chessman.

Wells and Chessman knew each other well. They had, in fact, led a sit-down strike together on November 1, 1950, coaxing thirteen of the sixteen Death Row inmates to refuse to return to their cells until San Quentin authorities agreed to their demands for window screens, better food, longer exercise periods, and, of all things, fountain pens. At the time, Warden Duffy said that Wells "intimidated the other men and had them under his control." After the "incipient riot" was broken up by prison guards (they gave themselves up peacefully), Wells and Chessman were sent to solitary confinement for twenty-nine days; Wells was allegedly beaten and racially taunted during this time, Chessman was left alone. At any rate, Wells and Chessman were not unsympathetic to each other's causes, thus Chessman pinned perhaps too much hope on the outcome of his erstwhile comrade's case.

Wells, meanwhile, was scheduled to die on April 9, 1954—ostensibly for throwing an ashtray, but really for the sum total of his chronically difficult prison career, as well as perhaps because he was black—but he had petitioned Governor Knight for executive clemency. Wells, through the efforts of Charles Garry, became a cause célèbre, and the campaign to spare his life produced fifty thousand signatures. The campaign, unlike Chessman's, portrayed Wells's life as one devastated by poverty, racism, and mental illness, and it benefited from the winds blowing from the American South, where the civil rights movement was just beginning to get some traction. According to the Civil Rights Congress, a left-wing organization that had taken up Wells's cause, "Wesley Wells is a victim of a government policy that enforces second class citizenship on the Negro people. We must not allow a California version of Mississippi justice."

Governor Knight, under intense pressure during an election year, granted Wells a commutation in April 1954.

Charles Garry would go on to fame as the lawyer for the Black Panther Party during their many brushes with the law in the late 1960s. In his memoir, he referred to Wells as "the first Black Panther."

Chessman was not so fortunate.

On May 3, Chessman received a telegram from the governor rejecting his application for a reprieve and "all possibility of clemency."

Longstreth received a telegram from Asher the same day: "Governor today denied reprieve or clemency." Chessman was to be executed, as scheduled, on May 14. In a way, the rejection by the governor only confirmed to Chessman that he should never have compromised, though he did not regret trying.

"Whatever happens, I shan't regret my attempt at compromise," he told Honour. "Unfortunately, as the matter has turned out, my situation doesn't permit compromise, won't tolerate it. So back I must go to the legal wars. While I have no ideological truck with the gentleman, Lenin once made a provocative statement: 'There is no such thing as an inextricable situation.' Now I wonder. We soon shall see. And right here I believe I should add that if this isn't an inextricable situation, I hope I never have occasion to run into one. How do I feel, really? Disappointed, Alan. A little sad. Still hopeful, but, if necessary, ready to die, thankful for the book. No self-pity. No bitterness. No anger. No wasting time cursing the malignant gods. Know, all of you, that I'll be in there pitching to the last. And then . . . well, if ten o'clock on May 14 rolls around and the courts have turned me down, I'll join hands with oblivion."

Longstreth wrote Chessman to offer as much encouragement as was possible under the circumstances. He said, "Few of us in this life accomplish anything of much merit, and you can say and believe, honestly, fairly, humbly, and sincerely, that you have accomplished something worthwhile with *Cell 2455, Death Row*. You have repaid whatever debt you might have owed to society. But let's forget society. You've repaid Hallie and you've repaid Serl. Carry that thought in your heart, Caryl, and it should help . . . You have achieved a status never before touched by anyone in your position. You're tops. Whatever else there is before you—and whatever else there is behind you—Caryl, you've accomplished something fine and good, clean and wholesome."

Longstreth again offered to do anything, anything "inhumanly possible," to help Chessman continue his embattled existence.

"I don't understand, Caryl. I can't believe that the law is such a peculiar thing that it can fail to take into account a man's positive intelligence and still refuse to carry out an order if a mind becomes unhinged. It doesn't make sense. But then what, at this point, does? Nothing."

On May 4, the official publication date of *Cell 2455, Death Row,* Chessman was fighting for his life. He told his agent, "Right now I'm as close to the gas chamber as it's possible to be—and still have a chance. A very slim one. That's the way it is, Joe."

Rather than bask in the glow of great reviews and good advance sales, the author was spending all of his hours preparing an airtight legal case. If it did not succeed, he had prepared an airtight will, naming Joseph Longstreth literary executor and Rosalie Asher executor of his estate. The will called for all monies to go to Rosalie Asher, less Longstreth's agency fee. And another thousand dollars would go to Lucy Ann Short.

As close as he would come to commenting on the book's reception was via the bittersweet observation: "The sum and substance of all these stories is that the book is fine, but not the author." Governor Knight, perhaps prodded by the media attention the author was receiving, was moved to comment on Chessman's case. He expressed his "repugnance" at taking a life where none had been taken, but he felt the crimes were sufficiently "atrocious" to warrant the sentence.

"I, of course, am in perfect accord with the Governor that the crimes are not very nice ones—but it's not too good an idea, in my opinion, to gas the wrong guy," Chessman said. "This difficult spot doesn't keep me from being very glad indeed that the book is being so well received. I'm most pleased and most grateful."

For the sake of Longstreth, who he had come to realize was as loyal a friend as he was likely to find, Chessman said, "I hope you don't feel that my sense of humor has deserted me. It hasn't and won't. And right now, Joe, I need it. I think I'd spend eternity sneering at myself if I suddenly were to emerge a whiner or crier. And whatever happens, don't feel too badly. Let's be glad at least that I was able to get this one book out. For me, that's a tremendous consolation—and I've been looking Death in the eye all my life. So if he calls May 14 I shan't be meeting an ominous stranger. He lost his power to menace a long time ago. Of course, there will be regret, but the regret will be more than compensated in ever so many ways I'm sure I don't need to set out."

Meanwhile, in New York, the book was the talk of the town. Its eye-catching dust jacket was in every storefront window and Prentice-Hall was devoting its full publicity staff to *Cell 2455, Death Row*, buying a full-page ad in the Sunday *New York Times* to promote the book as well as to inform the public about the author's legal plight. Longstreth appeared on Arlene Francis's *Home Show* on NBC-TV, though much of what he had to say was inexplicably bleeped out by network censors. People all over the country had begun to flood the governor's mansion in Sacramento with letters, pleading with Knight to spare Chessman's life.

In Chessman's letter to Knight, he said, "I'm not asking for my freedom, Governor. Guilt or innocence aside, I accept without bitterness the fact I probably don't deserve it . . . initially, I ask only a 91-day reprieve, from May 14 to August 13, 1954. I ask only the opportunity to be heard, to prepare and file with you a competent application for commutation of my death sentences to life imprisonment with or without possibility of parole, at your discretion.

"I ask that you take into consideration the fact I have a meaningful literary future, that, with my writing, I can salvage something good and useful from a tragically destructive past. In a practical way I can make up for the past. I want to do that."

Asher was working on Chessman's case, and a second attorney, Berwyn A. "Ben" Rice of San Rafael, who had been hired with part of the advance from the book, was working to gather evidence from the records of the original trial and subsequent findings to prove his innocence of the Red Light Bandit crimes; barring that, Rice was charged with showing that Chessman did not get a fair trial in 1948. This contention that would be convincingly laid out by William M. Kunstler; unfortunately, Chessman was one year in the grave when Kunstler's book *Beyond A Reasonable Doubt?* was published. Kunstler would go on the join Charles Garry as a prominent lawyer for left-wing causes, including the Black Panthers', over the next decade.

Chessman, while expressing a stoic resignation about the possibility of going to the gas chamber, was torn by the sudden fame. He began to have some regrets about the "false hopes" raised by *Cell 2455, Death Row*, expressing them to Longstreth, "Perhaps, just perhaps, I would have been wiser never to have written the book and to have continued to stand alone, defiantly, rebelliously. That way I wouldn't have been missed; my death then would have meant nothing to no one, would have hurt no one.

"Right now, Joe, I'm having it driven home that Chessman isn't as tough a guy as he thought he was; he's finding out that hurting his friends can tear him up. Why, dammit why, can't the State find some way of, say, gassing me three or four times and eliminating all the other hurt????? After all, I'm the guy who's supposed to be punished, no one else. Oh, no doubt about it, capital punishment is a very fine thing! It must be; I've heard people say so."

Longstreth, writing to Asher on May 4, said simply, "I still can't believe that one week from Friday will be the end to Caryl's strange life." He echoed this same feeling two months later, when Chessman was facing a new July 30 execution date. He told Asher, "I've completely resigned myself to losing Caryl, and it grieves me. He could have been saved, years ago. I wonder, metaphysically, why it didn't happen."

8

Down to the Wire

O**N THURSDAY, MAY** 13, 1954, fifteen hours before he was scheduled to die in the gas chamber, Caryl Chessman was saved by a
legal technicality. This, his third stay of execution, was as close as
he came to dying until his ninth stay, which failed, was granted on
May 2, 1960. Even Chessman thought he was a "goner."

As he described it to Longstreth in a letter four days later, "Two
bells would mean the stay had been rescinded, that the death watch
was coming to take me downstairs to await the morning and oblivion.
At six-fifteen, after living the longest hour in my life, I put on my
earphones to listen to Bill Guyman's California news commentary. At
the outset, he gave a lengthy resume of the case, stating that whether
I lived or died in the morning still hadn't been finally decided. He
went on to other news. I went on with the waiting. Just at the end
of the broadcast, he stated a bulletin just had been handed him: the
execution was definitely off. Judge Keating had refused to rescind the
stay order he previously had made."

The recently hired Berwyn "Ben" Rice's efforts at Marin County
Superior Court were credited with turning the trick. Others hadn't
shared Chessman's high opinion of Rice, who was seen by Longstreth
and Freeman as a self-aggrandizing money hog with a rocky marriage
and a fondness for booze; even the assistant attorney general, Clarence Linn, had warned Asher off Rice, and the ubiquitously nasty
gossip columnist Bill Hendrick included a notice at this time that
"At Larkspur's Blue Rock Inn, Lawyer Ben Rice with wife talking to
the bar-flies about the U.S. Supreme Court decision on San Quentin

convict-rapist Caryl Chessman." Because Rice got results and because he knew a lot of people above- and below-board, they let the doubts pass, though his repeated requests for money would continue to haunt Longstreth and Asher, guardians of Chessman's estate. By June 1954, Rice was already threatening to call off his investigation if he didn't get another $225 for fees and $1,300 for "expenses," none of which were itemized in his billing (Longstreth suspected he was padding the account with liquor bills). Asher found the situation delicate because of Rice's "many connections at the prison," and the fear that, if she made an enemy of him, her ability to help Chessman would be compromised.

Chessman, who'd paid Rice an initial fee of $750, was nonetheless grateful, citing "the loyalty of you [Longstreth], Frances, Miss Asher, Ben Rice, Alan, and all the others" as having helped "sustain me." He even found room in his heart to thank Monroe Stearns and Prentice-Hall.

The legal maneuvers that were going on prior to his being granted this ninety-day stay of execution by Governor Knight were threefold: 1) Bernice Freeman presented a letter to the governor asking for him to reconsider; 2) Rice sought a stay in a local court in order to present medical evidence that Chessman should not have been allowed to represent himself at his original trial; and 3) Asher phoned Supreme Court Justice William O. Douglas to ask if he would consider a petition of habeas corpus (Douglas, as it happened, was away from Washington for two days, on a hiking trip). Meanwhile, Rice had also dug up some compelling evidence in Los Angeles vis-à-vis the transcripts of the original 1948 trial—that is, that the man hired by the prosecutor, J. Miller Leavy, to transcribe the notes, was Leavy's brother in law, a falling-down, blacking-out alcoholic.

As it happened, Longstreth did hop on an airplane to Sacramento to present his letter in person to the governor. The visit was short and hectic; he barely had time to talk to his new friends, Bernice Freeman and Rosalie Asher. He did not go to San Quentin, but his effort still earned him points with his now-famous client.

When he was able to concentrate again on writing, Chessman picked up a San Francisco newspaper on May 16, 1954, and saw that

Cell 2455, Death Row was on the bestseller list. Not only that, but Chessman's bestselling book, his stoicism in the face of his execution, his nearness to death—dramatized by this last-minute stay—and the media attention accruing to all of these things had turned Chessman's sudden fame into something more substantial. That is, the average American began not only to know his name but to be open to the possibility that what he insisted—that he was innocent of the Red Light Bandit charges—might be true.

One ghost from his past, Lucy Ann Short, resurfaced. Asher had suspected this would happen. Claiming that she hoped to see Chessman before he died, Lucy Ann asked members of the Los Angeles press corps to intercede on her behalf. Her efforts yielded a fruitful story in the *Los Angeles Daily News* of May 15, 1954. Headlined "Who Is Lucy Ann?" and written by Paul Weeks, the story touched off a small media storm. Though it has been suggested over the years that Lucy Ann was careful to hide her identity out of fear for her physical safety and her daughter's, she was uncharacteristically forthcoming in these stories. In fact, in Weeks's story, Lucy Ann willingly removes her disguise, telling readers, "I am called 'Judy' in the book, for Caryl wouldn't use my name. I had heard that the book was about Caryl's life, that it was a book which might serve to keep others from following in his footsteps. Of course, I gave my permission."

While the stories about Lucy Ann Short did not register nationally, the localized flurry was enough of a distraction that Chessman did not want to risk the story leading to new revelations. He dropped any attempt to see Lucy Ann, who was still genuinely fond of Chessman and disappointed by the rejection. She had even written her ex-husband a letter in which she said, "You and I, Caryl, lived a full and happy part of our lives together. I'll not forget it nor have I regretted it. I would do it all over again if it were possible." Explaining the situation to Longstreth, Chessman noted, "Lucy gave the *News* a copyrighted story about her marriage to me. It's done sympathetically, and she identifies herself in it as the 'Judy' in the book. Among other things she tells how my agent—for the book—called and asked clearance from me for the parts of the book in which Caryl tells of me—of us. Thought you should know all this, if you didn't already. The story was given front page treatment on May 15."

Chessman, meanwhile, had enough good news to carry him through these rocky waters. That is, his name and fame—which had only recently spread beyond the borders of California—was on the verge of crossing the ocean. The British edition of *Cell 2455, Death Row* was in production and a contract was being drawn up for the Italian edition. Wenzell Brown's review in the *Saturday Review* of May 22, 1954, was ecstatic ("It will be surprising indeed if a more astonishing book is published anywhere this year"). The distinguished sociologist and author Harry Elmer Barnes wrote, "The most remarkable portrait of a criminal career and personality ever produced . . . Nothing comparable to it has ever appeared in print." The *New York Times's* Orville Prescott, in an otherwise prissy review, said, "An arresting addition to the annals of crime . . . a dramatic and interesting book." The *Los Angeles Daily News* chimed in with, "One of the best books of its kind ever written." *Argosy*, the noirish men's magazine, published the book's first chapter in its June issue, under the title "I Am Waiting to Die."

As a result, the book moved up to number 3 on the bestseller list, competing against Elmer Davis's *But We Were Born Free* and Norman Vincent Peale's *The Power of Positive Thinking* (coincidentally, a perennial bestseller for Prentice-Hall).

The only sour note was sounded by *Newsweek*, but it had nothing to do with the book. In the May 24 issue, *Newsweek* ran a story about Chessman's legal battles; in it, they revealed the existence of Frances Couturier. Curiously, the *Newsweek* reporter ignored the potentially more explosive and titillating matter of Lucy Ann, Chessman's ex-wife and mother of his child, while conjuring up some romantic implications about a woman who, for all the world knew, was only a friend of the Chessman family. In an interview granted only because she hoped it would help Caryl's cause, Frances acquitted herself well and probably helped soften his public image by insisting he could never have committed the crimes attributed to the Red Light Bandit. In a letter to Asher earlier in March, the gushingly naive Frances said, "I can't for the life of me see how they could condemn a man without proof," which elicited a pitying "Dear heavens!" from the seasoned lawyer. After the *Newsweek* piece appeared, CBS-TV showed up at Frances Courturier's doorstep. Again, she handled herself well, garnering sympathy for Caryl's plight as well as her own difficult situation, single moms with two young children being somewhat exotic in those days.

On May 27, 1954, Chessman's thirty-third birthday, he turned eagerly to the features section of the *Chronicle*. To his own astonishment, *Cell 2455, Death Row* had reached number 1 on the bestseller lists in San Francisco and Los Angeles. In New York, it was at number 12 and moving up fast.

Chessman's royalty statement from Prentice-Hall for the period January 1–June 30, 1954, gives a clear indication of the phenomenal interest in his story. Though the book had officially been published for only one month, 17,852 copies had sold, as had "condensation rights" to *Pageant* magazine, "reprint rights" to *Argosy*, "German serial rights," and "Swedish book and serial rights." Despite being docked his advance and two emergency cash advances, Chessman still cleared $5,597.13 in royalties.

The sheer numbers, and consistency, of book sales were welcome for the cash infusion they signaled and, of course, they were a boost to Chessman's confidence; no, they were like gasoline flowing directly into the furnace of his outsized ego. But something else was taking place; something profound psychologically and, yes, spiritually, was stirring to life inside Cell 2455. Acceptance on such a grand scale was the tonic he had craved since his boyhood, since the early illnesses robbed him of his love of music and art, since the car wreck robbed him of his mother and turned his father into a broken wretch, since his own first forays into crime had been unable to fill the empty hole in his soul. Caryl Chessman was, in his own way, undergoing a transformation as pronounced as that of his old prison cellmate, Bill Sands. That he would likely never again walk the streets a free man like Sands, that he would never fully lose his reputation as a "monster" and a "sex terrorist," was surely centermost in Chessman's mind. That he continued to transform himself over the next six years, still resolved to reinvent himself through the power of the written word, is a testament to the resilience of his evolving spirit.

■

EVEN THE RELATIONSHIPS with his most loyal champions, Longstreth, Asher, and Freeman, were repaired in the wake of his execution stay. Chessman may have acted irresponsibly and bluntly with these friends, but it was he—not they—who was staring at a date with the gas chamber while also standing on the verge of international literary fame. These two opposing titanic forces—death and fame—must have made him feel such intense pressure that he required an iron will not to go off the rails.

By the end of May, Longstreth had softened enough to tell Asher, "Having been through what he's been through, and facing still more of the same inhuman living, I'm amazed that he doesn't chain smoke, have T.B., develop ulcers and go completely berserk. It only takes a second of putting yourself in his shoes to discover that he's a person with some tremendous source of hidden strength which is untappable by the average human."

Longstreth also remarked that Chessman's letters "have been so sane and so sensible. They have been short, touching, and really beautifully written." Asher felt the same way, relating to Longstreth that her four-hour visit with Chessman on May 8 was "surprisingly unexhausting" and that "I find it hard to unearth the proper words to describe his attitude. It isn't resigned, in a sense of having given up hope; yet the hope that remains seems reasonable. Perhaps to say he is matter of fact would best cover it—or his statement that he'll go if he has to but he won't like it a damned bit. Joe, I think for the first time I felt a real sincerity in the man. We had a truly good talk. I wish I might have taken notes, my memory being what it is, for he was talking well, almost brilliantly. While I realize that the impact of his personality may still be influencing me, I am really inclined to believe that he wants a stay in order to finish the other two books, his short stories and novelette. . . . He talked a good deal of his past and of his present attitude toward long time associates. He realizes that perhaps he deserves to die for other things he has done—but says it hurts all the more to be dying for something he didn't do. And either that makes sense or I'm acquiring a prisoner viewpoint myself."

During Asher's visit, an unnamed San Quentin lieutenant told her that he hoped Chessman would get a commutation.

■

THIS SEA OF calm was soon filled with tidal waves. Judge Keating of the Marin County Superior Court denied Rice's request for a writ of habeas corpus. Asher and Rice immediately made plans to take the writ to a higher court, filing it with the California Supreme Court on July 16. When it was denied there on July 21, Judge Fricke set Chessman's new execution date for July 30, 1954, the absolute minimum amount of time allowed for doing so. The old judge had gone beyond the call of duty in the Chessman case; he had, it seemed, become Chessman's mortal enemy, and he wanted this upstart prisoner dead, the sooner the better.

While all these legal machinations were going on, Chessman briefly entertained fantasies of getting some writing done on his *Death Row Diary* sequel, which he'd now retitled *Trial by Ordeal*. Prentice-Hall and even some New York bookstores had already expressed urgent interest in the new book. But, with nine days to live, he was too preoccupied with legal matters to bask in further literary glory. Ben Rice was new to the case and wouldn't have time to digest six years of litigation history without Chessman's full attention. "One wrong move and I'm kaput," he said.

An investigator named Bill Linhart had been hired to interview the jurors at Chessman's original trial. Freeman vouched for Linhart as "honest and sincere" and said he "will do all he can at a minimum of cost." He'd already spent five days in Los Angeles, during which he'd interviewed six jurors, five of whom were prepared to say that Judge Fricke's instructions prior to their deliberating Chessman's fate made them feel "that there was nothing to do except to bring in a death sentence." Linhart told Asher that he had some promising leads that would potentially save Chessman. But Rice, who wanted to use the jurors' affidavits to accompany the petition to the State Supreme Court, distrusted Linhart, telling Asher he was "not the caliber of man he needs"; she suspected Rice had other motives.

The Linhart-Rice clash drove Asher to distraction, and she was inclined to cancel her first vacation in ten years to referee their bickering. She had the added worry of having to put her frail, elderly mother in a Sacramento hospital. The impasse found her quoting William Steig's motto ("People are no damned good") to Longstreth, with the proviso, "Emphatically, though, I don't include you in that classification."

To add to the surreal media swirl around Chessman, a Hollywood film version of *Cell 2455, Death Row* was close to becoming a reality. Columbia Pictures had bought the rights from Prentice-Hall for $15,000, and they were in the process of hiring someone to write the script. Chessman was surprised and angry that the sale was "so cheap," telling Longstreth—in a letter he asked the agent to destroy upon reading—"we have sold out my life at a mighty cheap price, for a picture such as is planned is a mortal cinch to put me in the gas chamber."

Still, he desperately needed the "substantial sum of money" that would accrue to placate the pockets of Rice and others. And he took enough casual interest in the project to write Longstreth, "Idle Thought Department: Steve Cochran would make a darned good adult Chessman."*

There was one hang-up. California Department of Corrections rules and regulations forbade the use of the voice or the likeness of any prisoner in a film. In response to a request from Monroe Stearns at Prentice-Hall, Chessman, undeterred, granted his consent to "the use of my photographic likeness and a recording of my voice in connection with any movie which may be made of my book."

Warden Teets had, however, had opened Chessman's mail from Stearns, which asked for the above consent, and upon reading the request, sent Chessman this curt and clear message: "It is noted in

---

* Cochran (1917–1965) was a second-tier lead actor who, with his slicked-back black hair and muscular frame, had made an impressive gangster, "Big Ed Sommers," in Raoul Walsh's *White Heat* (1949).

letter you received today from Prentice Hall that you are asked to sign a letter stating you are willing to be photographed in San Quentin and also to have your voice recorded, in connection with the possibility of a movie of your book. Your attention is called to the fact that neither of these can be permitted."

Chessman also asked Stearns for a chance to read over the final script before the filming began. He not only wanted a picture with "punch and meaning," he would not approve any script that suggested he might be guilty of the Red Light Bandit crimes. Should a film like that be made, he wisely reasoned, it would damage any legal case he might have down the road. He also did not want to make trouble for Warden Teets, who had treated him fairly up to that point.

Perhaps envious of the success enjoyed by a criminal, the Hollywood gossip columnist Louella O. Parsons* baited Columbia Pictures' executive Jerry Wald into saying, "There is no intention on the part of Columbia Studios of glamorizing the life of Caryl Chessman. To the contrary, his sordid story will be handled as a horrible example and perhaps a lesson to boys who might be starting out as Chessman did and ending up where he is." Parsons added that she hoped the movie will "serve as a horrible example to delinquents and not be glamorized by pity for the man who wrote it."*

Parsons's diatribe, of course, nauseated Chessman. "It's nothing but a spuriously pious attempt to pander to emotion and hysteria—the very things that are defeating solution," he railed to Longstreth. "Moreover, I happen to be innocent of the Red Light crimes and right now more than ever I'm trying to prove it. . . . Of course I shouldn't be glamorized but neither should I be reviled."

---

* Louella O. Parsons (1881–1972) was Hollywood's most feared snoop, cementing her reputation for viciousness with a long tenure as head of the Hearst newspaper empire's movie department. The thrice-married Parsons trafficked in scandal, and her innuendos appeared in a nationally syndicated column and radio program. She helped suppress the greatest American film ever made, *Citizen Kane* (1940), spearheading the drive to sue Orson Welles, deny him ad space in Hearst papers, and intimidate theaters from booking it. In a way, then, it was a badge of honor for Chessman to be singled out by Parsons, who by 1954 was a caricature of the put-upon gossip and was running on fumes.

∎

GIVEN THE FEELINGS of his client—which he shared—Longstreth put his efforts into overdrive to stop the film sale, insofar as it had been detailed (inaccurately, as it turned out) by the likes of Wald and Parsons. The final approval rested with Joseph Longstreth, the agent, and he refused to sign any document that sold the story so cheaply and to a bunch of Hollywood hacks in the sway of Cold War hysteria. Due to his efforts, Wald had been called off the project and replaced by two other producers, Wallace MacDonald and Jack DeWitt, whom Longstreth described to Chessman as "fair-minded men."

The final result, *Cell 2455, Death Row*, first released by Columbia Pictures in April 1955 and then rereleased in early 1960 to take advantage of Chessman's imminent demise, was as fair a representation of Chessman's book as could be expected in the Hollywood of the 1950s, riven as it was by charges of Communist infiltration, the "naming of names" to the House Un-American Activities Committee, and the blacklisting of those who were named. A trio of Hollywood journeymen did the deed—Wallace MacDonald produced the film, Jack De Witt wrote the screenplay, and Fred F. Sears directed.* Chessman, or "Whit," was portrayed by two brothers, as an adult by William Campbell and as a teenager by Robert Campbell. Serl Chessman was portrayed by Allen Nourse and Hallie by Diane De Laire.

The *Los Angeles Times* reviewed the film the week it opened at four large downtown theaters and four drive-in theaters in the suburbs. The reviewer called it a "brutal story, made more brutal by indelicate telling" and said that its impact "on young minds will probably be unhappy. At several points during the show the audience laughed at some hair-brained [*sic*] scheme of Whittier's, but it was not laughter of derision. It was laughter at the stupidity of cops." Campbell's portrayal, they said, "isn't convincing."

Despite the initial response, Columbia gave it the full press push and they played up the angry young rebel angle to take advantage of

---

* Though Longstreth found them "fair-minded," these were not the cream of Hollywood's crop. After *Cell 2455, Death Row*, Fred F. Sears went on to direct *Earth vs. The Flying Saucers* (1956).

the attentive audience for such fare, a process started in 1953 with *The Wild One*, starring Marlon Brando as the leader of a motorcycle gang. When asked, "Hey, Johnny, what are you rebelling against?" Brando's character answered existentially, "What've you got?" (Brando, in fact, became one of Chessman's most high-profile champions.) Three months after *Cell 2455, Death Row* was released, this theme created a sensation with the release of *Rebel Without a Cause* and the nearly simultaneous death in a car crash of its star, James Dean. At the time, Dean was riding high as the star of *East of Eden*, an ad for which appeared next to the *Times*'s review of *Cell 2455, Death Row*, as did ads for Jacques Tati's *Mr. Hulot's Holiday* and Walt Disney's *20,000 Leagues Under the Sea*.

The four-page "Pressbook" that Columbia released to reporters on *Cell 2455, Death Row*'s film release offered twelve different "publicity and advertising mats" emblazoned with such "timely" notices as "Hot as Today's Headlines! The Condemned Man the Whole World Is Watching . . . Caryl Chessman!" and "The Shock Event of the Screen Year: Actually Written in the Death Cell at San Quentin!"

The *Les Misérables* angle was also emphasized: "*Cell 2455, Death Row* describes how a desperate teen-ager named Whit, steals food for his hungry, impoverished family." Also emphasized was the Robin Hood angle: "He preyed on other criminals, 'Hijacking the hijackers' until this too became too hot for him to handle." The "Red Light Bandit" tag was airbrushed to "Lover's Lane Bandit" and, of course, none of the sex crimes are shown, or even hinted at in the movie, in which "Whit" comes off as a deeply misunderstood stick-'em-up thief in a desperate race to save himself with his typewriter.

In the accompanying press kit, prepared for the 1960 reissue of the film, Columbia's publicists encouraged theater owners to "Make sure that local news editors—newspaper, radio and TV—incorporate your picture and playdate into the hottest story of the year, Caryl Chessman's fight for life" and "Set up a lobby display of local newspaper headlines around the Chessman story, and try for special newspaper display ads plugging their own coverage!" and "Invite local clergy and other civic and social figures to comment, on the picture and on the Chessman story."

■

UNABLE TO DANCE around the fringes of Chessman's criminal past, Longstreth put into words, on June 1, 1954, what everyone connected to his case had long thought: If he was innocent of the Red Light Bandit charges, why didn't he simply reveal to the world who did the crimes?

"It's scarcely a new or novel idea," he wrote Chessman, "but its clear logic cannot escape anyone. Nothing is worth the protection of a guilty party, and the proof of who the real Red Light Bandit is would be one of the great moments of time. Don't think I'm being simple or stupid by making such a relatively obvious remark; however, there have been so many hints and innuendos—why not the naked truth? I'm still holding to enough illusions, Caryl, to believe firmly that nothing can, in the final analysis, defeat simple truth."

On June 8, adding more subterfuge to the Red Light Bandit mystery, Chessman responded, "You're right, Joe: nothing can defeat simple truth, but truth isn't always simple—and the state should not require any cabalistic analysis. Neither is the matter of proof simple, especially after six and a half years. Ironically, my problem doesn't involve protecting a guilty party so much as it does protecting innocent ones. Some day I hope to be able to explain all this to you."

In the meantime, Chessman had his hands full, working every waking hour with Ben Rice, preparing his case in time to survive beyond July 30.

■

UPON HER RETURN from vacation—she had ultimately decided to leave "with a clear conscience"—Asher visited Chessman at San Quentin and Rice at his Sausalito home. She found Chessman optimistic and Rice pessimistic about the chances for survival. Chessman expected the State Supreme Court to deny his petition, which would allow him to petition the U.S. Supreme Court. He put a great deal of stock in the jurors' affidavits, though Asher thought the idea "speculative" at best and "chasing rainbows" at worst. Rice gave her another sob story about his finances, claiming to have only fourteen dollars in his checking account. Chessman, confident of his earning capacity, estimated that he would gross $25,000 for 1954, and was already taking steps toward softening the tax burden by itemizing all of his expenses, including legal fees. This, while staring at a date with the gas chamber in two weeks!

He not only carried on as if he were not a dead man walking, he became a veritable dead man writing. It was during this time that he began writing, secretly and against prison officials' wishes, his second book, published the following year by Prentice-Hall as *Trial by Ordeal*. The secrecy regarding his writings after *Cell 2455, Death Row* was warranted. Though Chessman worked under the premise that his literary work constituted his own "property," the state could, with equal force, argue that he, as a resident on Death Row, had no civil rights beyond testifying in court, making a will, or acknowledging the sale of property. Thus, they could argue—as morally reprehensible as it would seem—that he had no "right" to be writing at all, not to mention selling his literary work in the public marketplace. Until this nebulous legal area was cleared up by some definitive judicial decision, Chessman was operating in the dark and took every precaution to hide his work from prison staff. He not only faced possible legal troubles—not that there was much more they could do to someone already facing two death sentences—but so did Asher and Longstreth for being parties to the secrecy.

Chessman told Asher in early July that if he didn't have his writing on which to focus he would be "deadly bored." He longed to get off the row and "into the yard" (the prison's general population) and even began thinking again of ultimately being released from prison. "Although he swears that if he ever gets out, he'll never again be a problem, I shudder at the very possibility," she wrote Longstreth. She also mentioned "the girl" who was "in need of money now, rather than having it set aside for her education," a veiled reference to his daughter by Lucy Ann, now ten years old.

It is a tribute to Chessman's confidence and calmness under pressure that as an execution date beckoned, he was still making plans for the day he won his freedom.

■

ON JULY 25, Asher made arrangements to pick up Chessman's effects at the prison, following his execution. She stayed at the Fairmont Hotel in San Francisco, visited Chessman one last time and stood ready for any last-second legal maneuver that might save him. "I can't see anything, short of a literal miracle, which will save him," she wrote Longstreth. "Caryl intuitively feels 'something' will save him. I'm afraid my role during our interview was largely as prophet of doom. He wearily responded, 'I honestly believe this is it,' and I'm not sure but what I believe it will be better for Caryl. At least his problems, worries and fights will be over once and for all."

Chessman may have thought this was curtains, too. He gave George Flowers, a reporter for the *Press-Telegram* (a Long Beach daily), a statement, which he dubbed "voice from the grave," to be printed alongside the story of his execution. Flowers was another member of the press corps whom Chessman befriended; he'd agreed, at Chessman's request, to be a witness at the execution.

Frances Couturier, meanwhile, had moved in with Bernice Freeman in San Rafael, prompting Asher to ask, "How long suffering can you be?" Freeman had another motive, besides altruism, for putting up Frances. She was preparing a *Chronicle* story about Frances that would appear under the pandering headline, "Why I Love Chessman" (a story Asher would later call "nauseous"). Asher's feelings toward Chessman at this point were harder than ever to gauge, but this comment to Longstreth was a bit catty at the time though it proved prophetic: "If Caryl finishes another book and if it sells, I would hate like hell to see Frances getting large sums of money. You know as well as I that she couldn't handle it. Of course, it's none of my business, but if there is going to be a sizeable estate, I'd like to see Caryl live up to his press releases and actually do a little good."

On July 28, 1954, two days before he was scheduled to die in the gas chamber, Chessman got his fourth stay of execution, signed by Judge Jesse W. Carter of the California Supreme Court. This was granted only to give Chessman and his legal team enough time to prepare a petition to the United States Supreme Court.

Again, the maligned Rice was to thank for this break. He traveled to the "Trinity Alps,"a vast wilderness area in northwest California where Carter was vacationing. Somehow, after hiring a trail guide, Rice was able to track down the judge. In his retelling, Rice made it sound like Stanley's stumbling upon Dr. Livingstone in the Congo, replete with a "hair-raising donkey ride over narrow mountain trails" and the stay order itself written out in longhand on a tree stump. Had that gambit failed, Rice was prepared to fly to Washington to file Chessman's self-penned twenty-three-page petition with the Supreme Court—a petition Asher felt was "legally just no good."

On July 30, Chessman wrote Longstreth, "I'm beginning this letter to you at exactly 10 A.M. It's a good feeling to be able to do so, Joe. For this could have been the end. Instead, it's a new beginning."

It was clear from this letter that Longstreth was now his close friend.

"Had the case been resolved otherwise," he wrote, "I had planned to write you last night after being taken downstairs [to the waiting room outside the gas chamber]. All of your letters and your two telegrams have been received. Just as you could find no appropriate words to say goodbye, should it be, I can find none to express my appreciation for your friendship, your humaneness, your concern, your help. All I can tell you, Joe, is that there is a sustaining warmth inside me. It carried me through the week. . . . I recognize gladly that my days no longer belong to me; that is, if it hadn't been for all those who have faith in me, I would even now be dying. This realization has strengthened my determination to justify that faith and put my time to as good and as creative a use as is within my power."

One of the unintended consequences of Chessman's good fortune was that his stay of execution cleared the 10 A.M. time slot on July 30 for two other Death Row inmates to be executed four hours earlier than they'd expected. James Franklin Wolfe, forty-two, and Joseph Johansen, twenty-six—both of whom were convicted of murdering another prisoner while serving life sentences in Folsom Prison—were originally slated for a 2 P.M. gassing. However, the gas chamber was now open for business earlier, and Warden Teets did not want to waste the precious four hours these men would otherwise wait until their deaths. This turn of events angered State Attorney General Edmund "Pat" Brown, who demanded that the governor stay the executions of Wolfe and Johansen. In a statement released to the press, Brown said, "There's no reason why a man who can write a book should have an advantage that these two other apparently friendless people do not have."

This would not be the last time that Caryl Chessman would run afoul of Pat Brown. From the intensity of his anger, it's clear that Brown—who was governor in 1960 when Chessman died—long held an animus toward the prisoner "who can write a book."

Chessman had seen Frances the day before, and now he knew she loved him. Though he stopped short of saying he loved her, he told Longstreth, "There's so much that is phony and selfish and self-pitying in this world, to share her nearness and her hopes is an experience that has done much for me."

Finally, Lucy Ann had succeeded in visiting Chessman at the prison, with no press fanfare. She remarked that she'd received the latest payout from Longstreth, who was sending the agreed-upon seven thousand dollars in chunks, as the money from royalties trickled in. Chessman noted that her visit was pleasant and that he was "truly glad" that she "had been able to make a good new life for herself, that she now has the children and the home she always wanted."

■

CELL 2455, DEATH ROW continued to sell briskly during the summer of 1954, as Chessman's ordeal competed with, and ran parallel to, a capital case unfolding in Ohio. Like Chessman's, this case attracted nationwide attention. On July 4, 1954, Marilyn Sheppard, the pregnant wife of a prominent Cleveland osteopath named Samuel H. Sheppard, was beaten to death in her bed while her husband was allegedly sleeping in another room downstairs. Though he suffered neck injuries during a fight with a "bushy-haired intruder," Dr. Sheppard was soon arrested and accused of the crime. Before his case came to trial in October 1954, he was at the eye of an intense national media storm that raged all summer across America and harkened back to the Lindbergh baby kidnap and murder trial of Bruno Hauptmann. Cleveland newspapers in particular, were, arrayed against Sheppard, echoing the sentiment of the Los Angeles dailies during Chessman's Red Light Bandit trial. One headline proclaimed, "Why Isn't Sam Sheppard in Jail?" and another, "The Finger of Suspicion"; they all but tried, convicted, and sentenced Dr. Sheppard in print long before a jury could. Sam Sheppard's trial, from October to December, played out like a nationwide soap opera—it was revealed, for example, that he had had a three-year affair with a nurse prior to his wife's murder. Imagine the collective gasp of shock this revelation caused in the placid Ike era.

Perhaps on some collective subliminal level, Sam Sheppard's trial served as a backdrop against which Americans could reexamine Caryl Chessman's case and his fate. At some point, it must have dawned on many people that, though there were parallels between the two cases, Chessman was never accused of murder and never had the advantages of privilege and money enjoyed by Dr. Sheppard, who lived in a pricey lakefront home in a nouveau riche suburb of Cleveland. And even after Sheppard was found guilty of murder of his wife and baby by a jury in late December, the doctor was not given a death sentence.*

Meanwhile, Chessman languished on Death Row for crimes during which no one was killed. He continued to write and fight for his life. Perhaps the many cracks in the perfect suburban veneer that were revealed in the Sheppard case helped prompt sympathy for Chessman's less blood-soaked case. Or perhaps sympathy was engendered by the many cracks showing elsewhere in American society, including the push for civil rights, the weariness over HUAC's Communist witch hunts, and the rise of a new American musical form that offered an escape, if not a rebellion, from the self-righteous blandness and

---

* The Sheppard case continued to produce headlines long after the guilty verdict. Dr. Sheppard's mother committed suicide by shotgun in January 1955, and his father died of a stomach hemorrhage two weeks later. Sheppard, proclaiming his innocence, was released from prison in 1964, got a new trial in 1966, and was acquitted. A popular TV series, *The Fugitive*, was aired starting in 1963, using many aspects of the Sheppard case as the basis for the series. The "bushy-haired intruder" was, however, transformed into "the one-armed man." Sheppard became, among other things, a pro wrestler and an alcoholic and died of liver disease in 1970.

conformity of the Eisehower era. On July 5, 1954, the day after Marilyn Sheppard's murder, an unknown Memphis truck driver named Elvis Presley entered Sun Studios to record his first three singles. By May 1955, when Bill Haley and the Comets released "Rock Around the Clock," which stayed in the number one position on the Top 40 charts for two months, the cracks in America's social landscape had turned into fissures. Against the backdrop of these sweeping changes, Chessman was no longer seen, by a certain segment of the hip and the young, as the monster the press had created. Rather, he was just part of this wider, shared rebellion. And a damn good writer to boot.

■

CHESSMAN'S PUBLISHING FAME had Longstreth exploring residual publishing opportunities. The most promising, money-wise, came from *Confidential*, one of the ubiquitous "true crime" magazines that flourished in the 1950s and traded in kiss-and-tell romance and sensationalized crime stories—the more lurid the better. They had in mind a story about Chessman and Frances Couturier that would combine both elements, playing up Chessman's sexual assault crimes and Frances's stand-by-her-man innocence—a "Beast Meets Beauty" romance. After talking with the editors, Longstreth rejected the proposal. He wrote Frances, staying with Freeman in San Rafael for the summer. Informing her of his decision to reject the offer, he explained that *Confidential*'s plans "were lurid and sensational to such a degree that I couldn't see the value for you or Caryl; quite the contrary. . . . I don't think any amount of money is worth a sensational or lurid story. Sensational, perhaps, in a good way, but they weren't interested in something good."

After Longstreth returned from an August trip to visit family in Indiana, he received a much more promising offer from *Saga* ("True Adventures for Men"), a magazine not unlike *Confidential*. On October 22, 1954, Ed Fitzgerald, the editorial director of *Saga*, solicited an article by Longstreth's now famous client. For the then princely payment of five hundred dollars, Fitzgerald wanted Chessman to write a four-thousand-word piece explaining "What I Would Do With My

Life" if he were spared the trip to the gas chamber. What Fitzgerald was asking for was fantastical, almost backhandedly cruel—that is, asking a condemned man to ponder "getting his life back." By "getting his life back," Fitzgerald meant the whole Hollywood ending: being released from prison after obtaining a new trial and proving his innocence of the charges that had landed him on Death Row.

Fitzgerald wanted to know: "Would he get married? Is the girl he was thinking of marrying still seeing him regularly and still interested in his future? What kind of work would he want to do? What means would he want to seize to prove his usefulness to society and thus prove his gratitude for the second chance at life?" This, of course, presumed that if Chessman were able to get a new trial and prove his innocence, he would be required to "prove" anything to anyone or to express gratitude for having been wrongly incarcerated on Death Row for more than seven years.

Regardless, Fitzgerald was expressing a curiosity that many thousands of people had about this enigmatic man who, through his remarkable book, had suddenly entered their lives and touched their hearts. Chessman was sufficiently well known across America for Fitzgerald to reap big sales at the news racks for such a sensational story.

Plus, five hundred bucks was nothing to sneeze at in 1954, especially when the recipient had Ben Rice on his payroll. Another legal investigator, Pauline "Polly" Gould, was also hired by Asher, behind Rice's back, and she managed to secure some solid affidavits regarding the chronic alcoholism of Stanley Fraser, the court reporter and transcriber including one from a witness who saw Leavy conveying his staggeringly inebriated brother-in-law home in a cab. This occurred during the period of time when he was allegedly transcribing the shorthand court proceedings from Chessman's trial. Gould also had become "drinking pals" with Fraser's temporarily estranged wife, from whom she was securing damning evidence. (Longstreth sardonically told Asher, "Congratulate Polly for me on being a drinking pal of Mrs. Fraser. I'd like to be someone's drinking pal."). Gould also warned Asher that Rice had left behind a "wave of resentment" in Los Angeles. To put it bluntly, he was widely considered both a lush and a jerk, and Gould refused to work for or with Rice. Asher trusted Gould instinctively, an impression confirmed upon meeting her in person in August. "In two days she turned up more than any of the others did in weeks," Asher assured Longstreth.

It is curious that while Rice, Linhart and Gould—not to mention the undeserving Frances—got paid, Asher and Longstreth were working largely out of pocket. Their faith in Caryl as a writer at this point equaled their growing fondness for him as a redeemable human being. Their loyalty was something Chessman would henceforth not take for granted.

Longstreth warned Asher, "Allowing a tiny sum to be spent, and planning to have it retrieved later, can become the thin edge of the proverbial wedge, especially in this case. Caryl has become a little loose with funds; in all fairness, I think we can admit that it is excusable and understandable. I always try to remember that he is the one facing death. . . . Most of us can't face life."

He apprised her of Chessman's financial agreement with Critics Associated. That is, that his annual available income could not exceed ten thousand dollars, a clause he insisted on for tax purposes. Everything beyond that went into savings and trust funds for various parties, as per his will.

However, strange breaks began to occur in the case, pulling Asher deeper into the maelstrom and making her more willing to go beyond the call of legal duty. One such break came in mid-August 1954, when Chessman received a telegram at San Quentin from an inmate at Los Angeles County Jail. "This," he told Asher, "may be the break we've been waiting for." He supplied no other details, but asked her to go to Los Angeles and "hear the man out, no matter how irrelevant his conversation may be, or may seem."

■

A PERIPHERAL ISSUE suddenly emerged as a stumbling block in Chessman's bid for a new trial, or even a fully sympathetic public hearing. The fate of Mary Alice Meza, the young woman who was a victim of one of the Red Light Bandit sexual assaults, came to public

PRENTICE-HALL, inc. *Publishers*
70 FIFTH AVENUE · NEW YORK 11, N. Y.

ROYALTY STATEMENT

FOR THE SIX MONTH PERIOD ENDED JUNE 30, 1954

TITLE: CELL 2455, DEATH ROW

AUTHOR: CARYL CHESSMAN

COPIES	SALES	RATE	ROYALTY
0,000 REGULAR TRADE EDITION SALES	22,706.24	17%	3,860.06
1,715 REGULAR TRADE EDITION SALES	3,894.13	21%	817.77
5,687 SALES OF 50% DISCOUNT OR HIGHER	11,092.13	10%	1,109.21
35 COUPON M O ADVG SALES	138.13	5%	6.91
366 FOREIGN SALES	868.15	10%	86.82
49 TEXT SALES	163.63	10%	16.36
7,852 TOTALS	38,862.41		5,897.13

TOTAL COPIES SOLD (In all above categories)

SALES TO BEGINNING OF THIS PERIOD .... # -
"   THIS PERIOD................................. 17,852
TOTAL SALES TO DATE................................. 17,852

EARNINGS THIS PERIOD - ROYALTIES 5,897.13

EARNINGS THIS PERIOD - RIGHTS

"CONDENSATION RIGHTS TO PAGEANT MAGAZINE" ... 1,000.00 @ 50% ...   500.00

"REPRINT RIGHTS TO ARGOSY" .... 1,500.00 @ 50% ...   750.00

"GERMAN SERIAL RIGHTS" .... 1,500.00 @ 50% ...   750.00

"SWEDISH BOOK AND SERIAL RIGHTS" ....   800.00 @ 50% ...   400.00
                                             4,800.00   2,400.00
CHARGES AGAINST AUTHOR'S ACCOUNT   8,297.13

INITIAL PAYMENT 1,200.00

CASH PAYMENT 5-14-54 ....   750.00

CASH PAYMENT - JUNE 2, 1954 ....   750.00
                                                                         2,700.00

NET AMOUNT DUE_____JOSEPH E. LONGSTRETH_____5,597.13

5.312-F2-1M-6/54

From 1954 until his death in 1960, flush royalty statements like this one were familiar sights to Caryl Chessman, the sole means by which he was able to sustain his legal battle for an extra six years. *Author's collection*

notice. She had been institutionalized at Camarillo State Hospital since October 9, 1949. The diagnosis was "schizophrenic, paranoid type, possible thyrotoxicosis" (a thyroid condition that may have contributed to her condition). Despite the insistence of the *Los Angeles Herald & Express* reporter Clyde Leech that Meza had "never known a seriously ill day in her young life," she had actually suffered from deep mood swings ever since high school and was failing most of her

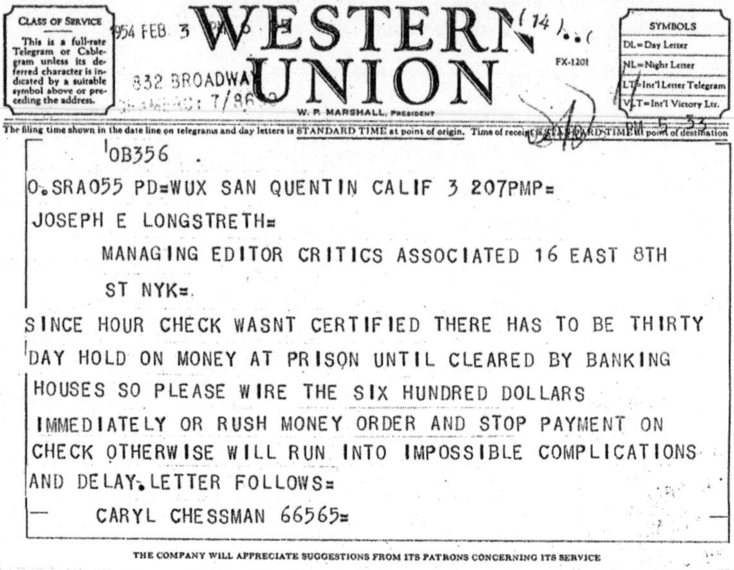
CLASS OF SERVICE
This is a full-rate Telegram or Cablegram unless its deferred character is indicated by a suitable symbol above or preceding the address.

1954 FEB 3

WESTERN UNION

W. P. MARSHALL, PRESIDENT

FX-1201

SYMBOLS
DL=Day Letter
NL=Night Letter
LT=Int'l Letter Telegram
VLT=Int'l Victory Ltr.

The filing time shown in the date line on telegrams and day letters is STANDARD TIME at point of origin. Time of receipt is STANDARD TIME at point of destination

OB356 .

O.SRA055 PD=WUX SAN QUENTIN CALIF 3 207PMP=

JOSEPH E LONGSTRETH=

MANAGING EDITOR CRITICS ASSOCIATED 16 EAST 8TH ST NYK=.

SINCE HOUR CHECK WASNT CERTIFIED THERE HAS TO BE THIRTY DAY HOLD ON MONEY AT PRISON UNTIL CLEARED BY BANKING HOUSES SO PLEASE WIRE THE SIX HUNDRED DOLLARS IMMEDIATELY OR RUSH MONEY ORDER AND STOP PAYMENT ON CHECK OTHERWISE WILL RUN INTO IMPOSSIBLE COMPLICATIONS AND DELAY. LETTER FOLLOWS=

CARYL CHESSMAN 66565=

THE COMPANY WILL APPRECIATE SUGGESTIONS FROM ITS PATRONS CONCERNING ITS SERVICE

The urgency of Chessman's financial needs, precariousness of his existence, and trust he had in his agent, are evident in this telegram sent from San Quentin on April 7, 1954. *Author's collection*

classes before the Red Light Bandit attack. Meza, raised Catholic, told one doctor, even before the sexual assault, that she was "possessed," and requested an exorcist be contacted.

Camarillo, located twenty-five miles north of Los Angeles in Ventura County, was a notorious place, California's equivalent of Bedlam. In fact, scenes from *The Snake Pit* (1948), one of the most lurid movies ever made about life in an insane asylum, were filmed here. Camarillo housed more than seven thousand mentally ill patients, the largest population of any such institution in the country; among the most famous were jazz sax legend Charlie Parker and actress Frances Farmer.* Though the date of her admission to Camarillo—more than a year and a half after the Red Light Bandit attack—made their claims about cause and effect dubious at best, a group of Los Angeles citizens were nonetheless pushing for a civil action lawsuit against Chessman on Meza's behalf, presumably because they noticed that their favorite Death Row monster was earning money from

* Camarillo State Hospital was closed down in June 1997 and converted into the campus of California State University Channel Islands.

a best-selling book. The symbolic power of her plight only under-scored, in the public's eye, the heinousness of the original crimes. The poor girl was driven mad by a blow job.

"What people won't do for money!" Longstreth wondered in a letter to Asher. "It might, though, turn into an excellent thing for Caryl. Can you agree that it might? In other words, wouldn't a real case along the lines you suggested mean that everything about the girl would have to be brought into the open? If so, surely the picture would become so black that it would begin to look as if Caryl had been convicted on the testimony of an idiot."

An equally vocal group in Los Angeles had emerged to take up the cause of Caryl Chessman. This group was led by a pair of psychia-trists, Dr. William F. Graves and Dr. Isidore Ziferstein. Graves had been the senior medical officer at San Quentin prison but on May 11, 1954, had resigned in protest over the state's plans to execute Chess-man. At the time of his resignation, Graves wired Governor Knight, "I am convinced he is not the red-light bandit." Two months later, on July 23, he addressed an open letter to Knight urging executive clemency for Chessman. In it, he said he had talked with Chessman twenty-five to thirty times while he was the staff physician at the prison, and he was sure that Chessman could not have committed the Red Light Bandit crimes.

Though Graves's efforts caused some embarrassment to the governor, he wasn't moved to change his stance toward Chessman. Ziferstein was a prominent Hollywood psychiatrist who had been well connected in both the celebrity and activist communities since the 1930s. Longstreth had donated some of his own money to the doctors' committee to print and circulate copies of the peti-tion they had drawn up to spare Chessman's life. Ziferstein also obtained a copy of the commitment papers for Mary Alice Meza and issued a statement, along with other prominent psychiatrists, that her condition in 1954 was not the result of the Red Light Ban-dit attack in 1948.

Dan Ziferstein, Dr. Ziferstein's son, recalled, "My father's office was one of the action central points. He had an office at the house, a nice big place in Hollywood." Among those who regularly gravitated to the Ziferstein salon were Phyllis Kirk, an actress and girlfriend of Mort Sahl; Shirley Spector, sister of the music producer Phil Spector, with whom Dan Ziferstein had gone to Hollywood High School; the Reverend Steve Fridgeman, a Unitarian minister who was locally famous; Dr. Linus Pauling, Dr. Edward Gorney; and the blacklisted filmmaker Dalton Trumbo.

Among Dr. Ziferstein's other left-wing causes was the plight of Mexican laborers. To that end, he contributed money and time to a feature film collaboration called *Salt of the Earth*, which featured some of Hollywood's talent who had been blacklisted since the HUAC hearings, including Herbert Biberman, director; Trumbo, screenwriter; Paul Jarrico, producer; and Will Geer, actor.*

"My father was very left wing," said Dan Ziferstein. "He went to Russia a number of times, and studied their psychiatric methods. . . . My mom got sick of all of it and was ready to divorce him. Normally, he didn't get involved in the causes of convicted criminals, but Chessman's case was special to him. It was about the ability to, or possibility for, reform. My dad felt that this guy was on his way to being reformed. Chessman was one of these typical guys who was a career punk criminal, but just like some druggies age out of their cravings, Chessman was growing up and he was serious about being a citizen instead of an outsider. And, of course, he was making money, royalties, and maybe very likely wasn't addicted to crime or criminality. My dad met with Chessman several times at San Quentin and came away very impressed with him."

Dr. Ziferstein often compared the Chessman case to that of the Rosenbergs', that is, as a "misuse of capital punishment."†

---

* Work on *Salt of the Earth* began in 1951, though the film wasn't shown publicly until 1954. Even then, the film—about a Mexican-American mine workers' strike in "Zinc City, New Mexico"—was suppressed and largely remained unseen. Since then, it has been selected by the Library of Congress as one of 100 American films to be preserved in perpetuity and, because of resultant sales on DVDs and videos, the Ziferstein family still receives regular checks for residuals.

† On July 19, 1953, Julius and Ethel Rosenberg were executed after being convicted of treason in spying for the U.S.S.R. Their case was, to many Americans, the culminating event of the Cold War.

■

WITHIN A WEEK of the public revelations about Meza, Asher confessed to being "much more optimistic" as she shared some confidential details to Longstreth in an August 23rd letter. Among the breaks in the case was the continued good work of Gould, whom Asher now trusted after a day spent accompanying the private investigator on her Los Angeles rounds. Though Gould confessed to Asher that she found Chessman personally unlikeable, she was more affected by his unfair treatment and called the bungled preparation of the trial transcript "an encroachment of liberties." Asher also met Drs. Graves and Ziferstein on her trip; she found both to be "dreamers" (read: do-gooder liberals) but Ziferstein "a shade more realistic." Ziferstein was particularly dismayed at the profligate manner with which Chessman had dispensed his funds, rather than using the money stream from the book to fund the effort to save his life.

Graves, who worked closely with several church groups, was spearheading the anti–capital punishment angle. Among the church leaders who'd come forward to help was the Reverend Herbert H. Richardson of the North Redondo Chapel in Redondo Beach who'd known Caryl Chessman as a boy and wanted to publicize the "good things" he'd done. The goal of their group at the moment was to secure the services of a prominent attorney who could pull the Chessman case further into the legal spotlight, focusing particularly on the transcript preparation. Though George T. Davis wasn't mentioned, within the year, he did just that.

Among the other confidences Asher shared with Longstreth was the matter of Mr. Fraser, the alcoholic transcript preparer. She had met with some of the witnesses of the man's stumblebum behavior, who told her, "He and his wife would get really drunk; neighbors would call the police; the Frasers would leave before they arrived, park their car in a service station and sleep there, using the car as a bathroom as well as a bedroom." At the moment, with Polly Gould on his tail, Mr. Fraser was "in hiding."

The pièce de résistance, though, was Gould's meeting with a friend of Governor Knight. The friend said that two things were needed:

1) a delay until after the election (pardoning or giving Chessman clemency would harm the governor at the polls); and 2) a detailed report on the appalling matter of Fraser's transcript preparation, so that he could present it personally to Knight. However, this friend of the governor, like all political insiders, had his price—it would cost five hundred dollars for "expenses" and two thousand for "services." Asher's perception of the man was as "one of the Hollywood types who's used to being flattered out of all proportion," but she was willing to go along with the plan, if it got results.

Finally, Asher admitted that, without phoning ahead, she had tracked Frances down in Glendale, "cabbing out for what seemed endless miles." Theirs was more of a confrontation than a friendly visit. Asher told her outright not to talk to any more journalists and that no more money from Chessman was forthcoming for the forseeable future, because all of it was needed to save his life. Asher depicted Frances as flighty and simpleminded ("I do feel sorry for the girl, for she is so far out of her own mental league"), and was particularly incensed over the engagement ring that she'd bought with Chessman's money, a shopping expedition on which she was accompanied by Bernice Freeman. Frances claimed that she hadn't wanted the ring to be publicized, blaming the story on "Harley" (as she now called Warden Teets), but Asher knew better. "A small thing, but I will not have her getting inflated ideas as to her guile and my gullibility." Asher was taken aback to learn that Longstreth was so well loved in the Couturier household ("Incidentally, dear, when did you become 'Uncle Joe'? The appellation really stopped me"). In all, she spent an hour with Frances and the two kids, "and it was the longest of my entire trip."

Two days later, Longstreth received "a lengthy and rather maudlin letter" from Frances, who was upset that she might have hurt Chessman's chances for survival. He felt duty-bound to explain the "Uncle Joe" nickname to Asher ("it started with her children, and she has taken it up. . . . I even sign letters to her that way now, since it pleases her."). He wrote a placating letter to Frances, assuring her that what she'd done had been with the purest motives. He also emphasized that he would never question any action or motive of

Asher, that "she worked for Caryl for years when he was penniless, and with no real hope of ever having a penny. That speaks for itself and can never be taken away."

■

BEFORE CHESSMAN COULD respond to the good news of the *Saga* offer, he had something considerably more exciting to relate to Longstreth. The U.S. Supreme Court had denied "without prejudice" his writ of habeas corpus in the U.S. District Court, and Chessman was adamant that this was legally "better than a review." A review would have meant that the U.S. Supreme Court would then have jurisdiction and final say on the case; what they ruled would leave him no last resort. If they ruled against him, then that was it, the end of the road. Instead, the denial without prejudice meant that he could do what he had been trying to do since 1948: get a new trial.

He excitedly said, "I now am in a position to win, to overthrow these death sentences and even all the 1948 convictions. I have no cinch, of course, but a real fighting chance. I mustn't muff it."

He had become so buoyed by the possibilities that he allowed himself the ultimate dream that Fitzgerald, the editor of *Saga* had planted in his brain: not just his life, but his freedom.

He wrote Longstreth, "Joe, there's nothing I'd like better than to clear myself of these red light charges, do my time on parole violation, and then come to New York and work for CA, learning the writing and publishing business from the ground up. For me, that would be a dream come true."

The news regarding *Cell 2455, Death Row*'s reception remained good. Chessman had earned nearly $15,000 in the first seven weeks of publication. Foreign rights had now been sold in Great Britain, Italy, France, Germany, Sweden, Spain (to be sold in all Castillian-language countries), Japan, Austria, Norway, Finland, and Greece. In addition, the serialization rights had been sold to *Revue* magazine in Germany; *Bild-Telegraf*, a daily newspaper in Vienna; *El Diario de Nueva York*, the largest Spanish daily in the United States; *Die Huisgenoot*, the largest Afrikaans magazine in

South Africa; and *France-Soir*, the largest afternoon newspaper in France.

Somehow, Chessman found time to complete the article for *Saga* by November 12, 1954. Skirting the prison censors, he snuck it out of San Quentin attached to a letter to Longstreth. He requested that Longstreth send it along to *Saga*. If *Saga* accepted the article, he instructed Longstreth to take his agent's fee and then send the rest of the payment to Frances. If *Saga* wavered, he instructed Longstreth to toss the article in the trash. The way that Chessman suggested Longstreth communicate the successful completion of this mission was to write him back at prison and use the locution "I placed the 'life' material" and then "rattle on blithely on another subject." In closing, he said, "Please destroy this letter. You'll be hearing from me in the regular way soon."

This act of otherwise understandable deceit, in the wake of his having granted permission to use his voice and likeness for the movie version of *Cell 2455, Death Row*, may have been the straw that broke Warden Teets's back. Asher had warned Chessman and Longstreth when the *Saga* article was proposed about the possible consequences. The warden, it's safe to assume, had never had a prisoner who'd attained the notoriety of Chessman. He had been as patient as he could be in accommodating Chessman's myriad requests, above or in addition to requests from nearly 6,000 other prisoners in his charge. In a way, Teets had himself to blame for this state of affairs. After all, it had been he—Harley O. Teets—who'd suggested back in 1952 that Chessman, rather than constantly fighting with prisoners and against prison authorities, get it all off his chest by putting his life story down on paper. Chessman had done just as he'd suggested, and the result was an international bestseller.

Perhaps this is why Teets had cut Chessman unprecedented slack—even allowing him to continue using a separate cell on Death Row as an "office." This arrangement had originated with Warden Duffy who, under a judge's order, had allowed Chessman to use a vacant cell to conduct legal research and case preparation that would otherwise have been impossible in the cramped confines of Cell 2455. Had Duffy known that this arrangement would lead to Chessman's career as a best-selling author, he surely would have refused, nipped it in the bud before Longstreth even entered the picture. Teets was, therefore, caught in a tough situation. As Chessman presciently noted in an unpublished manuscript, "If prison officials could have foreseen the furor that would follow the publication of Chessman's 'Cell 2455, Death Row,' it is an open question whether they would not then have suppressed his writing altogether." Teets had been cooperative with Chessman but was also sensitive to the public perception that the famous inmate was being "coddled"; he also faced the wrath of his boss, Richard McGee, director of the Department of Corrections.

However it transpired, the comforts of separate office space were to be short-lived under Teets, who, as the offers poured in for Chessman, must have felt like Colonel Klink in the TV series *Hogan's Heroes*. His captive was up to something, he just did not know what it was.

■

A NEW DATE for execution had been set for January 14, 1955. His humor still intact, Chessman told Longstreth in a late-November letter, "Here we go again???!!! Talk about an endurance contest! I'll bet if one of your writers submitted a piece of fiction involving the sort of fix I'm in and the time involved that you'd politely suggest he change brands. Me, all I'd like to do is change geography."

Meanwhile, the famous prisoner was heating up the keys of his trusty Underwood. In between his legal preparations and letter writing, he had continued to type manically on his sequel to *Cell 2455, Death Row*, to be called *Trial by Ordeal*. He projected the length to be six hundred manuscript pages and the completion date to be "within 45 days," which would mean it'd be ready to go to Prentice-Hall just hours before he would be readied for the gas chamber. Unfortunately, on November 21, 1954, the Underwood went belly up, after churning out hundreds of thousands of words in the previous 11 months. "When I immediately undertook an examination of my friend's innard I wasn't sure whether I was making a diagnosis or a postmortem," he told Longstreth.

With a typewriter borrowed from Asher Chessman soldiered on, barely losing ground. He assured Longstreth that *Trial by Ordeal* would not be bogged down with "technical legal jargon"—which had been the source of much of the haggling by Prentice-Hall editors in *Cell 2455, Death Row*—nor would it be "a series of essays or sermons." It would pick up the narrative where the previous book left off, at January 1, 1954, soon after the best-selling author met his agent. He did not want to tack on a "question-mark ending" nor did he want to rush to the finish line before his case was resolved, one way or the other.

"If I complete it now (before my fate is decided), we have another question-mark ending," he reasoned. "If I wait, we have either 'history' (a dead author) or a more satisfactory solution. The question now is: What is going to happen to Caryl Chessman? I don't believe I should end the book until I can answer that question . . . it will give the book far more punch and appeal."

Finally, he noted: "Just one year ago yesterday I received the first letter from you and wrote you for the first time. From the standpoint of our relationship it has been a happy year. I'll say again what I have said several times before: I'm an amazingly lucky guy to have found such a truly fine agent and friend. I sure never dreamed a year ago that I would be writing today. Who knows? Maybe a year from now we'll be looking back on 1955, and then, a couple of years from then I might even be knocking on a door marked CRITICS ASSOCIATED (with a fat manuscript under my arm, of course)."

Allowing himself to dream, perhaps egged on by the assignment from *Saga*, Chessman requested Longstreth to send him some books on playwriting and TV writing. He would seem to be in the perfect place to inspire the writing of plays, with Death Row's stationary staging, the cell being the setting for his scenes and the *deus ex machina* perhaps being the gas chamber—or a miraculous legal victory.

Longstreth sent him a book by Lajos Egri* and advised his client, "There is probably bigger money in plays than in anything else. The author gets large, large percentages of all subsidiaries, not to mention

---

* Though Egri's book is not specifically named, it had to have been one of the two popular guides Egri had in print in 1954, either *How to Write a Play* (Simon & Schuster, 1942) or *The Art of Dramatic Writing* (Simon & Schuster, 1946).

a nice weekly percentage of the box-office gross; however, successful plays are as rare as fresh dragon eggs."

Longstreth shared with him the details of his own freelance excursion along these lines—a libretto for a thirty-minute operatic version of James Thurber's *The Unicorn in the Garden*, on which he was collaborating with the composer Russell Smith.*

All this shop talk helped Chessman end the year on a quietly hopeful note. Even on Christmas Day, Chessman did not take a day off from his labors. In a letter dated December 25, he wrote to Longstreth and Honour to thank them for their Christmas gift—the book *Editor to Author*, an anthology of correspondence by Maxwell E. Perkins, the famed Scribner's editor who had shaped the literary vision of Thomas Wolfe, F. Scott Fitzgerald, Ernest Hemingway, and Marjorie Kinnan Rawlings, among many others. Chessman may have also enjoyed toying with the fantasy that his two agents felt he belonged in such exalted company.

The legal shadows had not gone away. Chessman continued to labor into the night, seven days a week, in his cell. Death stood with his scythe just on the other side of the New Year, grimly, patiently, waiting. The filing with the State Supreme Court had been delayed by Ben Rice's severe case of the flu, and then the hired legal expert had sniffed out some promising clues in Los Angeles and had gone off to track them down (and no doubt enjoy the nocturnal distractions of the city). The impression Rice gave was that his sleuthing might lead to the revelation of the real Red Light Bandit.

Rosalie Asher was not nearly as optimistic. She argued Chessman's habeas corpus petition in San Francisco on December 7, 1954. Though she sardonically noted that "it was an exceedingly well-dressed presentation: [Attorney General Clarence] Linn in striped trousers and morning coat, me in red velvet," she allowed that "I've a feeling the decision may not be favorable. . . . It all seems so horribly precarious."

---

* Russell Smith (1927–1998) studied with Aaron Copland and Edgar Varèse. In 1953, Smith had won the coveted George Gershwin Special Award, which marked the young composer as a rising star in American classical music. He and Longstreth did complete their comic opera based on Thurber's story, and it has been performed more than one hundred times in various productions over the years.

Linn anticipated the possibility that Chessman would file another petition for habeas corpus, "alleging they refuse to let him send out a book he has written, and attaching the manuscript [for *Trial by Ordeal*] as an exhibit." Linn—whom Chessman described as "an obese Don Quixote"—offered Asher one piece of advice in passing: "Stay away from Rice."

Asher sent a graphologist friend a sample of Chessman's handwriting—a letter written in October 1948, before he was a household name. The graphologist vowed that she would analyze the writing without regard to what she'd read about "the man and his life." The result, a two-page, single-spaced assessment, was sent to Longstreth in December 1954. The analysis opened, "Self-interest is the primary trait in this specimen of handwriting . . . Chessman has a varying ability to absorb emotional experiences as they occur. He feels deeply about the things which affect his ego, and hence is influenced by these long after they have happened, for they are not forgotten. . . . He has a fine memory, mostly for the things that pertain to Caryl Chessman. . . . He is never ruled by his heart."

The graphologist also found him instinctive, intuitive and secretive ("rather than deceptive"), creative without being imaginative, proud, extremely sensitive to criticism, determined, tenacious, stubborn, and domineering. She closed the analysis by saying, "He would steal in order to gratify himself, but I can see no indication of the desire or capability of committing sex crimes."

Despite the low regard in which handwriting analyses were held by psychologists, Asher's friend, it's worth noting, worked for Milton Bunker, the man who in 1915 founded graphoanalysis—the "science" of interpreting handwriting—as well as the International Graphoanalysis Society (IGAS) and *The Graphologist* magazine, both of which still exist today. Asher's friend seemed spot-on with this observation: "He is not generous in his judgements of other human beings. If he were in contact with other people, no doubt he would make enemies through his harshness. . . . Added to this is a degree of jealousy, argumentativeness, and a great deal of resentment—to society, to circumstances, to individuals. . . . It would be difficult to change him, for inwardly he feels superior to most of the human race."

■

CHESSMAN FINALLY GOT to meet Cheryl and David Couturier, Frances's children, on December 28, 1954. Like babes lost in the deep dark woods, the three Couturiers paid a visit to San Quentin prison to see their famous benefactor. To Chessman, they undoubtedly reminded him of all that he had been denied: family, hearth, home, and love. He had earlier asked Asher how difficult it would be, legally, for Frances to change her name to Chessman, though they weren't yet married.

On the last day of the year, he received a letter from Longstreth that closed, "May 1955 bring you everything good and see the end of this terrible suspense that you have lived under for so long."

9

Trial by Ordeal:
1955 and Still Alive

THOUGH HE SELDOM took any legal machinations for granted, Chessman was caught off guard when Judge Louis Goodman denied his writ of habeas corpus. The execution date of January 14, 1955, still stood, and the state had every intention of carrying it out.

On January 6, Chessman wrote Longstreth, "Ouch! Times are tough! . . . I honestly didn't think there was a chance, in view of the Supreme Court's action, he would deny the petition out of hand. But he did." Time being of the essence, Chessman also sent his agent a telegram on the same day, which read:

SAW ROSALIE THIS AFTERNOON RICE AND DUFFY TONIGHT. SITUATION TIGHT BUT NOT HOPELESS. IN VIEW OF DEVELOPMENTS WILL YOU KINDLY WIRE THOUSAND DOLLARS TO BERWYN RICE, CHEDA BUILDING, SAN RAFAEL BEFORE FRIDAY EVENING FROM ROYALTIES. THIS IMPERATIVE. ROSALIE WILL CONFIRM SHORTLY. LETTER FOLLOWS. KEEP EVERY-THING CROSSED.

His new legal strategy was to ask for a stay of execution in order to take his case to the Court of Appeals, though Judge Goodman would, in all likelihood, deny this, too. That would leave, as the only option, approaching the U.S. Supreme Court once again and risk getting the ultimate final decision, which could go against him, leaving him holding an empty hand.

To address the latter possibility, Chessman used the advance money from his second book, *Trial by Ordeal*, to dispatch Asher to Washington. He was being further bled of money by Rice and Jerome Duffy, who were combing statutes and legal proceedings for some precedent that would work in their favor. Rice requested another thousand dollars to stay on the case, and Chessman dutifully sent along the precious funds. All his money woes notwithstanding, Chessman managed to keep one foot in the grave, so to speak, by reserving enough money for the cremation of his body and allocating a portion of his future earnings for Frances and her children.

He wrote Longstreth the sort of letter that was becoming all too familiar—another "possible last letter."

"At best, it appears I'm in for another close call," said Chessman, adding with admirable understatement, "This is something of a bitter pill to swallow. It's a strange experience to be led to believe by the Nation's highest court that, after these long years on Death Row, I finally was to be given an opportunity to prove my claims of a wrongful conviction—and ultimately to prove innocence—and then have a lower court judge summarily slam the door in my face. I offer this as a comment, not a complaint."

Chessman had long been a fatalist, which perhaps explains how he was able to remain sane during his twelve years on Death Row. His stoicism was part of the prison pose, described by Malcolm Braly, a writer who was among San Quentin's general population at the same time: "The emotions of grief and uncertainty were no part of the pose we struggled to maintain with each other. Our ideal convict, like the Hipster, was a zombie of coolness. Hard, smart, utterly certain. This attitude was designed to say: You can herd us like animals and feed us on slops, but you can't break our spirits." Chessman took this attitude to a new level.

"It appears," he told Longstreth, "I shall never fully understand the workings—or machinations?—of Fate."

He again came face to face with the ultimate paradox of his situation: "In one sense, Death Row was the best thing ever to happen to me, for, resist and hate as I might, it brought maturity, many friends and the chance to write and, in some small way, to accomplish something worthwhile with my writing. Naturally, the hard thing to face is not death itself, but its futility . . . just when I find I can be an asset both to myself and others death must intervene. Well, if it comes, so be it. I'm ready again, and thankful at least for what I've been able to do, the friends I've made, the meaningful things these last several months have held. I'm sure you understand."

Longstreth rushed a check for four thousand dollars through Prentice-Hall—part of the advance for *Trial by Ordeal*, completed in manuscript form—to pay off Chessman's legal bills. He tried to maintain a note of calm and optimism, but it was hard when even his mother's Christmas candies, which she'd sent to Chessman, were returned as "not permitted."

"You'd be surprised at some of things I've got crossed!!" he wrote "Or would you? It hurts!!!"

Despite his frustrations with Chessman, expressed in letters to Asher, Longstreth was far more deeply touched by his condemned client's plight than he might have felt comfortable sharing with her, or admitting to himself. Two days later, Longstreth wrote Chessman, "Outside, it has turned dark. Inside—at least inside me—it is a bit dark also. I have not lost hope—far from it; however, one must face reality, difficult as it may be. If this should be my last letter, which it will not be, I should wonder indeed what to say. What mere words are there to express bitter thoughts? A grasp of the hands might say more: a tear in an eye might help communications: a jerky out-breathing might convey something. The cold, typed page is another thing."

Even as Longstreth was writing this letter on January 10, Chessman was granted a stay of execution by Judge Denman "until the order of the United States Court of Appeals for the Ninth Circuit."

Chessman attributed the turn of events to an uncharacteristic premonition that he'd had during a visit from Frances. Thinking it was the last time she'd see him, Frances was distraught. Perhaps to placate her, or himself, Chessman voiced an overpowering feeling that his life would be spared. As he put it, "While we were talking, I did some mental calculation and then I did what could have been a foolish thing. I told her I was certain I wouldn't die this Friday, and somehow I knew I was telling the truth. Nothing mystic, but a cold and hard determination, coupled with hardheaded faith in one federal judge, convinced me I wouldn't be put to death this Friday. . . . I would have given anything to have seen the expression on her face when she learned Judge Denman had granted the stay and the certificate of probable cause to appeal."

While Chessman was "grateful beyond words" for the stay, he felt (correctly, it turned out) that "the hysteria surrounding the case would reach a new high." He also knew that he still faced the gray, grim monotony of Death Row, even as he read in the newspaper about the culmination of a trial involving a Bay Area stevedore who confessed to having had sex with his stepdaughter, cutting her throat, dousing her body with gasoline and igniting it; the judge gave him a life sentence, to be served at San Quentin. As Chessman looked around the row, he was put in mind of Siegfried Sassoon's poems from the frontline trenches during World War I, about "citizens of death's gray land" who drew "no dividend from time's tomorrows."

He was bitter about the prosecutors' intractable efforts to block even a fair review of his case. He still wanted lie detector tests administered to himself and all the police officers who arrested and interrogated him in January 1948.

Art Ryon, a reporter for the *Los Angeles Times*, met with Chessman at the prison. Ryon, who was sympathetic to Chessman's situation, was compelled to ask if spending the rest of his life in prison were really a viable alternative to dying, quickly and efficiently, in the gas chamber.

Chessman, calling it "an unfair question," nonetheless answered, "If I were just going to rot here like a vegetable it would be no alternative. But I have found that I can do something creative, even if I am confined. What good would I be to anyone, including myself, if I were six feet underground?"

Ryon was impressed by Chessman, describing him as "a very very articulate young man" who "talks rapidly, using a ready vocabulary." He noted Chessman's "expressive tapering fingers" and his "wavy . . . well-trimmed and combed" hair. Chessman told him about his pending second book: "I have hoked it up with some emotional and dramatic stuff but essentially it's a studious examination of capital punishment." He also said he'd already completed eight hundred pages of notes for a third book, which he wanted to call *These Places Called Prisons.**

He told Ryon that he'd spent most of the $30,000 or so he'd earned from his first book. He said that much of it had gone to make his father's estate solvent; some went to Frances; and some went to "charities." When asked which charities, Chessman turned mysterious, saying, "I don't want to say. People think you're—well, they think the wrong thing."

Even as he expressed his congratulations over the stay, Longstreth found himself worrying about Chessman's health.

"Now, my friend, Doctor Longstreth advises a rest. Anxious and eager as I am, as many, here, are for #2, and though we realize that there are always legal matters and such that must have immediate attention, none of these things are of much consequence if you wear yourself out completely in their doing. How you've stood up under it all is beyond anyone's comprehension; it's super-human."

Adding to the sense of optimism was the successful launch of the French edition of *Cell 2455, Death Row*, [*Cellule 2455, couloir de la mort*], author's copies of which arrived at San Quentin.

This was followed by a sign of Warden Teets's backlash against his Death Row protégé. Chessman's article, "What I Would Do With My Life," appeared in the March 1955 issue of *Saga*, a copy of which landed on the warden's desk in early February. On February 3, he wrote Longstreth a terse note that betrayed some anger: "We find no record in our files of an authorization for him to submit this article for publishing. Can you advise us how this publication received his story?"

Longstreth tried to put his best face on the *Saga* article in a cordial, cooperative—albeit cautiously worded—letter dated February 7 to Warden Teets.

"I am rather surprised that you have no record of this *Saga* article. . . . As I understand it, Caryl's correspondence had been severely cut

---

* These notes were perhaps confiscated by the prison staff, as they are not among the papers in Joseph Longstreth's possession.

about that time, and he was too busy with other things to give the necessary time to the piece. I suppose there wouldn't be any record in your files of the actual article because Caryl gave verbal answers to the questions to Miss Rosalie Asher and she typed them and forwarded them to us."

This ruse worked, at least on the surface, because no further sign of trouble came from San Quentin over the next two weeks. Nonetheless, Teets must have been simmering with frustration, asking himself, "How gullible do they think I am?" Had he carefully read the *Saga* article, however, the warden would have been pleasantly surprised to learn how much credit Chessman gave him for his own literary redemption.

In addition to Chessman's five-hundred-dollar feature, the March 1955 issue of *Saga* (Vol. 9, No. 6) contained the story of a rescue of lost hikers on Mount McKinley; a chronicle of the life of Doc Holliday, "the West's greatest gunman"; articles with action-packed titles like "Fight to the Finish" and "I Sailed the Atlantic—Almost," as well as *Saga*'s "Girl of the Month" photo spread. Despite the high-titillation factor of these other items, Chessman's was the month's lead article.

The editor's note gave it the proper dramatic coating:

When you read this article, its author may already be dead. Or he may still be waging his dogged battle for life. In 1948, Chessman was convicted of being California's 'Red Light Bandit,' who prowled at night in a police-type car equipped with flashing red spotlight, waylaying young couples in lonely spots, robbing them and inflicting atrocious sex offenses on the terrified women.

Staring at this purple prose from across the article's opening spread was a full-page photograph of Chessman, sporting a pin-striped, wide-lapeled sport jacket, his hands crossed on the table in front of him. He looked as handsome, suave, relaxed, and smiling as Eddie Fisher or Bobby Darin. Readers were no doubt thinking, "How could this be the monster, the sex terrorist, known as Caryl Chessman?"

The article recounts Chessman's ordeal of waiting for a final decision by the U.S. Supreme Court on his stay of execution the previous October. Brilliantly anticipating the sort of audience to which *Saga* played, he used boilerplate expressions like "The chips were down" and "The stakes were high." And he laid his legal travails out as clearly and concisely as one can to an audience with no patience for legalese, peppering it with asides such as "six years, six eternities, of living in the shadow of the gas chamber . . . of watching nearly five dozen men take that last grim walk past my cell."

While Chessman openly admitted to a life of crime—"hijacking bookies and 'knocking over' collectors for a huge bookmaking syndicate in the [Los Angeles] area"—he apologized for not being "southern California's notorious Red Light Bandit."

He took personal, somewhat egotistical inventory. "There stood a battered-faced, 190-pound, 33-year-old six-footer, a guy who had been through one of the damnedest experiences in modern times. He'd spent more years, months and days in Death Row than any doomed man in California's history, waging an obstinate, seemingly impossible battle for survival." He accurately described himself as "a ruthlessly self-disciplined work horse, a voracious reader, reasonably intelligent, something of an enigma. A complex guy, probably, both dreamer and realist, with a violent past."

In response to Fitzgerald's question "Would you get married?" Chessman told the readers of this racy magazine (*Saga* "Girl of the Month" awaited ogling on page 36) "yes," he would. And he singled out Frances, by name, as the object of his affections, replete with a photograph of her sporting a nice dress and solid (not *Saga*esque sultry) heels outside the front gate of San Quentin—the very essence of the faithful, gold-hearted woman waiting for her man outside the death house. She was, Chessman wrote, "A pretty, blue-eyed, brown-haired young woman. . . . So far as we are concerned, the unusual thing is my situation, not the way we feel toward one another."

He shared her background with his new circle of intimate strangers: Frances was born and raised in Maine, was married too young to a navy man, moved with her husband and one child to Glendale after his discharge. In a statement laughable for its paternal earnestness, Chessman writes, "Her husband, however, wasn't ready for marital responsibility." When she was pregnant with their second child, the navy man flew the coop. They divorced. Her only means of income was working as a waitress in a Glendale restaurant where Serl Chessman regularly dined.

Though Chessman referred to his father as "an elderly man," the sad truth was that Serl Chessman was just fifty-seven, an age that even in 1955 could hardly have been considered "elderly." True, broken by poverty, failure and grief over his wife's recent death, Serl possessed the spirit of a defeated, broken-down man. The pert Frances might have rekindled more than merely an aging man's desire to provide lodgings.

Despite Chessman's fantasies about his father—"The children were a wonderful medicine for him . . . he was the only grandpa they had ever known"—Serl's home was not located inside a Dickens novel and he had only just reached middle age. Since no written record of his father's thoughts can be found, one can only guess at Serl's state of mind. Nonetheless, it stands to reason that after years of having to nurse an invalid wife, he may have found someone he could love in Frances.

Could it be that his failing health was the ultimate curse, the final indignity in a life of nearly Kafkaesque misery? Could Caryl, it's worth pondering, have stolen, by proxy, his father's object of desire from him? Could this—her writing of love letters to his son in faraway San Quentin—have been the final blow?

Chessman first met Frances in 1953, when she drove Serl Chessman to San Quentin for a reunion with his son. "She discovered that I was a human being," wrote Chessman, who commenced an impassioned correspondence with her that lasted until his father died of a heart attack.

By that time, they each saw something in the other. Frances's prospects were not great after Serl's death. With his departure, the house was prohibitively expensive to maintain. Without some windfall, she would soon be out on the street with a seven-year-old boy and a four-year-old girl. Chessman wrote that she "shyly offered a love that was selfless and sacrificing and warm. She believed in me and had become convinced I was innocent of the Red Light crimes. If I had a future, she wanted to share it with me. David and Cheryl wanted me to come home and be their daddy."

Chessman admitted to his *Saga* confidants that he and Frances were engaged (he had yet to share this information with Longstreth or Asher). "Moved by her love and loyalty," he told them he had slipped an engagement ring on Frances's finger through the bars of his San Quentin visiting cell, though he admitted Frances had brought the ring along on her visit, having purchased it with money he'd provided. Perhaps in a wave of gratitude during the last hours of an execution date that was ultimately overturned, he made this one gesture of affection, a down payment on a legacy.

Because writing, arguably more than the love of Frances and the "beautiful dream" of their prospective marriage, had provided his redemption, he told *Saga* readers that it would "play a full time part in my productive life." If freed, he wrote, "I would go to New York and learn the writing and publishing business from the ground up at Critics Associated, under the tutelage of Joseph E. Longstreth, the agency's managing editor. Joe Longstreth is my literary agent; he is also one of the finest and most understanding friends I have ever had, a warm, human and gifted man."

Were Chessman to stray from the straight and narrow, he was certain "Joe wouldn't hesitate, if less drastic therapy failed, to bend an encyclopedia over my head."

The most truthful passages in the *Saga* piece were these: "I like to think that my future began the day I started my first book here in Death Row" and "Long after I should have been dead, I wrote myself back to sanity."

He mentioned his plans for a trilogy, with *Trial by Ordeal* to be followed by *These Places Called Prison* [never completed]. And he harbored distant hopes for resurrecting what he called "a gentle satire of Hollywood," the oddly titled and never published *Nov Smoz Kapop?,** and giving it an "overhaul."*

He also mentioned some "whimsical, Runyonesque shorts I turn out when the face of Death Row gets to looking especially dour and

---

* The five-hundred-twenty-two-page, twenty-five-chapter manuscript for *Noz Smoz Kapop?* is in Longstreth's archive.

formidable." These include the unpublished "The Gladiator, the Dis-robing Danseuse and L'Amour" as well as a genuinely funny story called "A Corpse for Christmas." He made reference to an "off-beat, allegorical boxing yarn I just completed," which could have been either a short story called "Young Man With a Right Hand," which is still unpublished, or a novel-length manuscript called *The Kid Was a Killer*, which was not published until 1960. He completed the novel and submitted it to prison officials to be "cleared" for publication, but Teets confiscated it. It took years of efforts by Davis and Asher to get it back.

Chessman expressed understandable ambivalence about the idea that he might be required to, in Fitzgerald's words, "demonstrate his gratitude" if he were freed from prison. This segued into a confession that, though redundant, is one only Chessman could have made:

"Death Row is doubtless the best thing that ever could have hap-pened to me. Since I was 16, it was a race between Death Row and the morgue as to which would claim me first. Luckily for me, Death Row won." Death Row "forced on me the sustained, rugged psychological shock therapy I needed, needed desperately. . . . It took the kill-or-cure medicine of Death Row to give me a future."

■

SEEMINGLY PACIFIED AFTER the *Saga* dustup, Teets allowed Nerin Gun, correspondent for *Swiss Illustrated,* a Zurich-based magazine—Gun lived in New York City—to interview Chessman at the prison. The warden went even further. He allowed Mr. Gun to be accompanied by his wife, Joyce.

Chessman was impressed enough with Gun to agree to part, tem-porarily, with four of his most precious possessions—his only photo-graphs of himself as a child. Chessman sent them to Gun by way of Longstreth, with the note, "All four show me as a moppet. One is with my mother (the writing on the back is hers). Another shows me with my maternal (adoptive) grandfather. Both were taken at Saugatuck, Michigan. The two of me alone were taken in Los Angeles." While Gun's article was, in the scheme of things, a minor addition to the

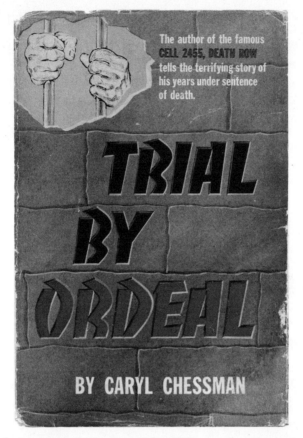

Trial by Ordeal, published by Prentice-Hall in 1955, was Chessman's second book. Though it received warm reviews, the book did not reach the sales figures of *Cell 2455, Death Row. Author's collection*

growing Chessman archive,* its importance was in being available to an audience in Europe, where *Cell 2455, Death Row* was selling briskly. By this time, the book had already been published in French, German, Spanish, Swedish, Finnish, Norwegian, and Dutch editions, and the translation rights had been sold to publishers in Japan and Greece, though no books had yet appeared. Also, serial rights were sold to magazines in Israel, Portugal, Australia and the Philippines.

Handling Chessman's photographs as an intermediary for Gun

---

* Nerin Gun, as a survivor of the Dachau death camp in Poland, had a kindred bond with Chessman. He would go on to write a definitive account of Dachau's liberation (*The Day of the Americans*, 1966), as well as an acclaimed biography of Eva Braun (*Eva Braun: Hitler's Mistress*, 1968).

allowed Longstreth to make the observation that Caryl's penman-ship—always impeccably neat and precise—was "strikingly similar" to his mother's. Indeed, two separate handwriting analysts approached Critics Associated, expressing an interest in writing a profile of their now-famous client, based on what his handwriting said about him. Longstreth turned down both requests, perhaps fearing that it would reveal, for public consumption, some of the less flattering things turned up by Asher's graphologist friend the previous year.

By March 1955, *Cell 2455, Death Row* had earned $23,425.57, $6,750 of that coming from the sale of movie rights to Columbia. Royalties and subsidiary earnings (sales to foreign publishers, whose royalties had not started rolling in) brought another $8,297.13. All legal bills, taxes on foreign sales of his book, payments to "Judy" (Lucy Ann Short) and Serl's debts had been paid to date, bringing Chessman to a break-even point. Though he had no money in the bank, the literary lion of San Quentin was feeling good about his financial prospects.

One sour note was sounded amid all this media frenzy and pub-lishing success. Chessman had long harbored a dream of joining the Mystery Writers of America, Inc., a prestigious group whose advisers included Rex Stout, Kenneth Millar [Ross MacDonald], and Georges Simenon, the prolific French writer who created the famous fictional detective Maigret. On the strength of his book's publication and his past dabblings in the mystery-noir genre, Chessman applied and sent a check for the membership fee. The MWA responded with a letter rejecting his application and returning his check, though they sent it by way of Longstreth. Their justification: "a person convicted of a felony and serving sentence is not eligible for membership, under the terms of our constitution." Longstreth responded to this rejection with a letter to the MWA that angrily refuted the implications of the MWA's pussy-footing missive (e.g., "You will, I am sure, understand that this matter has caused us all considerable questioning among ourselves"). He was much more deeply offended by the rejection than was Chessman, who'd grown accustomed to upturned noses.

At this point, Department of Corrections Director McGee, with Chessman his real target, unilaterally banned publication of all writ-ings by all condemned prisoners. If he couldn't stop Chessman writing, he would put a halt to the publishing of his work. McGee's reasoning: "Invariably books written by condemned men involve their own cases. Consciously or unconsciously they are designed to influence people about the man or the case. Under present law, cases involving the death penalty are never finally adjudicated until the man is executed."

By this twisted logic, McGee was saying that a condemned man was free to write and publish all he wanted after he was dead. This arbitrary stance also did not justify McGee's confiscation, via Teets, of Chessman's purely fictional novel *The Kid Was a Killer*. Nor did it justify the seizure of the completed manuscript of his next book, already scheduled for publication by Prentice-Hall, *Trial by Ordeal*. That is, when Chessman tried to convey property rights to this manuscript to Asher by a written assignment and to hand over the manuscript to her, Teets stepped in. Acting on the orders of State Attorney General Pat Brown, Teets confiscated the manuscript and the assignment documentation. This sour legal note for Chessman had potential legal importance to *all* future prison authors. Brown, who would go on to become Chessman's most deadly nemesis, had expressed displeasure the previous year over Chessman's publication of *Cell 2455, Death Row*. It was his interpretation of the law that the State of California did not allow a prisoner the right to publish and earn royalties—that is, to "own" the manuscript he'd written. Until its ownership was decided, the book's publication was delayed (Longstreth refused to negotiate a final contract with Prentice-Hall until this was ascertained).

Chessman was admirably calm about this battle being waged on his behalf by Asher, with the offered pro bono assistance of famous trial attorney Melvin Belli (no doubt smelling limelight for himself). Belli told the press that this writing ban "smacked of thought police" and admonished Brown and the prison officials: "Even in the Dark Ages prisoners were allowed to have their works published." Brown's assistant, Clarence Linn, added insult to injury by insisting, "The prison people can take the manuscript out in the back yard and burn it if they choose to do so."

Through all this, Chessman was cognizant of the need to play nice and stay on the good side of Warden Teets, his host for the foreseeable future. Perhaps his placid composure was due to the fact that, as it came to light later, he had already arranged to have smuggled out of prison another copy of his *Trial by Ordeal* manuscript. Thus, when Prentice-Hall announced on May 26 that they would publish his book, Brown, Linn, Teets and McGee must have been spitting mad over having been outwitted by the famous sly fox on Death Row.

■

OF MORE IMMEDIATE seriousness, Chessman's request for a new trial was turned down by the Court of Appeals. He was thus required to put aside all literary endeavors and concentrate again on saving his life, now due to be taken from him on July 15, 1955. "While my chances for ultimate survival have been considerably lessened, my spirits haven't dampened," he wrote Longstreth. "I'm still the same guy."

Typical of the legal thicket through which Chessman traveled was this account to Longstreth, from May 19, 1955: "So it has become dates and more dates, by the bunches. This one, as all the others before it, may be 'it' and it may not. I rather doubt that it will. Here's why. The U.S. Supreme Court is scheduled to begin its annual summer vacation May 31 and will not reconvene until the first Monday in October. While we shall prepare and file all the necessary papers as soon as possible, it will be impossible to do so before the last day of this month when the court goes out of session. Hence, if a stay is not granted, we'll be foreclosed from seeking review of the case by the Supreme Court, hardly a tenable situation, especially since that court denied our last petition 'without prejudice' and presumably thought, in doing so, I would be granted hearings in the lower federal courts, which didn't turn out to be the case. The stay will be sought next month, after the certified copies of the papers making up the record are forwarded to the clerk for printing. If granted, we will have 90 days from May 6 in which to prepare and file the petition for writ of certiorari, and it will be the second or third Monday in October before a decision on whether or not to review is announced."

Though death stood over his shoulder, Chessman wished Long-streth a happy thirty-fifth birthday on June 3: "I do sincerely hope that your 35th year is far and away the most gratifying one ever, both personally and professionally. I shall never forget all you've done for me, nor your friendship. . . ."

Chessman pressed on with his attempt to regain ownership of his next manuscript, litigation over which had stalled. He kept his mind active by reading the stream of material Longstreth mailed him. He was impressed with an article by Walter Kerr, "Killing Off the Theatre," and expressed his desire to write "legitimate drama," and by Malcolm Cowley's book *The Literary Situation* (1954). "If I ever get out from under these death sentences and am free to devote myself to creative effort, my first undertaking would be to attempt a play," he insisted to Longstreth, signing off his May 5, 1955, letter to his agent, "It was a year ago yesterday the book was published. Where, where has the time gone?" After reading the letter, Longstreth sent him a copy of *The Devil's Disciple* by George Bernard Shaw.

Soon after this package arrived, Warden Teets forbade any further literature to be mailed to Chessman without his permission. He was, it seems, still smarting from the deception surrounding the *Saga* article, and he was feeling the heat from his boss, Mr. McGee.

■

WHILE CHESSMAN DEALT with his summertime execution date, another California capital case briefly took his off center stage. This was the case of Barbara Graham, thirty-two, the third woman to be killed in San Quentin's gas chamber. Graham was convicted of murdering Mabel Monahan, a sixty-one-year-old widow who was believed to have more than $100,000 in cash stashed in her house. (Graham's lawyer was Al Matthews, who'd worked on Chessman's 1948 case as "legal adviser" and introduced Rosalie Asher to Chessman.) Graham was one of three convicted of Mrs. Monahan's death, which resulted from a beating administered when it was learned that she didn't have the expected motherlode on the premises. The pair convicted along with Graham were hardened criminals named Emmett Perkins and Jack Santo, who were suspects in other murders. It was more than likely that one, or both, of the men did the actual beating of Mrs. Monahan, but both refused to testify at Graham's trial.

While Graham was indisputably a "shady dame," it's hard to imagine a petite woman, as she was, administering a fatal beating to a woman who was not nearly as elderly and frail as the prosecution purported. Nonetheless, Graham was scheduled to die in San Quentin's gas chamber on the same day as Perkins and Santo. She was never actually on Death Row with Chessman (Perkins and Santo were). While awaiting execution, Graham was incarcerated at the state women's prison in Corona. The day before her execution, she was transferred from Corona to San Quentin, and placed in the holding cell around the corner from the gas chamber on the lower floor of North Block.

To circumvent what Teets feared was a potential media circus, Graham was scheduled to die first thing in the morning, and Perkins and Santo would be executed side by side in the afternoon. As planned, all three were executed on June 3, 1955, within a few hundred feet of where Chessman sat in Cell 2455, six floors above the air-locked chamber. Contrary to the Teets's wishes, however, the day was a media circus after all.

On the morning of her execution, the attractive Graham ate a hot fudge sundae. She then applied crimson lipstick as she was prepared for the procession of "thirteen steps" between the holding cell and the gas chamber, a stroll now commonly known as "dead man walking." Bernice Freeman, the *San Francisco Chronicle* correspondent who had befriended Chessman, described the scene she witnessed: "Right to the end, she was dressed as if for a luncheon in one of San Francisco's swanky hotels. She wore a well-fitted champagne wool suit with matching covered buttons. Her brown high-heeded pumps were a fashionable contrast. Small gold pendants fell from her ears, and on her left hand was Hank Graham's gold wedding band."

However, at a little after her scheduled departure time of 9:05 A.M., the authorities called to postpone the execution until the California Supreme Court could hear a new argument from her attorney.

This legal plea was rejected. An hour later, as the prison guard was taping the stethoscope over Graham's heart, a second call came in, causing a further legal delay in her inevitable rendezvous with death. The psychological torment of this ordeal was nearly intolerable. At one point, according to eyewitnesses, Graham asked tearfully, "Oh God, why do they torture me?"

By 11:30, Graham was finally readied for her date with death. She asked for the sleeping mask to be placed over her eyes, the only person in San Quentin history to opt for the mask. Her reasoning for wearing it, as she bitterly told the executioner, was, "I don't want to watch those sons of bitches watch me die!" She was led into the chamber by two priests—one on each arm—strapped into the chair, a tube attached to the stethoscope on her chest, so that the doctor could examine it from outside the chamber. She was told that the easiest way to go was to wait until she heard the cyanide pellets plop into the vats of sulfuric acid, then to count to ten and inhale deeply. As the priests and prison captain left her, Graham's last words were, "Good people are always so sure they're right." Santo and Perkins died in the same chamber at 2:30 that afternoon, grinning, chatting amiably and glowering at the witnesses, with Santo's last words being, "Don't you fellows do anything I wouldn't do."

Similarities between Graham's and Chessman's stories are unavoidable. Hers, like his, was made into a Hollywood movie (and a best-selling book), *I Want To Live!*; the 1958 film was directed by Robert Wise. Susan Hayward was nominated for an Academy Award for her performance as Graham in the film, and Alan Alda was nominated for an Emmy Award in 1977 for his made-for-TV portrayal of Chessman in *Kill Me If You Can*. (Neither won.) In hopes of attracting a young audience, Wise included a scene with Graham/Hayward snapping her fingers to a hepcat combo that featured the jazz icons Gerry Mulligan, Shelly Manne, Red Mitchell, Art Farmer, and Bud Shank.

Other than this brief side trip into popular culture, the film depicts Graham's life and death accurately, due largely to the reliable reportage of Ed Montgomery, from which Graham's film biography was fashioned. Montgomery, a *Los Angeles Times* writer, was sympathetic to Graham. He felt she'd been given bad legal advice and railroaded through the system. He also knew Chessman and was sympathetic to his plight.

Like Chessman, Graham had some literary gifts (poetry, mostly) and a relatively high IQ (114). Unfortunately, she—also like Chessman—

had a long and detailed criminal record, making it doubly easy for society at large to hate her (triply easy, in her case, as a "loose" woman). The conservative newspapers in Los Angeles, where her crime (like Chessman's) took place were unanimous in loud, sustained condemnation. Not to overstate the case, the 1950s were simply a time when any vestige of appearing out of step, or overly gifted and intelligent was deemed suspicious.

As great as Hayward's performance was, the real star of *I Want to Live!* was the set designer, Victor A. Gangelin. Because cinematographers were not allowed to record visual images of an actual gas chamber, the filmmakers re-created the scene at a Hollywood backlot with almost perversely accurate detail. Hired consultants simulated with eerie accuracy the experience of an execution by lethal gas. Moviegoers saw the testing of the equipment, the synchronizing of the time on the wall clock via Western Union, the agonizing silence of the "airlock test"—opening and closing the chamber's door by means of a miniature steering wheel-like lock—and the actual outlay of death-dealing chemicals. The cyanide pellets, like little eggs or mothballs, were placed inside cheesecloth bags that were then dipped like crab nets into buckets of acid on the side of Graham's death chair. And the last several minutes of *I Want to Live!* are exactly as eyewitnesses had depicted Graham's last minutes in their written accounts of her execution. The result is as close to an actual execution by gas as has ever been filmed. Indeed, there was very little "Hollywood" in the film. As such, it was considered "shocking" at the time. Nearly half a century later, it's still capable of eliciting a visceral response in a viewer, shuddering revulsion coupled with heartstopping tension.

For anyone wanting to understand what awaited Chessman at the end of his twelve-year struggle for a retrial, a viewing of *I Want to Live!* is mandatory.

■

ANOTHER STRUGGLE, ONE with wide repercussions, had ensued over Chessman's future literary endeavors. As required by the Rules and Regulations of the California Department of Corrections, Chessman had submitted his next book-length manuscript (published as *Trial by Ordeal*) in mid-1955 to the "Warden of Care and Treatment" to be approved for publication. No manuscript that contained libelous or pornographic material, was critical of the prison policies or law enforcement in general, glorified criminal behavior or drug use, would be approved.

Chessman had to clear these formidable hurdles, as he had with *Cell 2455, Death Row*, but he also had to clear an unforeseen hurdle: McGee's arbitrarily issued ban on all writing for publication by condemned prisoners. Until the issue of whether Chessman could make a living, or reap profits from, his published work, Warden Teets forbade him to work on anything but legal matters. Over the next two years, until the publication of *The Face of Justice*, Chessman played a cat-and-mouse game with prison staff over whether he possessed the right to write for a living. The special privileges he had been given, such as the use of an adjoining cell as an office, were suddenly determined—or reinterpreted—by Warden Teets as only for work related to his legal proceedings. *Trial by Ordeal* was eventually cleared for publication but prison officials had also seized a copy of the novel *The Kid Was a Killer* and sat on it for the next four years. It was finally published, as a paperback original, by Gold Medal in April 1960, a month before Chessman died.

■

Bound copies of Chessman's second book, *Trial by Ordeal*, were available to the media at the end of June, and the book was published officially on July 11, four days before Chessman's scheduled date with the gas chamber. Before the irony of that situation could be played out, Chessman was, granted a stay of execution by U.S. Supreme Court Justice Tom Clark on July 5. Justice William O. Douglas normally handled requests for stays of execution from the Western states, but because he was on his summer vacation, Clark was covering for him. It was a fortuitous substitution, since Douglas was not favorably disposed toward Chessman (in fact, he issued Chessman's final death knell in 1959). Although Chessman and his advisers had no way of knowing this—given the hundreds of legal maneuvers to be employed in the ensuing years—Chessman would not face another execution date until October 24, 1959.

Interest in the book, meanwhile, was explosive. Much of this was sparked more by curiosity than by controversy—was this guy a one-book wonder?—but it also reflected a growing concern among the general public about the capricious and subjective nature of the death penalty. The sympathy for Chessman's case in particular, which had begun with *Cell 2455, Death Row*, was now widespread. Foreign publishers were lining up for translations. *Pageant* magazine ran part of the book in their September 1955 issue, and many newspapers solicited excerpts via Critics Associated.

How had the manuscript for *Trial by Ordeal,* a copy of which had been confiscated from Asher, gotten to Prentice-Hall? Among Chessman's unpublished papers, he recreated the scene. "When I read that Clarence Linn had said the manuscript could be destroyed, I had a talk with another convict," wrote Chessman. "He may or may not have been a condemned man. I must protect the men involved at all costs." In this memo, Chessman said "five or six persons" were involved "in the complex scheme" and that it was "strictly a convict deal." He had given a carbon copy of *Trial by Ordeal* to one convict in "three separate installments" and it left Death Row "in some trash." Further elaborating, Chessman wrote, "Convict No. 1 turned it over to Convict No. 2 who was told to hide it within the prison" while Chessman awaited the legal decision on his original manuscript. For weeks, the carbon copy was "hidden in one or another of the prison shops, and it changed hands frequently." Eventually, one of the prisoners in this scheme was able to get it out of the prison. As to how this was done, all Chessman would say was "A minimum security prisoner could have left it lying around and by prearrangement an outsider could have picked it up and mailed it." None of this could have been accomplished, however, without a sympathetic San Quentin guard or two agreeing to look the other way.

In mid-June, Longstreth wrote Bernice Freeman, thanking her for yet another sympathetic *Chronicle* profile (published that week, headlined "Chessman Frets") and to tell her that "advance encomiums for the book are already piling up, and I think the reviews are going to be fantastic! This is a real publishing coup, and Caryl Chessman, if he must, can die knowing that despite everything he has left the world a better place."

While interest in the book was high, the publisher's interest in its author's fate was low. Even before the books were released and distributed, Prentice-Hall got off on the wrong foot. On June 22, Asher received a letter from the editor, Monroe Stearns. The book's dedication, he said, had to be altered. The letter did not ask for a revision from the author, or suggest changes; it simply told Asher—not Chessman—that it had been altered. Rather, it had been killed. Chessman had originally singled out a number of friends whose help over the years had sustained him. Stearns said that "we felt it in bad taste; in fact, so fulsomely expressed as to tend to bring ridicule upon the author." Even more high-handedly, Stearns said, "Mr. Chessman, and for that matter, no other author, should assume that he may dedicate a book to whomever he wishes."

The altered dedication read: "To My father, in memoriam, and My friends."

Asher, Chessman, and Longstreth should have known at that point that the time was ripe to part company with Prentice-Hall. To their everlasting regret, however, they continued their association.

■

DESPITE THE CHANGE in his fortunes, the stresses of Death Row took their toll on Chessman's health. In July 1955, he began vomiting blood and collapsed in his cell. He was examined by a prison doctor, who diagnosed a bleeding ulcer and prescribed acid-neutralizing pills and another medicine that acted on the ulcer itself. Unfortunately, one side effect of the latter was blindness. Chessman decided to gradually lower the dose of these pills on his own, while giving up smoking, drinking coffee, and even exercise for the foreseeable future, while also downing gallons of milk. Gradually, through his own regimen of self-medication, the pain of his ulcer subsided, though it remained a chronic problem, like his asthma, until his death.

Two months later, Chessman was officially reprimanded, along with two other Death Row prisoners (Bart Caritativo and Robert Pierce), for concealing "forbidden property" in their cells. The properties in question were book manuscripts. All of this material was impounded and held by prison authorities. For Chessman, this meant that the prison now held the manuscripts of two books (the last to be published in his lifetime), and he had good reason to believe he'd never see them again.

In October, Chessman's legal fortunes improved with the arrival George T. Davis. Davis had read all the stories about Chessman, as well as both of his books. He'd followed Chessman's case closely and was fascinated by the man himself. He confessed to wanting to meet the enigma in Cell 2455, and he got a chance when Chessman contacted him, out of the blue. The defendant, it turns out, was just as curious about Davis, a man the famed World War II correspondent Ernie Pyle had once predicted would be the state's governor.

Only weeks before meeting Davis, Chessman had fired his previous attorneys, Rice and Duffy, who'd picked his bank account apart like twin worms devouring a carcass. It was not an amicable parting, with Chessman flying into a table-pounding rage at a San Quentin conference ("Goddamn you, you _____," Chessman was quoted by an Associated Press reporter. "When are you going to get out here when you can spend more than 20 minutes with me?").

Rice told the same reporter that, now that he and Duffy had won his stays, Chessman wanted to "hog the whole show."

At the time, Davis, based in San Francisco (at 98 Post Street) was the best-known defense attorney in the Bay Area, perhaps in the nation. He'd attracted national, if not international, notoriety for his successful defense of the alleged Communist labor leader Tom Mooney. Mooney had been wrongfully imprisoned in San Quentin for twenty-four years for his alleged role in a bombing at a "war preparedness" parade. Davis managed to wrest Mooney's case out of California's hands and place it in the lap of the U.S. Supreme Court;

Mooney was eventually freed. Davis was hoping to employ the same strategy with Chessman.

"California was determined never to give Chessman a retrial," Davis told me in a 2003 interview. "Our only hope was to get the case into a federal court."

Davis's past legal cases had not escaped the notice of the FBI. Among his sins, found in documents housed in Chessman's FBI file, were such innocuous doings as having been the Northern California campaign manager for Harry S Truman's 1948 presidential campaign, and the vice president of the National Lawyers Guild in 1937. In one particularly eerie letter from J. Edgar Hoover to then Vice President Richard M. Nixon in February 1960, the FBI's power-mad director warned the red-baiting Nixon that Davis "has a long record of association with questionable activities in California" and was "an adventurous opportunist."

Though officially Davis became Chessman's co-counsel of record, with Asher, he was the new lead dog from their very first meeting at San Quentin in October 1955. Chessman instantly took a shine to him, for his informal manner, sense of humor, and strength of ego. He had met someone as hardheaded as himself, though it's amazing Davis wasn't put off in their initial meeting by Chessman's high-handed remark about this case being "the most important challenge" of his already estimable career. Davis saw the case as a chance for him to bring capital punishment into mainstream discussion. A bitter foe of the death penalty, Davis was at that point in his career taking only capital punishment cases. He saw the Chessman case as his "chance to drop a bomb on capital punishment."

"We say taking a life is wrong and then set the example," said Davis in 2003. "No case is good enough to justify capital punishment. The Chessman case, of course, turned out to be the epitome of anti–capital punishment. My ability to propagandize, my ability to speak against that subject was opened up in a way that had never been done before. . . . I won't say it's the first time that the world was ever thinking about it, but I'll say that because of the media and because of the nature of that case, I think that probably more people thought about capital punishment at that time than had ever thought about capital punishment before."

Despite his enormous reputation (and fee), Davis was willing to take the case even though his client was, at the moment, flat broke. Their agreement was unorthodox. Davis would take the case, he said, if Chessman would write a book about it, the royalties from which would pay his initial ten-thousand-dollar fee. The reason for this arrangement, besides the dire shape of Chessman's finances, was that Davis also wanted to test the legality of the writing ban placed on his client by Teets under orders from the Department of Corrections. Chessman would not be able to pay him without an income from writing; Davis could argue that they were denying his client due process and, indirectly, denying the lawyer the right to be paid.

Or, as Chessman dramatically put it in the book that was born of this deal (*The Face of Justice*), "Put squarely in issue would be my constitutional right to the effective assistance of counsel, as well as those fundamental constitutional guarantees prohibiting the suppression of the citizen's right to speak freely and not have his property seized arbitrarily by the state at its whim."

■

THE REST OF 1955 comprised a series of confusing legal maneuvers that had one simple motive: to get Chessman a new trial by proving that his original trial had not been a fair one. To do this, the tireless Davis worked the trial transcript angle. That is, in January 1948, halfway through Chessman's Los Angeles trial, the court reporter Ernest Perry had died. In a bind, Judge Fricke followed the advice of the prosecuting attorney, J. Miller Leavy, hiring the latter's brother-in-law, Stanley Fraser, to complete the transcript of the shorthand record. Without a valid and complete transcript of a trial, the mandatory appeal of a death sentence had no legal basis. Fraser's transcription was a travesty. Fraser was, by the testimony of many people, a hapless and hopeless alcoholic.

Here, then, are the steps that Davis took until the end of the year:

- October 17, 1955: The U.S. Supreme Court was prodded to remand the case to U.S. District Judge Louis E. Goodman, who had originally denied Chessman's writ of habeas corpus on March 17, 1950, for a hearing on the disputed transcript.
- December 8, 1955: Davis filed a motion to transfer the defendant to the custody of the U.S. Marshal (e.g., to become, temporarily, a federal rather than a state prisoner).
- December 22, 1955: Judge Goodman denied this motion.
- December 29, 1955: Davis filed a motion to disqualify Judge Goodman on the basis of "personal bias or prejudice" against Chessman.
- December 30, 1955: Conveniently, Judge Goodman got to rule on the motion against himself. And, predictably, he refused to disqualify himself. At this same hearing, the judge suggested that Chessman be sent to Alcatraz (Federal) Penitentiary in order to better facilitate his legal battle. As a state prisoner, he would be treated as a temporary resident but given more space in which to work on his legal preparations.

The absurdity of the legal tangle carried on into the new year, reaching something of a peak, or nadir, on January 4, 1956, when Goodman reversed himself and said that Chessman was going to stay put at San Quentin, making it seem as though it was Chessman who had petulantly turned down this offer. Actually, Davis made a phone call to the warden at Alcatraz who knew nothing about this matter, despite Goodman's insistence that he did. All he could offer, to accommodate Chessman, was a primitive cell in solitary confinement and a "conference facility" (one tiny room) far from Chessman's cell. Davis and Chessman didn't turn down this offer. It was not a serious offer to begin with. Judge Goodman should have, by all standards of legality and decency, been pulled from this case on the spot.

On top of all that, Chessman was so broke by the end of the year—or, as he put it, "we ran out of nickels to place in the judicial slot"—that he had no choice but to file an affidavit to proceed in forma pauperis.

He was, like a character in a Dickens novel, now a pauper.

10

"King of Death Row"
(1956–1957)

THE YEAR **1956** began with another series of mind-numbing legal maneuvers intended to get out of the intractable Judge Goodman's striking range. They didn't work. Judge Goodman would, like Death with his scythe, follow Chessman all the way into the gas chamber in May 1960, and even beyond—giving him one more hour to live, a stay that was, like one final insult, denied him by a misdialed phone number.

The last best hope for avoiding Goodman's long arms rested with the transcripts from Chessman's original 1948 trial. Most of these seventeen hundred pages were completed by Stanley Fraser when the original court reporter, Ernest R. Perry, died before the trial proceedings were over. (Perry had transcribed the first 646 pages.) Davis was planning to accuse Fraser and Leavy of conspiring to produce a fraudulent transcript. Perry's shorthand notes, he argued, were "undecipherable to a large degree" and that Fraser was "incompetent" to transcribe the notes.

The notes' indecipherability were attested to by Molly Kalin, a Pitman shorthand adviser Chessman secured as an expert witness.*

The charge of incompetence against Fraser was more compelling. Between 1940 and 1951, Fraser had been arrested ten times for alcohol-related crimes (drunken driving, public intoxication, public nuisance,

---

* Pitman shorthand, devised by Sir Isaac Pitman (1813–1897), was second to Gregg shorthand in popularity.

Federal District Judge Louis E. Goodman's 1957 ruling on the trial transcripts was the one Chessman could never shake, though he would fight it for three more years. Though Goodman greased the skids to the gas chamber, he did give Chessman one final hour-long stay of execution on May 2, 1960—a stay that was never consummated. *Author's collection*

domestic disputes, etc.). The owner of a liquor store next door to Fraser's house testified that he frequented her establishment in the years 1947 to 1949 and was often already drunk when he came in to buy liquor (though by admitting this she risked losing her license for selling it to him). He once entered her store "with his trousers open and urinated on the floor." She also noticed that many times during the period when he was working on the transcripts, she saw him pull up in his car in front of his house and then fall into the gutter getting out of the car, "spilling papers from his brief case." Neighbors testified that he repeatedly battered his wife when drunk; one police report noted that Fraser was arrested for drunkenness while in the act of working on his trial notes. His family doctor testified that Fraser was a "chronic alcoholic"; his dermatologist testified that he treated him for a skin condition from 1947 to 1949 that was known to afflict "winos." Finally, in August 1953, Fraser tried to commit suicide with an overdose of Ipersol barbiturates and was committed to Camarillo State Hospital—the same "snake pit" where Mary Alice Meza resided.

Drunkenness, noise complaints, driving infractions, arrests, police reports, wife-beating, incapacitation—the predictable trajectory of a "bottoming out" drunk. Any judge looking at this dispassionately and fairly would declare Fraser unfit to be employed by the court, that he would only compound his own personal problems by jeopardizing Chessman, who was fighting, soberly and with every legal means at his disposal, for his life. Not Judge Fricke in 1948 and not Judge Goodman in 1956. Not when the defendant was the monster and sex terrorist Caryl Chessman.

■

REGARDLESS OF THE strength of their case vis-à-vis Fraser's incompetence, Team Chessman was handicapped going into the courtroom. Chessman was so broke he was now a pauper, and he also faced a "dreadful tax mess" by April 15. He didn't even have money for his own copy of the original transcript; Davis and Asher had to rely on a "daily record" of the proceedings prepared by the court reporter, a paltry substitute. Nonetheless, Goodman ruled that Chessman had adequate time and provisions, and he ordered that the transcript hearings proceed as scheduled, January 16–25, 1956.

On a slightly comical note, prison officials refused to allow Asher to buy new clothes for Chessman to wear during his week-long appearances in the San Francisco courtroom. Instead, they supplied two sets of clothes for Cell 2455's famous resident: one gray suit and one sport jacket and pair of slacks. The suit, at the recipient's request, was tailored to fit. Asher confessed to being relieved by this turn of events. "At least he's satisfied and we save money," she told Longstreth.

From January 17 to January 25, 1956, Davis worked tirelessly and brilliantly in Judge Goodman's courtroom to undermine the notion that these transcripts were valid and fair. His arguments and the testimony and exhibits he presented filled one thousand pages of transcript. The highlight, or lowlight, of the proceedings was the three-day grilling of Fraser, who was shown to be unsurpassably incompetent at his job. When asked to read the shorthand notes on the witness stand, he was unable to do so, though he'd been hired to transcribe them. The state's expert witness, who had praised Fraser's work, also proved incompetent to read from the shorthand notes. And yet, Davis was denied permission to present his own expert witnesses, including Kalin, to refute the prosecution's claims that the transcript was valid.

So it went. It was another deck stacked against Chessman.

Judge Fricke took the stand, at Davis's request. Fricke, who'd sentenced twice as many men to death as any other judge in California history, wasn't going to let this fish avoid the skillet. Under Davis's grilling, Fricke admitted that Leavy had hidden his family relationship with Fraser from him and that, against his orders, had hidden the transcripts from 1948 to 1954 in Fraser's brother's garage. Fricke said he was unaware that Fraser had worked outside court with prosecution witnesses to reconstruct testimony to their liking, an unethical if not illegal act. Nor was Fricke aware of Fraser's lengthy arrest record for alcohol-related infractions. None of these things apparently mattered. The outcome was a fait accompli.

Chessman sent Longstreth a handwritten note "from the Cage," in which he said he "feared the decision will go against us at this point." He anticipated having to appeal Goodman's pending decision. "While it will mean more months on Death Row under difficult conditions, I'm positive I'll come out OK in the end, for these hearings really opened up crucial doors," said Chessman, feeling more optimistic than anyone else on his team. "They say it gets tougher and then tougher than that. Believe me, 'they' are right, but what the hell, I guess that's an occupational hazard of being a condemned man."

Chessman's prognostication proved correct. On January 31, Goodman tendered his ruling: no fraud was attached to the transcripts. Not content to stick the dagger in, the judge gave it a twist. He said not "a scintilla of verity" existed in Chessman's petition. This was a clear enough sign of his prejudice toward the defendant, and surely grounds for his disqualification to rule further in the case. From a purely mathematical standpoint, four thousand errors and nineteen hundred "emendations" in a trial transcript qualifies, at the very least, as a "scintilla." After it was over, Davis and Asher sat with Chessman, drinking coffee and discussing strategy. Chessman likened it to "awaking from a nightmare," and Davis—shell-shocked at the rarity of losing a case—told his client, "I think I'm just beginning to appreciate fully what you have had to face for seven and a half years."

In *The Face of Justice*, Chessman painted a somber picture: "We discussed immediate, practical aspects of the case, and then it was time for me to go. We knew what my return to Death Row could mean: that I would never leave the prison again—alive."

Asher summed up the ruling to Longstreth: "We never had a chance." She confessed to being worried about Chessman; he hadn't performed on the witness stand as well as she and Davis had hoped, failing to get some of the relevant statements they'd prepared on the record. "George expressed it by saying that when Caryl was testifying, he got the feeling that he just wasn't there," she wrote. "Being out of San Quentin and off the Row, in San Francisco and visiting George and me without bars between us had a tremendous impact on Caryl—he said that having to go back was like going back to a new death sentence."

Then, Asher wrote something curious: "We had some lengthy conversations which I'll not commit to writing but which disturb me in the sense that I'm uncomfortably aware of a dreadful non-legal responsibility—a situation I can't feel I created, but which exists, and one which is exceedingly difficult to cope with. Oh, God, Joe!"

Longstreth guessed that the "non-legal responsibility" was "not of your making," as he told his friend. "Never let emotions of any kind stand in the way of your responsibilities to yourself. You come first with you, and unless you do, you're of relatively little value to others. It is the strong person who is needed by others, and when that strength of character is overcome, then the use to the 'other people' ceases to exist and the 'ex' strong person finds himself on the outside, overcome and cast aside."

Her response indicated that it had more to do with ethics than emotions. Apparently, Chessman had enlisted her in some subterfuge related perhaps to his love life and she had to decide "whether a lie is ever justified by circumstances. . . . I have been able to forestall certain steps which I cannot condone."

Later that year, quashing any rumors that there might be a romantic bond between her and Chessman, Asher wrote Longstreth about an article by Frank Olson, to appear in the *Harvard Law Review*, in which he quotes Chessman "complimenting" Asher. "I'm not exactly enthusiastic about seeing in print that quote from Caryl. Of course we know (don't we?) that Caryl is motivated only by gratitude for my having helped him through the years; but I'm afraid more cynical readers might have another interpretation."

Longstreth told Asher that he felt "impending doom about the future." He felt that *"this* was Caryl's chance" and he either choked or deliberately blew it. *"This* was 'put up or shut up' as far as Caryl is concerned. I'm sick at heart if he flubbed it . . . but one must try to face facts," he wrote. "Any pleas for more hearings will fall on totally deaf ears until and unless Caryl names the real Red-Light Bandit."

Even though Asher didn't share Longstreth's pessimism, it proved warranted. Though the rest of the year was consumed with an effort to appeal Judge Goodman's rancorous ruling, that appeal was rejected by the U.S. Court of Appeals on October 18, 1956.

Throughout that ten-month period, Chessman still clung to the dream of getting a new hearing in a courtroom in Los Angeles, which would lead to a new trial and his exoneration of the Red Light Bandit crimes. Interviews had been conducted with former jurors, former criminal associates of Chessman, and witnesses to Fraser's ongoing Crazy Guggenheim act, and had been transcribed. Chessman still wouldn't name the Red Light Bandit, but he gave Davis and Asher some leads to pursue that he said would prove his alibi for the Red Light Bandit crime "conclusively."

Meanwhile, on television, radio, and suburban hi-fi consoles, a new American cultural hero emerged, as did a new musical genre. Elvis Presley's first hit single, "Heartbreak Hotel," was released on January 27, 1956, and topped the charts by April. This was followed, like a torrent of blows to America's midsection, by his "I Want You, I Need You, I Love You," "Don't Be Cruel," "My Baby Left Me,"

"Hound Dog," "Love Me Tender," and "Any Way You Want Me." By July 1956, he had earned $6 million in royalties. On September 9 and again on October 28, 1956, Presley performed on *The Ed Sullivan Show*, performances seen by fifty-two million viewers, or one in three Americans (and almost every American under, say, age twenty-one). In all, for the year, Presley's singles held the top spot on the charts for twenty-five weeks. Rock 'n' roll was here to stay.

And so was Chessman. Throughout the summer of 1956, the "Save Chessman" movement gained steam, and *Trial by Ordeal* received friendly notices, though its sales did not match the numbers of *Cell 2455, Death Row*. Chessman seemed to think the fall-off was due to Prentice-Hall's editing, though his complaints were not nearly as vociferous as they had been before. Longstreth blamed Prentice-Hall's publicists for not taking advantage of all the "free publicity" related to Chessman's case. ("This is Prentice-Hall's fault, pure and simple. . . . P-H and Stearns have been scared of this book from the very beginning.") Their "fear" of *Trial by Ordeal* undermined that book's success. The book sales should have been "quadrupled." He was "annoyed" enough with Prentice-Hall to suggest that Chessman approach another publisher for his next book.

More likely, though, *Trial by Ordeal* was the inevitable sophomore slump. Flagging sales may have also reflected some weariness with his case on the part of the reading public. Or perhaps they were absorbed in other matters, like the reelection campaign of President Dwight Eisenhower. His opponent, again, was Adlai Stevenson, the former governor of Illinois, whom he had trounced in the 1952 election. Eisenhower had suffered a heart attack in 1955, and Stevenson had gained a growing measure of support from younger voters who responded to his call for a "New Politics" movement. Even so, he could still not live down the "egghead" nickname that Ike's running mate, Richard Nixon, had stuck on him in the 1952 campaign. Nixon, who himself was a highly intelligent man, was simply pandering to the anti-intellectual impulse that had fueled his earlier HUAC witch hunt, launched his career, and, of course, devalued civic discourse for the decade. Despite making gains, Stevenson still lost the election to the likeable if fragile Ike, who seemed more focused on his golf game than on the nation's business.

Despite the less than stellar sales for *Trial by Ordeal*, Chessman labored on and the offers poured in. On January 12, 1957, German publishers were making pitches for a third book, *The Kid Was a Killer*, the manuscript for which still awaited clearance from prison censors. That same week, Swedish and Finnish editions of *Trial by Ordeal* arrived in Longstreth's office; the Japanese edition of *Cell 2455, Death Row* was due out in August, and the British edition of *Trial by Ordeal* was due out in October. The *Harvard Law School Record*, a weekly publication for alumni and students, was working on a special feature about Chessman, due out in April. Chessman was now a sufficiently reliable seller that Prentice-Hall immediately responded to Longstreth's late January request for an "emergency advance" of four thousand dollars on future earnings from his two books.

Not everything on the writing front went smoothly.

"We lost another round in our determined efforts to pry *The Kid Was a Killer* loose from San Quentin," Chessman told Longstreth. "This, too, has been a tough fight, but I always was a slow starter. I'm really warmed up and primed to fight both for my life and the right to write. George and Rosalie have been doing a damned good job every inch of the way and both will keep punching until I leave S.Q. behind for good. Meanwhile, I'm holding up in good shape. I even think I have that ulcer just about whipped."

The writing "ban" temporarily declared against Chessman the previous year was now, partly through bureaucratic entropy, allowed to continue. Adding to Chessman's difficulties of earning money with his writing, the prison had begun severely restricting his mail, both in and out. Chessman was permitted to write to a limited number of people; he had to cut Longstreth from his list, henceforth communicating with his agent via Asher. (This explains a large gap in correspondence with Longstreth that began to pick up again in late 1957.) Packages of foreign editions of his books were returned to publishers; magazine subscriptions (*Writers Digest, Author and Journalist*) were refused delivery, and even requests for autographs were now denied. Letters of some importance and urgency were lost, particularly frustrating when Chessman was trying to unsnag his IRS problems. Even the length of visits by Asher and Davis were reduced by half an hour. The prison also instituted a more stringent frisking process. Visitors were required to walk through an "inspectoscope," which used X-rays to search for concealed metal objects. Asher and Davis objected to this; Davis even consulted his physician about the medical effects. (Davis lived to be ninety-five, dying in February 2006.)

One brief flicker of good legal news arrived on February 26, when Judge Denman of the Ninth Circuit's Court of Appeals issued a certificate of probable cause to appeal Goodman's ruling. This was only a preliminary to the appeal itself, but it did buy a few more months' respite.

More ominously, while Chessman was in San Francisco in January, San Quentin officials ruled that there would be no more "special unlocks" on Death Row. This meant Chessman would not get special permission to use the extra cell where he had previously done "legal research." In his absence, they also cleared his legal cell and dumped its contents inside Cell 2455. Upon his return, he found that he now barely had room to turn around in his cage. Thus, for twenty-two hours a day, Chessman sat nearly paralyzed by the crush of his possessions inside this cramped space. Rather than succumb to despair, he told Asher that he would spend the time learning shorthand by the Pitman method, in order to break the code of the transcripts.

Chessman's loss of a legal cell prompted a story in the *San Francisco Chronicle*. When asked why his cell was taken from him, Teets said that it was needed to house a new resident: Burton Abbott. Abbott's murder/kidnap trial created a media storm that at least temporarily blew away Red Light Bandit references, although echoes of the Red Light Bandit trial could be found in Abbott's case. The prosecution sought the death penalty under the Little Lindbergh Law, Penal Code Section 209 (kidnapping with bodily harm), that had gotten Chessman his two trips to the gas chamber. There was one major difference: Abbott's alleged victim was killed in the process.

Abbott was an accounting student at the University of California at Berkeley when he was convicted of abducting and murdering

fourteen-year-old Stephanie Bryan in May 1955. Her body was found
two months later in the hills outside Berkeley; some of her possessions
were found in Abbott's basement in Alameda. Abbott also owned a
cabin in the woods near where Bryan's body was discovered. The girl
had been sexually assaulted before her murder, which, according to
the prosecutor, provided Abbott with "perhaps the greatest sexual
satisfaction of his life."

Besides sharing a cell on Death Row, Chessman and Abbott
eventually shared an attorney as well: George T. Davis. Abbott hired
Davis after all his appeals were lost and his plea for clemency from
Governor Knight turned down. His execution date set for March 15,
1957, Abbott settled into Chessman's old law cell in March 1956. His
presence within shouting distance of Chessman was a conundrum.
On the one hand, there was someone else on Death Row more reviled
by the public than Chessman; on the other, his kidnap/murder of an
innocent teenager had disturbing echoes of the attack on Mary Alice
Meza, now institutionalized at Camarillo State Hospital. Also, that
the two condemned men shared an attorney equated them somehow
in the minds of the newspaper-buying public.

■

THE WRITING OF *The Face of Justice* was a monumental struggle
against prison restrictions, requiring physical stamina, emotional
strength, sharp wits and courage. It may not have been Chessman's
best book, but its writing could very well have been his most remarkable accomplishment. Seldom has an American author faced such
odds against seeing a book in print. While the word "gulag" may be
too fraught with contemporary political overtones to be entirely fair,
Chessman's effort to write his book against the wishes of the state
recalls the struggles faced by Alexandr Solzhenitsyn during his years
in a Siberian gulag as the guest of the Soviet Union.

Chessman's writing regimen for *The Face of Justice* was as follows:
During the day he paced his cell, mentally outlining the book. At
night, from eight in the evening until four in the morning, he wrote
by longhand with a ballpoint pen on a legal pad. From four to six, he

copied all he'd written in shorthand, sprinkling each page with legal jargon, signs and symbols (e.g., "Sup Ct No. 117963"). After transcribing his work into shorthand, he tore up the longhand pages and flushed each one down the toilet ("With practice I soon could tear up paper without making a sound.") At six, as the new day on the row clattered into action, he stopped work. After two or three hours of sleep, he was sometimes yanked from his cot so that his cell could be searched top to bottom for contraband writing. Under such conditions, hiding a manuscript in the usual places was futile. Thus, Chessman hid his manuscript in plain sight, among his legal papers. With the camouflage of legal jargon and indecipherable squiggles of Pitman shorthand, the guards didn't suspect these "legal papers" were actually the manuscript of *The Face of Justice.*

From the time of his morning coffee and milk at eight in the morning, until six in the evening, when he settled back into his writing routine, Chessman was "a scrupulous observer of all rules and regulations." He wrote letters in the morning, and at eleven thirty was given a two-hour recreation period during which he played cards, chess, or Ping-Pong in the corridor outside his cell, or simply paced and talked to other Row residents. A nap in mid-afternoon brought his sleep total to anywhere from four to six hours out of twenty-four. From six to eight in the evening, he typed up his shorthand notes. Each day his goal was to complete three usable manuscript pages (which meant ten to fifteen original longhand pages). Because for years he'd used only a typewriter to write, the grueling longhand sessions turned his fingers into "arthritic-looking talons."

Adding to his obstacles, guards had increased the number and frequency of nightly patrols, after a Death Row resident, a religious fanatic suffering from paranoiac delusions, tried to commit suicide. The suicide attempt left the man half paralyzed. He told prison doctors that he had been slashed by a razor blade and knew there was a conspiracy by the other Row residents to kill him. He said this conspiracy, which included the Protestant and Catholic chaplains, was led by Chessman. He had become fixated with Chessman because the famous author had forcefully rejected his proselytizing efforts. "Since I was the most notorious prisoner on Death Row, and an agnostic at that, he inevitably saw himself as God's chosen instrument to reach me," Chessman wrote. "It was his holy duty to convert me, to wrest my black soul from Satan's clutches."

Though the man was clearly insane, the prison guards went into overdrive in their efforts to shake down the cells looking for the razor blades he said his attackers had used. Chessman "sweated it out."

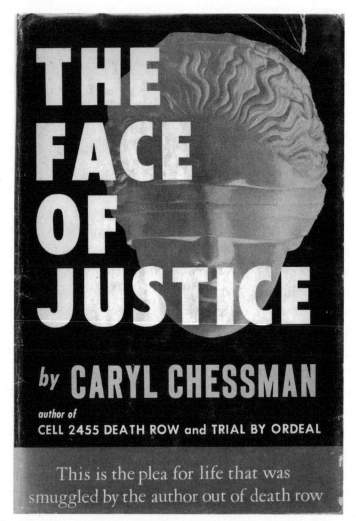

The Face of Justice, published by Prentice-Hall in 1957, was the book the manuscript for which was allegedly smuggled out of prison. *Author's collection*

■

OTHER SAN QUENTIN inmates felt the wind from Chessman's case, especially those harboring dreams of writerly success. There were hundreds of these ink-stained wretches, including Malcolm Braly. After the clampdown on Chessman led to his smuggling his manuscript out of the prison, Braly recalled how the supervisor of education for the general population sent the "goon squad to shake down the ed building and take anything that looked like it was becoming a book. They raised a net-full—sonnets, sagas, a clutch of the dirty stories we wrote and rented out for a pack [of cigarettes] a night, and two novels under contract to be published [including his own, which was eventually published as *Felony Tank*]. It was a twenty-four-hour shitstorm."

Before this turn of events, San Quentin's regular prisoners were not entirely sold on Chessman's efforts. As Braly put it, "We felt he was a showboat, who might still live if he could find the sense to compromise." But one of Braly's friends who was in charge of running the film projector weekly on Death Row assured him, "That man is all guts." After 1956, the thousands of prisoners—despite what any of the wardens or editorialists subsequently wrote about this time—were in Chessman's corner.

Braly wrote, "A federal judge dismissed this suit contemptuously [Chessman's writing and smuggling out *The Face of Justice*]. And it seems to me this miserable attempt to silence a condemned man and hustle him to his death is the sorriest abuse of free speech since the notorious Sedition Act, and I hope this memento mori has the power to bring some reflex of shame to anyone who lent his hand to it."

■

CHESSMAN DID NOT need to see the movie *I Want to Live!* or read firsthand accounts of Barbara Graham's last hours to be aware of the physical and psychological impact of execution by gas. Over the twelve years he was housed at San Quentin, he witnessed the fear and trembling and, in some cases, lapses into madness of his fellow Death Row inmates in the face of their impending executions. One of the most dramatic and widely reported involved Robert O. Pierce, a twenty-seven-year-old black man convicted of the 1953 murder of an Oakland cab driver and condemned to die at San Quentin.

Pierce's fate was perversely intertwined with Chessman's in March 1956, when William Hendricks wrote a "tell all" article in the *San Francisco Examiner* about San Quentin's Death Row. His primary source of information was the unreliable Pierce, who insisted that Chessman was "the king of Death Row" and that "a clique of Chessman hero worshippers help the convicted Los Angeles rapist run the show."

Hendricks was all too eager to print Pierce's description of Chessman verbatim, without double-checking with any other Row residents. No other Row residents, of course, would talk to Hendricks because of his sensationalized reporting. Hendricks was well known at San Quentin, having sniffed around the place for years as the news and gossip columnist for the *Examiner*'s Marin County bureau. Loud-dressing and loud-mouthed, Hendricks was best known for a column that appeared in the Sunday *Examiner*. In 1949—five years before Chessman was a world-famous author and cause célèbre—Hendricks devoted his column to the newly arrived "Red Light Bandit," describing Caryl Chessman as a "hunching. . . . absolutely ruthless bruiser" with a "genius" I.Q. He also noted that Chessman sported "pink ribbons" around his ankles, a backhanded way of reinforcing the image of this controversial inmate as a sexual deviant.

The "pink ribbons" were actually heavy-duty red string that prison officials issued to inmates who asked for it, the only means by which they could keep their institutional slippers securely on their feet. Hendricks knew this, of course, but chose to characterize it differently in his article, and it was this sort of first impression of Chessman that stayed with Bay Area readers over the years. After that column, Chessman refused to speak to Hendricks, and admitted to fantasizing how, if he ever agreed to another interview with him, he'd do his talking "nonverbally." Most of the other prisoners on the Row followed

Chessman's example. This did not stay Hendricks's hearsay-fueled verbal assaults on Chessman, however, especially after 1954, when *Cell 2455, Death Row* was published to great reviews and large sales.

For a period of about a year, Pierce was Hendricks's main source of information inside Death Row. Yet Pierce was arguably insane. Though an associate warden was quoted in one of Hendricks's columns saying Pierce was "no better or no worse" than the average prisoner on Death Row, the truth was more dramatic. As Chessman put it, "Pierce was about as 'average' as a mangy, hydrophobic dog might be said to be representative of the canine species." He was "short, squat and steatopygic," and in Chessman's informed estimation, "an aggressive psychopathic personality" who should be in a mental institution. "The worst place for him—and for the prison—is prison."

Even prison officials seemed to agree, as they'd penned Pierce up in a special section at one end of Death Row dubbed the "Iron Curtain." The irony: Pierce was so dangerous he had to be cordoned off from other killers. Prior to his incarceration at San Quentin, Pierce had done a long stretch in a mental institution and, after his release, joined the army, from which he was discharged for "bad conduct." Back in his hometown of Oakland, Pierce fell in with a gang of petty criminals. To impress them, he embarked on a brief crime spree that ended when, in the course of a pathetically bungled robbery in which he netted seven dollars, he beat Charles Rose, an Oakland cabdriver, to death. For this murder, he was sentenced to die along with one of his partners, Smith E. Jordan.

In San Quentin, Pierce desperately wanted to impress others with his toughness. Of younger inmates like Pierce, Chessman said, "To them being a 'con' is a badge of merit. They pattern themselves after the weird villains that emerge from the fertile but uninformed brains of Hollywood and television scriptwriters. . . . [Their] ranting is calculated to prove to you they are 'solid' (right guys) . . . they use 'benny' (Benzedrine), 'tea' (marijuana), and 'junk' or 'H' (dope). . . . They are prodigious but inept liars."

Underneath the bluster, though, was a terrified man who hero-worshipped Chessman, wrote the journalist Bernice Freeman. She interviewed Pierce (at his written request) soon after he arrived at San

Quentin in 1954. About that encounter, she wrote, "I found myself face to face with a convict so terrified that he couldn't sit still. Pierce's large dark eyes rolled, huge drops of perspiration poured down his face, and his hands moved crazily about like weeds in the wind. When he tried to talk, his lips formed words which didn't come out. I've never seen a more frightened man."

The only way she could calm him down was to talk about Chessman, whom Pierce called "wonderful. . . . He's always doing something—making legal papers for himself and helping the other guys who don't have no money for lawyers."

When she asked Pierce why he'd wanted to talk to her, he made a desperate plea with her to use her "influence" to save his life. Then, when she denied having any influence, he began twitching uncontrollably and begging her, babbling and blubbering to such an extent that Freeman later noted, "I had never seen anyone act like this before, and while I felt sorry for the man, I wanted to get away from him as quickly as possible."

Over the next two years, Pierce's hyena-like laughter could be heard throughout the Row at all hours, as could the beating of his fists and palms on his table and cell bars. All the other prisoners loathed Pierce. He, in turn, came to develop and nurse a personal animus toward Chessman, presumably because he, like Freeman, would not use his "influence" to save Pierce's life.

When Pierce met Hendricks, he saw an opportunity to extract some revenge on Chessman and to plead his own increasingly desperate cause. By the time Pierce gave Hendricks the "King of Death Row" scoop, he and Jordan were eighteen days shy of an execution date and awaiting word on appeals.*

Hendricks dutifully reported all of Pierce's wildest conjectures, one of which was splashed in Page A1 headlines of the March 21, 1956, *Examiner*: CHESSMAN DEATH ROW KING, CONVICT AVERS.

Jordan's and Pierce's appeals were turned down. Whatever loose strands and pink ribbons had been holding Pierce together came

---

* The "King of Death Row" sobriquet oddly echoes the "King of Rock 'n' Roll" honorific that had been bestowed on Elvis Presley by 1957. Perhaps it was an instance of cultural subliminal suggestion.

unwound. He went stark raving mad, destroying all the plumbing in his cell and screaming himself hoarse, night after night. Eventually, he had to be placed in a soundproof isolation cell. The day before his and Jordan's joint execution, the two doomed men were transferred from Death Row to the holding cell in the prison basement, just "thirteen steps" from the gas chamber. They were set to die, side by side, on April 6, 1956.

The headline of the April 7 *Examiner* news story (not written by Hendricks) told the grisly tale: SHRIEKING KILLER DIES IN DOUBLE EXECUTION.

The story reported: "Despite security measures rarely matched in the prison's history of 355 executions, the 27-year-old Pierce, a bull of a man, failed only by a margin of inches in an effort to commit suicide, fifty seconds before he was to enter the gas chamber. He slashed at the jugular vein in his throat with a two by three inches piece of broken mirror but missed the artery he had sought."

"I'm innocent," he screamed. "I swear to God I'm innocent!"

"The witnesses saw five guards," the *Examiner* continued, "like hunters struggling with a trapped gorilla, carrying Pierce into the gas chamber. A guard held each of the prisoner's hands and feet, and the fifth guard held an arm lock on his head, while steering the writhing Pierce and the other guards into the gas chamber. They dumped him into a chair. The astonished witnesses, unaware of the suicide attempt, saw a large red patch spread across Pierce's back."

It was ten A.M., and all the while the blood-spattered Catholic chaplain had been administering last rites to Pierce.

Pierce's right wrist and then his left were strapped down.

"But now he had kicked his feet free. Somehow, in the battle, a guard managed to drape a blue jacket over Pierce's back, presumably to hide the spreading red patch that now covered the entire back of his white shirt. The red patch seeped through the jacket."

Then he stopped fighting long enough for Jordan to be ushered into the chamber. Jordan grinned and winked absurdly at the witnesses, then gave them a V sign. Putting up no struggle whatsoever, he was quietly strapped into the other chair within arm's reach of Pierce. The door was shut, and the two of them sat there waiting for the cyanide pellets to be dropped:

"Suddenly, like a roped tiger trapped by jungle natives, the 27-year-old Pierce made a supreme effort to burst the bonds that held him. His massive shoulders rose high in the chair (and his mutilated throat was revealed). For seconds, it seemed he would make it. But his bonds held."

"God, you're a dirty son of a bitch!" he screamed.

At 10:06, the cyanide pellets were dropped into the sulfuric acid vats.

"Pierce looked at the fumes, curious."

"God, you dirty . . ." he bellowed.

From the other side of the gas chamber came a prayer. It was the prison chaplain.

"Father have mercy on them . . . have mercy on them."

"You dirty . . ." gasped Pierce, and then his head jerked back as the fumes hit him.

"Have mercy on them . . . Father forgive them for they know not what they do," came the voice of the priest.

Warden Teets called it "the most difficult execution we ever had."

For Chessman, the deaths of Pierce and Jordan were numbers 66 and 67 to have taken place while he was on Death Row. He made a statistical notation of their deaths in his papers, then turned back to the work he had to do on another appeal of his own death sentences. Whenever he needed inspiration, he said he "took out a *memento mori* I kept for the purpose—an inspiring, full color picture of the gas chamber downstairs—took a good look at it, and, with the help of my demon, went back to work."

■

THE FRUSTRATIONS OF the writing ban, the legal setbacks, and Frances's possible eviction for not paying rent finally got to Chessman. In late May 1956, there was a "beef" on the Row involving three other inmates; Chessman was cited for having "encouraged" it. He admitted to Teets that he "blew my top" at the "victim," who had been gloating about having been given a new trial, rubbing it in Chessman's face. This instigated the outburst from Chessman, to which Teets "intimated he would have acted much the same under the circumstances." The other prisoner had been a troublesome presence on the Row and afterward was removed altogether from the rest of the unit. Nonetheless, for his outburst, Chessman was sent to solitary confinement—eight days in the "hole."

Davis and Asher both felt that prison officials were looking for any pretext to be rid of Chessman, and this was a convenient way to create the impression that he didn't "deserve" to have his *The Kid Was a Killer* manuscript returned or his writing ban lifted. Asher was not in any position to be sympathetic toward Frances. She'd loaned the future "Mrs. Chessman" enough money to pay the rent, only to learn that Frances had recently been spotted in Las Vegas.

"I've given up all efforts to understand/analyze Frances," Asher wrote Longstreth. "My hands are washed."

Longstreth's take on Frances was only marginally more generous: "She's just a gal who's squeezing everything she can out of anyone she can," he said. "Oh, it's not deliberate or malicious—just a part of her being. She's more to be pitied than blamed."

■

ON JULY 5, 1956, Chessman received the sort of letter that every author dreads: *Trial by Ordeal* was being remaindered due to lagging sales. Prentice-Hall wanted to know if Chessman was interested in purchasing any of the 4,842 copies in stock for sixty-six cents each. Asher was more upset over the news than Chessman, who pondered a way to buy all the copies from Prentice-Hall. Asher wrote Longstreth, "While I wasn't looking forward to any fortune, I did have hopes of a relatively substantial check in September."

By August, Chessman had decided he wanted to purchase fifty copies of the remaindered edition of *Trial by Ordeal*. At that point, however, Prentice-Hall had reconsidered its decision to remainder the book, pending a story on Chessman in the October issue of *True*, a men's adventure magazine not unlike *Saga*. The article, by Wenzell Brown, turned out to be, in Longstreth's estimation, "a pack of lies." "The facts are dramatic and exciting and controversial enough without distorting them and linking Caryl, however vaguely and indirectly, to 'Bugsy' Siegel and all the other awful names that were literally dragged in, willy nilly, without rhyme or reason . . ."

In October, Bernice Freeman was in New York to pick up a journalism award and appear on television. She visited Longstreth during her trip East. Though she had just recovered from a lengthy illness that had required hospitalization, she told Longstreth she was worried about Asher's health. In addition to years of heavy smoking, Asher, at Chessman's beck and call, appeared to be working herself into the hospital.

A livid Longstreth wrote Asher, "When Caryl wants you, don't just jump. He, like everyone else, despite his plight, must learn that other people have feelings and responsibilities and he doesn't always come first."

But Asher was not having any of it. Fresh from a visit to Chessman on November 15, she wrote Alan Honour, "He is in amazingly good shape and still keeping busy." On December 10, she wrote Longstreth that Chessman was "in a good, good mood (how he thrives on work!) and we had an interesting and, somehow, touching, conversation."

Through Asher, the indomitable Chessman told Longstreth to "be ready for a surprise" by February or March, one that "doesn't involve 'kids.'" This was to be the manuscript of *The Face of Justice*, the smuggling of which led to a contentious lawsuit that pulled his agent, his lawyers and even Bernice Freeman into its net.

Meanwhile, Critics Associated was on a roll. Honour's book for young adults, *Cave of Riches: The Story of the Dead Sea Scrolls* (Whittlesey House) had been published and was selling briskly, as was a new children's book by Longstreth, *Little Big Feather* (Abelard), selected by the *New York Times* as one of year's ten best.

After all the worry about the health of Asher, Freeman, and Chessman, Longstreth himself ended up in the hospital for the final week of 1956.

■

CHESSMAN SPENT VALENTINE'S Day 1957 in solitary confinement. A shakedown of his cell had unearthed a copy of the manuscript of *The Face of Justice*. One copy of this manuscript had already been smuggled out of the prison and was undergoing editing at Prentice-Hall for its impending publication. As a result of that smuggling, Chessman was still being banned from writing for publication. Teets, worked into a lather by the ruse, angrily told the press, "He's accumulated the damnedest collection of transcripts and legal papers that you could imagine." In addition to the manuscript, guards found a letter Chessman had written, but not mailed, to Governor Goodwin Knight, allegedly gloating over "how he beat us."

Denied proper writing material while in "the hole," Chessman wrote a petition to Superior Court Judge Thomas Keating on eleven sheets of toilet paper, asking the court to force the prison authorities to return all the legal material they'd confiscated along with his manuscript. The judge denied the petition, but the gesture, reported in the two San Francisco daily newspapers, won Chessman some public sympathy. Toilet paper!

■

BURTON ABBOTT'S EXECUTION was a surreal foreshadowing of events in Chessman's life. Abbott was scheduled to die in San Quentin's gas chamber on March 15, 1957; his appeals were lost and his pitch for clemency denied. Davis's only hope was for a stay of execution from Governor Knight in order to appeal a point of constitutional law with the State Supreme Court. On the morning of the execution, Knight was at the Naval Air Station in Alameda waiting to board an aircraft carrier for a cruise around the bay. The only way for Davis to reach him was to go on live television, in hopes that Knight, or one of his staff, was watching. Alerted to Davis's appearance, Knight called the lawyer at 10:00 A.M., offering a one-hour stay. At 10:40, after the State Supreme Court turned down Davis's appeal, he asked Knight for another one-hour delay to make a similar case in a federal court. At 11:00, Knight agreed to the stay.

However, due to a faulty connection in the ship-to-shore communication, the phone call from Knight's clemency secretary (Joseph Babich) didn't reach the prison until 11:20 A.M. The cyanide pellets had been dropped into the vat of sulfuric acid at 11:18. Prison officials said it was too late to stop the procedure without endangering the lives of the witnesses and staff (which was untrue). Abbott died, perhaps needlessly. The next day, an editorial in the *San Francisco News* asked, "Does anybody in San Francisco feel good about what happened when grown men played a gruesome game of Beat the Clock, with Burton Abbott's life the prize?"

The papers didn't ask the same question on the morning of May 3, 1960.

■

WARDEN HARLEY O. Teets was found dead of a heart attack in the living room of his home at San Quentin on September 2, 1957. He was only fifty years old. Whether the stress of executions like Abbott's and Pierce's had taken their toll or whether Chessman's ongoing drama had worn him down is not known, as he left no written record or memoir. Teets had recently confided to friends that each execution he arranged "takes something out of me." The biggest controversy during his six-year tenure was an investigation into charges of brutality in the psychiatric department, a probe sparked by articles in the *San Francisco Chronicle* by Pierre Salinger (later President John F. Kennedy's press secretary). Teets was replaced by Fred R. Dickson. A longtime veteran of the prison system, Dickson had served as an associate warden at San Quentin under Duffy, then on the staff at Chino, then as a prison coordinator for the state of Washington.

"If Duffy looked like a professor of economics and Teets a successful small-town dentist," wrote Kenneth Lamott, "Fred R. Dickson looks every inch the part. A large, beefy man, he talks like an old-line police captain, but he has done graduate work at Chicago and Berkeley."

■

DESPITE SETBACKS AND struggles, 1957 was an exceptionally good year, legally, for Chessman, the culmination of his having Davis in his corner.

On April 8, 1957, the U.S. Supreme Court granted a writ of certiorari, meaning that Goodman's ruling on the transcript was temporarily put on hold, pending a full hearing in state court. On August 29, 1957, Davis and Asher won an even larger victory when the California Supreme Court vacated its judgments of 1950 and 1951, reversing denials and dismissals and rescinding its upholding of Chessman's original convictions. These decisions cleared the field, so to speak, so that Chessman would get an open and fair hearing on the transcripts.

Those proceedings began to take shape on September 10, when Chessman was transferred from San Quentin to Los Angeles County Jail, where he resided until late February 1958. He was accompanied by a five-foot-long pine box that resembled a small coffin. Inside the box were the legal papers and documents that Chessman was given permission to use for his defense. This made for an interesting news photograph that ran widely in newspapers. In it, the neatly dressed and well-groomed Chessman—gray suit, light blue tie—walked with his hands cuffed in front. Beside him, like a royal retinue, two armed Los Angeles police officers huffed and puffed, each holding one end of the coffin. As the men grappled with their heavy load, Chessman spoke with reporters. He was confident about getting a new trial, he said, but he never took anything for granted.

"I don't know that I ever held any hope," he said. "It's like being a soldier on the battlefield. You never know for certain when you may be hit."

Without the money he'd earned from his writing, he told the reporters, "I would have been dead long ago. Justice comes expensive in the state of California."

Chessman's official address for those six months was Tank 10-A-2 Rear, Los Angeles County Jail, 306 North Broadway, Los Angeles 12, California. The hearings themselves, on the "adequacy of the transcript," would take place in November, and Chessman had two months of hard work ahead of him.

One foil with whom Chessman would no longer have to contend was Judge Fricke, who on October 17, 1957, asked to be excused from presiding over the disputed transcript hearing. Before stepping down, Judge Fricke took one last opportunity to insist that he was not "prejudiced" against Chessman, as the famous defendant had long claimed. Nonetheless, the two nemeses faced each other one last time in court on December 19, 1957. This time, the tables were turned; Chessman questioned Fricke on the witness stand during his "resettlement of transcript" hearing. The irony could not have been more profound. Here was the tired old man who had, in a fit of judicial pique, upheld Chessman's two death sentences in 1948. And here was that same young man, now a world-famous author, still fighting for his life ten years later. Despite Fricke's animus toward Chessman, surely the old judge must have secretly admired his doggedness, his refusal to go gently into that good night. Yet, Fricke never softened toward Chessman, at least not in public.

When Chessman pressed him on the competence of Fraser to transcribe the court proceedings, Fricke maintained his stern demeanor, even lecturing Chessman, "The prosecution did not select Fraser. I did. . . . You probably don't know me as some of these other gentlemen do. I don't know of anyone who could tell me what to do."

Another thing that Chessman probably didn't know about Judge Fricke was the fragility of his health. He had twice been hospitalized in the previous nine months for treatment of throat cancer. One month after this final court appearance, Fricke died at St. Vincent's Hospital in Los Angeles, after an operation.

■

CHESSMAN WAS CONFIDENT that Fricke's replacement, Judge Herbert V. Walker, was a less tempestuous or prejudiced arbiter. This was confirmed when Judge Walker ordered that Chessman's team be provided, at no charge, a complete set of photostatic copies of the original shorthand notes of the 1948 trial. Judge Walker appointed

Davis to act as Chessman's chief counsel, his "reasonable fees" to be paid by the county.

During the negotiations of these fees, the details of the Davis-Chessman alliance came to light. Davis admitted to reporters that Chessman had originally paid him "about ten thousand dollars" cash and had assigned the royalties from *The Face of Justice* to the lawyer, "until an additional forty thousand dollars had been received." This revelation—that the famous, polo-playing lawyer was getting fifty thousand dollars—may have harmed Chessman's efforts. For one thing, it engendered bitterness in Asher and Longstreth, both of whom had gone for months without being paid and tendered many services pro bono. For another, it handed ammunition to the anti-Chessman forces, which began circulating the idea that the sex terrorist was swimming in money and bilking the system by enriching himself on the state's dime. With figures like fifty thousand dollars tossed around the newspapers, it was hard to convince the public of the truth that Chessman was, in fact, broke.

When Chessman brought the matter of his insolvency to Judge Walker's attention, a woman in the gallery stood up and said, "I'll give five hundred dollars for that lawyer (pointing at George Davis)," to which Davis jokingly replied, "I'll accept that offer!" (He later requested this be stricken from the record.)

Judge Walker didn't need convincing. He broke with precedent and allowed Chessman the use of a private room on the ninth floor of the Hall of Justice. This was Chessman's office for the next two months, a haven where he could do legal research. During this time, Chessman's confidence soared. This optimism was etched on his face in a photograph taken in his Hall of Justice office. He is seated at a large wooden library table, on which are scattered piles of books and manila folders. His entire being seems focused on the book in his hands, his face exuding an almost boyish wonder, perhaps even amusement. The sentiment is not shared by the two Los Angeles County sheriffs assigned to guard him. One guard with a buzz cut stands ramrod stiff at the door while the other sits across the table from Chessman, warily sizing up the famous prisoner.

Chessman was confident he would prevail on all fronts: He would get a new trial, *The Face of Justice* would sell well and his novel, *The*

Kid Was a Killer, would be published soon. Part of this confidence was the result of being away from San Quentin's crushing Death Row for several months.

On September 22, 1957, finally free to write Longstreth after the ban implemented by Teets was lifted, Chessman sent a newsy letter asking his agent if he'd "write and confirm to me that, in the capacity of literary agent, you will handle the book [*The Kid Was a Killer*] and will be free to do so without delay." He was seeking a court order for the manuscripts of *The Kid Was A Killer* to be turned over to him. (San Quentin officials had confiscated his only copies; unlike *The Face of Justice,* he wasn't able to fashion a secret version.) He would then assign them to "Mrs. Frances Couturier," who would arrange for its publication—a prospect that did not please Longstreth and sent warning flags up all over Asher's home front. Chessman's affidavit stated that the novel was "a valuable literary property; that it promptly will find a publisher; that I already have had movie and television offers on it; that it will be handled by a reputable and established literary agent, Joseph E. Longstreth." The efforts encountered an additional hurdle—the manuscripts were in one county (Marin); his present legal procedures were in another (Los Angeles).

In the interim since their last exchange of correspondence, Longstreth had also relocated. He was now living in Richmond, Indiana, having moved home to take care of his ailing parents. He'd also relocated Critics Associated there, and the home he and Honour set up in Richmond was their first real one. They both loved the peace and tranquility of the rural setting, as well as "breaking the mental routine with physical work." Chessman now jokingly referred to them as "farmers."

Chessman's confidence was buoyed by the September 1957 release of *The Face of Justice,* though once again he had doubts about Prentice-Hall's ability to promote it properly. Already by late September, he was complaining to Longstreth that the book appeared to be "a mystery to local news media," that "the Face has remained faceless" and suggested that the agent "give P-H a gentle push."

Longstreth felt the "vibrant spirit" in Chessman and was glad for it, saying it was "like old times" and suggesting that he and Alan

were fixing up a guest room just in case Chessman's plans for freedom bore fruit ("We really look forward to your knock on our door").
Chessman responded appreciatively to the offer and said the "vibrant
spirit" was more like "vibrating spirit"—"I feel like a guy hooked up
to one of those belted vibrator reducing machines." His most pressing
business was to locate two competent Pitman shorthand writers to
assist with his case, their fees to be paid by the court.

The insertion of Frances in the literary business may have been
necessitated by the serious illness of Asher. Her condition, Chessman
insisted, had been "aggravated by harassment" of the Marin County
District Attorney, who was prosecuting a case involving the smuggling
from prison of the manuscript of *The Face of Justice*. But the truth is
that Asher's health woes were likely brought on by the cumulative
effect of nearly a decade of stress related to Chessman, and her own
chain-smoking. Despite her illness, she flew to Los Angeles to visit
Chessman at the Los Angeles County Jail. She was dressed to the nines;
according to the *Los Angeles Times*, she wore "a black suit, large pearl
earrings and a black cloche hat." After the visit, Asher told reporters,
"If and when I am sufficiently recovered, I want and intend to join in
Mr. Chessman's defense. I am utterly convinced that the cause is a
meritorious one." She also said that Chessman had told her who the
"real" Red Light Bandit was but she'd promised to keep it secret. Her
illness coincided with Davis's shoulder injury incurred from a fall off
a horse while playing polo. As soon as he'd recovered, by mid-October,
Davis raced to Los Angeles, only to be felled by the flu, necessitating a
doctor's care in San Francisco. Davis asked to be relieved of his job as
chief counsel and returned the wages paid to him by the county.

Despite the lack of consistent legal aid, Chessman was able to locate
another qualified Pitman shorthand writer, Frank Hanna. Hanna had more
than fifty years of experience covering hearings in the U.S. House and
Senate, as well as having served as Official Reporter for the United States in
international cases in London, The Hague and in Canada. His other paid Pitman expert, Molly Kalin, finally got to testify in court. Kalin said that court
reporters were "wont to ignore shading of certain symbols while taking fast
notes." She insisted that Perry ignored "the shape as well as the shading and
the side on which reporters make loops or circles," which would "give an

entirely different connotation" to the transcribed testimony. She compared a random page of Perry's shorthand notes with Fraser's transcription of them and insisted that the notes—allowing for possible ignored shadings, shapes, loops, and circles—could have an entirely different meaning. Kalin's testimony contradicted the state's Pitman shorthand expert, seventy-four-year-old Bessie Lill, who had called the tainted transcript "reasonable and fair."

Chessman also enlisted the aid of the American Civil Liberties Union, which was supplying its Los Angeles representative, Abraham Lincoln "Al" Wirin. Wirin's task was to initiate court action to free the manuscript of *The Kid Was a Killer*, the potential funds from which Chessman desperately needed for what he called a "life-or-death hearing."

Chessman was lucky to get Wirin, a battle-hardened, Harvard-educated civil libertarian who, when hired by the ACLU in 1931, was the nation's first civil rights attorney. His presence was double-edged. On the one hand, Wirin added prestige and experience and helped make the case a national story; on the other, he was a diehard lefty who bore the scars of labor battles. In the 1950s, the words "labor" and "left-wing" and "activist" meant "Commie pinko." Indeed, one finds several notices in Chessman's FBI file about Wirin's previous legal experience, the obvious inference being that he was a "Communist" or a "subversive." Wirin, whose health was failing, was ably assisted by another ACLU lawyer, Paul Posner, who was greatly impressed with Chessman. In fact, Chessman was given permission by the judge to hire Paul Posner as his new chief adviser, with fees to be paid by the county, to augment the help provided by Wirin.

Meanwhile, in another part of the country, President Eisenhower had to send federal troops into Little Rock, Arkansas, to put down what amounted to a rebellion by the state government and the city's residents. These right-thinking, red-blooded Commie-hating people did not want to allow nine black children inside Central High School, as per the 1954 U.S. Supreme Court's *Brown v. Board of Education* ruling against "separate but equal" public education facilities. But on September 24, 1957, the attempts to buttress segregationist policy were put down by armed force.

In Los Angeles, Frances Couturier was able to visit her erstwhile fiancé for an hour, and the reporters noted that Chessman "brightened perceptibly" and "smiled often when he looked at her." Though in earlier days she had been somewhat titillated by the idea of press coverage of their presumed romance, she was now trying to conceal her face and identity. Her relationship with the press was now aloof, at times hostile. When pressed about marriage plans with Chessman, she angrily retorted, "Our relationship isn't a question of love. This is all on a legal basis, understand . . . strictly business."

She allowed that she felt a debt to Chessman and his father, for having taken her and her children in after her husband deserted them. "They opened the door for me, and I'm keeping at least one door open for Caryl. This is simply a gesture of friendly help. Society is cruel and I know it. I'm just offering Caryl friendly help and doing what I can for him."

Despite the cooling of their relationship, Frances was now in charge of relaying Chessman's messages to Longstreth by phone ("I have given her instructions that she is to repeat my message verbatim to avoid any confusion").

■

ON THANKSGIVING DAY, Chessman was served something better than turkey and trimmings—a ruling by Judge Evans that the manuscripts for *The Kid Was a Killer* be released, with one being sent to Longstreth by airmail. The other manuscript was delivered to the courtroom by San Quentin officers, one of whom handed the parcel to the prisoner personally. Chessman was elated. He was already basking in using his "local contacts" to secure a lucrative movie deal, and he foresaw that "judiciously chopped," the novel would be a hot property as an eight-part serial, as well as a simultaneous paperback and hardcover edition. He was excitedly anticipating Longstreth's reaction to the book. Chessman said, "I tried to produce a novel with guts and dramatic impact—and at the same time to say something."

Chessman's report to Longstreth on the transcript hearing was also positive. Fraser had been forced to submit to two days of cross-examination by Chessman, in the process admitting that he "often added words to the transcript as well as often failed to transcribe symbols" from Perry's notes.

Longstreth responded to Chessman's manuscript on December 12, 1957. His was the sort of letter every writer dreams of receiving from an agent. It is reproduced almost in its entirety here:

> *The Kid Was a Killer* arrived late yesterday, and with a roaring fire in the fireplace (it's zero outside), a scotch and soda and the dogs at my feet, I opened to page one. I must be frank with you, as usual, and say that I was worried. I had everything crossed that I could find, for I was slightly afraid of this novel. I was afraid it would be overdone. I was afraid it wouldn't even be a novel.
>
> Caryl, I think it is absolutely tremendous! It is compelling beyond description, and with phrases throughout which ring clear and crisp, sharp, without equivocation, and which smack of true creativity. Your characterizations are extremely well handled, with Maura emerging, in a very short space of time—indeed she doesn't last that long in the book!—as a very warm and believable character.
>
> Despite everything, our sympathies remain with the Kid, and we hurt with and for him, searching desperately for the love which he cannot find, and having found, loses. He's real, he's believable, he's—the Kid. Even the minor characters are acutely drawn. Borden is excellent, and The Angel could almost steal the book if you hadn't handled him so skillfully. Janey, despite the fact that she disappears for such a lengthy time, which is generally considered not comme il faut for a novel, remains very much a part of the picture and comes across as a person to be remembered, indicative of qualities which were inherent in the family initially.
>
> I could go on and on. Obviously, I like *The Kid Was a Killer* and am genuinely enthusiastic about it. I could say, with some justification, that the book is contrived, which

any novel is, almost by definition. And yet it has a reality which overcomes any such defect.

Longstreth felt that serialization possibilities were "tremendous," as were the film potentials ("just don't promise anything . . . but whip up whatever enthusiasm you can and put them onto us."). He thought they should approach *Playboy* and *Esquire*.

> Caryl, several years ago, when I first read *Cell 2455, Death Row*, that night, a Saturday, I felt the presence of a writer. *The Kid Was a Killer* proves that Alan and I were right, and that despite criticisms of your work, we have been right in maintaining to everyone that their reactions were false. I think you will do still better work, eventually, perhaps things less apparently tailored, but you have produced a book with body and soul, with guts and giggles, and tears, and rest assured that we are going to do everything we know how to do and can think of to do to make this a success. Congratulations.

It was the sort of letter that affirmed a writer's very being. One can only imagine the tonic it must have been for Chessman as he sat inside his Los Angeles cage.

"Since I have only a very few minutes to get this typed before lights out, excuse pliz [sic] if my words seem a little disjointed. Maybe, too, I'm slightly intoxicated by your reception of The Kid! I've been figuratively pacing the floor like papa in the maternity waiting room until your critical appraisal came. . . . I'm tremendously pleased that you liked the ms. so well. I'm not being ironical or sarcastic when I say what you know to be true: that the author is the last man to be able to say whether he's written a good or bad book. Hence, your reaction is a big boost to me, especially since I know you wouldn't have pulled your punches if I'd written a turkey."

With such a reception, in fact, Chessman carried his zeal a bit too far, telling Stuart Daniels, the publicity director for Prentice-Hall, who was in Los Angeles promoting *The Face of Justice*, that Longstreth was free to arrange any deal he wanted, "the best deal as fast as he can." Given Chessman's recent displeasure with Prentice-Hall, he was in the enviable position of biting the hand, so to speak. Chessman was, figuratively speaking, showing his ass—not the most politic thing to do to someone whose job it is to promote your writing. Chessman had already contacted the producer and director Walter Wanger about film possibilities. Longstreth had approached Doubleday.

"The best holiday season ever to you and Alan!" he practically shouted in a December 16, 1957, letter.

Asher wrote Longstreth about her "pride in Caryl" for the good news about the high quality of *The Kid Was a Killer*. She also expressed her growing frustration with Davis ("what I might say would be less than ladylike").

Chessman followed with a letter on December 30 that was filled with good humor and promise. "If you ever took a look at the price tag of this thing called Justice in the Chessman case, you'd do a double somersault backwards."

About *The Kid Was a Killer*, Chessman wrote, "That sense of accomplishment and genuine pleasure hasn't diminished since receiving your reaction to The Kid. . . . Odd, isn't it, Joe, that 'The Kid' was written in a death cell when I really didn't think I had too many days left and, under pressure, was fighting a last-ditch battle for survival. Now the Kid has been rescued from a big safe and it's very possible I may soon win this legal war."

In his most optimistic moments, Chessman fantasized that Judge Evans would reject the transcript that Fraser prepared in its entirety and rule that no usable transcript could be prepared from Perry's notes. At that point, Chessman could be released from custody (in the technical sense, without leaving the jail), then arraigned again, released on bail, and "then walk out the front gate on bond sometime this spring! Incredible to contemplate, isn't it? Yet that is exactly what I'm fighting for and certainly, from the fine way the case is progressing, is a distinct possibility. . . . Let's hope 1958 is our year."

Once again, the year ended on a promising note.

11

A Faith Worse Than Death
(1958)

CHESSMAN SPENT HIS first New Year's Day in ten years outside San Quentin prison. He was not free, of course, but being in Los Angeles energized him, as did the relative openness of the county jail and visits from old friends and new fans. Asher's illness was a good excuse for her to pull away from Chessman's long-distance battle; she had soured at the "figurehead" status to which she was relegated as Davis's co-counsel and developed an allergy to his ego. ("It's nice on the sidelines; just hope I can stay here," she wrote Longstreth. "Personally and delightfully I've heard nothing from George. Apparently, he has visited L.A. once or twice, more or less casually dropping into the courtrooom.")

Though Davis said he hadn't healed from his polo injury, the truth was he was too busy handling other cases in Honolulu, Korea, and Tokyo to focus on Chessman's case. From the outset, he had taken Chessman's case, just as he had Abbott's, for the high-profile opportunity to proselytize against capital punishment. The unorthodox deal he'd struck with Chessman—the client writing his lawyer's "biography" (Davis was the "face" in *The Face of Justice*, though the book was dedicated to "Rosalie Sue")—also gratified his ego. Davis was one of the great attorneys of his day—certainly more formidable than Asher—and yet Chessman was being handicapped by his "casual" approach.

This left Chessman to do most of the legal research and some of the court presentations, with assistance from the ACLU's Wirin and Posner. Indeed, with their help, Chessman didn't get a pound of flesh but he did get an ounce of satisfaction at J. Miller Leavy's expense by being allowed the final word in the proceedings. He followed Leavy's presentation by spending three hours making his case, an articulate and gripping performance that may actually have hurt his chances, satisfying though it had been. After the one-hour mark, his appearance was seen as grandstanding by the press, something Asher saw coming six hundred miles away in Sacramento and something Wirin and Posner were powerless to curtail.

Even after the proceedings concluded on Valentine's Day, Chessman believed there was "an excellent chance" that Judge Evans would reject the Fraser transcripts and rule that no usable transcript of the original trial was available; thus, a new trial would be mandated. If, on the other hand, the judge ruled that the transcript was usable, with "emendations"—the four thousand corrections and changes suggested by Chessman and the many expert witnesses—then he was prepared to appeal the ruling, heading back to the U.S. Supreme Court. "I still remain confident of an ultimate legal victory, vindication, and freedom," he wrote Longstreth. "If I didn't, I'd fold up my legal tent and quietly steal away to the gas chamber."

The judge indicated that he would need two weeks to make his decision and that Chessman could stay in Los Angeles until then.

During that time, two reporters from *The Daily Trojan*, the student newspaper of the University of Southern California, interviewed Chessman in the court's jury room. The reporters, Joe Nevens and Jerry A. Burns, were immensely impressed with Chessman and managed to compose a two-part series of articles and interview transcripts that are as good as any that were ever written about him.* The reporters were slightly in awe of Chessman at first, writing about "chatting amiably with one of the most controversial criminal figures of modern time." But they warmed to him, describing Chessman as "friendly, well-spoken with a firm and well-modulated voice." He seemed "honest,

---

* J. Edgar Hoover must have agreed, because copies of this article are included in Chessman's FBI file.

sincere and willing to help." His "vocabulary, his speech, his intelligence were as good as that of any middle-class intellectual." He "no more fits the stereotype of a rapist-robber-convict than does your university adviser." The photographs that accompanied the article showed Chessman to be well dressed in his sport jacket and tie, relaxed and clearly enjoying himself. He told the reporters that he was determined to become a novelist "worth his salt" and "given another ten years I may make the grade." That is, after he was in a position "to give these death sentences back to the State of California unused."

His cheerful demeanor was short-lived. On February 28, 1958, Judge Evans ruled on the transcripts, which now comprised 1,200,000 words of revisions. Records of corollary proceedings were now housed in sixty volumes. The ruling went against Chessman. Evans accepted, "with emendations," the transcripts as "fair and accurate."

This may have been the most bitterly disappointing defeat of Chessman's twelve-year legal war. He'd made a good case on his own, presented it thoroughly and professionally and, for the most part, without his legendary arrogance. He had brought to light hundreds of embarrassing aspects about the original trial. He had, in short, bested Leavy, arguably the best prosecuting attorney in Los Angeles. However, in this retelling of David v. Goliath, Goliath walked away with the decision.

Despite this, Chessman put his best face forward to the press. Dozens of newspaper, radio, and television reporters and photographers rushed the front of the courtroom after Judge Evans left the bench. Images of Frances Couturier crying at the decision were broadcast far and wide, as were those of Chessman trying to hold his own against the onslaught of questions. He told one reporter that he had "additional legal maneuvers up my sleeve, enough to keep the courts busy for another five years." As he was being led away by deputies, Chessman said, "I'll still do what I can. The Constitution gives us the right to every legal avenue."

Judge Evans's ruling and the news that Chessman's tax problems from 1956 and 1957 had not been resolved to the satisfaction of the IRS arrived at the same time. Chessman's accountant, Douglas Olin (also

Asher's accountant) had had his hands full trying to unsnag the financial records since he was hired at the time of the publication of *Cell 2455, Death Row*. As Chessman's legal expenses mounted, his income dwindled; he made a total of $12,194.44 in royalties for 1957. Asher eventually loaned him eight hundred dollars to pay his tax bill.

The eight-hour drive back to San Quentin in the state's black station wagon on March 11 may have been the longest of Chessman's life. "No prophecies," he told the assembled press in the parking lot of the Hall of Justice. "I got every fair shake in the hearing. I have no complaint about that."

He seemed resigned to the possibility now that he would not cheat death.

"In ten years I've seen everything there is to see on Death Row. I don't want to see any more of it," he said, then seemed to realize he was presenting too vulnerable a flank to the press sharks. "I don't mean to seem dejected. I guess I could do another ten years up there and survive."

Though he wasn't prepared to throw in the towel, he also didn't want to throw good money away, not if it was a pointless exercise in delaying the inevitable trip to the gas chamber. "If I believe I'm dead, then I'm through. I don't want any cliff hanging, no hanging by my fingernails. . . . My money could be used posthumously to a better purpose. Maybe for the education of youngsters."

It is no small wonder that in the sudden darkness of a return to San Quentin's "gray death cell" and his failure to get a new trial Chessman didn't at least consider turning to religion or toward something, *anything*, spiritual for solace. He certainly had every opportunity to do so, as the prison religious leaders visited Death Row daily and often stopped by his cell to chat.

Chessman's lack of religious faith was not an affectation, nor did it come without serious reflection. On more than one occasion, he described himself as an avowed "agnostic" and whenever a questionnaire demanded a religious affiliation, that's what he wrote. It was because of this—his having listed "agnostic" as his religion—that the cemetery authorities in Glendale claimed as the reason they would not allow his cremated ashes to be buried alongside his parents in the famed Forest Lawn Cemetery.*

The word "agnostic" was coined by T. H. Huxley in 1870 to describe a person who believes, as Huxley and Chessman did, "that the human mind cannot know whether there is a God or an ultimate cause, or anything beyond material phenomena."† Chessman's agnosticism didn't prevent him from discussing theology or metaphysics. On the contrary, he enjoyed discussing religion with the four chaplains (two Protestant, one Roman Catholic, and one Jewish) at San Quentin when they made their Death Row rounds. And they, likewise, enjoyed the challenge of picking Chessman's brain and penetrating his formidable defenses.

Chessman's most frequent foil was Byron E. Eshelman, a Protestant minister who came to San Quentin from Alcatraz in 1951 and was there throughout the rest of Chessman's stay. Eshelman devoted a large part of his remarkably candid 1961 memoir, *Death Row Chaplain*, to his relationship with Chessman. Relying largely on notes taken while on the job, Eshelman provided an invaluable firsthand window onto Chessman's day-to-day existence. During their discussions, Eshelman noted, "sparks usually flew."

In one of their encounters in 1958, after Chessman returned from Los Angeles following his failed transcript hearing, Eshelman found the famous prisoner fuming. He was still mulling over the testimony of two jurors from his original 1948 trial who had shown up on January 28, 1958, as state's witnesses against his appeal for a new trial. One, Mrs. Nana L. Bull, had admitted writing a letter to the *Los Angeles Times* after the trial in which she said Chessman had "got what was coming to him" and that he should have "been dead already." The other, Mrs. Mary E. Graves, said that she felt Judge Fricke was "a very

---

* Partly because no final resting place was made available to him, Chessman's ashes sat in an urn on Rosalie Asher's bookshelf until 1974, though Longstreth had repeatedly petitioned for them to be buried on his Indiana farm.
† Nicholas Murray described Thomas Henry Huxley (1825–1895) as a "formidable Victorian autodidact" who became "one of the leading scientists, controversialists and communicators of the nineteenth century." He was also grandfather to Aldous Huxley, one of a group of intellectuals who in 1960 went to Sacramento to personally petition Governor Edmund Brown to spare Chessman's life.

honorable man" but Chessman was "anything else but," and that the ten-year delay in his execution was "a perfect disgrace, a shocking development and disgusting."

But what really bugged Chessman was how Mrs. Graves had admitted asking "God for guidance and got the answer that I should be found guilty." He told Eshelman, "That kind of religion burns me up . . . this is not religion but some kind of superstition. . . . It isn't that God is a super great being up in the sky and handling a switchboard with calls coming in from every direction, while He is sending down the answers. This old girl calls up and God says, 'Down with Chessman.' I can't swallow it."

As Eshelman saw it, Chessman was as angry at this woman as she was at him and that the two of them were "rationalizing their neuroses."

The minister's observation sent Chessman on a tangent about psychology: "Neurotic, psychopathic—these are epithets more than diagnoses. But even accepting the diagnosis, as I do, I can't go along with your idea that in predestination we're all puppets dangling on a string. Say you were free to do as you wanted, you'd do about the same as you're doing now, wouldn't you?"

Boxed in, Eshelman landed his final punch before moving on to the next cell. He told Chessman, "We are not free and it doesn't matter what our rationalizations are. There is a theological explanation behind all of the psychological ones. . . . I think you agree with me, but just have different words for it."

To which Chessman said, "OK . . . time!"

■

ONE OF THE many prison inmates whose paths crossed Chessman's during his twelve-year residence at San Quentin was a young hellraiser, a former Preston School of Industry inmate, and a convicted thief from Bakersfield named Merle Haggard. Haggard went on to become one of American country music's most distinctive artists, a First Amendment champion, and a maverick within the notoriously conservative genre.

Haggard met Chessman in 1958, while serving a sentence for armed robbery, and he credited the condemned man with turning his life around. Haggard, sixteen years Chessman's junior, had continued to be a hellraiser even after being sent to San Quentin; he ran a gambling and alcohol operation out of his cell. A guard caught him one day, visibly intoxicated, and he was thrown into an isolation cell by the prison authorities.

Haggard said, "It was a situation that occurred accidentally in San Quentin where I was detained in what they call the Shelf, which is the jail within the prison. I got busted for making beer and did seven days on the shelf, and while I was there I had a couple of conversations with Caryl Chessman."

The Shelf was attached to Death Row. Prisoners could not see one another, but they could talk openly to each other.

"It was awful close to the fire," Haggard told the television talk show host Larry King in late 2004 about Chessman (they were discussing Scott Peterson's recent transfer to San Quentin's Death Row). "I was just across the alleyway from him. . . . They hung this Red Light Bandit thing on him. Nobody believed he was guilty, but he became a political prisoner. Somebody had to execute him or get fried themselves. The guy didn't kill anybody but they were going to kill him anyway. That's what can happen if you get the reputation that he had."

The conversations with Chessman forced Haggard to confront his situation. As soon as he got off the Shelf, he volunteered to work at the jute plant, took high school equivalency courses, and played in the prison's country music band. At his second parole hearing, in 1960, Haggard was given a five-year sentence, which included two years and nine months in jail and two years and three months on parole; he left prison ninety days later.

Haggard recalled the experience of being among Death Row prisoners: "I couldn't see them, but I could hear them. We were on a silent system on the shelf and I was there for seven days for making beer. And while I was there I could hear prisoners such as Caryl Chessman, I heard him talking about getting a life insurance policy in the mail and that was interesting. And that was where I decided to change directions in my life. When I went to prison, I had a lot of escapes on my record. And at the time, I was in what they call a closed security and did not get to have a guitar until about a year into my sentence. And finally, I was able to participate in some of the musical functions and finally wound up in what they call the prison band and played for different events every Wednesday night."

Haggard told Larry King, "I'm sixty-seven years old, and I was twenty years old at the time. And I still have dreams. I still have nightmares. There is nothing, not even a country music career, worth going to San Quentin for. I got to talk to Caryl Chessman, who was the world-famous Red Light Bandit that was executed, I think, on circumstantial evidence only. It was not really his style. I really don't think he was guilty. I have had a lot of time to think about that."

■

SIX MONTHS PASSED between letters from Chessman to his literary agent. In that time, the optimism of January had vanished. Chessman was back at San Quentin, agonizing over legal and financial troubles, and pondering his next moves. Not that it mattered in the long run, but—in the adding-insult-to-injury department—he had been evicted from his world-famous Cell 2455 while he was away in Los Angeles; he now occupied Cell 2458. Stuck for twenty-two of every twenty-four hours inside this tiny cell, his books and papers suffocating him like a shroud and his writing and correspondence strictly controlled by prison officials, Chessman saw only one glimmer of light at the end of his tunnel: *The Kid Was a Killer.*

With *The Kid*'s anticipated sale as a book, film-script, and magazine serial fueling him, Chessman soldiered on. He had hoped that the novel would sell quickly to a hardcover publisher. Longstreth worked feverishly to make that wish come true, but Doubleday, Simon & Schuster, Knopf, Abelard-Schuman, Frederick Fell, Citadel, Harper, Scribner, and Putnam had all passed on the book, and MGM and Columbia had passed on the film rights. The only bite he got was from the French publisher Presses de la Cité, which agreed to bring it out the following spring. Oddly, this meant Chessman's novel would appear in translation in another country before it would appear in his own country in his own language.

Chessman grew more restive in Cell 2458, despite Longstreth's February pep talk:

> My dear Caryl, being disturbed and hurt and worried over the so-far rejections of *The Kid Was a Killer* is the most natural and understandable thing in the world. In fact, the straight-away acceptance of your first three books is definitely the exception to the rule, yet I am very disturbed for your sake that this has happened, to date, with *The Kid*. I know how much more important it is to you, in your delicate situation, than it is to most authors, and though it is slight comfort, in fact, no comfort at all I suppose, it is the experience which has been shared by countless authors, myself included. I DO understand your position and your concern and your disappointment. In fact, I match it with my own. But one of our most successful books was rejected thirteen times, and there are so many examples of that kind of thing in publishing. None of us can afford to give up now; we're not that kind, and you most certainly are not.

Chessman was hurt enough by the rejection, coming on the heels of his loss in court, that he had, via the increasingly unreliable Frances, instructed Longstreth to return all scripts. In the course of pleading with Chessman to reconsider such an impulsive move, Longstreth explained his strategy vis-à-vis Prentice-Hall. Chessman had not, after his brush-off of Prentice-Hall's publicist Daniels, wanted his former publishers to get a look at the manuscript. He fantasized mass success with another house so that he could gloat from behind the bars of his cage as Stearns and all the other know-it-alls kicked themselves repeatedly.

Longstreth's logic was sound. Doubleday, which had expressed an urgent preliminary interest, had already turned it down; Doubleday had, in fact, dropped the project so quickly that Prentice-Hall wouldn't doubt they were being offered a "virgin script." Longstreth had gotten numerous inquiries from them, plus a letter from Stearns saying that "P-H considered themselves your publisher and were interested in furthering your career." By striking then, hoping for a quick sale, Longstreth reasoned that he and Chessman could dictate new, more generous terms. Stearns quashed that fantasy, rejecting the script "in a summarily cynical fashion."

Chessman's career publisher had rejected his novel! That wounded him to his core, opening the door to the cancer of self-doubt.

By June, when he next contacted Longstreth, Chessman dispensed with the niceties (he had to get special permission from Warden Dickson to write his agent, who was permanently banned from the correspondence list). He wasn't hostile, just frustrated by lack of progress. "I have to be realistic and hard-headed," he told Longstreth. His decision was final: Longstreth was to offer *The Kid Was a Killer* to a paperback publisher, preferably Dell or Gold Medal. Chessman reasoned that, though he shared Longstreth's confidence that eventually a reputable publisher would agree to bring out a hardcover edition, the time sequence involved was too deferred. "We gambled for high stakes with it and, through a great many weird circumstances beyond our control, time has run out. . . . To put it graphically and inelegantly, I could very easily be dead by that time if I remained broke, and the money wouldn't help me in hell."

He needed cash. Period. "$2500 or $3000 now would be as helpful as $10,000 might in another setting," he said. He was appealing Judge Evans's ruling in State Supreme Court and had prepared a two-hundred-fifty-page opening brief; he needed twenty copies of the brief, for various legal channels. The cost of this printing process—this was before photocopying machines—was more than one hundred dollars, with another hundred dollars in "miscellaneous costs."

After reading a copy of the brief Chessman had sent him, Longstreth marveled at its clarity and drama. It was, he felt, a model of philology, opening with references to Socrates and embracing the whole history of the Western legal tradition; he was impressed enough with it to believe it was "saleable, perhaps in paperback form." For the first time, in his book-length polemic, Chessman folded the issue of capital punishment into his case. Curiously, for someone who, to death penalty abolitionists, acquired near-martyr status, he didn't personally exploit this issue until late in his stay at San Quentin. Prior to 1958, and the defeat in the Los Angeles transcript hearings, he had been able to keep the gas chamber's shadows at bay by immersing himself in his writing and his battle to prove his innocence of the Red Light Bandit crimes. Now, the tide had turned against him on both fronts, and he could no longer deny the possibility—rather, the probability—that he would be gassed.

Even if the legal brief was not published, it was yet another writerly milestone for Death Row's dynamo. In the three years since *Cell 2455, Death Row* was published and under the most trying conditions and restrictions, Chessman had written and published two books, one 309 pages, the other 271 pages; written one full-length novel of sixty-five thousand words, which was being published in France; prepared hundreds of pages of legal documents; argued two cases before two judges, written a twenty-thousand-word piece for *Saga*; dictated a series of articles to Molly Kalin called "Lost—A Last Chance at Life," aimed at the magazine market ("Lost" was, literally, lost in the mail); he had written several lengthy short stories (unpublished) and carried on correspondence with countless friends and associates—the letters to Asher and Longstreth alone in that time comprise more than 250 pages. He had also taught himself playwriting, screenwriting, and Pitman shorthand.

And yet, no contract for *The Kid* had been signed. Time was running out. He was growing desperate enough to suggest to Asher that he withdraw the manuscript from Longstreth and sell it on his own from his death cell—that is, to essentially fire Longstreth.

Longstreth, who had already, as per instructions, dispatched the manuscript to Dell, Pocket Books (which had earlier published a successful paperback edition of *Cell 2455, Death Row*), and Gold Medal, took this in stride, and felt no ill will toward Chessman. He told Asher, "I still have a big spot in my heart for him and for his situation. When, Rosalie, do you suppose it will end? It has been such an ordeal for him; in some ways I imagine the Green Room sounds rather inviting at odd moments."

Chessman was no doubt seeing red, not green, when he perused the *Los Angeles Times* on June 9, 1958. The lead story in the paper's local news section (page B1) was headlined, 2 'RED LIGHT' BANDITS BEAT AND ROB MOTORIST; the subhead read: NEW CHESSMAN-TYPE HOLDUP WAVE FEARED. The opening sentence: "A 'red light' highway robbery reminiscent of Caryl Chessman in his heyday had police and Sheriff's deputies on the alert throughout the South Side yesterday."

A twenty-six-year-old "power saw operator" staggered into the Seventy-seventh Street Police Station after he claimed that he was pulled over by two men in a car with a red spotlight, dragged from his car, "stomped," and robbed at gunpoint. The victim's description of his assailants matched the height and weight of Chessman—6 feet tall and 200 pounds—that were related by some victims of the "Red Light Bandit" spree.

■

MONEY AND PUBLISHING weren't Chessman's only woes. His relationship with Frances had deteriorated. Most relationships between prisoners and spouses or girlfriends suffer from neglect and absence; but in this case Chessman had never consummated his relationship with Frances, though she wore his engagement ring. He was the generous benefactor for her two children, often sending her money before paying his lawyers, the IRS, and other creditors. That he had no legal reason or requirement to do so—that he seemed to be doing this out of an old-fashioned sense of moral duty—had gone unrecognized by the press, perhaps even by himself.

Meanwhile, Frances (whom he now called "Fran") was bouncing checks all over Los Angeles. She was increasingly deceptive in her dealings with him and his friends. She was also "associating" with some unsavory people of whom Chessman did not approve. In early June, he "ordered" Frances by letter to come visit him at San Quentin to discuss all this. Asher told Longstreth that Chessman "is all set for a showdown. I won't definitely predict that a complete break-up will follow, but I certainly wouldn't be surprised."

Asher visited Chessman on June 19 and found him looking "very very tired" and thin. She doubted that he would "throw Frances to the journalistic wolves," but that the publicity that might accrue from their breakup could actually be more sympathetic toward him, given the sort of trouble Frances was in.

Finally, after avoiding his summons for two weeks, Frances came to see Chessman in late June. The visit did not go well. In response to a "frantic summons" now directed to her, Asher visited him on July 3, and the encounter left her shaken. She admitted to Longstreth that she was "dreadfully worried about him; and so, for that matter, are all who have seen him." Because he claimed not to have been able to sleep for three nights, Chessman was not, according to Asher, "exactly coherent in the telling of the story" but she did learn that Frances had been up to much mischief. She was "leaving the children alone, night and day, and as a result is in danger of being charged with child neglect." She had also "been going with several men, one of whom she wants to marry." She had stopped writing to Chessman, hadn't even sent him a birthday card in May (though he was still paying her bills), and "lied to him consistently." Asher "pitied" Frances, though she "cannot overlook her opportunism."

As a result of this breach with Frances, Chessman was "in worse condition than on occasions when he was so close to the gas chamber." The prison guards put an extra watch on him; he was "dangerously near the breaking point." Asher told Longstreth to "Just keep your fingers crossed and hope that Caryl's phenomenal strength can see him through this crisis. I have never felt more sorry for anyone in my life."

Longstreth's attempts to reach out to his friend were rebuffed again by prison censors. His letters of consolation were returned unopened, accompanied by a short note from Warden F. R. Dickson: "We are returning your letter to condemned inmate Caryl Chessman inasmuch as you are not on the subject's approved correspondence list. Special permission was granted to Mr. Chessman in June to address one letter to you. Your reply to that letter was delivered to him."

■

IN OCTOBER, CHESSMAN was returned to Los Angeles County Jail (same address: Tank 10-A-2 Rear), where he awaited a new hearing on November 19. He hadn't lost hope or heart, despite the lack of funds and his breakup with Frances. He told friends that he was "still managing to ride this legal tiger." He gave a series of interviews to the press and was filmed by newsreel cameras. The *Los Angeles Times* said that he "played the role of an educated gentleman. . . . His replies were almost poetic as he answered an outpouring of questions." When asked about his suit and tie, he said, "Yes, they're clothes I wore here during my last court visit. The people at San Quentin must have more faith in me. They saved my city clothes for this trip." He joked with the same press that had turned him into a monster, saying, "I read the editorials and letters to the editor regularly. Then I rush to the mirror to see my horns and fangs and the saliva dripping from my lips. But I never find I look that way." He even remarked on the superiority of Los Angeles weather: "It certainly is a lot warmer than where I just came from, but I understand it isn't anywhere near as warm as where I'm going."

With characteristic chutzpah, Chessman was counting on a petition to the U.S. Supreme Court for a writ of habeas corpus that would give him "immediate discharge from custody on the grounds that California's judiciary has deliberately failed to proceed within a reasonable time to thrash this record dispute out and willfully has failed to proceed in the way the U.S. Supreme Court ordered it to. Without being foolishly overconfident, I'm reasonably hopeful the Supreme Court may decide California has played one strange stunt too many and hence will order my release."

Even facing the final stages of his battle for earthly existence, Chessman found time to do a favor for an old friend, Neva Hull. He had known Mrs. Hull since he was "practically a toddler" and she now lived in Indiana, was married with two kids, and was an aspiring humorist. Chessman, who was free to write anyone he wanted from the Los Angeles jailhouse, wondered if Longstreth would take the time to look at her manuscript. By way of explanation, he told his agent, "She's really got a side-splitting brand of humor and is quite an unstuffy and interesting person but serious about her writing. She doesn't know I'm writing you and you won't have an albatross hung around your neck. I really believe with the guidance and criticism you can give she could do something equal to *Auntie Mame* [by Patrick Dennis, 1955] or *Please Don't Eat the Daisies* [by Jean Kerr, 1957]. Neva's got that itch to give the world a chuckle and I've carried her as far as I can by remote control."*

■

IN LATE OCTOBER, James Whitfield Ellison, managing editor of Gold Medal Books in New York, wrote to Chessman about his manuscript for *The Kid Was a Killer*. Ellison was seriously interested in publishing the book but also wanted some substantial revisions to be made. Chessman wrote Ellison back on November 3, 1958, his letter a brilliant polemic that, more or less, told Ellison why he wouldn't be making those revisions. The letter is worthy of George Orwell, who also had—as Ellison had suggested about Chessman's manuscript—been accused of being more advocate than novelist.

"To be candid," Chessman responded,

> the dilemma confronting me may be attributable to the fact that, at bottom, I am more a pamphleteer than a novelist. You are aware, I'm sure, where and under what conditions *The Kid* was written, as well as the strong feelings and convictions I have concerning its central theme.
>
> Let me put it this way. We (society if you will) are faced with a staggering social problem called crime. The individual units of that problem we call criminals, and among those are some whose antisocial conduct seems wholly senseless, alien and "evil." We have an unhappy faculty for righteous oversimplification in our approach to the problem they pose; philosophically, as a collective social entity, we subscribe to the notion that the answer

---

* Mrs. Hull's book was never published.

is to deplore, excoriate, editorialize, be indignant, get tough, jail and kill off. This, of course, is no answer at all, as evidenced by our rising crime rate. On the other hand, neither is the answer blindly to maintain, without more, they (these violent ones) are really nice boys. Actually they are, by their distorted response to reality and by our standards of interpersonal relationships and ideas of social responsibility, sick personalities.

The psychiatrists recognized some years ago, and gradually under scientific disciplines and away from the shrieking headlines, their view of this violent and seemingly altogether amoral group crystalized. An increase in knowledge, unfortunately, does not invariably imply either acceptance per se by the scientists or society (witness Galileo) or uniform deductions to be drawn from that knowledge. Thus, a schism developed; the psychiatrists disagreed among themselves on the precise nature of this type of character disorder, its genesis, its treatment and its cure. Meanwhile, as a part of a too familiar historical process, the public took a tentative diagnostic label (aggressive psychopathic personality), shortened it to psychopath, converted it into a frightening epithet, and thereby added another weapon to their arsenal. Not only was a tragic cultural lag perpetuated, it was extended and those who advocated a rational and sensible approach to the problem of the "psychopath" (allegedly one of the worst of them is writing this letter) were shouted down as coddlers.

Now back to my novel. I purposely didn't author a traditional crime story, or, in fact, a crime story at all; similarly, I purposely didn't make the Kid a criminal. I did make him a "psychopath," intentionally—because, in dramatic terms, to use an overworked phrase, I wanted to bring the psychopathic personality into sharp focus (and criminality, while simply one means by which he overtly finds expression for his rebellious and violent affliction, might have obscured the issue). My thesis was that the "evil" in him (and in any of his kind) is not an inexplicable mystery, and by necessary implication that it is social folly to regard it as such. My goal was to explain, not to explain away. Obviously, I failed, for you say: "One point seems to be to be obvious: The Kid must be mysterious. He must represent to us a terrifying, even an exciting entity. The evil that seems to be part of him must flow in him as naturally as blood. You must not explain his being away. Leave him opaque and his force will be that much greater. Let him live in us whole and unexplained. Don't allow psychology to take the place of drama."

I am sure my dilemma now will be clear to you. I cannot in good conscience leave the Kid's being opaque, since if I did so I would be betraying the very thing that motivated and impelled me to write *The Kid*. You can reply, fairly, then that if I am so concerned with my thesis (or message) I should write fact pieces or pamphlets. Well, as you know, I already have had three books, largely autobiographical, published along these lines, and *The Kid* represented an effort on my part to effect a transition from non fiction to fiction. My trouble is that, assuming the time and opportunity to do so, it would be too easy for me to tailor *The Kid* to fit your specifications. All I would have to do is abandon for that period what I believe in deeply and what cries out in me for expression. There is no sarcasm in that last sentence, only recognition of the cutting kind of irony that has marked the last several years of my beleaguered existence. Hence we come to the purpose of this letter: Granted that psychology can't be permitted to take the place of drama, how, in this particular instance, can the two be successfully fused to produce a book that will be a commercial success and also one that will say something that will hold the reader and arouse in him an awareness of the problem with which The Kid seeks to grapple?

A day after he wrote this letter, Chessman wrote to Longstreth and told him to send the manuscript to Dell. Though he wasn't totally

opposed to the idea of compromise and revisions—if Longstreth shared
Ellison's view—he was absolutely consumed with his legal battle.
Though Wirin and Posner were still offering advice, he was going it
alone almost entirely. "I must be working night and day for the next
several weeks on the case and any time that I took from this critical
legal work proportionately would reduce chances of success." He
also knew that, once he was returned to San Quentin on December
12, the prison officials would forbid his working on any writing that
did not directly involve his legal case. Chessman apparently figured
he'd burned his bridges with Gold Medal, though they did, in fact,
publish his novel, with only minor chopping, in 1960. Though Dell
didn't publish the novel, by a coincidence of timing, they ran a friendly
piece about Chessman's "right to write" in the December 1958 issue
of their popular magazine *Inside Detective.*

To avoid jail censors, Chessman dictated letters from his Los
Angeles cell to his friend, Molly Kalin, the Pitman shorthand expert.
She took his words down in shorthand and later typed up the letters
and mailed them from her Los Angeles home, at 840 Sayre Lane.

Health woes continued to afflict his legal counsel; Wirin had to
withdraw completely from the case due to a heart condition. Even
so, Chessman still held out hope for a discharge from custody and a
battle in Washington. In the courtroom, he had the singular privilege
of calling the presiding judge (Evans) to the witness stand and cross-
examining him for an entire morning. At the noon recess, the judge
said he would testify no longer and would not allow another judge to
be appointed. Chessman described the case as "snarled up worse than
it ever has been."

One other thing was snarled, or knocked, up. Asher's suspicions
about Frances were realized when Chessman learned in November
that she was several months pregnant. This was only months after
taking the money Asher had loaned her to pay her rent and blowing
it in Las Vegas, and then siphoning much of the advance for *The Face
of Justice* away from the efforts to save Chessman's life. Chessman
tried to maintain a cool front about this news, saying that the guy
who'd knocked Frances up—a black man—was "some excellent fellow she is living with." He said that this explains "her strange and

tragic actions over the last several months and finally her attempt to disappear completely—with all the reserve funds I have. Naturally, she still has my good wishes but I am still baffled by the fact she felt it necessary not only to betray me in so many ways but to practice so many small and great deceptions on me and many of our friends. I think the less further I say about this the better it will be, not that I am disturbed by it any longer. It is just that I feel the thing to do is to put her out of my mind completely."

Chessman still felt a "moral obligation" to help Frances and her kids.

About Frances, Longstreth wrote, "Your attitude is a mature and wise and intelligent one, and the only way to size up the deal. Some day, I hope we, and Alan, have a long, long talk about pink string and cabbages and kings."

Chessman got more bad news. Prentice-Hall had decided to remainder *The Face of Justice*. Was he interested in the remaining copies for seventy-one cents apiece?

■

JOE LONGSTRETH WAS pulled further into the spiral of bad news surrounding all things Chessman when he learned, via a December news story in the *New York Times*, that a Marin County Grand Jury had indicted him on "a charge of conspiring to smuggle the manuscript of *The Face of Justice* from the prison." The indictment was the brainchild of the county D.A., a publicity hound named William O. Weissich who was fond of calling press conferences in a bid for front-page coverage in Bay Area papers. Weissich had been unable to determine in his investigation how the manuscript slipped past prison officials and ended up in New York. He filed three felony conspiracy indictiments against Longstreth, Davis, and Prentice-Hall.

As Chessman wrote Longstreth, "How in the hell you could conspire with me to smuggle out the book when you didn't even know anything about the book's existence until after it had left the prison is entirely beyond my comprehension. I'm furious enough to bite bars over this. . . . If this sample-sized Don Quixote, in his frenzy to get

In March 1957, to dispel rumors that he, or anyone, was Chessman's "ghost writer," Joseph Longstreth showed reporters the original manuscript for *The Face of Justice*, which was smuggled out of San Quentin's Death Row. As can be seen, Chessman was not taking any chances either, having signed and fingerprinted each page. *Courtesy Peg Longstsreth*

his name on the front page, gives you too rough a time, I hope you politely tell him to drop dead."*

Longstreth took Weissich's indictment in stride. Though he was angry, he was prepared to fight to the finish, a determination fueled in part by the humiliation of having the warrant for his arrest sent to the home of his

---

* Curiously, Weissich did "drop dead" in 1986, murdered by Malcolm Schlette, an arsonist he had sent to San Quentin in 1955 and who had harbored a grudge for thirty-one years.

ailing father in Richmond, Indiana. Longstreth appeared before Indiana Superior Court Judge John Brubaker and was released on five hundred dollars' bond. He then met with the local sheriff and prosecuting attorney, as well as some friends of his who were lawyers. The prosecuting attorney advised him to return the warrant, calling it "inadequately worded." That stalled Weissich sufficiently, as did a sternly worded message to him by Bernice Freeman that Longstreth had nothing to hide. Longstreth vowed to Asher, "I will not, repeat, WILL NOT be pushed around by a publicity happy anybody!"

Chessman was as apologetic to Longstreth as he was angry at Weissich. "Needless to add, anything I can do to help you be promptly cleared of these utterly absurd charges I will do. . . . What he [Weissich] is actually charging you with is a conspiracy to help me exercise my constitutional right to freedom of speech."

Chessman's letter of December 14, 1958, dictated to Molly Kalin, was his last to Longstreth for some time. On December 17, he was escorted from the county jail, dressed exactly as he'd arrived—in a gray flannel suit and light blue tie—and with two county sheriffs toting his mini-coffin of legal papers alongside him. He, his papers, his typewriter, and a three-guard entourage were loaded into a station wagon, which pulled away in the direction of San Quentin State Prison, what he described to Longstreth as "my little gray home on Death Row." Chessman did get a chance to exchange quips with the assembled press, telling them, "I'll be back and this time I hope to come back a free man." When asked if he was worried that he'd come to the end of his legal road, he said, "You lose your capacity or inclination to worry after ten and a half years."

The senior officer in charge of the transport detail, Harry Sargent, later told the press that Chessman was a "model prisoner" and "congenial" company. However, he said, "Once he gets there [prison], he turns hard, just like that. He's all con again."

When Chessman returned to San Quentin, he learned, as he suspected, that the restrictions on his correspondence and his writing were still in place.

Longstreth felt a surge of kinship with Chessman and thanked him for his offer of help. "We might indeed be fighting together, side by side, in the future, which wouldn't faze me a scrap. I've always admired your guts and always will."

Nonetheless, he wished "In spite of all this sinister nonsense . . . a merry Christmas and that 1959 proves to be the best year ever for both of us."

Davis was in Korea in early December, defending an American soldier charged with murdering a Korean woman, when Weissich sent out his indictment. He returned to California within several days to deny the charges. Unfortunately, Davis then leaped into another controversy that could not have helped Chessman's legal battle, at least in the court of public opinion. That is, on December 22, Davis told the press that would defend two men accused of the murder-for-hire of Olga Duncan, a recently married pregnant woman from Santa Barbara. The Duncan murder was as sensational, gruesome, and publicly villified as the Abbott case. As in the Abbott case, Davis's connection with the alleged perpetrators of such a heinous crime reflected back on Chessman. Every story for the rest of the trial, in fact, noted that "Davis is the lawyer credited with the strategy of keeping Caryl Chessman, notorious red light bandit alive for more than a decade" (never mind that Davis only met Chessman in 1955).

In December, Longstreth learned that he had developed skin cancer. To treat it, he would have to spend part of the Christmas holidays in a Cincinnati hospital.

"Things don't come singly, do they?" he wrote Chessman at year's end. After a second thought, he added, "I'm telling *you*?"

12

The Coming of Governor Brown
(1959)

WHILE HIS TWO gubernatorial predecessors, Earl Warren (later Chief Justice of the United States) and Goodwin J. Knight, both signed off on Chessman's execution, Edmund "Pat" Brown, elected California's governor in November 1958, was the man put in the hot seat over the case. A self-proclaimed "death penalty opponent," Brown nonetheless allowed the fate of Chessman to be decided by political expediency rather than deeply held ethical views on capital punishment.

Brown's reputation as a death penalty opponent is, in retrospect, fairly solid. This was due in part to a public relations campaign that Brown himself waged once he left elective office. It was also due to his lucky timing of being governor when the U.S. Supreme Court had, effectively, declared a moratorium on executions by, in Brown's words, "ordering retrials in the penalty phases of most capital cases still under appeal." Thus, during the last three years of Brown's gubernatorial career (1963–66), he was spared having to face as many tough calls as Warren and Knight.*

---

* Between 1972 and 1976, the U.S. Supreme Court did officially declare a moratorium on capital punishment. That is, with the *Furman v. Georgia* decision, the death penalty was seen as a violation of the Eight Amendment against "cruel and unusual punishment." With this one stroke, all state death penalty laws and death sentences were overturned. By 1976, the U.S. Supreme Court reversed itself, and on January 17, 1977, Gary Gilmore became the first person executed in America in nearly ten years, by a firing squad in Utah.

Brown's memoir *Public Justice, Private Mercy: A Governor's Education on Death Row* (1989) suffers from selective memory about these matters. The author congratulated himself for mercy and glossed over anything that didn't reinforce it. Perhaps more than any other fault, Brown is guilty of the pot–calling–the–kettle black when he characterized Chessman's books, only one of which he admitted to having read, as "self-serving." No event brings out the "self-serving" nature of any politician quite like an execution, and Brown was not immune to this occupational hazard. Indeed, with the exception of his handling of the Chessman case, Brown was one of the most canny politicians of his time. He was personable, charming, smart, and, perhaps most important, he had the burning ambition one needed to take aim at the White House.

Twenty-nine years after Chessman died on his watch, Brown wrote, "I became known as an outspoken foe of capital punishment." Insisting that he paid a political price for his reputation as a "softie," Brown nonetheless handily defeated Richard Nixon, a former vice president, in his 1962 reelection bid, a victory that came despite the fact that Nixon, still reeling from the razor-thin loss of the U.S. presidency in 1960, tried to make political hay out of the lingering Chessman and death penalty controversies. In February 1960, obviously believing he would be the Republican presidential nominee, Nixon dropped by the San Francisco studio of KQED radio station and took questions from a panel of journalists. Throughout the event, Nixon repeatedly used his trademark, "Let me make it perfectly clear" before answering any question with anything but clarity. As for the Chessman case, a hot topic, Nixon pushed the death-penalty-as-deterrant meme: "Many of us have forgotten that kidnapping was pretty general in this country a few years ago. . . . As a result of the amount of kidnapping, there was passed the Lindbergh Law . . . which made kidnapping a capital crime and called for the death penalty. Today, as a result, you seldom hear of kidnapping . . . I think that the capital punishment for kidnapping, therefore, has proved to be an effective deterrent. . . ."

Brown noted in his memoir, "Richard Nixon made it such a major issue during the 1962 gubernatorial campaign that at one point I was sure I'd lose and seriously considered dropping out."*

Brown's views on capital punishment, while more progressive than many of his peers, were always a work in progress and considerably more complicated than he let on in his golden years. Indeed, throughout his career, Brown had wavered from one extreme to the other on the death penalty as well as on the fate of Caryl Chessman. At the start, as San Francisco's district attorney, he was a hard-nosed prosecutor who pressed for the death penalty in nearly every capital case on which he worked. He became the state's attorney general in 1950, and for the eight years he held this office, he vigorously pursued executions for those on San Quentin's Death Row. Chessman was among his bêtes noires even then. In fact, Brown wanted Chessman dead so badly as far back as 1952 that he himself was nearly prosecuted for contempt of court after he called the judge who'd given Chessman a sixty-day stay of execution "softheaded."

Elected governor in 1958, Brown took the oath of office in January 1959. Once settled into his Sacramento office, he proclaimed himself an ardent opponent of capital punishment. While he did make some important decisions on this front, Pat Brown was anything but a pushover for death penalty opponents, and he now avoided going anywhere near the Chessman case unless forced to do so. Of the fifty-nine death penalty cases that crossed his desk during eight years as governor, Brown sent thirty-six men to San Quentin's gas chamber. His predecessor, Goodwin Knight, had sent forty-one of forty-seven to their deaths. Brown undoubtedly would have sent more had the U.S. Supreme Court not ordered retrials on the penalty phases of all capital cases on appeal around the nation in 1963. Thus, taking Pat Brown's full record into consideration, it's disingenuous of him to suggest,

---

* In 1966, when Ronald Reagan defeated Pat Brown for governor, it has been said that the death-penalty issue helped the Republican challenger. If that's true—and it may simply been have a case of the notoriously flinty California voters having wearied of Brown after two terms—then Chessman, it could be argued, had an even more profound impact on American history than has previously been noted. He not only cost Brown his dreams of higher political office, he blew wind in the sails of what, in the 1980s, became "the Reagan Revolution," the fallout from which America is still feeling.

Edmund G. "Pat" Brown was California's governor from 1959–1967, though his animus toward Chessman dated back to his days as the state's attorney general. *Author's collection*

as he did in his memoir, that the status quo for those facing death sentences changed dramatically during his tenure in Sacramento.

Chessman's is an obvious case in point. Brown did give Chessman a sixty-day reprieve on February 18, 1960, a day before his scheduled execution, in order to allow the state legislature to determine, or reconfirm, the validity of the state's death penalty. That action was motivated by a phone call from his son, Edmund G. "Jerry" Brown, who had just left a novitiate in a Jesuit seminary after nearly four years to enroll at the University of California at Berkeley.* This reprieve, which Brown said demonstrated his distaste for the death penalty, was actually much easier to grant than he implies.

---

* As Pat Brown described the conversation to Orville Schell in 1978, "I was up in that great big old Governor's mansion in Sacramento by myself. He called me and said, 'Dad, you're not going to let Chessman die, are you?' And I said, 'Well, son, I have no power to commute his sentence. I've asked the Supreme Court and they've turned me down.' And Jerry said, 'Well, you can give him a reprieve, can't you? And you can go to the legislature and ask for a moratorium on the death penalty.' I said, 'Jerry, there isn't a chance in a thousand the legislature would pass such a bill.' He said, 'Dad, if you had one chance in a thousand to save a man's life, shouldn't you take it?'"

That is, the Assistant U.S. Secretary of State, Roy R. Rubottom Jr., warned Brown by urgent telegram that Chessman's February 1960 execution could ignite "hostile demonstrations" during President Eisenhower's planned trip to Uruguay the following month:

THROUGH OUR EMBASSY IN MONTEVIDEO THE NATIONAL COUNCIL OF GOVERNMENT OF URUGUAY HAS TONIGHT BROUGHT TO THE URGENT ATTEN- TION OF THE STATE DEPARTMENT THE GRAVE CONCERRN OF THE COUNCIL OVER ANTICIPATED HOSTILE DEMONSTRATIONS OF STUDENT ELEMENTS AND OTHERS TO CHESSMAN EXECUTION WHEN OUR PRESIDENT VISITS URUGUAY MARCH 2.

The pro-Chessman sentiment was particularly strong in South America, where the Catholic Church's staunch opposition to capital punishment was embraced by the predominantly Catholic countries and where Chessman's *Cell 2455, Death Row* was a bestseller in Spanish and Portuguese editions. Among the mail received by Governor Brown was a clemency petition with 2.6 million signatures from Brazil and a note from an Ecuadorian man who said he would commit suicide if Chessman were put to death.

Again, expediency dictated Brown's policy.

Two other cases more vividly illustrate the paradox of Brown's record on capital punishment. They are the exceptions that prove his rule, so to speak. In both cases, the convicts' crimes were more violent and heinous than any for which Chessman was ever tried. Nonetheless, both of these convicts—killers, really—had their death sentences commuted by Governor Brown to "life with the possibility of parole." More remarkably, both convicts were eventually released from San Quentin Prison—from Death Row to freedom, no questions asked.

The first was John Crooker, a twenty-nine-year-old navy veteran and aspiring writer from Maine who'd enrolled at UCLA Law School in 1954. While attending classes, Crooker was hired by Norma and Frank McCauley as the live-in "houseboy" for their sprawling residence in the exclusive Bel Air neighborhood, just above Sunset Boulevard. Crooker did household chores and helped care for the three McCauley children; for this he got room, board, and pocket money. He also got Norma, the thirty-one-year-old "socialite wife" (as the newspapers dubbed her). Their torrid love affair simmered, as in James M. Cain's *The Postman Always Rings Twice*, right under the nose of the oblivious Frank McCauley. Crooker quit his job but continued to cuckold the husband. The couple, somewhat inevitably, separated, with Mrs. McCauley getting custody of the children. At that point, Norma ended her relationship with Crooker, who did not take the rejection well. He began stalking and harassing her, even threatening her with physical harm. Finally, on the night of July 4, 1955—one year to the day since the murder of Marilyn Sheppard in Ohio—Crooker broke into the McCauleys' Bel Air home and hid in the closet in Norma's bedroom.

Sometime in the wee hours of July 5, Norma returned from her social rounds; Crooker was there to greet her. When he emerged from her closet—where he'd pissed in jars and smoked cigarettes throughout his wait—Norma remained calm. A nervous and needy Crooker plied her with desperate pleas for reconciliation. Had she struggled or screamed, Norma might have survived—undoubtedly, the children and the maid would have heard her. Instead, exhausted, she fell asleep, at which point the thwarted Crooker became enraged. As he described it in a seven-hundred-word confession which he wrote out by hand for police after his arrest the following afternoon, "I put the knife in my coat pocket and knelt beside her for what seemed to be a long time. She was asleep. I took her throat in my hand and she awoke and started to scream." Crooker shoved his hand over her mouth, and stabbed her numerous times. "She still made sounds and struggled on the [chaise] lounge," Crooker wrote. "I choked her some more with some clothes around her throat and after a long time she was still and the house was still."

A detail not included in Crooker's account: Norma McCauley's five-year-old son, Kirk, discovered his mother's body in a pool of blood the next morning. Newspaper accounts record the pitiful words of the boy to the maid, "You'd better go in. Mommie is in a mess."

After writing out his confession, Crooker accompanied the police back to the McCauley mansion, where he agreeably walked them through the crime scene. They collected evidence at the scene but were lacking the murder weapon and the killer's clothing—all of which Crooker said he'd tossed in an incinerator. The next morning at the police station, Crooker—the UCLA law student—finally asked to speak to a lawyer, who advised him to repudiate his confession. Crooker and his lawyer, Raymond Simpson—who had taught a legal history class at UCLA, where Crooker had befriended him—then led the Los Angeles police and the county's legal machinery through a game of cat-and-mouse. The prosecution's glaring weakness was the lack of a murder weapon.*

Presumably, if we were to follow the logic of a James M. Cain novel, Crooker hoped that Frank McCauley, portrayed by the press as an embittered cuckold, would take the rap for him. Lurid headlines, of course, accompanied the trial's daily revelations, but Crooker cut a more sympathetic figure than Chessman had seven years earlier, mainly because he was clean-cut and handsome, and his lawyer kept a tight leash on his mouth. Some questions were raised about whether the confession was "coerced" or voluntary, a legal nicety not accorded Chessman, who had been held without a lawyer for almost three days in January 1948, interrogated around the clock, and beaten before he "confessed."

Despite all the legal maneuvers and every break in the book, Crooker was found guilty of murder at trial. It seemed so cut and dried that the jury needed only an hour to render its verdict and, upon further reflection, to recommend that Crooker die in the gas chamber at San Quentin.

As soon as he was sworn in, in 1959, Governor Brown, for reasons that are still unclear, took up the case for commuting Crooker's death sentence. Among his first acts in office was to convene a clemency hearing for Crooker on January 9, 1959. The justification for Crooker's

---

* Norma McCauley's body was found with a fur stole tightly coiled around her neck, and knotted on the side. She may have died from suffocation or strangulation rather than from the knifings, which would seem to have made the search for a knife moot. Either way, Crooker was a brutal murderer who had left nothing to chance.

hearing was that a three-man psychiatric committee at San Quentin had determined his mental condition to be "deteriorating"; San Quentin's chief psychiatrist, David Schmidt, reported that Crooker possessed a "passive-aggressive personality, with partial or acute hysteria" and that he might be schizophrenic. Brown later claimed that Crooker's mental incapacity was "aggravated by reported homosexual overtures from the Row's most notorious occupant, Caryl Chessman." This is a dubious accusation—and irresponsible, really, since Chessman had no way to rebut it, and no proof was offered. It was based on the word of a man said to suffer from "hysteria." One might just as easily make the armchair diagnosis that Crooker himself was a repressed homosexual and that he'd transferred these feelings onto Chessman, the famous author that he (Crooker) wanted to be; maybe his way of exacting revenge was to defame Chessman. Maybe, driven by shame over his latent homosexuality, Crooker killed Norma; maybe she knew he was a homosexual. Such speculation is at least as valid as Brown's speculation about "overtures" from Chessman.

One thing is known: from late 1955 to January 1959, Crooker and Chessman had been residents of the same Death Row. Chessman was an acknowledged leader, was looked up to by many residents, and resented by others. The sense of rivalry between Crooker and Chessman, if indeed there was one (Brown's assertions are based on hearsay), had plenty of time to fester and stew. And that's about all they could do, since Row residents were locked down twenty-two hours a day and were seldom in each other's company. Curiously, the name John Crooker never appeared in any of Chessman's writings, and, other than Brown's 1989 memoir, the name is not found in any related San Quentin literature.

Despite the brutality of Norma McCauley's murder, Crooker's death sentence was commuted by Governor Brown on January 12, 1959.

"My first decision about clemency was the easiest one I ever had to make," Brown later wrote. "John Crooker was young, attractive and intelligent; his crime, although terrible, was at least understandable [*sic*]." Brown glossed over the backlash from his commutation of Crooker, saying the "initial grumbles quickly faded away, especially as the Chessman case began to occupy more and more of the world's attention."*

The second case with an indirect link to Chessman and Governor Brown was even more macabre. It involved Edward Simon Wein, the so-called Want Ad Rapist. From early 1955 through October 1956, Wein staged a one-man reign of terror in Los Angeles. His modus operandi was to answer classified ads in person. Meek in appearance, Wein did not present an immediate danger. Thus, he easily gained entry into homes. If the seller was a woman and if she lived alone, or was without male protection, Wein tied her up, raped her, and robbed and ransacked the residence. One of Wein's victims was a fourteen-year-old girl ("He threatened to kill me and my little brothers and sister if I made any noise," she testified). After his arrest, Wein was prosecuted by J. Miller Leavy, who'd prosecuted Chessman in the same courtroom in 1948. Of "Eddie" Wein, Leavy said, "This fellow puts Caryl Chessman to shame. He makes Chessman look like a rank amateur, a schoolboy."

Despite Wein's claims of innocence—of the whole thing being "a tragic case of mistaken identity"—and his insistence that the police had set him up—saying, "a half hour after I was arrested a Hollywood detective said they were going to make a Chessman out of me"—the jury found him guilty on all counts (six counts of rape, six counts of "sex perversion," three counts of robbery, two counts of kidnap, five

---

* Inspired by Chessman's example and, after May 2, 1960, being the prison's best-known living wannabe writer, Crooker penned a hundred and seven-page play called *M'Naghten's Madness*, about a Scotsman who was declared "criminally insane" after being imprisoned for murder; the play was never produced or published. Even Brown admitted that it was "not a particularly good play." Prodded by a British writer, Brigid Brophy, who'd been corresponding with Crooker, Brown, who as State Attorney General had made sush a big deal about the unfair advantage that Chessman had over other prisoners because "he could write a book," commuted Crooker's sentence even further, in late 1966 offering him "the possibility for parole." In 1972, when Ronald Reagan was governor, Crooker was released from prison altogether—that is, a murderer was allowed to go free right under the nose of a renowned "law and order" governor. In 1978, Crooker visited Brown, then in private legal practice, at his Beverly Hills office, a visit the retired governor later recalled as "pleasant." Meanwhile, Norma McCauley was dead, her three children grew up without a mother, and Kirk McCauley was supplied with a memory that launched a thousand nightmares.

counts of kidnap for the purpose of robbery). He received his death sentence, as Chessman had, because he'd moved his victims from room to room and thus fell under Section 209, or the Little Lindbergh Law, which laid out the guidelines for kidnap. Wein was sentenced by Judge Leroy Dawson to die in the gas chamber at San Quentin and he soon joined Chessman and John Crooker on the Row.

Wein's request for clemency landed on Governor Brown's desk on June 5, 1959. Brown was sympathetic to the arguments that Section 209 (Little Lindbergh) was a "legal swamp," another nicety not extended to Chessman. Brown shared the view of Judge Jesse Carter, who had dissented in Wein's earlier (failed) appeal to the State Supreme Court and had previously issued two stays to Chessman for the same reason, a distaste for Section 209 with its vague definition of what constituted "kidnap." Carter stated: "Under the rule of this case a robber who shoves his victim against a wall is eligible for the gas chamber." Brown commuted Wein's sentence on June 4, 1959 to life without parole. The linchpin for him was Wein's "mental history"; he'd been diagnosed as "psychotic or borderline psychotic" just weeks before his first rape and had tried to commit suicide with an overdose of Nembutal two weeks before his final attack in 1956. San Quentin psychiatrists determined Wein to be "sociopathic, antisocial, emotionally immature with psychoneurotic and psychosexual disturbances." However, he was not legally insane, and he was aware of the consequences of the criminal acts for which he stood trial.

Governor Brown commuted Wein's sentence even further in December 1966, to "life with the possibility of parole." Wein, said to be a model inmate who played piano for the prison's Christian Science services, was paroled from San Quentin on September 16, 1974, a free man. Barely one year later, in November 1975, Wein was arrested for the murder of a housewife in the Westchester section of Los Angeles, and the rape-beating-stabbing of another woman in the Palms neighborhood. The modus operandi: answering want ads in person. In June 1976, Wein was convicted of both crimes and sent back to San Quentin. The death penalty having by then been struck down by the U.S. Supreme Court, Wein spent the remaining years of his life behind bars.*

These two cases—Crooker's and Wein's—should have offered some perspective to California's authorities regarding their contemporaneous treatment of Caryl Chessman. Yet another case came to light in January 1958, when the convicted murderer Howard Gibson was asked to testify at Chessman's transcript hearing. Gibson, who had stabbed his wife to death on January 12, 1948, was present in the Los Angeles jail when Chessman was brought in after being arrested on January 23, 1948, and charged with the Red Light Bandit crimes. Gibson substantiated Chessman's claim that his face and body were covered with bruises after his "confession" was beaten out of him by police. There was one undeniably odd aspect to the courtroom scene ten years later. This time, Gibson, responsible for his wife's death, was a free man, having been paroled from San Quentin in 1956—he had, said the *Los Angeles Times*, "paid his debt to society." Whereas Chessman, whose alleged victims were still alive, faced extermination.

The essential mystery of Chessman's case resides in such inequitable treatment. Chessman's Red Light crimes, if indeed he was guilty, left no corpses, did not take any mother away from three children, nor did they leave a trail of blood and grief (other than his own mother's), and yet he was called a "monster" and a "terrorist" by the same governer who allowed murderers to go free. Were one to "grade" criminality, Chessman's crimes were far less egregious than Wein's, Crooker's, or Gibson's. One could argue, then, that Chessman's parole would have been far less of a gamble and far less of a potential danger to society than the leniency shown toward those other ruthless killers.

Of such flimsy threads did the curious case of Caryl Chessman seem to have been woven from start to finish.

---

* Eddie Wein dodged the death penalty by two years. In 1978, the gas chamber at San Quentin was reopened for business.

■

BESIDES THE ARRIVAL of Pat Brown in Sacramento, 1959 saw Chessman watching with a mixture of anger and bemusement as the antics of Marin County District Attorney Wiessich backfired worse than a hand-cranked horseless carriage. Longstreth had managed to delay his own extradition to appear in court by taking his case to the governor of Indiana, Harold W. Handley. And George Davis, no stranger to milking the press, had made mincemeat out of the zealous prosecutor in the daily papers. Nonetheless, the hearings over the smuggling of *The Face of Justice* continued.

In mid-January, Longstreth flew to California to testify in the case of the smuggled manuscript. Not taking any chances, he hired John Thorpe, a sharp young lawyer from San Jose, to represent him in this frivolous lawsuit. All the Bay Area newspapers covered the hearings in Marin County with banner headlines, the Oakland paper running front-page stories for three days running. Asher was much more culpable for having received the manuscript and then passing it on to an unsuspecting Longstreth (and, thus, Prentice-Hall), but she escaped with a reprimand. An itinerant printer and former convict named Joseph Parham, confessed to helping smuggle the manuscript out of the prison, but Asher and Davis both thought he was a plant by Weissich, someone paid to take the fall and to save the D.A.'s face, if not his behind, which at that point were hard to distinguish one from the other.

While out west, Longstreth had a liquid lunch with Rosalie and dinner with Bernice Freeman and her new husband, Bob Davis. Due to the restrictive visiting hours, he wasn't able to schedule a trip to San Quentin to see Chessman, and he sent his regrets.

"It was grand seeing you, Joe, even if you had to be arrested to get to California," Asher wrote him upon his return to snow-bound Indiana. Curiously, the February edition of *American Home* magazine featured a spread on Longstreth and Alan Honour's converted farmhouse. Honour had expressed anxiety over having anything to do with the article, then reconsidered, only to have his quotes and photos excised by the editors. It was just as well with him. This was

1959, and two men living together, presumably sharing a forbidden lifestyle, would have raised more than eyebrows.

Frances Couturier's daughter was born on Valentine's Day, 1959. Asher wrote Longstreth, "Fran is, or purports to be, quite happy, though the miscegenation angle caused the other children some difficult times." She was not married to the man whose child this was.*

Chessman finally got some good publishing news in March. The latest flurry of legal maneuvers had, apparently, raised his international profile again, resulting in a spike in sales of all three books. Prentice-Hall was sufficiently impressed that they held *The Face of Justice* back from the earlier plan to remainder it. The infusion of cash was like lifeblood to Chessman's legal war chest, though Asher confessed to spending her long overdue lawyer's fee on a blond wig, among other sartorial accoutrements. Copies of the French edition of *The Kid Was a Killer* (*Fils de la Haine*, published by Presses de la Cité, 1959) arrived at the same time. (This was good news since, as he was preparing his tax returns by April 15, he learned that his total income in 1958 had fallen to $2,745.67.)

This was counterbalanced by the sad news of Judge Jesse Carter's fatal heart attack on the Ides of March. Without Judge Carter's July 1954 stay of execution, Chessman would not have had time to bask in the success of his first book, *Cell 2455, Death Row*, and he would have had considerably less of a precedent for future stays. Carter had, in short, given Chessman a fair shake. Upon his death, Asher wrote her client, "The good guys are beginning to go, and that ain't according to the script."

On March 16, Asher wrote Longstreth, "I heard a most interesting tale as to the real reason for Caryl's original arrest. In parts it's incredible; but it could easily be reasonably accurate. Comes (indirectly, let me add) from the Syndicate. But, at this stage, even if it's true—so what? I see no way in which the information could be used to help him now." She was probably right that the information was of little

---

* Curiously, according to Asher's "niece," Bonnie Fovinci, the lawyer's longtime romantic companion was also a black man.

help to Chessman, but it's entirely within reason that someone from within the Los Angeles Police Department who had gotten wind of the corruption of the late 1940s on the force had decided to come clean and, perhaps, save the life of a man unjustly convicted. Nothing, to this date, has come of this, however.

April brought more good news and bad news. On April 8, Mr. Ellison from Gold Medal wrote again and said they would publish *The Kid Was a Killer* "with revisions." But, on April 21, the State Assembly defeated a proposal, 43 to 35, that would have put an eight-year moratorium on the death penalty, substituting life imprisonment without parole for those already on Death Row, including Chessman. And on April 26, the Supreme Court denied Chessman's motion to file a petition for habeas corpus.

Death was beginning to rattle the bars on Chessman's cage. The point of no return may have come on July 7, 1959, when the state supreme court affirmed Chessman's original convictions. On August 10, Judge Herbert V. Walker, the judge Team Chessman had hoped would be more lenient than Judge Goodman, scheduled Chessman's execution for October 24, 1959. To add to the misery of this news, August brought temperatures in excess of 100 degrees several days running. Needless to say, Death Row was not air-conditioned. Thus, the clearance given by the prison officials for Chessman to work on revisions of *The Kid Was a Killer*, for publication by Gold Medal, was a mixed blessing. How does one work under such meteorological and psychological conditions?

The pressure, the heat, the dwindling hope for a commutation or reprieve, the loss of Frances's affections—all of these things undoubtedly contributed to a profound sense of frustration for Chessman, who finally broke on August 15, 1959. He and another Death Row inmate, Lawrence Wade, a convicted murderer from Alameda County, began arguing across the corridor about baseball, of all things. Wade was lauding the San Francisco Giants, goading Chessman into defending his "hometown" Los Angeles Dodgers. The next day, during exercise period, the pair continued their discussion of the national pastime with their fists. The brief fight was broken up. Associate Warden Walter Achuff told reporters, "They are pretty poor fighters. About all they did was get some exercise. Tempers get short where they are." Still, they were both sent to isolation for two days and denied exercise for five more.

Asher wrote Longstreth, "Caryl looks reasonably good, especially considering his recent 'beef' with one of the other condemned men, of which you might possibly have read. I really believe that the brawl was not of his own making and that he could scarcely avoid it; in any event, it happened. And, strangely, it appears to me (psychiatrist junior grade?) that the physical release also has served to ease some of the emotional tension which was building up in him."

Asher prepared for a possible trip to Washington, to argue the case in front of the Supreme Court. Instead, she went to Brazil to appear in a television documentary about capital punishment. On October 2, Asher reported from Brazil to Longstreth about the "utterly fantastic and unbelievable" reaction to Chessman. Best-selling Portuguese editions of all his books were everywhere, including *The Kid Was a Killer*. A pro-Chessman, anti–capital punishment movement was gaining ground throughout South America, headed by a prominent industrialist named Giacomo Franco in São Paulo. Franco had been to San Quentin to meet with Chessman on three separate occasions, all of the visits recorded on film to be shown on Brazilian television. Chessman spoke in Spanish, in which the Portuguese-speaking Franco was also fluent. Based on these meetings, Franco said, "I am personally of the opinion that Chessman is a completely rehabilitated personality. I feel that he can be of great service to society. . . . in speaking to youth, showing crime doesn't pay. . . . He can teach a vivid lesson." Asher described Franco as a "strange, driving, ambitious but good man." He gave Asher an impassioned letter about Chessman to hand-deliver to Warden Dickson.

Franco also gave *L.A.* magazine an interview in late 1959. In it he described how his petition drive for clemency created a groundswell of support among "all levels of society . . . from the Supreme Court right down to the ministers and lawyers and university students and plain people. . . ." At one São Paulo professional football (soccer) game, nearly everyone in the stadium, including "some world champion players" signed it. He said that he was so confident in Chessman's rehabilitation that "I would certainly offer him a home, a place to write, if Chessman should find it psychologically or economically impossible to live in the United States. In fact, I would be pleased to have Mr. Chessman come to live in my home. I would be ready to send the plane ticket at any time."

Otto Gill, the president of the Brazilian Bar Association, had personally appealed to Governor Brown in July, saying, "Public opinion throughout the civilized world would rejoice over a favorable decision in this case." That same month, a group of Brazilian women had sent a petition to spare Chessman's life to Brown via Vera Ribeiro, Brazil's entry in the Miss Universe pageant held in Long Beach, California.

Emboldened by her trip to Brazil, Asher wrote Longstreth, "Caryl has already told the authorities he will not accept a commutation to life without possibility of parole, or any relief predicated on an assumption of guilt," wrote Asher. "I disagree and have told him, assumptions aside, if he's still alive we can at least continue to try and prove his innocence. . . . I also accused him of, consciously or subconsciously, wanting to play the martyr; but he insists this isn't true and he's a little tired of everyone psychoanalyzing him. . . . So be it . . . but I WANT TO WIN THIS CASE!"

Asher had a friend who was close to Cecil Poole, Brown's clemency secretary. There was cautious optimism that he could help Chessman. She warned Longstreth that Assistant Warden Nelson "hated" Chessman.

Asher's "in" with Cecil Poole amounted to nothing. Neither did a petition to commute Chessman's sentence signed by Eleanor Roosevelt—as well as slightly lesser luminaries Aldous Huxley, Harry Golden, Ray Bradbury, Steve Allen, Theodore Bikel, Walter Wanger (whose house Chessman was allegedly casing in 1948)—which arrived on Brown's desk on October 14. The next day, an executive clemency hearing was held in Brown's office. George T. Davis argued on Chessman's behalf, citing the severity of the punishment for crimes that left no one dead, as well as its outmoded connection to the Lindbergh baby kidnapping, the mental illness of Mary Alice Meza, and the mitigating factor of Chessman's already record-length stay on Death Row. Brown countered by questioning Chessman's "usefulness" to society. "Even if I do act, will there ever be a chance of Chessman contributing anything to society?" said Brown, ignoring the existence Chessman's three books that had launched a worldwide reassessment of capital punishment. "I can find no indication of his barest desire to express contrition for his acts. The depravity of his character seems fairly well assured."

Though he hinted broadly to the press after the hearing that he might spare Chessman's life, Governor Brown announced on October 19 that he refused to grant clemency. Chessman's execution, set for October 27, would proceed.

Back in Indiana, Longstreth told a reporter for the Richmond newspaper that, on October 27 at 1:00 P.M.—Chessman's scheduled execution time—he planned to play the piano, "Something Caryl would like, perhaps 'Moonlight Serenade,' Then I'll pray." In a fit of anger, he also told the reporter, "Caryl Chessman has never taken a life. . . . Yet they are going out of their way to see that he dies. They even seem eager for it. Where is the Christianity in this?" He predicted that Chessman "will die with far greater dignity than he has been shown by the people willing to put him to death . . . Caryl is alone, friendless and penniless in a death cell, but he has created a niche in history. . . . He will live whereas the people who are killing him and putting him to death will die."

Brown's decision was hailed by conservatives, including District Attorney McKesson, who said Brown "had placed the responsibility of his office above personal inclination." J. Miller Leavy, a bit more realistically said, "Regardless of the reasons for Governor Brown's denial of the commutation, at long last the proper administration of justice in the Chessman case is one step closer."

Though Brown may have been deluded enough to think he was placing the responsibility of his office above personal inclination, the denial of commutation left him open to charges of wishy-washiness; it also raised doubts about his professed aversion to the death penalty. If any case called for a Solomon-like act of judicial decency, Chessman's did. But Brown, playing politics more than moralist, succumbed to the hysteria of the right wing. Chessman didn't do himself any future favors by attacking the governor's decision, but his bitter assessment of Brown's motives was, in retrospect, correct: "It was the politically expedient thing for him to do. He has made his bid, made his verbal bow and paid his homage to hysteria. He has now emerged as Presidential timber."

Governor Brown's decision was countermanded almost immediately.

On October 21, George Davis flew to Washington to confer with Supreme Court Justice William O. Douglas, to whom he'd applied for a stay of execution prior to Brown's decision. A second petition for a stay was sent to Justice Douglas by John Thorne, representing Longstreth in the Marin County Superior Court's manuscript smuggling case, as Chessman's presence was requested as a witness for the defense. On October 24, Douglas granted a stay of execution three days before Chessman's scheduled execution, "pending the timely filing and consideration of a petition for certiorari."

Chessman was informed of the decision by Lawrence Wade, the Death Row inmate whose love of the Giants had irked Chessman in the heat of August. "He was as excited as any of the prisoners," Chessman told the reporters who had assembled in Achuff's office for a press conference. "So much death is always present with us that any time one of us can escape it, it encourages all of us. Friday will be a very busy day instead of my last."

In the midst of all this, the comical book-smuggling indictments were dismissed by the District Court of Appeals at the end of October (the dismissal was upheld by the State Supreme Court on December 23, 1959).

"Congratulations! I'm so happy for you I could burst," Asher wrote Longstreth. "I haven't had the opportunity to see the actual

Pages 321–322: People around the country, including Wanda Kohls of Chippewa Falls, Wisconsin, were fascinated by Chessman. Ms. Kohls told this author, "For some reason the Chessman case intrigued me, and I followed it for about ten years. I didn't think he was guilty, certainly not enough to deserve the death penalty. Another thing that kind of bound me to his story was that as a child he'd had encephalitis. I too had that disease as an after-affect of the measles when I was ten years old. At that time, I was used as a 'guinea pig' for treatment as there was no known cure for it." *Courtesy Wanda Kohls*

CONVICT BLAMES CIVILIZATION
'Different' Chessman Dies

CARYL CHESSMAN
Dies With Dignity

Editor's Note—A former Evening Telegram city editor, George Flowers, now assistant managing editor of the Long Beach, Calif., Independent, and Caryl Chessman, who met death in the gas chamber Monday, sat down in January of this year to revise a statement prepared earlier for release in the event of Chessman's death. The statement, originally made in 1955, was revised to conform with the existing situation and was released by the Independent following Chessman's death Monday. Flowers was an employe of the Evening Telegram for about 10 years.

BY CARYL CHESSMAN
Copyright 1960 by Long Beach Independent, distributed by The Associated Press.

LONG BEACH, Calif. — (AP)— These words are not intended for publication unless the state of California has finally taken its vengeance. I should like to ask the world to consider what has been gained.

I know that there are many who

waisted. It seems irony that most of my childhood was spent in institutions that were designed to correct my ways and mend my manners. They failed to do that and, I am sorry, I failed to respond to that treatment. Yet it seems to me that someone could have penetrated to me, someone could have reached me when I was only a perplexed and befuddled boy.

That is the time to stop crime, to rehabilitate. Boys can be reached and changed, and that is a job society must accomplish.

Now I am gone. Whatever use I might have been to society is canceled by an act of vengeance. Capital punishment is not a penalty. Many times, in these last few years, I have realized it might

be a blessing to end this tormented struggle and this inhuman harassment.

I have seen the poor, the friendless, the mentally ill, led to the chamber of execution. I have felt that society has each time, shirked its responsibility. These were the mistakes of civilization. Instead of correcting mistakes, society erases them. Out of sight, out of mind.

You ask me if I have a confession to make. I have not. In my lifetime I was guilty of many crimes, but not these for which my life was taken. You ask me about a future life. I believe there is none. Caryl has gone to oblivion, so that society can forget one sorry lifetime.

Conflict Chessman Created
Seethes on After His Death

SAN QUENTIN, Calif. (AP)—The bitter conflict Caryl Chessman created in life seethed on today after its execution, finally carried out after 12 suspense-

innocent of the crimes that cost his life.

Just before taking the last 13 steps into the death chamber, Chessman told Warden Fred Dickson he was not the red light

He was strapped in the chair at 10:02 a.m. The potassium cyanide pellets were dropped into a pan of sulphuric acid at 10:03:5.

As the first fumes rose, Chessman took a deep breath. His head

---

Six Condemned Men Stag
Brawl On Death Row

CARYL CHESSMAN

SAN QUENTIN, Calif. (AP)—Officials of this northern California penitentiary were to decide today how to punish six condemned men — including Caryl

Chessman — for a New Year Day brawl on death row.

The fight broke out after prison's 24 death row inmates were admitted to their recreation room to watch holiday programs on television. They had just seen in the Rose Bowl parade.

James Merkouris, 44-year Los Angeles killer of emerged from his cell and began yelling and swinging at other mates. Louis Nelson, prison ciplinary officer, said Manuel Chavez, 27, hit Merkouris with a wooden stool, whereupon Merkouris is dashed the television set to pieces on the floor.

Chessman, death row was sentenced to die Feb. 19, knocked Merkouris down and straddled his chest. The four others, Charles Clyde Bates, 19; Marion Lir 45, and Donald L. Cash, 32, pummeled Merkouris.

Guards restored order and the six back in their cells.

Were You Count

THE EVENI

THE EVENING

THE WEATHER
ly cloudy to cloudy;
nued cool.

Sevent

VOL. 71 — Upper Wisconsin's Great Home Newspaper — SUPERIOR, WIS

OTESTS BITTER
uropeans Denounce
hessman Execution

NDON (AP)—Europeans to-itterly denounced the execution of Caryl Chessman. Two youth demonstrations were red from Latin America, and a, the Middle East and Asia

dramatic argument for abolishing the death penalty. Raimondo Manzini, director of the Vatican newspaper L'Osservatore Romano, which had appealed for mercy for Chessman, wrote

In the Scandinavian nations, which have no death penalty, the papers called for an end to capital punishment everywhere. "A parody of justice" said the Paris Combat, left-wing but non-

THE MIL

Chessman Lawye
Fought to Very E

CHICAGO'S AMERICAN, TUESDAY,

[Continued from first page]
Gas Chamber; Cruel America.
A few voices raised in belief

forced sexual perversion against two young women,

He died as he said he would

abou
cludin
ing to
eared
that

Denies Guilt--
Chessman Dies
With Wink, Grin

SAN QUENTIN—(UPI)—Caryl Chessman died in th gas chamber Monday with a smile and a wink, ending 12-year legal battle for life that went to and beyon the moment of death.

Except for an appeal that was too late and a misdiale telephone number his life might have been spared for at leas an hour.

• • •

A federal judge in San Francisco was trying to reach San Quentin to grant a one-hour stay when the cyanide pellets splashed into a vat of sulphuric acid beneath the green death chair at 10:03 a.m. (11:03 a. m. CST.)

Among his last words, "Tell Rosalie goodbye."

Chessman Case
Stirs Anti-U.S.
Demonstrations

LONDON — (UP)— The ex

Chessman's Ex-Wife Sure He Will Die, Doubts Guilt

Part 1

Los Angeles, Calif. – AP – On Aug. 8, 1940, a 16 year old high school girl married a boy of 18 with dark, curly hair and a bad reputation. His name: Caryl

so completely closed that she agreed to talk to newsmen who traced her only if they would promise not to use her name.

She told a story of a brief

the littlest. Then in 1941 he came home one night and dumped a sackful of money on the bed.

"The bed was just covered

escape this time, as he had previous seven, through leg maneuvers or action by the go

"I think he will be executed

LINE 10 A.M. MONDAY
essman Readies Final Bid to Escape Execution

QUENTIN, Calif. (AP)—Caryl Chessman pre-a "final" talk with two of his attorneys today more can be done to prevent his execution in the ber, scheduled for 10 a.m. Monday.

neys, A. L. Wirin and her, got nowhere with u to Gov. Edmund Sacramento Thursday. meet with Chessman today.
told them that he stood statement of last Tues-e is powerless to act re is some unexpected t of a critical nature. sight.
ess, Wirin told report-re confident that when s are down the gover-o the same thing se." The last time was when Brown granted a 60-day reprieve. ernor said nothing to that impression, Wirin

hessman, sentenced to ay, was convicted of g 17 crimes in a 20-d. See story, Page 2. t the execution went

would be allowed on the prison grounds Sunday night, the eve of the execution. Newsmen had been admitted in the past.

The governor's office announced it would flash the word when the death-dealing cyanide pellets are dropped in the gas chamber. Newsmen at the viewing area in the prison aren't permitted to leave until the execution is over.

Chessman was sentenced to death in 1948 for kidnaping for robbery with bodily harm. He was convicted of being Los Angeles' "Red Light Bandit."

He has been on San Quentin's death row for nearly 12 years, successfully fighting off eight execution dates.

PREDICTS REPRIEVE

Wirin, predicting Brown would spare Chessman, said: "As a man of honor he can't do anything else. It would be an unconscionable and godless act to let Chessman die. "We take the position that the matter continues to be in the

LETHAL CHAMBER — If Caryl Chessman is ber which is designed to kill a man in 15

Ex-Wife Denies
Chessman
Had Daughter

CARYL CHESSMAN'S former wife said Thursday as far as she knows the robberbyrapist never had a daughter despite his claim that fear for her life kept him from naming the real "red-light bandit." The woman, now remarried, said through an attorney that she had no children by Chessman. "I don't know either of a wife before, during or after my marriage to Chessman," she said. Chessman's attorneys said after he was executed that he did not identify the real bandit because he was afraid for the life of his 17-year-old daughter.

OFFICIALS of Forrest Lawn Memorial cemetery in Glendale, Calif., steadfastly refused to accept the ashes of Chessman. Offers of a final resting place for the convict author continued to flow in from Europe, South America, Mexico and many places in the

Justice or Revenge-
Chessman Adds Fuel to Death Debate

By BERNARD GAVZER
Associated Press Writer

Nearly 200 convicts in the United States will scratch this day off the calendar as another step closer to doom.

Their predicament would get no more attention than usual but for one of their number—Caryl Chessman—scheduled to be executed next week in San Quentin's gas chamber.

Chessman—through his books dramatizing his case, through his self-acquired legal knowledge helping him stave off execution for 11½ years—vigorously stirred up an old, impassioned controversy.

Can modern man continue to exact "an eye for an eye, a tooth for a tooth?" Is the death penalty justice or vengeance? Is it the ultimate deterrent to keep man from violence?

In Chessman's California, the recently refused Gov. 's plea to abolish ... But the argu... ...nist on the death

... justifiable punish-...king of, another's ... will to live de-...iminals from con-... crime. Execution ... to make certain ...es not kill again.

Those against the death penalty say:

Capital punishment has proved no more a deterrent than less severe punishment. Juries are reluctant to levy the death penalty and thus some murderers go unpunished. Murderers who have been paroled rarely commit another murder; they are the best parole risks. Crime rates and murderous attacks on police in abolition states are no greater, and in some cases lower than in death penalty states. Capital punishment is morally wrong, psychologically unsound and discriminatory; the condemned are often the poor, the weak and the ignorant. It is punitive, retaliative, revengeful and stands in the way of rehabilitating wrongdoers.

Forty-one states inflict the death penalty for about 30 different crimes; not the same crimes are capital in every state. But the death sentence is most often given for murder. Of 49 executions in 1959, 41 were for murder, 8 for rape. Executions are largely private. Death is imposed in the electric chair, the gas chamber, on the gallows or by the firing squad.

Some abolitionists say that if capital punishment is inflicted for its deterrent effect, it is surely illogical to kill the convicted person painlessly, rapidly and pri-

so much secrecy. If the state really believes that execution is necessary to deter others, it should execute openly and unashamed."

Today, across the world, there is a definite trend toward doing away with the death penalty. Thirty-five foreign countries have abolished it. The United States, one of the few major nations in the Western world to retain it, in practice does not inflict it with any regularity or frequency. The number of executions has steadily declined, reaching a low of 48 in 1958.

Yet, there is a recurrent demand for the death penalty—particularly in the wake of vicious crime.

Upon the ordinary citizen who wants to live quietly and peacefully, the issue of capital punishment may never intrude except occasionally when he reads headlines in his newspaper.

Whom should he believe—the people who say the death penalty stops murder or the ones who say it doesn't?

"It is common sense to know that capital punishment works," say many policemen, police chiefs and some jurists, clergymen, prosecuting attorneys. "There is no fate man fears more," they say. Police point it up with personal accounts of criminals carrying fake weapons or unload... rather than risk a shoo... could pu... ...

But ... warden... talki... ...ers—...and o... cuted ...pu...

"I ... man ... sa... give ... t... they ... they co... that is ... alty," ... one pe... thought ... to the c... The abo... our mand ... than 8,000 ... crimes of ... occur unde...

New York Institute of ...says a roll call of ...capital punishment in...James V. Bennett, dir...U.S. Bureau of Priso...ernors of Florida, Ca...nois and Ohio; man...criminologists, socio...chiatrists; such relig...as the Society of F...Methodist Church, ...Presbyterian Church ...U.S.A.; the Protestan...Church, the Union of ...Hebrew Congregation...an Catholic Church

Chessman Scorns Clemency

From Late Dispatches

CARYL CHESSMAN SAID Saturday he would die rather than ask Gov. Edmund Brown or clemency, ...ut the Californi...he chief executive ...he said ...he ould review he kidnap-...apist's case anyway.

Chessman, ...ho is scheduled ...o die in the San Quentin ...hamber Feb. 19, ...old a news con-...erence he would stick with ...he courts since Brown had ...ejected a bid for clemency ...ade by the convict-author's ...attorney last fall.

"I haven't ever gone to the governor for clemency. I have no intention of leaving the courts as long as there are any other courts left. I don't intend to ever say another word to the governor," Chessman said.

Brown's statement on the ...se was based on a ruling by ...federal Judge Louis E. Good-...ian, who Friday turned down ...Chessman's demand for a writ ...f habeas corpus. Goodman re-...used to issue the writ but ...uggested that the case might ...ell be considered by the ...California governor and the ...tate supreme court under ...heir clemency powers.

Chessman A To Reveal 'Real Bandi

SAN FRANCISCO (AF...Chessman's attorney, ...new evidence, says he ...save the convict-author...gas chamber by revea...name of the "real red l...dit."

"We know who he is ...he is," attorney George ...told newsmen Sunday nig...don't know wher...

Chessman Execution Begins on Schedule

Gas Pellets Dropped Acid

PROTESTS FAIL TO STOP EXECUTION — Shown are some of the families who gathered on a hillside near California's San Quentin Prison Monday carrying signs pro-

Disposition of Chessman's Ashes Now in Controversy

SAN RAFAEL, Calif. (AP)—Caryl Chessman's ashes remained at a mortuary here today, the object of a controversy over their disposition.

The convict-author who was executed Monday had directed that his ashes be inurned at Glendale's Forest Lawn Memorial Park in Southern California. His mother is buried there.

But a Forest Lawn spokesman, noting that Chessman was "unrepentant and an avowed agnostic," said Tuesday night the ashes would be refused. He said they would "detract from the spiritual values of Forest Lawn."

One of Chessman's attorneys, L. A. Wirin, said in Los Angeles he would recommend to Rosalie Asher, executrix of the convict's estate and also his lawyer, that a court order be requested requiring Forest Lawn to accept the remains.

Miss Asher went into seclusion after failure of her last frantic efforts to obtain a stay of execution. She was not present at the cremation at Tamalpais Ceme-

tery. There was no religious service.

A San Rafael newswoman, Bernice Freeman placed two rosebuds from her garden in the otherwise unadorned coffin.

Mrs. Freeman, who knew Chessman well, said he offered one of his eyes when one of her daughters, Pat Aldrige, was going blind. When another daughter, Bettie Johnson, also began losing her eyesight Chessman made a like offer, Mrs. Freeman said.

Mortician Harry Williams await instructions from Miss Asher.

George T. Davis, another of the convict's attorneys, said the execution of the death row author, who was convicted as the Los Angeles red light bandit 12 years ago, was "a regrettable mistake."

Oshkosh Youth Committed for 80-Year Term

GREEN BAY (AP) — David Spanbauer, a 19-year-old Oshkosh youth arrested after a crime spree, Tuesday was committed to the state prison under the sex deviate law.

Municipal Judge Donald W. Gleason acted on the recommendation of the State Department

Whereabouts of Esther Person Is Sought

ASHLAND — (Special) — An effort to lo...

Appeals
...ve
...ail
...
...hessman's appeals
...orld-wide conflict.
...around of the News, ...
...mi
...Cal
...ary(AP)— The gov-
...day-ice announced
...tion of Caryl
...ed today.
...estir the cyanide pel-
...onsigned into the acid
...goldtin prison's gas
...been flashed in wait-
...now by a secretary
...could ...
...All ...
...origi ...
...happy ...
...ko of ...
...in the ...
...Acc ...
...been a ...
...and e ...
...averag ...
...there ...
...of thas ...
...piece o ...
...Caryl Chessman's 11½-
...cent... fined legal torture."
...will we He asked Gov. Ed...
...weight Brown Tuesday to spa...
...gold seman's life, although he a...
...that's aman should be kept be...
...such as he noted Chessman...
...Pleskcondemned for an offe...
...El Dordid not involve the dea...
...three yeather human being...
...during ti Giesler said his ple...
...and his as prompted by a ple...
...to visit Dilliam Hamling of Ch...
...tor and publisher of Rog...
...zine.

Chessman A Victim of 'Legal Tortur

LOS ANGELES (AP) ...criminal attorney Jerr... says condemned sex decision; but George Davis said it's really strongly worded. Davis is very much back in the act. I'm not at all pleased with this development and, though I want to discuss it with Caryl to see that I wouldn't be prejudicing his case in any way, I'm strongly inclined to withdraw, solely because of Davis's participation. I feel that vehemently about it."

Longstreth responded, "I know very well how you must feel about George Davis, Rosalie. I'd think he would be most difficult to work with. However, do you really 'want out' now? It may well be that the most exciting parts of this now famous case are yet to come. This last stay resulted in making the case, it seems to me, truly a cause célèbre. And as difficult as the day-to-day problems may be, I should think you could minimize them as far as personal relations with George are concerned and still keep your fingers in the pie."

Asher wrote on November 17: "Davis I can scarcely bear to talk about; he becomes more irksome day by day. I know you're right. If I can just maintain a certain amount of detachment, I can muddle along fairly well. But I'm afraid I've reached the peevish and petulant stage where it infuriates me to seem him grabbing all the glory; I've never before cared too much about headlines, but I do smart seeing Davis claim credit for work he hasn't done."

Chessman somehow found time to make the revisions on *The Kid Was a Killer* and was interested in seeing galleys and page proofs.

On December 14, 1959, the U.S. Supreme Court denied the writ of certiorari and Chessman was facing yet another execution date as the year came to an end. He may have suspected that this was his last Christmas on earth.

13

The Green Room Beckons

IN TIME, THE gas chamber took on a powerful and grisly symbolic aspect in America, though when it was introduced to the California state legislature in 1937, it was considered a far more enlightened form of extermination than its predecessor, the gallows. It was also chosen as more "humane" over methods then being employed by other states, like the firing squad in Utah and the electric chair in a majority of the other thirty-eight states where capital punishment was on the books.

Gassing was the brainchild of a Nevada toxicologist, Dr. Allen McLean Hamilton. When the Nevada state legislature rejected electrocution as "gruesome" in 1921, they chose Dr. Hamilton's newly devised method and thus became the first state to do so. Perhaps to make his idea seem more palatable, Dr. Hamilton originally intended for the condemned to be gassed in their cell while they slept, without being told ahead of time—thus, presumably, saving them hours or days of agonized waiting. When the dangers to other prisoners and prison staff were considered, the need for an actual airtight chamber was obvious.

To the rescue came Major Delos A. Turner, an army medical corps officer who fashioned an airtight chamber for this purpose; it was first used at the state prison in Carson City on February 8, 1921, to execute a Chinese-born gang member named Gee Jong, convicted of murdering a rival gang member. Because no stethoscope was attached to the prisoner and the hydrocyanic acid gas was manually pumped into the makeshift stone chamber—a converted tool shed—Gee Jong was left inside for thirty minutes to be certain that he had expired.

After Nevada proved that a gas chamber could work, ten other states, mostly bastions of the "old West," adopted gassing as the means by which they executed their convicts: Arizona, California, Colorado, Maryland, Missouri, Mississippi, New Mexico, North Carolina, Oregon, and Wyoming. Between 1930 and 1980, these states combined to put 945 men and seven women to death by gas. Though California got a relatively late start with its gas chamber at San Quentin—also known as "The Green Room"—the state has, to date, executed more prisoners by gas than any other: 192 men and four women between 1938 and 1994. During the time that Chessman resided there, San Quentin held 150 men on Death Row, seventy-four of whom were executed, a frequency and number surpassed only by the state of Georgia.*

In Chessman's time, the use of gas was widely felt to be the least cruel of all execution options. Even Elmer Barnes and Negley K. Teeters—both of whom, ironically, became staunch supporters of Chessman's claims of innocence—proclaimed in their definitive text-book, *New Horizons in Criminology* (another irony: it was published by Prentice-Hall): "Lethal gas, used by ten states, is certainly painless. It is a relatively pleasant form of meeting death, and humanitarian sentiment would recommend it as a universal method of execution (until capital punishment is abolished)." While Barnes and Teeters aver that the method is still seen as revolting, they make the bizarre claim that this is not because "gas is painful to the condemned men but that the spectacle of gradual expiration is 'torture to the spectator.' There is reason to believe, however, that asphyxiation is less brutal than electrocution, and far less so than hanging."

■

CALIFORNIA'S GAS CHAMBER at San Quentin is still the best-known judicial gas chamber in the world. It is housed in the basement of the prison's North Block and painted a light shade of green, which

---

* In May 2006, 560 men resided on Death Row at San Quentin.

explains its legendary nickname: The Green Room. This color—what would be called "sea foam" at a paint store but at San Quentin is sardonically known as "gas chamber green"—was thought to have a calming effect on those about to die, replacing the robin's-egg blue scaffolding of the gallows, a color chosen for the same calming reason. The orange straps on the chairs and the bright orange handle that opens and closes the chamber ("To Seal, Turn Right") made the room look slightly festive, like something one might find on a Caribbean cruise ship.

Built in 1938 at an iron factory in Denver, San Quentin's gas chamber is an octagonal metal box, six feet across and eight feet high. It has a thirty-foot chimney that disperses the lethal gas directly into the atmosphere above the prison. The entrance is a steel door closed by a large locking wheel onto rubber seals. There are windows in five of the eight sides through which witnesses can view the execution. Inside the chamber are two identical metal chairs with perforated seats, marked "A" and "B." Beneath the chair is a bowl filled with sulfuric acid mixed with distilled water, with a pound of sodium cyanide pellets suspended in a gauze bag just above.

A Death Row inmate named Alfred Wells volunteered to install the gas chamber when it arrived from Denver. Wells was one of San Quentin's nastiest criminals, convicted of three counts of first-degree murder. He shot his half brother, his sister-in-law, and her boyfriend; before killing his sister-in-law, he took her baby away from her; when she was dead, he placed her baby back in her bloodied arms. Five years after helping to install the gas chamber, Wells was executed in it. He had, by then, converted to Christianity, with the help of Warden Duffy's wife, Gladys. He died clutching a letter to Mrs. Duffy, which opened, "My dear Mother Duffy, By the time you receive this I'll be resting in glory."

The first execution by gas of convicted criminals at San Quentin took place on December 2, 1938, when Robert Lee Cannon and Albert Kessell were put to death, side by side, for the murder of a prison warden during an attempted escape from Folsom Prison. Actually, the first gas execution at San Quentin took place in March 1938, when a 155-pound pig named Oscar, raised on the prison farm, was placed in

The gas chamber at San Quentin Prison is more familiarly known as "The Green Room." It is an octagonal metal box, six feet across and eight feet high, with viewing windows in five of its eight sides. Inside the chamber are two identical metal chairs with perforated seats. Beneath each chair is a bowl filled with sulfuric acid mixed with distilled water, with a pound of sodium cyanide pellets suspended in a gauze bag above it. Though gas is no longer used for executions at San Quentin, the chamber itself is the site of lethal injection executions today. *Leo L. Stanley Collection, Anne T. Kent California Room, Marin County Free Library*

a steel cage and then put inside the gas chamber to test its efficiency; a hundred witnesses came to watch Oscar die with nary a squeal.

Another large contingent came to watch Cannon and Kessell die, but the reactions were considerably less positive than for Oscar's performance. The *San Francisco Examiner* reporter, calling the gas chamber "California's new robot executioner," described its work: "The finished product was two men seated peacefully side by side, with heads bowed as in reverence; two men who might have been at prayer, except that they were newly dead, and their skin was blue and their distended lower lips were not pleasant to see." Rather than the "quick and painless" death they'd been promised, the reporter cited "undisguised feelings of revulsion and frank declarations by prison officials and physicians that hanging is a quicker, more merciful method of execution and widespread suspicions that the State's new lethal gas chamber is a chamber of horrors."

The *Examiner*'s description of Cannon's death was particularly

These two young men were the first to be executed in "The Green Room." They died, side by side, on December 2, 1938. *Leo L. Stanley Collection, Anne T. Kent California Room, Marin County Free Library*

harrowing: "Even as the lethal vapor rises about him, like a fog from a marsh, Cannon attempts a gesture that is obviously meant to show his contempt for death. It begins with a grin and a nod toward the fumes, and something that was possibly meant for a shrug and a flinging upward of the hands from the wrist and an almost supercilious curling of the lips. What the exact words are, nobody will ever know, but Cannon most certainly is telling those outside, as the first whiff of gas hits him, that this is an easy, easy way of dying. Abruptly he changes his mind. A second, stronger cloud of gas curls around his head. The sneer leaves his face, he throws his head violently back, as far as it can go, he strains fiercely against the ten unyielding straps, his voice rises to a shout and, as he gasps at the ceiling. There is terror on his face. Then he snaps his head back again, and with open mouth pointed at the ceiling, sucks in the deadly gas in quick, gasping breaths."

These death throes took place for the next five minutes, and even when the spectators thought the men were dead, they continued to move. Noted the *Examiner* reporter, "Several times this is repeated—the appearance of death, the long, long period of absolute quiet—and then the brief gasping. Once, Kessell stirs out of apparent death and yawns." Leo L. Stanley, the prison physician determined that it took fifteen minutes to kill Kessell, and twelve minutes to send Cannon to glory.

While Warden Court Smith declared the execution "flawless," he admitted, "Hanging is bad enough, but this—this is terrible." Yard Captain Ralph New—who would be fired two years later for "brutality" toward prisoners—said, "I don't like any part of it. I didn't like it when they executed the pig in the test trial. I like it less now. Hanging is the best method of execution." Father George O'Mara, who administered last rites to Kessell and Cannon and who'd previously witnessed fifty-eight hangings, was quoted, "It was one of the worst things I've ever seen. I'd rather have witnessed a dozen hangings than this execution." One state legislator, so disgusted by the event, introduced a bill to replace gas executions with the firing squad.

Despite all these initial reservations, the bureaucratic wheels were already in motion, and there was no turning back. Gas also had an undeniable pragmatic appeal; the cost to the state of a gas execution was $1.80, for the cyanide, acid, and a clean set of clothes for the condemned prisoner. Though both hanging and gas were used for executions at San Quentin between 1938 and 1942, gas became the sole means of execution in California after that. In 1942, Clinton Duffy—who'd replaced the disgraced Court Smith as warden in 1940—allowed a Death Row inmate the pleasure of dismantling the scaffold that held the gallows; the lucky prisoner was given an axe for this purpose, and he wielded it with relish. Soon after the prisoner finished the job, he too was dispatched in The Green Room. The wood from the gallows was used in the hobby shop that Duffy had set up. A letter opener made by an inmate from this wood, along with the last noose used in a hanging, sit alongside each other in a small museum just inside the main gate of San Quentin State Prison today.*

■

THE RISE IN popularity of the gas chamber in the United States was curious for its timing, coinciding with the mass gassings by the Nazi regime in specially designed extermination camps whose names—Treblinka, Bergen-Belsen, Auschwitz, et al.—will forever be linked with something patently evil. Though Nazi technicians had conquered the logistics of gas chamber extermination in the late 1930s,

---

* Ethel Leta Juanita "The Duchess" Spinelli, convicted of murder, became the first woman ever executed by gas in the United States when she was killed in The Green Room at San Quentin on November 21, 1941.

they did not begin employing it on a grand scale until 1942. This, of course, begs the question: Did the Nazi command choose this method because of its proven efficacy and cost-effectiveness in the United States? While this is probably unanswerable, the parallels between the lethal paraphernalia in the gas chamber at San Quentin and ten other state prisons around the country and the shower rooms of Treblinka, Bergen-Belsen, and Auschwitz are indisputable. Chemically, cyanide gas is nearly identical to Zyklon B, a gas form of hydrocyanic acid that was manufactured in bulk by IG Farben and used to exterminate millions of Jews, Slavs, homosexuals, gypsies, Soviets, and other peoples deemed *Untermenschen* by Adolf Hitler.

In April 1992, after California resumed use of the gas chamber to kill Robert Alton Harris—the first execution in the state, by any method, in twenty-five years—the American Civil Liberties Union filed a lawsuit proclaiming the use of gas to be "cruel and unusual punishment," and thus a violation of the Eighth Amendment. Among the affidavits filed was testimony from a Nazi death camp survivor who'd witnessed mass gassings. She stated, "Execution by gas is torture and it can never be anything less."

In 1993, California passed a law that allowed Death Row inmates to choose their method of execution: either gas or lethal injection. But, on October 5, 1994, District Judge Marilyn Hall Patel ruled that the gas chamber was an inhumane method of punishment and outlawed the practice in California.

On February 21, 1996, a three-judge panel of the 9th U.S. Circuit Court of Appeals unanimously upheld the ruling that gas chamber executions in California violated the Eighth Amendment to the Constitution because there was a risk that an inmate could suffer "horrible pain" for up to several minutes. "The district court's findings of extreme pain, the length of time this extreme pain lasts, and the substantial risk that inmates will suffer this extreme pain for several minutes require the conclusion that execution by lethal gas is cruel and unusual," Judge Harry Pregerson wrote. The last execution by gas in the United States took place on March 4, 1999, in Arizona, where Walter LeGrand chose the gas chamber one week after his brother Karl was executed by lethal injection. The Green

Room at San Quentin is still fully functional and ready to go, if gas were to be reinstated.

Five states, including California, still have gassing as an option on their books, though lethal injection is now the preferred method. Since 1995, when executions by lethal injection were begun at San Quentin, the gas chamber itself has still been used as the place of death, presumably to take advantage of the consoling green color scheme and the multiple viewing windows for spectators. The perforated metal chairs are simply removed from the Green Room and a modified dentist chair is moved in. This was, in fact, done on December 13, 2005, when former gang leader Stanley "Tookie" Williams was executed by lethal injection.

No other country in the world besides the United State still has gas on their books as a means of judicial execution.

■

THE CHAIN OF events attending a San Quentin execution were set to follow a strict regimen. Once the door of the gas chamber was sealed, the warden gave a signal to commence the execution. In a separate room, the executioner—whose identity wasn't allowed to be known to the prisoner or the witnesses—operated a lever that released the cyanide into the acid. This caused a chemical reaction that released hydrogen cyanide gas, which rose through the holes in the chair. (The actual chemical equation for this reaction is $2\ NaCn + H_2SO_4 = 2\ HCN + Na_2So4$.) In medical terms, victims of cyanide gas die from hypoxia, which means the cutting-off of oxygen to the brain. The initial reaction, physically, is a series of spasms, not unlike an epileptic seizure. Because of the straps, involuntary body movements are restrained. Seconds after the prisoner first inhales, he/she will be unable to breathe, but will not lose consciousness immediately.

A study of the execution records at San Quentin found that the average time it took the State of California to kill a condemned prisoner was 9.3 minutes. Prisoners usually lost consciousness between one and three minutes after the gas hit their nostrils; the doctor pronounced them dead in ten to twelve minutes. An exhaust fan sucked the poison air out of the chamber. And the seated corpse was then sprayed via a remote-controlled hose with ammonia, which neutralized traces of the cyanide that may have remained. After half an hour, prison medical staff entered the chamber, wearing gas masks and rubber gloves. Their training manual advised them to ruffle the victim's hair to release any trapped cyanide gas before removing him from the chamber.

Warden Clinton Duffy detailed the operation of the execution chamber in a series of articles called "San Quentin Is My Home" written in 1950 for the *Saturday Evening Post* (later compiled in the book *The San Quentin Story*). He said the operation of The Green Room included, "funnels, rubber gloves, graduates, acid pumps, gas masks, cheese-cloth, steel chains, towels, soap, pliers, scissors, fuses and a mop; in addition, sodium-cyanide eggs, sulfuric acid, distilled water, and ammonia."

Regardless of the gas chamber's consoling color scheme and the experts' consoling opinions of gas's painlessness, Chessman was all too aware of psychological trauma engendered by waiting for his own appointment. Between 1942 and 1956, 180 people were sentenced to die in the gas chamber in California. Over one-third of this number had their death sentences overturned, or commuted to life in prison. Chessman personally watched sixty-nine men make the last walk past his cell on the way to the elevator that would take them to The Green Room, located six floors below Death Row.

The media circus that attended Barbara Graham's execution in 1955 and Robert Pierce's execution in 1956 were anomalies, but the same elements of abject terror, bitterness, and professions of innocence were part of nearly every inmate's experience. They each handled it in their own way, and Chessman had, by the time of his death, twelve years to ponder the inevitable, as well as eight previous stays of execution. Eight times he had prepared himself to die, only to be told he could live for a few more weeks or months.

Just prior to his third death date, on May 14, 1954, Chessman told *Newsweek*, "I'm all ready. I'm a million miles away. It's difficult to explain but I feel . . . nebulous."

Having been spared then, as he would be three more times in the interim, he put his fantasy about his own death in the gas chamber down on paper in the prologue to *Trial by Ordeal*, published in 1957.

> You die alone—but watched.
>
> It's a ritualistic death, ugly and meaningless.
>
> They walk you into the green, eight-sided chamber and strap you down in one of its two straight-backed metal chairs. Then they leave, sealing the door behind them. The lethal gas is generated and swirls upward, hungrily seeking your lungs. You inhale the colorless, deadly fumes. The universe disintegrates soundlessly. Only for an awful moment do you float free. For a blackness that is thick and final swiftly engulfs you.
>
> Then—what?
>
> An improbable Heaven?
>
> Another Hell?
>
> Or simply oblivion?
>
> Soon you'll know. After long, brutal years of fighting for survival, your days are running out.

In a later chapter from the same work, he expanded on his fantasy:

> You inhale the deadly fumes. You become giddy. You strain against the straps as the blackness closes in. You exhale, inhale again. Your head aches. There's a pain in your chest. But the ache, the pain is nothing. You're hardly aware of it. You're slipping into unconsciousness. You're dying. Your head jerks back. Only for an awful instant do you float free. The veil is drawn swiftly. Consciousness is forever gone. Your brain has been denied oxygen. Your body fights a losing, ten-minute battle against death.
>
> You've stopped breathing. Your heart has quit beating. You're dead.

■

THE APPEALS TO Governor Brown made by Davis and Asher—Chessman himself refused to beg the governor for clemency—were shifted around on his desk like meaningless memos until at the very last instant his hand was forced. For example, when the deadline for Chessman's seventh stay was nearing its end in late October 1959—the second granted by the U.S. Supreme Court—Brown refused to act. Only after the stay was assured did Brown release a statement that appeared to pander to the right wing: "The record shows a deliberate career of robberies and kidnappings, followed by sexual assaults and acts of perversion . . . at the point of a loaded gun. One of his victims, 17 years old at the time, is still hopelessly confined in a mental hospital. . . . His attitude had been one of steadfast arrogance and contempt for society and its laws."

The mental toll that these political machinations took on Chessman is incalculable. Surely, such tension contributed to an incident that occurred on New Year's Day 1960. The twenty-four residents of Death Row were allowed to spend the day together in their recreation room, watching the various festivities on television. Perhaps the spectacle of the Rose Bowl Parade in Pasadena, the place that held his happiest childhood memories, sent a twinge of regret through Chessman as he sat in his assigned chair. Any nostalgia he might have enjoyed was cut short when a convicted killer, James Merkouris, provoked a brawl with several other Row residents. Another convicted killer, Manuel Chavez, hit Merkouris with a wooden stool. The injured Merkouris, in a rage, detroyed the television set, at which point, Chessman knocked Merkouris down, straddled his chest and pinned him to the floor until the prison authorities could arrive. The six men involved were escorted back to their cells. Chessman, ultimately, was spared any further disciplinary action, but this was cold comfort, not to mention a bad omen for the new year.

Again, in February 1960, Governor Brown was saved from making a decision by outside intervention. This time, however, he had a hand in it himself. Feeling the pressure from the world outside California—hundreds of letters in Chessman's defense arrived daily at his Sacramento office from around the world—Brown sent two members of his staff to Washington to sniff out possible means by which an intervention might get him off the hook. A pretext was found. President Eisenhower was due to visit Uruguay, where sentiment for Chessman was high. The U.S. Embassy in Uruguay had been warned by the Uruguayan government about possible demonstrations if Chessman was executed. The embassy, in turned, relayed this to the State Department in Washington. This was at midnight of the day before the scheduled event. Chessman had, in fact, already been moved from his sixth floor Death Row cell to the "ready room" on the ground floor, located thirteen steps from the gas chamber, for his scheduled 10:00 A.M. execution. Brown granted the sixty-day reprieve on February 18. Chessman, not realizing Brown had manipulated Washington for an intervention, was uncharacteristically thankful to Brown. "Tell the governor I'm very grateful," he said to Warden Fred Dickson, only moments after the call came in.

Brown had his pretext; he was off the hook.

Or was he?

U.S. Senator J. William Fulbright of Arkansas, a stalwart of Brown's Democratic Party, denounced the State Department for "unprecedented action in interfering with the normal carrying out of justice within a state." The *London Times* called Brown's decision "highly damaging to the repute of the law." But in California, Brown faced a wave of wrath from enraged citizens and the right-wing press. Cries for Brown's impeachment and recall were made on the editorial pages and in letters to the editor. Religious bigotry reared its head to further pollute public discourse on the Chessman case. Some suggested that Brown, a Roman Catholic, was under orders from the pope to spare Chessman's life. Others, out of pure anti-Semitic ignorance, were under the mistaken belief that Chessman was Jewish and, as one letter to the editor of a West Coast magazine put it, "We should kill that Kike in Death Row." Both Brown and Chessman were hanged in effigy—at last, the two longtime nemeses were now in the same boat!

An equally impassioned surge of support for Chessman resulted from this gambit, part of it inspired by a forty-five-minute documentary film, *Justice and Caryl Chessman*, that attracted sizeable audiences to movie theaters around the country in March 1960. The film was directed by Ed Spiegel, produced by Terrence Cooney, written by Jules Maitland, and narrated by the mainstream journalist Quentin Reynolds. The *New York Times* reviewer (March 3, 1960) was impressed by the filmmakers' "presenting their material objectively and attempting to avoid sensationalism." Among the most striking aspects of the film was the newsreel footage of Chessman, the first time many of his supporters actually saw and heard him. Due to prison restrictions, however, an actor who looked like Chessman was used to depict his life on Death Row. Though filming at San Quentin was forbidden, Spiegel and Cooney were allowed to shoot scenes at the California Institution for Men in Chino. They even secured the on-camera assistance of Chessman's arch enemy, J. Miller Leavy.*

Brown's "out" this time was to turn the matter over to the state legislature, requesting that they vote on a measure that would abolish capital punishment during the sixty-day reprieve for Chessman. Even so, it was an empty gesture, as the legislature's leaders in both parties had assured Brown they'd reject his request. So, in a sense, he allowed Chessman to be executed by passing the buck—and perhaps assuaging his guilt—to the legislature. It was a cagey political move but it backfired. He was perceived, rightly, as wanting it both ways. As a result, he had it neither way.

The measure never came up for a full vote in the legislature. It died in the State Senate's Judiciary Committee in March 1960, when a Democrat, Edwin J. Regan, broke a 7–7 tie with a "no" vote. This, despite a lengthy hearing at the new Capitol building in Sacramento, where Chessman's old nemesis, the former San Quentin warden Clinton Duffy, who, unlike Brown, showed the courage of his convictions by testifying against the death penalty, even if it meant Chessman

---

* In 1963, Leavy filed suit against Terrence Cooney over *Justice and Caryl Chessman*, claiming breach of contract for his having shown the film in theaters when it was planned as a television documentary. Leavy claimed that "he suffered humiliation and embarrassment because of his fear and apprehension that if the picture should be shown in theaters the public would think he was being compensated for his participation in the project, and he would be subjected to severe criticism." The ruling went in favor of Leavy, who received $7,500 as compensatory damages and $35,000 as exemplary damages.

would be spared. Duffy told the committee, "I do not believe in the death penalty, because its inequality is apparent. You have yet to find anyone executed who was wealthy."

The controversy over Chessman's impending execution was further buffeted by the storm gathering around the country over civil rights. In *Life* magazine, opposite the story about Governor Brown's Chessman "crisis," was an unrelated story about how an effort to desegregate lunch counters in Portsmouth, Virginia, had "erupted in violence," which *Life* editors saw as "the dismaying but uneasily awaited break in a display of nonviolent protest against southern segregation." Nearly three thousand black and white students and adults pushed, shoved, and chanted at a shopping center. One car full of white students carried the placard "Stomp Out Niggers"; another photograph showed disheveled white men holding hammers taunting peaceful black protesters. Police dogs were called in. Change was in the air in America.

■

AT THE END, only Brown could save Chessman, who had exhausted every other conceivable route for a retrial or stay. While Davis and Asher continued to file writs and petitions for review right up until the end, their only real hope was Brown, with whom Davis was said to be friendly (Davis was deeply involved in the state Democratic Party).

Friendship or moral courage aside, Brown was more interested in political expediency. He had visions of higher national office and fancied himself a "dark horse candidate" for the presidential nomination at the Democratic National Convention. Brown was a pragmatic politician before he was an idealist, and he was, like all elected office holders, willing to use a man's life to further his own career. All the finery of his intentions and his legendary Irish charm couldn't disguise this one basic truth: Pat Brown lacked the courage of his convictions when it was most demanded of him. Even the gesture of a commutation—which Chessman would have, more than likely, refused—was not forthcoming from the governor's office in Sacramento.

Chessman, for his part, had never wanted anything to do with begging the governor, recalling the vitriol that Brown had unleashed at him in his days as the state's attorney general. He had all but refused any deal that would commute his sentence to life in prison without parole. He repeatedly claimed his innocence and vowed to accept nothing short of total exoneration for the Red Light Bandit crimes. He left Brown little wiggle room, and the governor did not want to row against the public tide.

It was the single worst decision of Brown's political career. And it sealed the fate of Caryl Whittier Chessman.

14

"I'll See You in the Morning"

THE EMOTIONS SURROUNDING Chessman's case were so volatile by early 1960 that the California Supreme Court, in the end, pushed the execution date up by four days, to hasten the troublesome convict to his death.

The heightened tensions between the two sides were evident in a February 1960 exchange between George T. Davis and State Supreme Court Justice Clement Nye, who'd set Chessman's final execution date for Monday, May 2, 1960. The normally genial Davis bristled at the fact that, though executions at San Quentin were traditionally held on Friday, the judge did not want to wait the extra four days beyond the deadline of Chessman's final stay.

Davis demanded of Judge Nye, "Why the mad haste to set the execution date? Why must our court be the butt of the world's scorn? To kill this man now would achieve no more than world repugnance."

The judge responded with a snarling, "Are you implying that I, in my capacity as judge, would shirk my duty merely because of the world's opinion?"

■

WHEN THE TIME came for Chessman to make that walk, he was ready. He certainly had had enough practice, having narrowly missed the gas chamber on eight previous occasions and having watched ninety-three men walk past his cell on the way to The Green Room. After his twelve years of dodging death, he was honest enough with himself to accept the inevitable and somehow make peace with it. To the surprise and relief of prison officials and state politicians, he went with equanimity, no bitterness, and even a sense of humor. In short, he gave the state of California the spectacle it had wanted for so long: his ritualistic extermination.

Of course, even as the clock across the hall from his cell ticked down to 10:00 A.M. on May 2, 1960, Chessman and his attorneys still plotted legal maneuvers. He was polite and calm in his dealings with prison officials and the press. He was composed, even consoling, with the few people to whom he was close, including Rosalie Asher.

On Saturday afternoon, April 30, he held a two-hour meeting with Asher and Davis, at which he signed his will and added this codicil, post-dated May 1, 1960:

> I, Caryl Chessman, at the age of 38 years, being of sound and disposing mind and memory, and not acting under the fraud, duress, menace, or undue influence of any person whomsoever, do hereby make, publish and declare this instrument as and to be a codicil to my last will and testament executed by me earlier on this same date, hereby ratifying, affirming, and republishing all of the provisions therein contained. It is my express will and purpose by bequeathing my entire estate to Rosalie S. Asher, by naming her the executrix of my last will and testament, and by naming Joseph E. Longstreth as the literary executor, to insure that no letters, documents, manuscripts, or writings of any description actually authored by myself and unpublished, be published under my name without the express consent and approval of both Rosalie S. Asher and Joseph E. Longstreth; and I expressly so direct. This codicil was entirely written, dated and is be [*sic*] signed by me at San Quentin Prison on the above date. Caryl Chessman.

Afterward, Chessman held what turned out to be his last press conference, in the office of Louis S. Nelson, San Quentin's associate warden. Ten members of the press crowded in, representing national and international news organizations. Chessman shook hands with every journalist, after which another associate warden, Walter D. Achuff, explained that there would be "unrestricted" questions allowed.

Lawrence E. Davies, a correspondent for the *New York Times*, was one of those present, and he described Chessman as "chain-smoking but relaxed and even at times jovial." The questions the reporters asked the doomed man ranged "from the philosophical to the ridiculous."

Chessman told them that his chances were "fifty-fifty" and if his lawyers' final pleas were rejected, "I intend to walk in and sit down and die."

He also said, "I have proof [of my innocence] but it involves bringing in other people and other crimes. I am not going to tear down a house for a lot of people who have built lives for themselves."

However, he doubted that even if the court were given irrefutable proof of his innocence, they would admit their mistake.

"Did you ever think of the position that California would be in if it were shown to be wrong now after twelve years?" he asked rhetorically.

He emphasized further that Governor Pat Brown, the governor's clemency secretary Cecil Poole, and prison officials "don't want me to live. . . . There is no limit on the Governor's reprieve powers. It's a matter of his conscience. But practically speaking I doubt if he would grant another reprieve."

Chessman sardonically described, in response to a question, the size of his estate as "minus $18,000" He said that he was as prepared to die as he had been at all the previous scheduled executions.

"I try to have myself disciplined," he said. "To keep a check on my emotions and not act subjectively. I'm hopeful but this is something I've erected artificially. I'll start dying at 10:01 Monday morning and I don't intend to slice myself up in little pieces meanwhile. I have no masochistic pleasure in what I'm doing, I assure you."

When asked what advice he'd give a young man considering a criminal career, Chessman said, "I wouldn't give him any advice. But I'd try to help him have a feeling of belonging to society, not try to menace or coerce him or warn him about the gas chamber."

Some of this press conference was televised and the broadcast shown on television sets accessible to San Quentin's general population. Malcolm Braly, one of the prisoners in the general population, recalled, "He came out and sat on a desk to talk to reporters. He was at ease. I could sense how he liked the attention. He'd only been locked on Death Row for twelve years. They asked if he expected to die in the morning, and he smiled and said, 'Yes, they have me now. I think it's over.' When they broke for a commercial it was to advertise an air freshener. They gassed him the next morning."

■

As soon as he returned to Death Row after the press conference, Chessman found that the Row's television set had been moved in front of his cell, a privilege accorded all those whose time was "short." The guard handed Chessman a tray on which was placed the earphones for the television, in case he wanted to hear the programs.

Byron Eshelman, the Protestant chaplain, was speaking to Louis Moya, in the next cell, when Chessman was escorted back to the Row. The chaplain finished his conversation with Moya and moved over to Chessman, who told him wearily that the press conference had been "rough. I've got to be so careful—for my own interests and for this whole cause of abolishing capital punishment."

Eshelman asked if he was afraid of saying the wrong thing to the press. Chessman replied, "I wouldn't say anything I didn't believe, but it's more subtle than that. They're all looking for some little sign of weakness—and they're ready to pounce like a bunch of hounds."

He showed Eshelman the paperback edition of his novel *The Kid Was a Killer* that Longstreth had just sent him, as well as the dust jacket for the Italian edition of the novel. "I feel good to see it finally out," Chessman said, before discussing the legal maneuvers that still remained to him; his only hope, he decided, was for a justice on the State Supreme Court to change the balance of previous votes from 4–3 to 3–4. And that, in all likelihood, would have happened had Chessman been given a stay until June 1, when the newly appointed Appellate Justice Maurice T. Dooling Jr. was scheduled to replace

Justice Homer R. Spence on the California Supreme Court. Spence had already voted against clemency three times in the previous ten weeks, and Dooling indicated that he would have voted for clemency, commuting Chessman's sentence to life imprisonment.

"I've still got a chance," he said, then climbed onto his cot to rest, though he was unable to sleep.

■

FOUR DAYS EARLIER, in what turned out to be his last letter to Longstreth (dated April 26, 1960), Chessman exhibited the same calmness, but not the laconic sense of humor that surfaced as he drew nearer The Green Room's embrace. The overriding emotion of this letter was one of profound gratitude for having found a friend as loyal as Joseph Longstreth. Similarly, he admitted his own flaws as a sometimes nonreciprocating partner in that friendship.

"I want you to know I am deeply and abidingly grateful for your assistance over the last several years as my literary agent and friend. I am well aware of how trying and even at times how seemingly thankless have been your efforts on my behalf. Yet, knowing how intensely I felt about the things of which I'd written, you always persevered. As you know, for the last 12 years, mine has been a harsh world where, if you failed, you didn't live to get a commendation for a good try and a pat on the back. It has been a world without next-times, and so perhaps the iron disciplines I had to impose on myself to survive against almost impossible odds on occasion gave the impression that I was a brusque, unfeeling guy who gave no thought to the sensibilities of others in his drive toward a goal. I am certain, however, you know how far from the truth this is."

Chessman was also grateful, he told Longstreth, for having survived his ordeal without cracking; that is, "with my mental processes reasonably intact." He also expressed gratitude for being allowed by the trying circumstances to become "a better man and a more mature one," and was resigned to the knowledge that his legacy might not reside in his writings, to which he'd given every ounce of his being, but in the face that he'd supplied for the issue of capital punishment.

"I think now the issue—whether the death penalty has a defensible place in a civilized community or whether it is not an ugly and demeaning anachronism that confounds social progress and confounds solution for the problem of what rational social man can do realistically and humanely to control the violence that lurks in all of us—is joined . . . In time, I am satisfied, people will become aware that retributive justice is not really justice at all, and that violence is not an answer to violence."

Perhaps what's most remarkable about this letter, and several other letters Chessman would write over the next five days, was the complete lack of self-pity or rancor. The pity inherent in his fate could not be more obvious—having rehabilitated himself through writing, offered himself as a fount of knowledge about sociopathic and criminal personalities, and forged a successful writing career that showed no signs of slacking (and judging from many of the unpublished manuscripts he left behind with Longstreth, were capable of moving in any number of directions, including humor, plays, mystery fiction and novel-length works of fiction), he was nonetheless going to be killed.

As he explained to Dr. David G. Schmidt, chief psychiatrist of the prison (see Appendix: "And What If I Failed?", page 379 for the full transcript), Chessman already had plans for enough writing projects to "occupy me for another ten years." Among these were a biography of California Supreme Court Justice Jesse W. Carter, whom he admired (*The Face of Justice* was, in effect, Chessman's "biography" of George T. Davis, though it was much more than that); a play about François Villon ("French lyric poet and gallows bird"); a trilogy of novels; and a novelette (*Autumn and Eve*), a draft of which does exist among Longstreth's papers.

He wrote Schmidt: "And what if I failed? What if I collected rejection slip after rejection slip? Well, I am certain I would not fail finally, and I am quite prepared for rough going along the way. The pertinent point, in my judgment, is that, at 38, I am old as a psychopathic hoodlum but young for a writer. Many of the world's best authors did not reach their full powers until their 50s and even their 60s.

"There is irony, of course, in the fact I am discussing the future as though I had one, as though I did not have a date with the executioner 14 days and a few odd hours hence. However, be assured, I am completely aware of that date and, statistically, of the overwhelming possibilities I shall keep it."

Similarly, in his final letter to Longstreth he wrote: "I would like to live, and there is irony in the fact I am to be executed after 12 years and now that I seemingly would be able to accomplish considerable and constructive good with my writing to counterbalance those earlier, rebellious years. But here again I must face up squarely to the realities of my situation. And here, too, I must keep in mind that irony of this sort as well can be forged by others into a weapon for aiding in the establishment of a better and saner world for the generations to come."

He closed the letter simply: "Now, Joe, I must say goodbye. That is not easy, I admit, but it must be done. Good luck. As ever, Caryl."

If this penitent tone were all an act, it was an extraordinary feat indeed, because he kept it up to the very moment of his death.

Indeed, this very point was made by a Swedish librarian, Gudrun Linnarsson, who sent a letter, written in English, to Longstreth from Stockholm, dated March 3, 1960. She had just spent the previous two weeks reading all three of Chessman's books available in Swedish translations. She told Longstreth that she could find nothing in them that pointed to "criminal nature" or "bad character" or "psychopath." "On the contrary," Linnarsson wrote, "they display the feature of a person who is not only highly intelligent but also dignified, magnanimous, unselfish, valiant, firm of mind, essential. Were this not his real face, he would not have been able to sham it through eleven hundred pages of the Swedish editions without losing his cue."

She asked Longstreth to convey to Chessman her offer to marry him in order to save him from the gas chamber. She spiced the deal with an additional offer to provide a one-room flat for Chessman's "rehabilitation." She added that her offer of marriage and room and board held true for Chessman only, not other prisoners.

■

AT 3:30 P.M. on Sunday, May 1, Chessman was moved from his cell on Death Row. On his way down the line as he was escorted to the sergeant's office at the east end of the Row, Chessman shook hands with seventeen of the eighteen other residents as he passed their cells (the eighteenth was asleep). He made the traditional farewell from Death Row to each of them: "I'll see you in the morning." And each of the seventeen returned the salutation.

In the sergeant's office, he was asked to change into new "prison blues": jeans, denim work shirt, socks, and cloth slippers. Then he was taken by elevator to the ground floor of the prison, where he was led to a brightly lit holding cell located just around the corner from the gas chamber. To soften the execution process, perhaps, the holding cell—not even big enough to "hold" a cot, though it had a seatless toilet and a writing table that folded flat against the cell bars—was officially called the Preparation Room or "Ready Room." This was the same cell where Barbara Graham was "readied" five years earlier. Though the condemned could not see it from there, The Green Room was located just around the corner. It beckoned thirteen steps away, like a large deadly mouth.

His last meal arrived—hamburger, fries, and a chocolate milk-shake—but it remained mostly uneaten. Around dinnertime, George Davis visited for a few minutes and Rosalie Asher spent two and a half hours with him in his holding cell. She emerged to tell the assembled press that his situation was "desperate and critical" (indeed it was; though he had come just as close to dying in 1954, he had never actually been escorted off Death Row to the holding cell). Asher also said that petitioning Governor Brown was "a waste of time." A delegation of five had visited the governor that afternoon, to make a personal plea for Chessman's life. They were Steve Allen, Marlon Brando, Shirley MacLaine, author Eugene Burdick, who'd written the bestseller *The Ugly American* (1958), and Richard Drinnon, the chairman of a committee to abolish the death penalty. "I am powerless to act," Governor Brown told them.

■

ACCORDING TO PRISON records, between 6:20 P.M. and 12:30 A.M., Chessman received twelve different visitors in his holding cell. Somehow, he was also able to get some writing done—a great deal of writing, considering the circumstances. He was not allowed the use of his trusty Underwood typewriter in the holding cell, so he wrote all of his final letters on yellow legal pads in his firm hand, with nary a crossout or a misspelled word. Also noticeably absent from the cell was a bed, though a mattress had been thrown on the floor for anyone who could possibly sleep under such circumstances. Chessman eschewed the tonic of both sleep and religion, politely informing Father Dingberg, the Catholic chaplain, and George Tolson and Byron Eshelman, the Protestant chaplains, that he remained an agnostic. He asked Eshelman to come see him in the morning, and the delegation of clergy left him at midnight. He stayed awake and continued writing by longhand on yellow legal pads. Among the items he wrote were seven personal letters, which he handed to Warden Dickson in the morning, to be mailed after he was dead.

One of the letters, and typical of the sentiment, was written to the *San Francisco Chronicle* reporter Bernice Freeman, whom he'd invited to be a witness at the execution, an offer she could not bear to take him up on. A few days after his death, she was forwarded the letter from Chessman by Rosalie Asher.

> Dear B—
> I have asked Rosalie to be sure and say good-bye for me. The way things were going, I wasn't sure I would have time to get off a last note. But then I decided to take the time. So here I am—just a few feet and a few minutes from eternity and remembering you and our many talks. I don't need to say—but I want to—even though I am sure you know—how privileged I feel to have been counted among your friends. And let me add, simply, thanks for your many, many acts of kindness.

I hear you haven't been well. I am genuinely sorry, for if anyone deserves good health and happiness, it's you.

Bye.

    As always,

        Caryl.

P.S. Be sure and remember me to Bill.

Another letter was written to Mary Crawford, a journalist for the *San Francisco News–Call-Bulletin.*

This equally eloquent missive was five pages long—the first page typewritten in his Death Row cell, the other four handwritten in the holding cell. Among the thoughts contained in his letter to Crawford were the following:

> They say the child is father to the man. Tomorrow morning, barring last-minute court action, I shall be executed. The physical man will die. What of the child? What sort of person was this lad who, figuratively, sired Caryl Chessman?
>
> Initially, in these last hours of life, I must tell you frankly that memories of my boyhood are often blurred. The images of the present and the immediate future are sharper in my mind than are those of a dim past when I and the world each were young. It seems more like three centuries than three decades have passed since the tousle-haired eight-year-old I once was looked forward that May 1 spring day in the year 1930 to his 9th birthday 28 days hence. Now, so far as I know, the man that boy became—after 12 years on Death Row—has no more birthdays to look forward to.

Crawford had asked Chessman earlier what could have been done to reach that "troubled, rebellious youngster that boy became"? With death breathing down his neck, he, in neat, unwavering penmanship, wrote the final four pages of his last letter in trying to answer that and other questions. ("It is now past six A.M. Less than four hours remain to me, and, after a busy night consulting with attorneys Rosalie S.

Asher and George T. Davis and writing last personal letters to my friends, I'll return to your questions.")

After weighing various theories about punishment on youthful offenders, Chessman closed by saying, "I might have spent this, my last night on earth, cursing my plight and society. I didn't. Instead, even though I realized no matter what I wrote or didn't write my fate would remain unchanged, I put these pressures, these tensions to work. They are producing this letter. They will permit me to walk into the gas chamber and, paradoxically, die calmly. For I have learned the hard, the lethal way, to put them to work. I want to believe no man ever again will have to know the 12-year hell I have known, since, especially, there is such a reasonable, rational and humane alternative.

"Yet, as Voltaire said, 'The more ancient the abuse, the more sacred it is.'

"Sincerely, Caryl Chessman."

He had not slept for more than twenty-four hours. And only three and a half hours of life remained to him.

■

OUTSIDE THE GATES of San Quentin prison and for half a mile along the road leading into the complex, protesters and curiosity seekers had been gathering since Sunday afternoon, May 1, as had the reporters and photographers chumming the waters for some new ghoulish twist on this twelve-year-old story. A group of protesters marched from San Francisco to San Quentin, bearing signs ("Each Man's Death Diminishes Me," "Stop Legal Murders") and chanting to passing motorists. Someone set up a mock gallows outside the prison walls, someone else set up a lifesize mural of an executioner, accompanied by a giant banner: "The World Is Watching Us," a slogan that would appear at protests over the next decade and become an epoch-defining chant after the events at the Democratic National Convention in Chicago in August 1968 ("The whole world is watching!").

Adding to the ominous atmosphere of this occasion was the news that an American pilot and CIA agent named Francis Gary Powers had been shot down over the Soviet Union. His U-2 supersonic spy plane, filled with sophisticated Cold War gadgetry, had fallen into "enemy" hands, and he had been captured. Once again, America seemed on the brink of a nuclear showdown. Would this protest really matter?

As many as eight hundred people camped out along the side of the road Sunday night. Some slept in their cars. Some stayed up all night sitting around bonfires holding prayer vigils, singing hymns, talking, and drinking coffee. The scene was well lit by two prison spotlights, used for security, that beamed down from atop a hill. The earnest idealism of the youthful gathering was palpable. Indeed, their fresh faces in the photographs stand in stark contrast to the jaded countenances of the journalists and the grim visages of law enforcement personnel.

As the sun rose on Monday, May 2, Marin County deputies and prison officers moved in to force the growing numbers of people back at least half a mile from the San Quentin prison gates. Some of the more aggressive protesters—carrying signs bearing messages saying, "This Is Justice?" and "12 Years on Death Row is Enough"—were led

On the afternoon of May 1, 1960, marchers and demonstrators began arriving outside San Quentin State Prison to begin what would be an all-night vigil. *Author's collection*

Among those who participated in the all-night vigil was this earnest young couple, who are camped out in front of their mock gallows and banner. *Author's collection*

away by the county police. In the quaint parlance of the *San Francisco News–Call-Bulletin* correspondent Claude Hall, these young people were "given the bum's rush." This note was appended to one of Hall's photo captions, offering a glimpse of the mainstream press's real attitude toward these impassioned young people, in jeans and sneakers and hepcat's boots. Some sported moustaches; some had hair spilling over collars of army surplus jackets, a tiny inkling of the social maelstrom to come in the next decade.

It was too late by May 1960 to dismiss them as "Beatniks," too early to use the "hippie" perjorative. Many of these young people had been, or would soon go, to the American South to take part in voter registration drives and civil rights marches. Others would, in just four years' time, occupy university buildings a few miles down the road in Berkeley and listen to Mario Savio's demand for "free speech" and his urgent plea to "put your bodies upon the gears and upon the wheels, upon the levers, upon all the apparatus, and you've got to make it stop." Some would, in two weeks' time, be among the crowd of protesters outside the HUAC hearings being held in downtown San Francisco.* Still others would drift into the acid tests of Haight-Ashbury and the communal experimentations of Northern California's woodlands. Many of those who stood outside all night pleading for the life of Caryl Chessman felt the first winds of change on the road leading into San Quentin. Looking at photographs of these Save Chessman protests—in New York and Rome and Los Angeles and Sacramento—is like seeing the crack form in the complacent 1950s, a crack that would widen in November when John F. Kennedy was sent to the White House.

Among those who stood outside the prison that day was Marlon Brando, who after the rebuff from Governor Brown the day before stood at a police roadblock with the protesters. Many of the young protesters had come of age watching Brando capture their own nascent rebellions with his assortment of existentialist drifters and wounded rebels in the films *The Wild One* (1953), *On The Waterfront* (1954) and, most recently, *The Fugitive Kind* (1959), in which he played Val Xavier, a handsome drifter and rebel created by Tennessee Williams. The sight of their hero must have emboldened them, but Brando wasn't there to preen or be worshipped. He was seething with rage at the powers that be. He told reporters, "The tide against capital punishment is in full swing" and called the execution of Chessman, "A vulgar, stupid, unutterably sad act. . . . It will be a long time before we will be able to repair our damaged reputations."† Alongside Brando was the author Eugene Burdick.

---

* HUAC was looking into (what else?) "Communist activities," this time in Northern California, but the allegedly "open hearing" was in fact packed with members of right-wing groups who'd been given preferential treatment. Those excluded created enough of a disturbance to draw fire hoses, tear gas, and nightsticks; four students and eight policemen were hospitalized and fifty protesters were arrested.

† According to biographer Peter Manso, Brando agreed reluctantly to film *Mutiny on the Bounty* in October 1960, telling the press and colleagues the film "he wished to make instead: the story of Caryl Chessman."

Also upset with the proceedings was Governor Pat Brown's son, Edmund G. "Jerry" Brown Jr., who had just left the novitiate at a Jesuit seminary in Los Gatos because, as he told his biographer Orville Schell, "I'd gone as far as I could in following the rules and the ideas of St. Ignatius. His teachings run counter to the American flow."

Having recently enrolled at the University of California at Berkeley, Jerry Brown was at the time living within a few miles of San Quentin; today, as the mayor of Oakland, he lives only a few miles further away. In May 1960, he not only felt that the death penalty was wrong, he was at loggerheads with his family. His mother, Bernice, was a Protestant and, as his father told Schell, "She and Jerry weren't really simpatico. She was for the death penalty. Her father was a policeman. I think it bothered him terribly, particularly when Chessman died."*

Jerry Brown was hardly alone in his revulsion over Chessman's execution. Among the more prominent activists standing outside the Governor's Mansion in Sacramento during an all-night vigil on May 2, 1960, was Dr. Isidore Ziferstein. The Los Angeles psychiatrist had not just been fighting for Chessman's life, he was among the leading proponents of his innocence of the Red Light Bandit crimes. Ziferstein, whose clients included Judy Garland and, later, Robbie Krieger, the Doors' guitarist, was a familiar face on the sidewalk outside the State Capitol in Sacramento, a distinguished man in trenchcoat and fedora amid the more motley assemblage of university students and wannabe beatniks in berets. He had taken up Chessman's cause six years earlier, after the publication of *Cell 2455, Death Row,* and

---

* Jerry Brown, at the time a young, Los Angeles–based lawyer, also stood outside the prison protesting the death of Charles Aaron Mitchell on April 8, 1967, the 194th and last person to be put to death in San Quentin's gas chamber before 1992. As a two-term governor of California (1975–1983), he vetoed a death penalty bill passed by the State Senate in 1977, one superseded by the even more severe Proposition 7, passed in November 1978, removing three anti–death penalty judges that he'd appointed—a defeat that was widely depicted, even by the scholars Robert Jay Lifton and Greg Mitchell as late as 2000, as a "humiliation." Though he did no lobbying—finding it inappropriate to "twist arms on an issue of conscience"—Brown's veto was barely overridden by the State Senate. His unwavering opposition to this measure, contrary to the myth that such a stance spells defeat at the polls, did not stop him from being reelected in the same November 1978 election by the widest margin in California history, a profoundly unhumiliating fact. Brown the Younger, unlike his father, remained consistent in his beliefs regarding capital punishment.

Outside the prison on the morning of the execution, picket lines and sit-down strikes were organized on the road leading to San Quentin's front gates. A Marin County deputy sheriff shunts along this young man, clad in jeans, sneakers, and Army surplus jacket—or, gives him "the bum's rush" in the words of the photographer. The young man's long hair and defiant expression would be a familiar sight over the next decade. *Author's collection*

remained faithful to it until the end. During the final Sacramento vigil, he confronted Pat Brown point-blank with the question, "Are you unequivocally in favor of clemency for Caryl Chessman?", to which Brown could only say, "I am hesitating."

Dr. Ziferstein's son, Dan, and daughter, Gail, were eager adherents to the cause, too. They had held signs in protest marches in Los Angeles alongside their father. The Ziferstein siblings, in fact, were captured in a photograph that ran in *Time* magazine.

■

EVEN THOUGH CHESSMAN had already, and repeatedly, told the religious officials that he was going to his death an agnostic and was not interested in confessing sins or taking part in an eleventh-hour "conversion," both Father Dingberg and Rev. Eshelman were present on the morning of Monday, May 2, 1960. Eshelman provided one of the most invaluable records of Chessman's last moments, taking notes beside the holding cell;later that morning he admitted that "I came as close to breaking down and crying as I ever had at an execution. Walking home alone, I cried to myself. I'm crying now."

Eshelman arrived at 8:20 to find Chessman alert and relatively calm, given that he hadn't slept in more than a day and was scheduled to die within two hours. When he bid Chessman a good morning, Chessman said, "No good news, no especially bad news. All I can say is that this is a hell of a way to start a week."

The State Supreme Court had convened twenty minutes earlier and the radio in Chessman's holding cell was switched on, awaiting any news. Eshelman remembers that one of the songs that played while they waited was "Keep Your Sunny Side Up," midway through which—sensing the horrible irony—the guards switched to an all-news station. Chessman worked on a last letter to Rosalie Asher. A news flash broke in at 9:14 A.M. The State Supreme Court had denied Chessman's petition.

Chessman looked at the clock and said, "It's unfair they took so long. It's practically killed any chance to go further. . . . We'll have to face it. This is it."

At 9:45, Eshelman noted, "Chessman straightened papers on his table and told the guards, "Let's get packed and ready to go here. Let's get started with this white shirt routine."

Chessman admitted to feeling "foolish" with two members of the clergy, Dingberg and Eshelman, close at hand and not knowing how to avail himself of their comforts.

He told them, according to Eshelman, "I appreciate knowing both of you. I feel a little foolish about not having a religious faith, and seeing things like you see them. In fact, I feel like a damn fool. I thought I might have a feeling now, but it's just not there. It went out of me years ago and just never came back. I don't feel I should pretend about it when it isn't there."

Dingberg thanked Chessman for his candor and Eshelman told him, "Your life has left a tremendous impact on the world. Your books will be classics."

Chessman retorted, "In spite of being accused of such great ego, I don't believe my books will be classics, but I do hope they will have some effect on the whole problem of capital punishment."

As he paced around the holding cell, he told the clergy and the guards that he was "uneasy" and felt fear but was certain he'd be able to keep it under control. He talked about one prisoner he'd heard about who, while awaiting execution, was asked "if his ass twitched" and who told the guards, "It jumped clean out of the socket."

It was clear to all those who watched Chessman that his main concern in his last moments was that he depart with dignity, that he not break down, weep, beg for mercy. It was also important to him that he not make any last minute confessions to his alleged crimes. Thus, when Warden Dickson arrived to officiate at the execution, Chessman told him, "I just want to keep the record straight. I am not the Red Light Bandit. I am not the man. I won't belabor the point; just let it stand at that."

He gave Dickson all of the letters he'd written in the holding cell, and the warden promised to "take care of them." (He later turned the seven letters over to Rosalie Asher to distribute them to the appropriate recipients.)

Two members of the prison medical staff, including the Chief Medical Officer, entered the holding cell, asked Chessman to remove his shirt while they checked his vital signs and strapped a heart monitor onto his chest, over which he donned a crisp white dress shirt. The doctor asked, "How are the adrenalines working?" Chessman took this ridiculous question in stride, saying, "I can't tell you just how they're working, doc, but I know they're working."

Father Dingberg gave Chessman a lighted cigarette and shook his hand. Eshelman shook Chessman's hand and said, "I'm in your corner." He admitted later that "I wanted to say 'God bless you,' but I knew he didn't want me to."

Warden Dickson gave the signal to start at 10:01, at which point Caryl Chessman became a dead man walking. From an empty cell nearby, two guards removed a "traditional green carpet" and rolled it down the hall and around the corner onto the lip of The Green Room. This was so that, as part of the traditional courtesy the ritual demanded, the condemned wouldn't take his last "thirteen steps" on the cold concrete floor.

The door to Chessman's holding cell was unlocked. A four-guard detail then escorted him onto the green carpet. Resigned to his fate, he told one of the guards, "Inside of me I had a feeling the court would relent and let me live."

Chessman now sported his new blue slacks and white shirt, though the black rubber tube from the heart monitor dangled a few inches down his front. By prison regulation, he was not allowed to wear underpants, socks or shoes. The procession neared the rivet-covered door of the octagonal gas chamber, the door to which opened outward. As he padded by Dingberg and Eshelman, Chessman said, "So long, Father, so long, Reverend."

"He walked straight past us to the gas chamber and sat down in the chair," Eshelman noted. "He looked completely composed, hair combed, white shirt collar open at the neck. He smiled at the warden, and said, 'I'm all right.' Then he turned and said the same thing through the window, so that someone out there would be reassured."

■

INSIDE THE OBSERVATION room, which afforded a view of the proceedings through five separate windows, five guards and sixty spectators (referred to, politely, as "witnesses" by the prison) sat transfixed by the scene. Chessman had been allowed to invite five witnesses of his own (Asher and Freeman had declined the offer).

Perhaps expecting trouble or sensing the enormity of the occasion, which was being broadcast live across the nation by radio hook-up, the sixty-five spectators held tightly to the edge of their seats.

But if they had expected fireworks, Chessman disappointed them, for perhaps the first and only time. He quietly and expressionlessly entered the airtight chamber and allowed the guards, without mishap, to strap him into the chair marked "A". His only complaint was that the wrist straps were too tight, and they were quickly loosened by one of the guards. An electric stethoscope was affixed to his chest with adhesive tape and then hooked up to a line that led outside the chamber, where the prison doctor could read it and determine the time of death. According to William Kunstler's account, "One of the guards said a few comforting words to the silent figure in the chair and then the four men left the chamber. The last one out carefully shut the steel door behind him and twirled its spoked wheel until he was satisfied that the tiny cell was hermetically sealed."

Michael Burt McCarthy, a freelance journalist, visited San Quentin in 1978. He was one of the few members of the press ever given actual physical access to The Green Room itself. As a former San Quentin inmate himself, McCarthy claims to be the only felon who had ever sat in the death chair and gotten up to live another day.

"I wanted to come as close to describing what the condemned saw and experienced before death as possible," McCarthy wrote while seated in the "A" chair, the very seat occupied by Barbara Graham on June 3, 1955, and Caryl Chessman on May 2, 1960. "I noted the sixty-four nuts and bolts on the huge air-proof door, the dark green metal floor, the seven bullet-proof glass observation windows. The two to my left were where the Warden and the Executioner stood behind Venetian blinds, unseen by the condemned."

McCarthy continued his checklist: "One tan canvas strap, each arm; two tan canvas straps, each leg; one tan canvas chest strap, the black rubber tube on the right wall that is attached to the stethoscope taped to the condemned's chest; the overhead vent for suction removal of the gas; and the valve through which ammonia pours out, neutralizing the gas clinging to the body and Chamber walls. I got up and stepped behind the chairs. To the rear and just below each chair was a metal brace with a release hook upon which the Executioner hangs the one-pound bag of cyanide. Below each brace was the trough which holds the 97% sulfuric acid, 3% distilled water solution, mixed and released in the adjacent Mixing Room. Both apertures were lined with corrugated sheet metal—porous metal. The odor I smelled was derived from a minute film of cyanide-sulphuric residue from the 194 executions. Physically, it was harmless. Psychologically, it sent tremors of revulsion through me. I wanted out . . . I now knew enough of the sensation experienced by anyone who had ever sat in Chair A."

■

WARDEN DICKSON, STATIONED like the Wizard of Oz behind a window hidden by Venetian blinds, was told that everything was set. The time was registered as 10:03:15. Dickson gave the signal to the executioner who stood alongside him, also hidden from view by Venetian blinds.

■

WITH A CLICKING sound, the cyanide pellets were released into the bucket of sulfuric acid solution that was positioned under the chair, which was made of a metal mesh that allowed the rising poisonous fumes to sift upward toward the prisoner's nose and mouth.

■

MEANWHILE, DAVIS AND Asher had been dispatched to make a final plea for Chessman's life. Knowing that his petition for a writ of habeas corpus—filed on Saturday afternoon with the California Supreme Court—would probably be rejected, the two attorneys arranged for a cab to drive them down the street to the U.S. District Court. They arrived at the former at 9:00 A.M. and had until ten to get the stay, at either court, as that was the exact planned time for the cyanide pellets to be dropped into the vat and the vapors to be released into Chessman's lungs.

As Davis expected, the State Supreme Court rejected the petition, 4 to 3. That was at 9:20. He and Asher navigated the six blocks to the district court and presented their petition to Judge Louis E. Goodman. Because the fifteen-page document was too long to read in the allotted time, Davis had driven out to the judge's house the day before (a Sunday) to personally give him an advance copy. But the Judge Goodman still hadn't read it when Davis arrived at about 9:30. The attorney was desperate.

"The judge took the petition, and he started to read it, page by page," he recalled. "As he started to read it and turn the pages, I kept watching the clock. I saw that clock going from five minutes to ten, to four minutes to ten, to three minutes, and finally, when it got to just almost exactly one minute to, the judge said, 'All right, I'll grant the stay of execution.'"

That is, Goodman would allow Davis and Asher one hour to file an appeal to the U.S. Supreme Court (though Supreme Court Justice William O. Douglas had announced that the nation's highest court would not intervene in this matter). Regardless of the seemingly insurmountable obstacles that lay ahead, the two attorneys—who, by this time, were barely on speaking terms—were frantic that the

Chessman's lawyers George T. Davis and Rosalie Asher leave the Federal Building in downtown San Francisco after Judge Goodman's stay was not relayed to Warden Dickson in time to save their client and friend's life. A clearly distressed Asher had to be escorted by Davis and another, unnamed man, from the building. *Author's collection*

prison be called. The execution had to be stopped. Davis begged the judge to let him dial the direct line on his chamber phone, to save precious seconds. The judge told him that his secretary, Celeste Hickey, would dial it for him, to just give her the number.

"I gave the number to the secretary. She walked into an adjoining office just a few feet away, and I thought 'Boy, this is the cliffhanger of all cliffhangers,' because now it's thirty seconds before ten, and she's dialing, but all it needs is to get to the warden. At about five seconds to before ten, the secretary walks out and says, 'Could you give me that number again, Mr. Davis? I must have misdialed it.' [She had the correct number, GL 4–1460, but through sheer incompetence she'd neglected to dial the first "4"]. I gave her the number again, she dialed it again, she got the warden."

The judge told the warden to grant a stay of execution.

■

HAROLD V. STREETER, the reporter-witness for the Associated Press, filed a report that ran in editions of many of the country's afternoon newspapers that day. In his version, Chessman's "dark eyes" scanned the group of sixty spectators while the guards strapped him in the chair, then closed the airtight door behind them. Chessman looked for a familiar face, and found one in Eleanor Garner Black, a Los Angeles reporter. Streeter wrote, "He strains at the straps in an effort to lean forward toward her."

Black was one of two women to witness Chessman's execution; the other was Mary Crawford of the *News–Call-Bulletin* . Black and Crawford, thus, became the first women in California history to witness an execution by the state. In Crawford's eyewitness account, she wrote, "There were so many people there it seemed like going to a hanging in a public park. I stood about four rows back. The only other woman present stood close to the rail."

William Kunstler wrote, "As the invisible fumes swirled up toward his nostrils, he turned his head to the right where the witnesses were pressed up against the heavy glass windows. He was trying to say something but the hushed observers could not hear his words through the sound-proof glass. Eleanor Garner Black, a reporter for the *Los Angeles Examiner*, read his lips. 'Tell Rosalie I said good-bye. It's all right,' she repeated in a choked whisper. She then made a circle with her thumb and forefinger to indicate that she had understood. He just had time to smile once before his head fell forward on his chest."

Streeter wrote, "His smile vanishes. He grimaces but managed a deep breath. His face with its hawk-nose and protruding lower lip goes back as though he was looking at the ceiling."

It was at this point, 10:04 A.M., that the phone rang in the warden's office, though it could be heard clearly by everyone in the now ominously silent observation room. Eshelman noted "there was a whispering and commotion over where the warden stood," behind his Venetian blinds. The phone was answered by Associate Warden Louis Nelson. The caller was Celeste Hickey, phoning from Judge Goodman's chambers in downtown San Francisco. She told Nelson, "Judge Goodman has granted a one-hour reprieve."

Without consulting Dickson, standing a few feet and one door away, Nelson said, "I'm sorry, it's too late. The pellets have just been dropped."

Hickey turned and relayed the message to the judge and Davis and Asher.

■

THERE WAS SOME controversy at the time over whether, indeed, the call had been made too late. Some members of the medical community were certain that the chamber could have been cleared of fumes by the fans and the prisoner could have been revived. Dr. Isidore Ziferstein told reporters that Chessman could have been saved, that even if he had breathed some of the gas, injections of sodium nitrite and sodium thiosulphate, and a handkerchief doused with amyl nitrate, would have revived him in time.

At 10:04, Chessman was not dead.

He had told some friends that he would try to hold his breath for as long as he could. He had also worked out a prearranged signal with one of the reporters he'd invited as his guest, Will Stevens, that he would flash if he felt any physical pain. This he did, Stevens insisted, at 10:08. At 10:09, it was reported, that "his shoulders quivered slightly." In other words, Chessman was alive enough to make a hand signal *five minutes after* he was reprieved by a federal judge.

Nevertheless, Streeter falsely reported, "If this is your first execution, you will make the mistake of thinking the condemned man is holding his breath. He isn't. The first 15 seconds of the deadly hydrocyanic acid have blotted out his will. As a personality, as a reasoning human being, he is already dead." Because nowhere in his "eyewitness" account does he mention the last-minute reprieve—a fact known to every other reporter in the room—one can only guess that Streeter included the above as a cover for the prison officials failure even to give the controversial Chessman a fighting chance to live. It didn't work. The last-minute reprieve was widely reported

The sixty official witnesses are led out of the San Quentin's gas chamber within minutes of Caryl Chessman's execution. As they are leaving, the cyanide fumes are being dispersed into the atmosphere via the tall, thin smokestack (visible here at the top of the building) far above their heads. The prison's signature five-story gun tower is also visible at left. It is an otherwise beautiful May morning in California. *Author's collection*

Los Angeles Examiner reporter Eleanor Garner Black pulled herself together after witnessing her friend's execution. During the last moments of Chessman's life, according to the *Examiner* photographer, "he carried on a silent lip-reading conversation with Mrs. Black, who had attracted his attention with hand motions as he was strapped into the metal chair in the gas chamber." Black told onlookers that Chessman mouthed his final words to her: "Tell Rosalie I said good-bye." *Author's collection*

the next day, only further fanning the anger and bitterness of those who'd protested the execution.

The bureaucratic wheels had been put in motion. Certainly, Nelson weighed the scandal that would ensue from the spectacle of San Quentin staff scrambling frantically to rescue the famous Caryl Chessman, dust him off, and breathe him back to life in full view of horror-stricken reporters and members of the public. He could not bear the thought of that, and Warden Dickson later concurred with his judgment, telling television reporters outside the prison that he was relieved "the Chessman case was over with, one way or another."

■

At 10:12 a.m., the attending doctor noted that the stethoscope indicated that Chessman's heart had stopped beating.

The chamber's fans were employed and the dead prisoner was removed an hour later. A hearse from the Harry M. Williams Funeral Home in San Rafael arrived three hours later to retrieve the body. The following day, the remains of Caryl Whittier Chessman were cremated at Mount Tamalpais Cemetery in San Rafael.

Two days later, Isidore Ziferstein received a letter from Chessman, one of the seven he'd handwritten in his holding cell before his death. Chessman thanked the doctor for his years of fighting to abolish the death penalty.

He said, "I am sure the fact my life finally was forfeited will spur your determination to see this ugly practice of capital punishment

Outside the state capitol in Sacramento, demonstrators gathered in a circle around the bronze plaque of the state seal of California in silent reflection moments after learning the news of Chessman's execution. *Author's collection*

Governor Brown holed up in his Sacramento office during and after Chessman's execution. Brown's press secretary Hale Champion, was given the unenviable task of telling the gathered reporters that the execution had commenced. *Author's collection*

San Quentin Prison Warden Fred Dickson did not try to duck press after Chessman's execution. Here, he takes questions from the somber gathering. Chessman and Dickson had begrudging respect for one another. *Author's collection*

abolished. And that makes dying easier and gives my death an affirmative meaning it otherwise would be denied."

Within days of the execution, Governor Pat Brown contacted Dr. Ziferstein's son and daughter, having seen the photograph of them in *Time* magazine protesting in the streets of Los Angeles. In the days following the execution, Brown retreated to an office in Los Angeles to avoid the backlash; he was already beginning his campaign of damage control.

"He invited Gail and I up just to chat," Dan Ziferstein told this author in 2005. "It was in an office in Los Angeles within that same time frame. It was clear that he wanted to ease his conscience. He was very strong on how terrible crime was, showing us all these pictures of crime scenes. The feeling about Chessman, when I think about

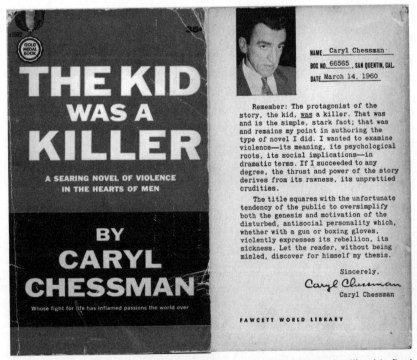

Chessman received advanced copies of his novel *The Kid Was A Killer*, his final publication, within weeks of his execution. On the back of the book, Chessman offered a corrective to his potential readers not to be misled by the public's tendency "to oversimplify both the genesis and motivation of the disturbed, antisocial personality." He closes with his characteristically neatly written signature. *Author's collection*

people on both sides, including the people against us, wasn't so much that he embodied any particular type of criminality but that the death penalty was a good thing. That people like him, and there were plenty of them, wouldn't do what they did if they were afraid of being executed. And we were saying that the death penalty was no deterrent."

Chessman had done what he said he would do. He had met death head on, with the sort of beatific dignity one finds in accounts of the final hours of the "heretics" and "humanists" killed by the Catholic Church in their periodic inquisitions or the witches dispatched by the Puritans. He prepared a final statement, to be publicly read after the State of California's dollar's worth of cyanide gas had done its work.

"When you read this," his statement read, "they will have killed me. I will have exchanged oblivion for an unprecedented twelve-year nightmare. And you will have witnessed the final, lethal, ritualistic act. It is my hope and my belief that you will be able to report that I died with dignity, without animal fear and without bravado. I owe that much to myself."

■

Two days after the execution, George Davis told government officials that the reason Chessman never revealed the identity of the real "Red Light Bandit" was that he was concerned about the well-being of his daughter, who was seventeen in 1960. Threats had been relayed to Chessman in San Quentin over the previous months that if he snitched the girl would be harmed. On the official government communiqué about this, now contained in Chessman's FBI file, J. Edgar Hoover had appended the handwritten note, "Such rot!"

In the final petition to the State Supreme Court, Chessman had named four people who could "clear" him of the Red Light Bandit crimes, all four of whom he'd met in prison prior to December 1947: William Wampler, Paul R. Judd, David H. Knowles, and Charles Saverine Terranova. Knowles, who was with Chessman the night he was arrested for the Red Light Bandit crimes, was convicted in 1948 under the Little Lindbergh Law for manhandling his victims during the robbery of a Redondo Beach clothing store. Though, like Chessman, he potentially faced the death penalty under this law, Knowles had long since been paroled from San Quentin prison. Wampler begged out of coming to Chessman's aid, citing fears for the safety of his wife and two stepchildren in Long Beach. Judd was never located.

George Davis told reporters that the Los Angeles Police Department had refused to let him see the file on the Red Light Bandit. Nonetheless, he said, he had been offered, for a price, information that proved that Chessman's conviction was part of a "vicious frame-up."

"We didn't buy," said Davis. "But he [the seller] was dead a month later. I don't know how he died, but he wasn't very old."

∎

WITHOUT ANY ACCOMPANYING religious service, Chessman's body was cremated at the Tamalpais Cemetery on Monday afternoon. Bernice Freeman placed two rosebuds from her garden on an otherwise unadorned coffin. Rosalie Asher did not attend. The mortician, Harry Williams, awaited instructions from Asher as to what should be done with the ashes. Two days later, Chessman's ashes were still at the San Rafael mortuary, as negotiations had broken down between Asher and Forest Lawn Memorial Park in Glendale over whether Chessman's ashes would be buried in his mother's grave. The spokesman for Forest Lawn said that Chessman was "unrepentant and an avowed agnostic" and that his ashes would "detract from the spiritual values of Forest Lawn."

∎

ON MAY 9, 1960, Joe Longstreth wrote Rosalie Asher a consoling letter, in which he also tried to console himself. "Of one thing I'm happy and sure: Caryl, personally, is at peace, and at peace, really, for the first time in his life. And he most assuredly has a life, even now, which few ever achieve. He was born to be something, and he was: it was the quirk of fate that his creative genius went in the direction it did. I'm not really a fatalist, but one sometimes wonders if his role was not, indeed, decreed in order to accomplish what, through devious paths, I believe he has and will accomplish."

The State of California wasted little time in returning to its status quo. On Friday, May 13, 1960, James Eugene Hooton was executed in The Green Room, followed by Richard Thomas Cooper on July 8, Robert S. Harmon on August 9, George Albert Scott on September 7, and, closing out a very dark year on Death Row, Raymond L. Cartier on December 28.

Over the summer, Longstreth buried himself in work on his Indiana farm. Just as he felt the "calm setting in" over his memories of Chessman, he visited a carnival in his hometown of Richmond. The main attraction of this traveling entertainment operation was a replica of a gas chamber, with a "live re-enactment" of an execution. The sign accompanying the sideshow read, SEE HOW CARYL CHESSMAN DIED!

About this, Longstreth wrote Asher, "I could vomit most of humanity up and trample it in the mud."

In August, Longstreth received a brief but urgent missive from Asher about some letters of Chessman's which she believed Bill Linhart had "stolen" and sold to the *Independent* in Richmond, California, which planned to print them. Linhart had been a private investigator for Chessman since 1954, and the letters in question had simply come into his possession as the natural accretion of six years of research; they weren't "stolen," per se. The letters, one to Danny Clarkson, and another to a woman named Genelle, date from 1952 and confirm the existence of Chessman's daughter, who is described as "a lovely strawberry blond." Asher worried that this revelation would "wreck her marriage." She admitted to contacting the reporter in an effort to "kill the story." She reserved her harshest words for Linhart, calling him a "stupid opportunistic oaf." In strictest confidence, she told Longstreth about how some of the staff at *Argosy* were able to get the letters away from him by slipping him a "mickey." ("Great private eye!" she gloated.) She told Longstreth that she was compiling material for her own book about Chessman, having chosen the tentative title, *Chessman: Twelve Years in Check.**

In early March 1974, Rosalie Asher quietly and unceremoniously arranged to have Chessman's ashes, which had been in her possession since May 2, 1960, scattered from an airplane west of Santa Cruz Island. Here, among the waters of the enchanting Channel Islands, where the world's remaining whales are staging a minor comeback and where rare flora and fauna find safe haven, the remains of America's best known bandit may find some eternal rest, if not serenity.

Thirty years later, while going through Asher's last effects, her niece Bonnie Fovinci found the urn in which Chessman's ashes had been contained from 1960 until 1974. It was sitting on a shelf in Asher's office.

---

* The book remains unpublished.

CHESSMAN'S LEGACY

An Afterword

MOST CRIMINALS FACING extermination at the hands of the state would, it stands to reason, try to locate the unique set of circumstances—social, cultural, psychological, biochemical, spiritual—that might explain the behavior that led them to their caged purgatory. It also stands to reason that most criminals facing extermination at the hands of the state would have time to sit and think about these things.

Until they take this self-exam, however, or make this self-inventory, they are irredeemable, a demonic "other" whose extermination is that much easier for the state to accomplish and its citizens to accept. Their extermination will bring tears to only those few close relations whose bridges they have not long since burned, and to death penalty abolitionists who argue that anyone's death at the hands of the state—no matter how irredeemable or "evil" they're deemed to be—diminishes us all. Had the State of California conformed to the then swift resolution of capital punishment cases for Caryl Chessman—that is, killed him by March 28, 1952, the date of his first scheduled trip to the San Quentin gas chamber—he would not have become the famous face that adorned the issue of capital punishment, and the best-selling author whose words and deeds rang out with clarion sound to the four corners of the globe and are still capable of haunting us nearly half a century after his death. He would have been known as the monstrous, cold-hearted Red Light Bandit—or, as one Los Angeles newspaper editorialist called him, a "sex terrorist"—and joined the dusty lore of such San Quentin legends as Diamond Reed, Leanderess Riley, Lloyd Sampsell ("The Yacht Bandit"), Eddie Wein ("The Want Ad Rapist") and Harvey Glatman, a rapist and murderer who photographed victims during and after his crimes in "every conceivable pose."

However, Chessman was given a stay of execution by Judge Jesse W. Carter—and eventually eight more stays of execution by other judges and in other courts—and was issued an ultimatum after one of these stays by Warden Harley O. Teets. Teets, weary of Chessman's defiance, dared him to "make some sense out of your life," if only to repay the judge for giving him another "chance." Because of these two seemingly miraculous events, Chessman was given time to locate the source of his criminal nature, relocate his prodigious instinct for self-expression, and create something—a literary legacy, if you will—that enough people appreciated to make him, in the last five years of his life, the most famous prisoner on earth.

As far as I know, I have read every book, article, and newspaper account pertaining to Caryl Chessman. I have also read Chessman's books and articles, many of them several times. While these were the work of a man who, like all authors, was careful about the face he presented to a reading public, the same cannot be said for his letters from Death Row. These letters, unguarded and unintended for publication, convinced the author that Chessman was someone who had changed, had undergone a profound transformation, and is thus worthy of respect for this transformation, even if his life of crime was worthy of the public castigation it has roundly received. One's view of Chessman tends to be based upon whether one believes this transformation to be "sincere." By that yardstick, this author hasn't a single doubt. The act of writing is hard enough under the best of circumstances. Under the circumstances that Chessman faced, including the most depressing "office" imaginable and the ultimate in "deadlines," a human, much less a writer, would not be able to, in Lincoln's words, "fool all of the people all of the time."

Thus, I share the view of Byron Eshelman, the San Quentin chaplain

Typical publications that made their pages available to Chessman after the publication of *Cell 2455, Death Row. Author's collection*

who befriended Chessman over the last decade of his life, seeing him on a nearly daily basis. In his 1961 memoir Eshelman wrote, "I believe that the state of California executed the wrong man." By that, Eshelman meant that Chessman may or may not have been the Red Light Bandit, but he was certainly "not the psychopath who had come to Death Row twelve years earlier." Eshelman noted that he'd watched Chessman change during his years on the Row. "I saw him grow and mature, and learn to channel the explosive forces within him into power for social good. From the viewpoint of our social understanding, his death was sheer tragedy. From the viewpoint of clinical psychology, his death was a terrible loss. From the viewpoint of Christianity, his death was a total negation of all that Jesus Christ tried to teach us."

In addition to books by and about Chessman, I consulted numerous books about prison life, incarceration, crime, and criminals in my effort to penetrate the minds of those who chronically commit criminal acts. Also, while none of the following books provided information specific to Caryl Chessman's life, they helped put into focus my thoughts about the human potential for change. In the words of Gitta Sereny, they offered a "renewal of an act of faith in the possibility of metamorphosis." Or, in the words of Helen Parkhurst, they offered testimony of "an authentic person who changed his own life." This idea is the very underpinning of all prison rehabilitation efforts—that is, that no human being is beyond recovery or redemption. In the final analysis, I decided that life, or at least my life, would not be worth pondering if I lost the capacity for believing in such potential. Indeed, my life as I know it today, with a loving wife and a beautiful son, a sober and occasionally serene outlook on the world, would be unthinkable without it.

Behan, Brendan, *Borstal Boy*
Braly, Malcolm, *False Starts: A Memoir of San Quentin and Other Prisons*
Ellroy, James, *My Dark Places*
Exley, Frederick, *A Fan's Notes*
Haley, Alex, ed., *The Autobiography of Malcolm X*
Mitchell, Joseph, *Joe Gould's Secret*
Naeve, Lowell, *A Field of Broken Stones*
Parkhurst, Helen, *Undertow: The Story of a Boy Called Tony*
Sereny, Gitta, *Cries Unheard. Why Children Kill: The Story of Mary Bell*
Stringer, Lee, *Grand Central Winter: Stories from the Street*
Winchester, Simon *The Professor and the Madman: A Tale of Murder, Insanity, and the Making of the Oxford English Dictionary*

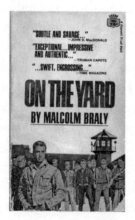

Malcolm Braly was in San Quentin when Chessman was executed. Though the two writers never met, Braly's earlier skepticism of Chessman as a "grandstander" changed to admiration. To some critics, Braly was Chessman's literary heir apparent, especially after his fourth novel, *On the Yard*, was published in 1967; he started the novel in San Quentin, was reprimanded, then completed it when he got out and was off parole. Tragically, after fifteen years of freedom, Braly was killed in a car accident in 1980. *Author's collection*

APPENDIX

"And What If I Failed?"

ON APRIL 17, *1960, two weeks before he was executed in the gas chamber, Caryl Chessman submitted the following document to Dr. David G. Schmidt, Chief Psychiatrist, San Quentin Prison. It was submitted in response to a series of questions put to him by Dr. Schmidt about the changes he had undergone during his twelve years on Death Row. This was, in effect, Dr. Schmidt's "debriefing" of the prisoner. After this, the State of California's book on Caryl Whittier Chessman would be closed.*

DOUBTLESS THE WISEST thing to do is to heed Voltaire's perceptive injunction and define the term. Maturation means to me maturing and maturing signifies a growing up; that is, an ability to respond to life situations, and particularly conflict or frustration, with intelligence, without avoidable, emotion-clouding heat, anger or hate, and with a reasonable degree of prudence. The mature person must have long range goals consistent with his skills and temperament. He must be able to relate to others and be able to sympathize with their aspirations and needs. He must be socially aware, although I do not think he must be a conformist in the opprobrious sense of that term. Rationally recognizing the imperfections in himself, in his neighbors and in his society, his dissent or protest against conditions, events or actions in which he perceives inequity would be, when made, of a constructive kind. He must recognize that there lurk primitive, violent impulses in all of us but that the advocacy or practice of violence not only demean him as a person; it invites and begets counter-violence, solving nothing.

By such standards, have I matured in my 12 year stay on Death Row? I believe I have, markedly. Not only have I grown up by the objective and subjective test by which maturity may be measured, I have grown older. And, a not uncommon phenomenon, either physiologically or psychologically, to some extent there has been a "burning out" of sociopathic reaction or reflex. Humanly, I still lose my temper, but increasingly (and, to be candid, as much a consequence of this aging process as self-discipline) I find myself trying to solve my problems with my pre-frontal lobes rather than smash at them—or a substitute for them—with my fists. It may be said that my basic character hasn't changed, that, figuratively in grudging compliance with the mental and physical demands of these passing years, I simply have exchanged rapier for bludgeon out of necessity, and hence that, at bottom, my psychopathy or sociopathy merely has found a more subtle form of expression. You, Doctor, with your special psychiatric training, are far better equipped to answer this question authoritatively than I am. My answer is perhaps a rationalization: If those character traits or that personality pattern which impelled me as a youngster into violent criminal conflict with society (and myself) remain basically unaltered or cannot be excised wholly, at least I know they can be usefully directioned. They can be made my servants rather than I theirs. Historical examples abound of men who, if they had been born into this period, would have been called psychopathic or sociopathic. Yet today we honor their names and admire their creativity.

As you know, I want to become a writer, and—here ego finds expression—I sincerely believe I possess the motivation, the self-discipline, the drive, the dedication and the gift of words to become a writer whose writings can enrich our literature and contribute significantly to some of the pressing social problems of our time. Yes, I am quite aware that notoriety has contributed appreciably to the success of my already published books. Yet, keep in mind, that

I did write them, not simply talk about wanting to write. And now that it has served its purpose both as a desperately needed purgative and as a means of dramatically focusing attention on the question of the validity of the philosophy and practice of retributive justice, I am through with biography. This transition already has begun. In a few days my novel "The Kid Was a Killer" will be published. I am sure it will furnish you a useful insight into its author, just as I believe it will help the public understand the sociopath and thus encourage that public to demand that, in dealing with him, the men in your profession must be relied upon rather than executioners.

I have at least enough writing projects in mind to occupy me for another ten years. I want to do a biography of the late Jesse W. Carter, Associate Justice of the California Supreme Court, a jurist who taught me to respect the law. As well, there is a play I desire to do about François Villon, French lyric poet and gallows bird, that has contemporary relevance. Further, I am itching to do a series of three novels, of today, a trilogy. And I want to try my hand at a novelette, which could be readily converted into a play, called "Autumn and Eve" and which, entertainingly not ponderously, with a Malibu setting, would examine the relationship of man and woman in a swiftly changing world.

And what if I failed? What if I collected rejection slip after rejection slip? Well, I am certain I would not fail finally, and I am quite prepared for rough going along the way. The pertinent point, in my judgment, is that, at 38, I am old as a psychopathic hoodlum but young for a writer. Many of the world's best authors did not reach their full powers until their 50s and even their 60s.

There is irony, of course, in the fact I am discussing the future as though I had one, as though I did not have a date with the executioner 14 days and a few odd hours hence. However, be assured, I am completely aware of that date and, statistically, of the overwhelming possibilities I shall keep it.

What do I really think of my past? Initially, I believe it is evident that I have in fact thought a great deal about it, tried to make some kind of sense out of it. I can't and I don't try to justify it insofar as shifting responsibility for it is concerned. It's there and always it is going to remain there (the changes have occurred in the black, overdrawn legend that has been built up in the public mind about me, where I have emerged as a slavering, snarling, sneering mocker of justice, an inhuman "monster" without a single redeeming value).

No, I can't change my past, Doctor; I can't erase it. I can't forget it. But I can realize I was a damned fool, and admit it. My responsibility, legally adjudicated punishment and the questions of guilt or innocence of my present crimes aside, does not end there, as I see it. I feel a need more fully to grasp the nature of what we can call the psychodynamics of my particular brand of folly (overtly expressed as criminality and psychiatrically diagnosed as sociopathy). In sum, I damn well don't want to engage in any more irrational conduct if I can avoid it. In this, obviously, I would need help, yours or someone like you who gave a damn about me and was professionally and personally willing to lend a hand. Reversing the coin, if I survived, perhaps I could be of some value to science and humanity by being a guinea pig. Tragically, my case is not atypical; there are thousands of youngsters filling reform schools, committing crimes, defiant and rebellious, who will end up in prison or shot dead or on Death Row.

Seemingly, although my awareness of this is only recent, another test of maturity in my case would be whether I would be willing to accept a commutation of sentence to life imprisonment, even without possibility of parole. Now, I would, and not because any newly developed animal fear of death or compromise of what I define as integrity or principle. The reason (at least the conscious one) is that, realistically, I must accept the fact that, in the context of my situation, I cannot expect more at this time. Only an irrational fool would, and this is a logical first step in my effort to think and act rationally, without folly. At this juncture, I might comment, editorially or philosophically, it would appear that another crucial test of maturity is that one must come to accept the fact that, by his standards, each of us will know injustice in our lives, and if, for the present, that injustice (real or imagined) is irremedial, that is no excuse or reason for us to seek what would amount to self-destruction. Restated, I do not want to wear, posthumously, a self-invited martyr's robes. To the contrary, I have become convinced a mature man in my position should and must prefer to live and thus have an opportunity to prove, if he can, that those who judged him so harshly were wrong. In this way, I would be helping those who know that gas chambers and executioners should have no place in our society to demonstrate with a concrete example the validity of their thesis.

Many reporters have asked me: If you were commuted, how would I react to anonymity or relative anonymity. The notion behind the question seems to be the suspicion (and mistaken) belief that I have become so intoxicated by seeing my name in the headlines that, on finding myself just another prisoner, I might become so disenchanted that I would attempt something sensationally irresponsible simply to feed my (conjectured) craving for notoriety. This is perfect but understandable nonsense. I have had my belly full and more of headlines and sensationalism. Inwardly, I wince every time I read one of these breathless and indignant accounts of myself as a cunning "fiend" with an oversized ego who, the writers would have it, cares nothing for his fellows and seeks only the false glamour of being a notorious character. Such reporting reveals far more about those who grind it out than it remotely does about me. There is nothing I desire more than to get out of the headlines. The place I want to see my name in the future is not on the front pages of a newspaper but in the title page of books. Finally, whatever my past, I want to be a man who can respect himself and who has earned the hard way the respect of others. I do not want the synthetic fame of a psychopath.

NOTES

I HAVE ENDEAVORED WHERE possible to indicate the sources of all quotations, statistics, and characterizations within the text itself. When this was not possible, pertinent material is included in footnotes. When a specific book or magazine article of Chessman's is not indicated as the source of a quotation, that item was extracted from the hundreds of pages of letters that he wrote from Death Row to Joseph Longstreth, Rosalie Asher, George Davis, and Bernice Freeman. The recounting of the Red Light Bandit crimes, the arrest record, and Chessman's 1948 trial are based on contemporary news accounts in the *Los Angeles Times*, *Los Angeles Herald Examiner*, transcripts of the trial proceedings, and the books *Beyond a Reasonable Doubt? The Original Trial of Caryl Chessman* by William M. Kunstler and *Caryl Chessman: The Red Light Bandit* by Frank J. Parker.

INTRODUCTION

p. XIII "offers from forty Brazilians to die in his place": *Time*, March 21, 1960, p. 16.

p. XIV "California rejected a moratorium on the death penalty": www.carylchessman.com

p. XIV "one of the sharpest and best-trained lawyers I've ever met": *Time*, March 21, 1960, p. 18.

p. XVIII "robbery, kidnapping, attempted rape and 'unnatural sex'": Parker, *Caryl Chessman: The Red Light Bandit*, p. 17.

p. xx "'My soul,' he famously announced, 'is not for sale'":
These and other quotes in the introduction are, unless
otherwise indicated, taken from Chessman, *Cell 2455,
Death Row*.

p. xx "a capital crime to kidnap a person for the purpose of
inflicting physical harm": Parker, *Caryl Chessman: The
Red Light Bandit*, pp. 93–117.

p. XXIII "the U.S. Embassy in Stockholm had to be surrounded
by police to protect it from angry protesters": *New York
Times*, May 3, 1960, p. A1.

PART I ■ THE BOY BANDIT

1: "DEATH ROW WAS THE BEST THING EVER TO HAPPEN TO ME"

p. 3 "raised Hallie by the dictates of the Good Book": *The
True Story of Caryl Chessman* by Clark Howard, "Hallie"
chapter.

p. 6 "a fivefold increase in ten years." U.S. Census figures.

p. 9 "when its 124,000 members would take pleasure drives of
the area." See *America First* by Alan Bisbort, pp. 123–25.

2: "WHICH WAY TO HELL?"

p. 21 Much of the story of the early crime career comes from
Chessman, *Cell 2455, Death Row* and Machlin and Woodfield, *Ninth Life*.

p. 29 "Chessman tried to dominate class discussions": *Time*,
March 21, 1960, p. 18.

p. 38 "attempted murder, of Glendale police officer Fred
Bovier": *Los Angeles Times*, February 4, 1941.

3: A SAN QUENTIN APPETIZER: CHESSMAN'S FIRST TWO VISITS

p. 41 The early history of San Quentin prison is covered in
definitive detail in Lamott's *Chronicles of San Quentin*,
pp. 3–118.

p. 47 "was hired as a guard at the prison": All biographical
information was derived from the Clinton T. Duffy Collection, Marin County Museum, San Rafael, California;
various personal scrapbooks; and interviews with Lt.
Vernell Crittendon, San Quentin Museum Association,
president.

p. 49–50 "Three days a week, he sat in the mess hall": *San Francisco Chronicle*, September 1–6, 1940.

p. 53 "as high as 90% in some states": Sands, *My Shadow Ran
Fast*, p. 209.

p. 55 "the worst industry in any prison in the United States":
Chronicles of San Quentin by Kenneth Lamott, p. 253.

p. 58 "highest in San Quentin history": *Newsweek*, November
2, 1959.

4: THE RED LIGHT BANDIT

p. 71 "lone women found savagely": *Black Dahlia Avenger* by
Steve Hodel, p. 347.

p. 71 "who grew up in Medford, Massachusetts": The life and
death of Elizabeth Short was reconstructed from accounts
in James Ellroy's *My Dark Places*, Steve Hodel's *Black
Dahlia Avenger*, and contemporary accounts in the *Los
Angeles Times* and *Los Angeles Herald Examiner*.

p. 78 "ended on the night of Friday, January 23, 1948": Reconstruction of the Red Light Bandit crimes, the scenarios
and Chessman's trial were derived from Kunstler's and
Parker's books and contemporary newspaper accounts.

p. 83 "their statements were voluntary, the law was satisfied":
David Goewey's *Crash Out*, p. 230.

5: SAN QUENTIN'S LEAST WANTED (1948–1952)

p. 117 "The fights that Chessman has been in over the *L.A.*
magazine": "The Case For Caryl Chessman" by Irwin
Moskowitz, Vol. 1, No. 11, p. 13.

p. 119 "Despite her cultivated appearance": Account of Wilson
de la Roi taken from Warden Duffy's personal scrapbooks,
Marin County Museum, San Rafael.

p. 125 "One day on Death Row was like any other day": Chessman detailed daily life on Death Row in *The Face of Justice*, pp. 202–207.

p. 128 "if Mr. Dies were on the Hitler payroll": *A Quarter Century of Un-Americana, 1938–1963*, edited by Charlotte
Pomerantz, pp. 15–30.

p. 132 "one long struggle not to be laughed at": *The Orwell
Reader*, pp. 3–9.

PART II ∙ THE TRANSFORMATION

6: THE COMING OF UNCLE JOE

p. 139 This chapter was largely based on letters to and from
Joseph Longstreth and Caryl Chessman, and interviews
with Mr. Longstreth by the author in 2002.

p. 152 He wrote Governor Goodwin Knight the following year.
L.A., "The Case For Caryl Chessman" by Irwin Moskowitz, Vol. 1, No. 11, p. 16.

7: AN IMPORTANT VISIT

p. 161 This chapter was largely based on letters to and from Joseph Longstreth and Alan Honour to Caryl Chessman, Bernice Freeman, Rosalie Asher, and interviews with Mr. Longstreth by the author in 2002. Much of the corroborating material can be found in Bernice Freeman's *The Desperate and the Damned*.

p. 183 "Wells had been in and out of prison since 1928": Bernice Freeman, *The Desperate and the Damned*, p. 136.

8: DOWN TO THE WIRE

p. 189 This chapter was largely based on letters to and from Joseph Longstreth and Alan Honour to Caryl Chessman, Bernice Freeman, Rosalie Asher, and interviews with Mr. Longstreth by the author in 2002.

p. 204 "Like Chessman's, this case attracted nationwide attention. On July 4, 1954, Marilyn Sheppard, the pregnant wife of a prominent Cleveland osteopath named Samuel H. Sheppard . . .": Fred McGunagle, *The Murder of Marilyn Sheppard*, Crime Library, www.crimelibrary.com/sheppard/.

p. 220 "Despite the low regard in which handwriting analyses were held by psychologists": www.igas.com.

9: TRIAL BY ORDEAL: 1955 AND STILL ALIVE

p. 227 The article recounts Chessman's ordeal of waiting for a final decision by the U.S. Supreme Court on his stay of execution the previous October. *Saga*, March 1955, pp. 8–11, 78–80.

10: "KING OF DEATH ROW" (1956–1957)

p. 254 "Meanwhile, on television, radio and suburban hi-fi consoles, a new American cultural hero emerged, as did a new musical genre . . .": Joel Makower, *BOOM!*, p. 20.

p. 257 "Abbott was an accounting": Freeman *The Desperate and the Damned*, pp 143–160.

p. 263 "Underneath the bluster": Freeman, *The Desperate and the Damned*, pp. 140–142.

p. 265 "Despite security measures rarely matched in the prison's history": *San Francisco Examiner*, April 7, 1956, p. A1.

p. 276 "Meanwhile, in another part of the country": Makower, *BOOM!* p. 228.

11: A FAITH WORSE THAN DEATH (1958)

p. 285 "coined by T. H. Huxley in 1870": Murray, *Aldous Huxley*, pp. 17–19.

p. 285 "Eshelman found the famous prisoner fuming":
Eshelman, *Death Row Chaplain*, pp. 205–206.

p. 287 "It was awful close to the fire": Merle Haggard interview,
Larry King Live, December 16, 2004.

12: THE COMING OF GOVERNOR BROWN (1959)

p. 305 "Of the fifty-nine death penalty cases that crossed his":
Brown, *Public Justice, Private Mercy*, p. xiii.

p. 307 "Roy R. Rubottom, Jr., warned Brown by urgent telegram":
Duffy, *88 Men and 2 Women*, pp. 134–138.

p. 307 "The first was John Crooker": Brown, *Public Justice,
Private Mercy*, pp. 5–20.

p. 311 "even more macabre": Brown, *Public Justice, Private
Mercy*, pp. 90–105.

p. 317 Franco also gave *L.A.* an interview in late 1959. *L.A.,* "A
Foreign Viewpoint," Volume 1, Number 11, p. 15.

13: THE GREEN ROOM BECKONS

p. 326 "Between 1930 and 1980, these states combined to put
945 men and seven women to death by gas": *Los Angeles
Times*.

p. 327 "Built in 1938 at an iron factory in Denver": All descriptions of the gas chamber's history taken from Clinton T.
Duffy's personal papers.

p. 328–329 "particularly harrowing": *San Francisco Examiner*,
December 3, 1938, p. A1.

p. 331 "nearly identical to Zyklon B": *Los Angeles Times*.

p. 336 "Brown faced a wave of": *L.A.,* Volume 1, Number 11,
"The Case for Caryl Chessman" by Irwin Moskowitz, pp.
11–13, 16.

p. 338 "Change was in the air in America": *Life*, February 29,
1960.

14: "I'LL SEE YOU IN THE MORNING"

p. 341 The description of Chessman's final days was woven from
newspaper accounts in the *Los Angeles Times, New York
Times, San Francisco Chronicle, Marin Independent,*
and *Los Angeles Herald Examiner*, as well as eyewitness accounts by Byron Eshelman and Eleanor Garner
Black and interviews with George T. Davis and Joseph
Longstreth.

BIBLIOGRAPHY

BOOKS

Adams, Randall, William Hoffer and Marilyn Mona Hoffer. *Adams v. Texas*. New York: St. Martin's Press, 1991.

Basinger, Jeanine. *Silent Stars*. New York: Alfred A. Knopf, 1999.

Bloch, Herbert A. and Gilbert Geis. *Man, Crime, and Society: The Forms of Criminal Behavior*. New York: Random House, 1970.

Braly, Malcolm. *False Starts: A Memoir of San Quentin and Other Prisons*. Boston: Little, Brown, 1976.

———. *On the Yard*. Boston: Little, Brown, 1967.

Brown, Edmund and Dick Adler. *Public Justice, Private Mercy: A Governor's Education on Death Row*. New York: Weidenfeld & Nicolson, 1989.

Chessman, Caryl. *Cell 2455 Death Row*. Englewood Cliffs, N.J.: Prentice-Hall, 1954.

———. *The Face of Justice*. Englewood Cliffs, N.J.: Prentice-Hall, 1957.

———. *The Kid Was a Killer*. Greenwich, Conn.: Gold Medal Books, 1960.

———. *Trial by Ordeal*. Englewood Cliffs, N.J.: Prentice-Hall, 1955.

Davies, Ioan. *Writers in Prison*. Oxford: Basil Blackwell, 1990.

Davis, Bernice Freeman. *The Desperate and the Damned*. New York: Thomas Y. Crowell, 1961.

Davis, George T. *San Francisco Trial Lawyer: In Defense of Due Process, 1930s to 1990s*. Berkeley: University of California, Bancroft Library Oral History Project. Interviews by Carole Hicke, 1993.

Duffy, Clinton T. with Al Hirshberg. *88 Men and 2 Women*. New York: Pocket Books, 1963.

Duffy, Clinton T. with Dean Jennings. *The San Quentin Story*. New York: Doubleday, 1950.

Duffy, Gladys with Blaise Whitehead Lane. *Warden's Wife*. New York: Popular Library, 1963.

Ellroy, James. *My Dark Places: An L.A. Crime Memoir*. New York: Alfred A. Knopf, 1996.

Eshelman, Byron E. and Frank Riley. *Death Row Chaplain*. Englewood Cliffs, N.J.: Prentice-Hall, 1962.

Goewey, David. *Crash Out: The True Tale of a Hell's Kitchen Kid & the Bloodiest Escape in Sing Sing History*. New York: Crown, 2005.

Hallinan, Joseph T. *Going Up the River: Travels in a Prison Nation*. New York: Random House, 2001.

Haggard, Merle. *Sing Me Back Home: My Story*. New York: Simon & Schuster, 1983.

Hamm, Theodore. *Rebel and a Cause: Caryl Chessman and the Politics of the Death Penalty in Postwar California, 1948–1974*. Berkeley: University of California Press, 2001.

Hardwick, Elizabeth. *A View of My Own: Essays in Literature and Society*. New York: Farrar, Straus & Cudahy, 1962.

Hodel, Steve. *Black Dahlia Avenger*. New York: Perennial, 2004.

Howard, Clark. *The True Story of Caryl Chessman*. The Crime Library, Dark Horse Multimedia, 2000.

Jackson, Joe and William F. Burke, Jr. *Dead Run: The Untold Story of Dennis Stockton and America's Only Mass Escape from Death Row*. New York: Times Books, 1999.

Knappman, Edward W., ed. *Great American Trials*. Detroit: Gale, 1994.

Kunstler, William J. *Beyond a Reasonable Doubt?: The Original Trial of Caryl Chessman*. New York: William Morrow, 1961.

Lamott, Kenneth. *Chronicles of San Quentin: The Biography of a Prison.* New York: David McKay, 1961.

Lamson, David. *We Who Are About to Die: Prison as Seen by a Condemned Man.* New York: Charles Scribner's Sons, 1936.

Machlin, Milton and William Read Woodfield. *Ninth Life.* New York: G.P. Putnam, 1961.

Makower, Joel. *BOOM! Talkin' About Our Generation.* Chicago: Contemporary Books, 1985.

Parker, Frank J. *Caryl Chessman: The Red Light Bandit.* Chicago: Nelson-Hall, 1975.

"Peek." *This Is San Quentin!* San Quentin: San Quentin Museum Association, 1944.

Phillips, Cabell. *The New York Times Chronicle of American Life, From the Crash to the Blitz, 1929–1939.* Toronto, Ontario: Macmillan, 1969.

Pomeranz, Charlotte, ed. *A Quarter-Century of Un-Americana, 1938–1963.* New York: Marzani & Munsell, 1963.

Sacks, Oliver. *Awakenings.* New York: Harper Perennial, 1990.

Sands, Bill. *My Shadow Ran Fast.* Englewood Cliffs, N.J.: Prentice-Hall, 1964.

———. *The Seventh Step.* New York: New American Library, 1967.

Stanley, Leo L. with Evelyn Wells. *Men at Their Worst.* New York: D. Appleton-Century, 1940.

Vila, Bryan and Cynthia Morris. *Capital Punishment in the United States: A Documentary History.* Westport, Conn., Greenwood, 1997.

Work Projects Administration of Northern California. *San Francisco: The Bay and Its Cities.* American Guide Series. New York: Hastings House, 1940.

NEWSPAPER AND MAGAZINE ARTICLES

Chessman, Caryl. "A Letter from Death Row," *Psychology Today.* February 1969.

———. "On Revenge," *L.A.*, Volume 1, Number 11, April–May 1960.

———. "What I Would Do With My Life," *Saga*, March 1955.

Hardwick, Elizabeth. "The Life and Death of Caryl Chessman," first appeared in *Partisan Review*, 1960.

McCarthy, Michael Burt. "The Journey to the Green Room," unpublished article.

Marine, Gene. "Seventh Execution of Caryl Chessman," *The Nation*, October 17, 1959.

Meister, Richard. "Who Hates Chessman?" *The Nation*. February 20, 1960.

———. "Politics and Chessman," *The Nation*. March 26, 1960.

Palmer, Stuart. "How Many More Chessmans?" *The Nation*, May 21, 1960.

The San Quentin News, weekly prison newspaper. Various back issues, 1941–1960.

Styron, William. "The Death-in-Life of Benjamin Reid," *Esquire*. February 1962.

Wechsler, Herbert. "Death Sentence: Its Pros, Cons. *Life*. May 9, 1960.

Various other unbylined articles in *America, Christian Century, Commonweal, Newsweek, Time, U.S. News and World Report*.

Also, accounts of his last hours by correspondents for the *New York Times, San Francisco Chronicle, News–Call-Bulletin* and *Los Angeles Times*, accessed by microfilm.

Caryl Chessman's FBI file: http://foia.fbi.gov/foiaindex/cchessman.htm. Voluminous correspondence between Joseph Longstreth and Caryl Chessman; Longstreth and Rosalie Asher; and Longstreth and Bernice Freeman.

Seven hundred articles pertaining to Caryl Chessman in Los Angeles newspapers, 1941 to 1960, searched via ProQuest, and in microfilm collections at the Library of Congress, Washington, D.C.; and the Olin Memorial Library, Wesleyan University, Middletown, Connecticut.

ORIGINAL UNPUBLISHED MANUSCRIPTS BY CARYL CHESSMAN

"Dust Thou Art?"; "A Voice From Death Row"; "Noz Smoz Kapop?" (522-page novel); "Pedro Was a Happy Man"; "The Gladiator, the Disrobing Danseuse and L'Amour"; "A Corpse for Christmas"; "Young Man With a Right Hand"; "Autumn and Eve"; "Crisis"; "Art for Arthur's Sake," "The People Versus Chessman: A series of six articles on the case and the man."

ACKNOWLEDGMENTS

THE STORY OF Caryl Chessman is like the proverbial iceberg. The tiny section above the water is available to anyone who can navigate a public library's reference shelf—look under "Capital Punishment"—or grasp the rudiments of Google. I had known about that tip for years, due to an obsession with the Beat Generation, countercultural history and all things California, especially all things related to the San Francisco Bay Area. Every time I listened to recordings of Lenny Bruce or Mort Sahl, I'd make a mental note, when Chessman's name came up as part of their stand-up routines, to find out more about the guy. But I never did. At least not until years later, when I came across a collection of essays by Elizabeth Hardwick (*A View of My Own*) in a secondhand bookstore. After reading her essay "The Life and Death of Caryl Chessman," I knew it was time to don the scuba gear and dive below the waterline. The opportunity to do so was provided by Jayson Whitehead at *Gadfly*, the late, lamented online magazine. The phenomenal reaction to the resultant piece, "The Curious Case of Caryl Chessman," convinced me that a book was begging to be written. That initial outpouring from *Gadfly* readers—all wondering, as I was, how Chessman, his case, and his writings could be so completely forgotten—still astounds me. So, thank you, Jayson, and thank you, readers.

Countless people kept the boat on the surface while I foraged down below. I owe profound thanks to several people who helped clear some seemingly insurmountable obstacles. These include Tom Anderson, for his tireless decades-spanning pursuit of the truth about Chessman's past; Athena Angelos, picture researcher and human being extraordinaire; Nick Bougas, for providing photographs that would have been impossible to otherwise locate and/or afford to buy; Wanda Kohls, for being an inveterate "collector of clips" and eager to share them along with her remembrances of the Chessman case; Thomas Riggio, for his early encouragement and whose obsession with Theodore Dreiser was an inspiration; Michael McCarthy, for sharing his own prison experiences and personal brush with San Quentin's "Green Room"; and Steve Hodel, the real "avenger" of the Black Dahlia whose book helped refocus my research and whose guiding hand led me as close to the truth as one will likely ever get.

In Marin County, I stumbled upon the Anne T. Kent California History Room of the Marin County Library System, which is housed in the most unique government building in the nation—Frank Lloyd Wright's Marin County Civic Center. The library here is blessed to have some indispensable collections of San Quentin–related material, including the papers of Dr. Leo L. Stanley. It is also blessed with two talented librarians, Laurie J. Thompson and Jocelyn Moss. Yes, "talented," because it's one thing to point out the shelves and explain the rules to patrons, but it's quite another to, as they do, steer them in directions they hadn't expected to go. Jocelyn Moss also holds down the fort as curator of the Marin Historical Museum in San Rafael and was generous in sharing the personal archives of Warden Clinton T. Duffy and other San Quentin–related material there. At San Quentin State Prison, Lt. Vernell Crittendon, the keeper of the flame for prison history, opened some cells onto Chessman's life, and death, and provided an entertaining tour through the holdings of the onsite museum. Tom and Katie Burke, the driving forces of Pomegranate Publications, provided hospitality and encouragement during my Marin County visits.

Others who have my deepest gratitude are Dan Ziferstein, for his remembrances of his father, Isidore Ziferstein; Ricci Terranova, for his remembrances of his father, Charles Terranova; George T. Davis, for racking his ninety-plus-year-old brain on my account, and for sharing the files and oral histories from his incredible sixty-year career in pursuit of due process (Mr. Davis died as this book was in production); Suzette Martinez Standring, my friend who casually dropped the bomb that she was friends, and former assistant to, the man who nearly saved Chessman, Mr. Davis; Gene Marine, a voice from the 1960s who warned me against turning Chessman into martyr or saint; Cheshire cat Tom Hearn; *Advocate* colleagues Alistair Highet and John Adamian for giving me journalistic freedom while all this was going on; and Parke Puterbaugh, for, as he has during more than thirty years of friendship and creative partnership, showing me the way on so many fronts.

None of this, of course, would have been possible without the persistence of Anne Zeman, who was my friend long before she was my agent and has proven herself peerless at both roles. And her husband, Mark Peel, America's great unknown wit, provided levity when called for and even when it wasn't. At Carroll & Graf, I am indebted to Philip Turner, editor in chief, for showing enough patience to properly hear me out, and to Keith Wallman, for facilitating all the myriad publishing details.

As the book's dedication indicates, I owe more than I can ever repay to Joseph Longstreth, who in the short time I knew him proved as gentle and honest as he appears in the hundreds of letters with Chessman he shared with me. I felt Joe standing at my shoulder as I wrote this book. I owe as much, if not more, to his wife, the unsinkable Peg Goldberg Longstreth, for her own remarkable character and courage.

Finally, I gladly accept my life sentence without the chance of parole in the custody of my wife, Tracey O'Shaughnessy, and our son, Paul James Bisbort.

INDEX

A

Abbott, Burton, 257–58, 269–70
Abbott, Donald, 37
Achuff, W. D., 117, 316, 343
ACLU (American Civil Liberties
   Union), 276, 331
agnosticism, 285
Alda, Alan, xvi
Allen, Brenda, 75
American Civil Liberties Union
   (ACLU), 276, 331
anti–capital punishment
   movement
   in California, 211–12, 213,
   351–56
   Chessman case and, xiii,
   245–46
   protests against Chessman
   execution, xi–xiii, xxiii,
   xxiv, 211, 351–56, 367
   worldwide, xiii, xxiii, 307,
   317–18, 336
arrests of Chessman, xviii, 22–
   23, 29–30, 35, 37–38, 77–82
Artie Shaw Orchestra, 50
Asher, Rosalie
   Chessman relationship, 119–
   22, 174, 193–94, 281

on Chessman's personality,
   173–74, 182–83
on Davis, 320, 323
description of, 155
as executor of estate, 186, 342
illness of, 275
last stay of execution
   attempt, 361–63
last visit to Chessman, 348
Longstreth relationship, 166
scatters Chessman's ashes,
   372–73
on transcript proceedings,
   253–54
on transformation of
   Chessman, 124
trip to Brazil, 317
automobile accident, 2, 13
automotive tourism, 9
Autumn and Eve (unpublished;
   Chessman), 346, 381

B

Baby and Child Care (Spock),
   127–28
Baby Boom, 127
The Badge (Webb), 73

"The Ballard of Caryl Chessman"
(Hawkins), xvi, xvii
Ballew, Floyd E., 86
Barbara (girlfriend), 19–21
Barnes, Elmer, 326
Barnes, Harry Elmer, xxii, 192
Bartle, Thomas, 86
Basinger, Jeanine, 7–8
Belli, Melvin, xiv, 235
Bemelmans, Ludwig, 81, 82
Beyond a Reasonable Doubt?
(Kunstler), xxii, 85, 187
Biberman, Herbert, 129, 212
bibliotherapy, 110
Birdman of Alcatraz (film), xvi
Black, Eleanor Garner, 363, 364,
366
Black Dahlia Avenger (Hodel),
71, 73–74
Black Dahlia murder, 71–74
The Blue Dahlia (film), 72
bookie joint robberies, 31–32, 37
Bovier, Fred, 37–38
Boy Bandit Gang, 30–33, 37
Braly, Malcolm, xxiii, 39, 224,
261, 344, 378
Brando, Marlon, 199, 354
Brazil, support for Chessman in,
xiii, xxiii, 317–18
brothel robberies, 31–32, 37
Brown, Edmund G. "Jerry," 306,
355
Brown, Edmund G. "Pat"
animosity toward Chessman,
204
on Chessman's crimes, 335
commutes Crooker's
sentence, 309–11
commutes Wein's sentence,
312
as death penalty opponent,
303–7
denies clemency for
Chessman, 184–85, 318–20
grants stay to Chessman,
335–36
orders confiscation of
manuscripts, 235

political aspirations of, xxii,
xxiv–xxv, 338
political expediency of
decision, 338–39
post-execution backlash,
367–69
Brown, Edward W., 114
Brown, Wenzell, 268
Bryan, Stephanie, 258
Buckalew, Benjamin, 44
Bull, Nana L., 285
bullwhip incident, 11–12
burglaries, 25
Burns, Jerry A., 282–83
Bushaw, Elaine, 86

C
California. *See also* Los Angeles;
San Francisco
in 1920s, 5–6, 9
anti–capital punishment
movement in, 211–12, 213,
351–56
building of state prison,
43–46
during gold rush, 41–44
California Institution for Men at
Chino, 64–65
California Penal Code, Section
209. *See* Little Lindbergh
Law
Camarillo State Hospital, 209,
210, 251
Cannon, Robert Lee, 327–30
Caperton, John, 43, 44
capital punishment. *See also*
anti–capital punishment
movement
Brando on, 354
Brown's views on, 303–7
California legislature
considers ban on, 337–38
Chessman on, 346, 351
Davis on, 245–46
Duffy on, 117–18, 337–38
moratorium on, 303
repercussions of Chessman
execution, xiii, 235–36

Carter, Jesse W.
 Chessman plans biography of,
  346, 381
 death of, 315
 grants stays of execution, 143,
  202–3
 on Little Lindbergh Law, 312
car thefts, 21–22, 23–25, 29–30,
 35, 37
*Caryl Chessman: Red Light
 Bandit* (Parker), 85
Cell 2455, Death Row
 (Chessman)
 blowups over editing of, 161–
  62, 169–73
 bought by Prentice-Hall, 145,
  154
 Chessman threatens lawsuit
  over, 171–78
 earnings of, 234
 film adaptation of, xv, xvi,
  196–99
 Longstreth on, 185
 publication of, 159–60, 182,
  186
 reception of, xxii, 179–81,
  187, 191, 192–93, 215–16
 submission of manuscript to
  Longstreth, 143–45
Chessman, Caryl
 childhood, and family
  childhood, 1–3, 8–9, 10–14
  childhood health problems,
   9, 10–11, 13–14
  daughter, 66, 67, 169, 201,
   370, 372
  engagement to Frances
   Couturier, 225–26, 230–
   31, 266–67, 292–93
  family moves, 5–6, 10, 13
  family poverty, 13, 15–16
  first sexual encounter,
   23–27
  humiliation at hands of
   Barbara's suitor, 19–21
  marriages, 35, 36–37, 66, 67
  musical ability, 10, 12, 141,
   193

named Carol, 4–5
 in school, 3, 10, 29, 36–37
criminal activity/
imprisonments
 acquires gun, 28–29
 arrests, 22–23, 29–30, 35,
  37–38
 Barbara affair in instigation
  of, 19–21
 begins serious theft,
  joyriding, 21–22
 Boy Bandit Gang, 30–33, 37
 car thefts, 21–22, 23–25,
  29–30, 35, 37
 escape from Chino, 64–66
 escape from Glendale
  Police Station, 22–24
 first thefts on paper route,
  14, 15
 at Folsom State Prison, 67
 at forestry camp, 30
 joins gang, 21
 overview of criminal
  record, xix
 parole from Folsom State
  Prison, 67, 75
 at Preston State Industrial
  School, 30, 33–34
 robberies, 30, 31–32, 37, 78
 at San Quentin, 38–39,
  54–61, 64, 66–67
 Red Light Bandit arrest/
 trial
 arrest, xviii, 77–82
 beatings in police custody,
  83, 84–85
 confession of, xviii, 83–85
 defends self at trial, xx, 93,
  97–98, 100, 101–2
 Hallie Chessman
  testimony, 102–5
 inevitability of outcome,
  92–94
 Jarnigan Lea testimony, 99
 Little Lindbergh Law and,
  94–96
 Mary Alice Meza
  testimony, 99–102

Regina Johnson testimony,
96–98
transcript of trial. *See* trial
transcript
on Death Row. *See also* stays
of execution
arrival on Death Row,
107–8
clemency application, 180,
182–85
daily routine, 125–27
develops ulcer, xxvi, 126,
243–44
extra cell, 135, 257
fight with Wade, 316
finances of, 207, 209, 210,
234, 247, 251
legal filings for other
prisoners, 134, 135, 264
price of living on, xxv–xxvi
sit-down strike, 184
solitary confinement, 184,
267–69, 316
Teets issues challenge, 131,
133–34, 376
transforming experience
of, xiv–xv, 124, 130–35,
193–94, 376
execution
disposition of body, 285,
367, 371, 372–73
execution procedure, 361,
363–66
final hours, 348–49, 356–60
final public statement, 370
last letters, xxvi–xxvii,
345–47, 349–51
last press conference,
342–44
last words, 364, 366
mental/emotional attitude
prior to, 341–46
protests against, xi–xiii,
xxiii, xxiv, 211, 351–56,
367
statements on death
penalty, 346, 351
stay of execution fails,
361–63, 364

will drawn up, 182, 186,
342
opinions and ideas
on crime, 61
on death penalty, 346,
351
execution imagined, 334–
35
on his childhood, 350
on his parents, 25, 166–67,
168, 230
on his sentence and
appeals, 150–51
Hitler assassination plan,
65, 66
on innocence claim, 151–52
on Little Lindbergh Law,
94–95, 150
on maturity, 379–83
on mortality, 170
on notoriety, 383
religious beliefs, 16–18, 159,
284–86, 349, 357
Robin Hood illusions of,
31–32
self-education of, 58, 64
on sociopathy, 382
on transforming experience
of Death Row, 224–25,
232
personality and relationships
Asher relationship, 119–22,
174, 193–94, 281
cynicism of, 34
descriptions of personality,
xx, 157–59, 173–74,
182–83
Duffy and, 54–56, 64, 65,
111–15, 117
egotism of, xx, 157–59,
193–94
Freeman relationship, 116,
156–59
handwriting
graphoanalysis, 220
intolerance of drugs and
drunkenness, 32–33
IQ of, 58–59
legal expertise of, xiv, 134

Longstreth relationship,
139, 145–46, 148–49, 152–
54, 193–94
as model prisoner in San
Quentin, 56–59, 61
mother's influence, 10, 12,
19, 140
reaction to editing of *Cell
2455, Death Row*, 161–62,
169–73
rebellion against authority,
xix, 23, 25, 30, 61
Sands friendship, 56, 60–61,
118–19
self-destructive behavior of,
169–70, 173–74
stoicism of, 1, 191, 224
teaching gift of, 55–56
writings. *See also Cell
2455, Death Row; The Face
of Justice; The Kid Was a
Killer; Trial by Ordeal*
as agent of transformation,
123–24, 193–94
articles, 206–7, 216, 227–32,
291
diary, 111, 119–20, 122
disputes over *Cell 2455,
Death Row*, 162–63, 170–
71, 172, 176
early aspirations, 34–35,
123–24, 140–41
overview, xiv, 291
proposed writing projects,
176, 346, 380–81
short stories, 120, 123, 160,
231–32
statement to Dr. Schmidt,
379–83
transformed by Death Row
experience, 123–24
unpublished works, 141,
176, 231, 291, 346, 381, 395
Chessman, Hallie Cottle
accident of, 2, 13
beliefs and attitudes of, 16–17,
19
childhood, education, and
marriage, 3–4

death, 122–23
encourages Chessman to
write, 34–35
relationship with Chessman,
10, 12, 19, 140
testimony at trial, 102–5
Chessman, Lucy Ann. *See* Short,
Lucy Ann
Chessman, Serl Whittier
business ventures, 10, 13, 34,
36, 75
Chessman on, 167, 168, 230
death, 124, 166–67
employment, 2, 4, 7–8, 13
and Frances Ann Couturier,
142–43, 167, 168
Longstreth's description of,
163
marriage, 4
suicide attempt, 13
visits Chessman after
confession, 84
*Chessman: Twelve Years in
Check* (unpublished; Asher),
372
Chino, California Institution for
Men at, 64–65
Chronicles of San Quentin
(Lamott), 45
CIO (Congress of Industrial
Organizations), 128, 129
civil rights movement, 276, 338
Clark, Tom, 241
Cochran, Steve, 196
Cohen, Mickey, 71, 76
Cold War, 128, 351–52
confessions, coerced, 83
Confidential, 206
Congress of Industrial
Organizations (CIO), 128,
129
"A Corpse for Christmas"
(Chessman), 232
Cottle, Hallie. *See* Chessman,
Hallie Cottle
Cottle, Charles and Abigail, 3, 19
Court of Last Resort, 150–52
Couturier, Cheryl, 142, 168, 221,
231

Couturier, David, 142, 155, 168,
   221, 231
Couturier, Frances Ann
   Asher on, 202, 214, 267
   breach with Caryl Chessman,
      276–77, 292–93
   daughter born, 315
   engagement ring, 214, 231
   Freeman *Chronicle* story on,
      202
   interviews by, 192–93
   irresponsible behavior of, 214,
      267, 292–93
   The Kid Was a Killer rights
      assigned to, 274
   Longstreth visits, 163
   love for Caryl Chessman,
      204, 225–26, 230–31
   as portrayed in *Saga* article,
      229–31
   pregnancy of, 298–99
   Serl Chessman and, 142–43,
      167, 168
   stresses upon, 179
Crawford, Mary, 350–51, 363
"Crime Doesn't Pay"
   (Chessman), 160
criminal activity
   in Bay Area during gold rush,
      42
   of Chessman. *See* Chessman,
      Caryl, criminal activity/
      imprisonment
   in Los Angeles of 1940s,
      69–74
   Los Angeles underworld,
      75–77
criminal behavior, encephalitis
   and, 12
Critics Associated, 141, 147–48,
   208, 268
Crittendon, Vernell, 47
Crooker, John, 307–11
Currier, Charles, 43

D
Daily Trojan article, 282–83
Daniels, Stuart, 279
Davies, Lawrence E., 343

Davis, Bernice Freeman. *See*
   Freeman, Bernice
Davis, Bob, 314
Davis, George T.
   Asher on, 320, 323
   on capital punishment,
      245–46
   on Chessman's legal
      expertise, xiv
   on Chessman's personality,
      159
   The Face of Justice as
      biography of, 281, 346
   fee of, 246, 272–73, 281
   hired to represent Chessman,
      xxii, 244–46
   injured, 275
   last stay of execution
      attempt, 361–63
   last visit to Chessman, 348
   represents Burton Abbott,
      258
   on setting of execution date,
      341
   takes Duncan murder case,
      302
   in transcript proceedings,
      246–47, 251–53, 281
Dean, James, 199
death penalty. *See* capital
   punishment
Death Row. *See also* Chessman,
   Caryl, on Death Row
   conditions in, 107–8, 109
   daily routine, 125–27
   Duffy on, 117–18
   price of living on, xxv–xxvi
Death Row Chaplain
   (Eshelman), 285
Death Row Diary, 176, 195.
   See also *Trial by Ordeal*
   (Chessman)
"The Death Song of Chessman,"
   xvi
debating team of San Quentin,
   59
de la Roi, Wilson, 119, 183
demonstrations. *See* protests
   against Chessman execution

Denman, Judge, 225, 257
desegregation, 276, 338
The Desperate and the Damned
  (Davis/Freeman), 55, 116,
  157, 165–66
DeWitt, Jack, 198
Diamond, Neil, xvi
Dick, Philip K., 35
Dickson, Fred R.
  Chessman execution and,
    358, 361, 366, 368
  Chessman works in office of,
    67
  as warden of San Quentin,
    47, 270
Dies, Martin Jr., 128
Dingberg, Father, 349, 356–59
diphtheria, 13–14
Don Pedro (Mozart), 141, 147
Doty, Harold, 17, 90–91
Douglas, William O., 241–42,
  320, 362
Dragnet, 73
*The Dream Endures: California
  Enters the 1940s* (Starr), 31
Duffy, Clinton T.
  books by, 52, 55, 112, 333
  Chessman and, 54–56, 64, 65,
    111–15, 117
  childhood and family, 47–48
  on death penalty, 117–18,
    337–38
  named acting warden,
    48–49
  on operation of gas chamber,
    333
  reforms San Quentin, 46–47,
    49–51
  relationship with prisoners,
    53–54
  Sands and, 51–54
  Seventh Step Foundation and,
    118–19
Duffy, Gladys, 48, 52, 57, 65–66,
  67–68
Duffy, Jerome, 224, 244
Duffy, William, 47
Duncan, Olga, 302
Durocher, Leo, 50

Dutton, Denis, xxv

E
Ecuador, xxiii
88 Men and 2 Women (C. Duffy),
  55, 112
Eisenhower, Dwight, xxiii, 255–
  56, 276, 307, 336
Ellison, James Whitfield, 295
Ellroy, James, 73
encephalitis, 10–12
Eshelman, Byron E., 285–86,
  344, 349, 356–59, 376–77
Estell, James M., 43, 44, 45
Euphemia (jail ship), 43
Evans, Judge, 277, 280, 282, 283,
  298
execution of Chessman. *See*
  Chessman, Caryl, execution
executions, procedures for,
  325–26, 332–33. *See also* gas
  chamber

F
The Face of Justice (Chessman)
  as biography of Davis, 281,
    346
  publication of, 274
  smuggling indictments, 299–
    301, 314, 320
  smuggling of, 117, 268–69
  transcript proceedings related
    in, 253
  writing ban and, 241, 246
  writing of, 258–60, 261
Fairbanks, Douglas, 7–8
*False Starts: A Memoir of San
  Quentin and Other Prisons*
  (Braly), 39
Felony Tank (Braly), 261
Fitzgerald, Ed, 206–7
Flowers, George, 202
*Flow My Tears, the Policeman
  Said* (Dick), 35
Folsom State Prison, 67, 75
Forbes, Colin, 83–84
Forest Lawn Memorial Park,
  371
Fovinci, Bonnie, 124, 315n, 373

Fox, Manuel, 84
Franco, Giacomo, 317–18
Fraser, Stanley, 125, 207, 213, 246, 249
Freeman, Bernice
    on Barbara Graham execution, 238
    on Chessman as teacher, 55
    on Chessman's personality, 155–59
    at cremation, 371
    and Frances Ann Couturier, 202, 214
    last letter from Chessman, 349–50
    Longstreth and, 164–66, 268
    prison guard relays message to, 116
    on Robert Pierce, 263–64
French, Jeanne, 74
Fricke, Charles, xxi, 93, 97, 121, 195, 252, 271–72
Fulbright, J. William, 336

G
G.I. Bill of Rights, 127
"Gabriella," 66
Gangelin, Victor A., 240
Garden Beautiful, San Quentin, 61, 62
Gardner, Erle Stanley, 150–52
Garry, Charles, 183–84
gas chamber
    depiction in *I Want To Live!*, 240
    first California executions, 327–30
    invention and adoption of, 325–26
    outlawed in California, 331
    procedure for execution, 332–33
    at San Quentin, 326–28, 360
gassing of Jews by Nazi regime, 330–31
Gaylord, Lucy Ann. *See* Short, Lucy Ann
Genelle, 66
Gibson, Howard, 84, 313

Gill, Otto, 318
"Gina," 66
Gissling, George, 139
"The Gladiator, the Disrobing Danseuse and L'Amour" (Chessman), 232
glandular rejuvenation, 61–63
Glendale, CA, 6–7
Glendale Police Station escape, 22–24
Going Up the River: Travels in a Prison Nation (Halliman), 62
Gold Medal (publisher), 241, 295, 298, 316
gold rush, 41–42
Goodman, Louis E., 223, 247, 249–53, 361–63
Goosen, Elliott, 83
Gould, Pauline "Polly," 207–8, 212–13
Graham, Barbara, 237–40
Grand, Donald W., 83
The Grapes of Wrath (Steinbeck), 6
graphoanalysis, 220
Graves, Mary E., 285–86
Graves, William, 116–17, 118, 211, 213
Great Depression, 16
Greco, Alex, 90–91
"The Green Room." *See* gas chamber
Gun, Nerin, 232–33

H
Haggard, Merle, xvi, 286–88
Halliman, Joseph T., 62
Hamilton, Allen McLean, 325
handwriting analysis, 220
Hanna, Frank, 275
Hardwick, Elizabeth, xv
Harris, Robert Alton, 331
Harte, Bret, 45
Hauptmann, Bruno Richard, 96
Hawkins, Ronnie, xvi, xvii
Hays, John C., 43, 44
Hearst, William Randolph, 69
Hendricks, William, 262–64

Hickey, Celeste, 363, 364
Hiss, Alger, 129
Hitler, Adolf, 65, 66
Hodel, George, 91
Hodel, Steve, xviii–xix, 71, 73–74, 77, 85, 91–92
Hollywood Ten, 129
Holohan, James B., 48
Honour, Alan, 141, 147–48, 170–72, 176, 314
Hopper, Hedda, 70
House Un-American Activities Committee (HUAC), 128–29, 198, 354
Hubka, Arnold, 83
Hull, Neva, 294–95
Hurlbut, Frank, 87, 100–101
Huxley, T.H., 285
hydrogen cyanide gas, 332–33

I
imprisonments of Chessman. *See* Chessman, Caryl, criminal activity/ imprisonment
Inmate Representative Committee, 51
international opinion on capital punishment, xi–xiii, xxiii, 307, 317–18, 336
I Want To Live! (film), 239–40

J
Johnson, Harry, 96
Johnson, Regina, 86, 94, 96–98
joyrides, 21–22
Judd, Paul R., 370–71
"Judy". *See* Short, Lucy Ann
Justice and Caryl Chessman (film), 336–37
jute mill, San Quentin, 55

K
Kalin, Molly
    Chessman dictates letters/ articles to, 291, 298, 301
    testifies in trial transcript hearing, 249, 252, 275–76
Keating, Thomas, 189, 195, 269

Kennedy, John F., xxiv
Kessell, Albert, 327–30
kidnapping laws, 94, 95–96
The Kid Was a Killer (Chessman)
    Chessman rejects revisions of, 295–99
    confiscation of manuscript, 232, 235, 241, 256
    court action on sought, 274, 276
    Longstreth on manuscript, 278–80
    manuscript released, 277
    publication of, 316, 369
    rejected by publishers, 288–91
Kill Me If You Can (film), xvi, 239
Knight, Goodwin, 165, 184–85, 269–70
Knowles, David H., 78, 79, 80, 83, 84, 370–71
Kohls, Wanda, 320
Korean War, 129–30
Kunstler, William J., xxi–xxii, 85, 96, 187, 360, 363–64

L
Lacey, J. Mark, 104
Lamott, Kenneth, 45
Lancaster, Burt, xvi
Lea, Jarnigan, 86, 97, 99
Leavy, J. Miller
    Chessman documentary and, 337
    on denial of clemency, 319
    prosecutes Wein, 311
    prosecutor in Chessman trial, 93, 97, 105
    at transcript hearing, 282
    transcriptionist hired by, 190
Leopold, Nathan, 68
lethal injection, 331–32
Levittown, 127
library at San Quentin, 110, 111
Lill, Bessie, 276
Lindbergh kidnapping, 95–96
Lindbergh Law (Federal), 95–96
Lindley, William Marvin, 150
Linhart, Bill, 195–96, 372

Linn, Clarence, 219–20, 235
Linnarsson, Gudrun, 347
Little Big Feather (Longstreth), 268
Little Caesar (film), 32
Little Lindbergh Law (California Penal Code, Section 209), xx, 94–96, 132, 312
Longstreth, Joseph
    Bernice Freeman and, 164–66, 268
    on *Cell 2455, Death Row*, 185
    Cell 2455, Death Row disputes, 162–63, 171–75, 178
    Chessman relationship, 139, 145–46, 148–49, 152–54, 193–94
    Chessman's description of, 231
    Chessman's last letter to, xxvi–xxvii, 345–47
    on Chessman's life and death, 371
    children's' books by, 142, 147, 155, 268
    first contact from Chessman, 141–45
    on Hallie's influence, 19
    homosexuality of, 153–54, 314
    indictment for smuggling of *The Face of Justice*, 299–301, 314
    on *The Kid Was a Killer* manuscript, 278–80
    as librettist, 141, 147, 219
    as literary executor, 186, 342
    personal background, 146–49
    photograph of, 300
    Rosalie Asher and, 166
    on transcript proceedings, 253–54
    visits Chessman, 154–56, 161–64
    visits Chessman family, 163
Los Angeles
    Chessman supporters in, 211–12, 213
    criminal activity in 1940s, 69–74
    criminal underworld of, 75–77
Los Angeles County Jail, 271, 294
Los Angeles' Dead End Kids, 37
Los Angeles Police Department
    1939 purge of, 31
    corruption of, xviii–xix, 70–71, 74, 76–77
    motivation for railroading Chessman, 93
Los Angeles Times interview, 226–27
"Lost—A Last Chance at Life" (Chessman), 291

M
MacDonald, Wallace, 198
Machlin, Milton, 35, 77, 85, 88–89, 163
mail restrictions, 256–57
marijuana, 32–33
Matthews, Al, 96, 103–4, 119, 150, 237
May, Robert J., 79–81
McCarthy, Michael Burt, 360
McCauley, Norma, 307–8
McDougal, John, 43
McGee, Richard A., 144, 164–65, 217, 235
media depiction of Chessman, xxi, 294, 321–22, 381–82
Meza, Mary Alice, 87, 94, 99–102, 208–12
Monahan, Mabel, 237
Montgomery, Ed, 239–40
Mooney, Tom, 244–45
Morrison, Marion, 6
Moskowitz, Irwin, xiv, 117
murder-rapes in Los Angeles, 71–74
My Dark Places (Ellroy), 73

My Shadow Ran Fast (Sands), 51, 115–16
Mystery Writers of America, Inc., 234

N
Nazi gas chambers, 330–31
Negri, Pola, 7–8
Nelson, Louis S., 342, 364, 366
Nevada first to use gas chamber, 325–26
Nevens, Joe, 282–83
New, Ralph, 49, 329–30
New Horizons in Criminology (Barnes and Teeters), 326
newsclippings, 321–22
newspapers, in Los Angeles, 69–70
Ninth Life (Machlin and Woodfield), 35
Nixon, Richard, 129, 255, 304–5
Nov Smoz Kapop? (unpublished; Chessman), 141, 176, 231
Nye, Clement, 341

O
Old Spanish Prison, San Quentin, 45, 46
Olin, Douglas, 284
Olson, Frank, 254
O'Mara, George, 330
On the Yard (Braly), 378
Orwell, George, 132

P
Panasuk, Esther, 87
Parham, Joseph, 314
Parker, Frank J., xxi, xxv, 85, 93
Parkhurst, Helen, 377–78
Parslow, Phil, 37
Parsons, Louella O., 70, 197
Pasadena, CA, 10–12
Pearl Harbor, 63, 64
Perkins, Emmett, 237–38
Perry, Ernest R., 249–51
Perry, Ernest W., 125, 246, 275
Phillips, E. D., 80–81

Pierce, Robert O., 262–66
playwriting/screenwriting, 218–19, 237
Poole, Cecil, 183, 318
Posner, Paul, 276, 282, 298
pot dealer incident, 33
Powers, Francis Gary, 351
Prentice-Hall
    alters dedication to *Trial by Ordeal*, 243
    buys *Cell 2455, Death Row*, 145, 154
    publicity for *Trial by Ordeal*, 255
    rejects *The Kid Was a Killer*, 290
    royalty payments, 193, 209
    sells film rights for *Cell 2455, Death Row*, 196–99
Presley, Elvis, 254–55
Preston State Industrial School, 30, 33–34
prison conditions in 1850s, 43–44
prisoner strikes at San Quentin, 49, 184
The Private Papers of Henry Ryecroft (Gissling), 139
prostitution, in Los Angeles, 75
protests against Chessman execution, xi–xiii, xxiii, xxiv, 211, 351–56, 367. *See also* anti–capital punishment movement
Public Justice, Private Mercy: A Governor's Education on Death Row (Brown), 304
public opinion on execution, xi–xiii, xxiii, 320–22, 335–40, 351–56
Punta de Quentin, 44
pursesnatching, and Little Lindbergh Law, 95

R
rape-murders, in Los Angeles, 71–74

Reardon, John D., 79–81
Rebel Without a Cause (film), 199
recidivism, 38–39, 52–53
redemption of criminals, 375–78
Red Light Bandit
   arrest/trial of Chessman. *See* Chessman, Caryl, Red Light Bandit arrest/trial
   crimes, xvii–xviii, 85–87, 92, 97–98, 100–101
   true identity of, xiii–xiv, 87–92, 199, 370–71
Red Lipstick murder, 74
Rice, Berwyn A. "Ben"
   fired, 244
   hired, 187
   problems with, 189, 195–96, 201, 207–8
   results produced by, 189–90, 203
Richardson, Herbert H., 17–18, 213
Road Camp No. 7, 35–36
robberies, 30, 31–32, 37, 78
Robin Hood (film), 7
Robinson, Jackie, 6–7
Rockwell, George Lincoln, 7
Roosevelt, Franklin Delano, 16
Rosenberg executions, 212
Rutledge, Andrew, 37
Ryan, Art, 226–27

S
Saga article, 206–7, 216, 227–32
Salembier, René "Robert," 82
Salt of the Earth (film), 212
Sands, Bill
   Chessman friendship, 56, 60–61, 118–19
   Duffy and, 51–54
   on recidivism, 38–39
   recollections of Chessman, 115–16
San Francisco, in 1800s, 42–43
San Francisco Chronicle, 156, 157
San Francisco Examiner, 262, 264

San Quentin News, 50, 108–9
"San Quentin on the Air," 50
San Quentin State Prison
   Chessman at, 38–39, 54–61, 64, 66–67. *See also* Chessman, Caryl, on Death Row
   construction of, 41–46
   contributions to war effort by, 63–64
   history of, 57–60
   inmate authors, 110–11
   jute mill, 55
   library and writing programs at, 109–11
   prisoner strikes, 49, 184
   transformed into model prison by Duffy, 46–47, 49–51
The San Quentin Story (C. Duffy), 52, 333
Santo, Jack, 237–38
Sauer, Kearney, 100
scar evidence, 88, 91–92, 102
Schmidt, David G., 346, 379
Sears, Fred F., 198
Sereny, Gitta, 377
The Seventh Step (Sands), 38–39
Seventh Step Foundation, 118–19
Sewell, Wilber Power. *See* Sands, Bill
Sexton, Fred, 91–92
Sheppard, Samuel H., 204–6
Shire, Talia, xvi
Short, Elizabeth, 71–74
Short, Lucy Ann (Gaylord)
   Cell 2455, Death Row payment, 169
   daughter, 66, 67, 169, 201, 370, 372
   marriage to Chessman, 36–37, 66, 67
   named in will, 186
   reveals identity to press, 191–92
   visits Chessman, 204
short stories, 120, 123, 160, 231–32

Siegel, Benjamin Hymen "Bugsy," 31–32, 71, 75
Simpson, O. J., 80, 96
Smith, Court, 49, 329
Smith, Russell, 219
Sonny (teen bully), 19–21, 28–29
The Son of the Sheik (film), 7–8
South America, anti–capital punishment sentiment in, xiii, xxiii, 307, 317–18, 336
Spector, Herman K, 109–11
Spock, Benjamin, 127–28
Stanley, Leo Leonidas, 61–62, 63, 329
Starr, Kevin, 31
stays of execution
    Feb 29, 1952, 143, 376
    Jun 23, 1952, 130–31
    May 13, 1954, 189–90
    July 28, 1954, 202
    Jan 10, 1955, 223–26
    July 5, 1955, 241
    Oct 24, 1959, 320
    Feb 18, 1960, 335–36
    May 2, 1960, 361–63, 364
Stearns, Monroe, 162, 163, 171, 172, 197, 243
Steinbeck, John, 6
Stephens, Albert Lee, 130, 143
Stevens, Will, 365
Stevenson, Adlai, 255–56
Stoker, Charles, xviii, 70, 75–76, 85
Stone, Gerald, 87
Stone Building, San Quentin, 45
Streeter, Harold V., 363, 365
Stroud, Robert, xvi
suburbia, 127–28
Sutter, John Augustus, 41–42
Swiss Illustrated interview, 232–33

T
Taylor, William, 37, 38
Teeters, Negley K., 326
Teets, Harley O.
    challenges Chessman, 130–31, 133–34, 376
    Chessman on, 144

    death, 270
    denies Chessman permission to appear in film, 196–97
    description of, 171
    leniency with Chessman, 216–17
    Saga article and, 216, 227–28
    as warden of San Quentin, 47, 112
Terranova, Charles Saverine, 88–90, 370–71
Terranova, Ricci, 89–90
testicular implantation, 61–63
Thatcher, Phil, 68
These Places Called Prison (unfinished, Chessman), 176, 231
Thicker 'n Thieves (Stoker), 70
The Thief of Baghdad (film), 7
Thomas, J. Parnell, 129
Thorpe, John, 314
Tiger Tizzy (Longstreth), 142, 147, 155
Time cover, xii, xiii
Tollack, Robert, 37
Tolson, George, 349
transcript of trial. *See* trial transcript
Trial by Ordeal (Chessman)
    Chessman transformation described in, 131–32
    clearance for publication, 241
    confiscation of manuscript, 235
    publication of, 241
    reception of, 242–43, 255
    remaindered, 267
    smuggled out of San Quentin, 236, 242
    writing of, 195, 217–18
trial of Chessman for Red Light Bandit crimes. *See* Chessman, Caryl, Red Light Bandit arrest/trial
trial transcript
    hearings on, 249–53, 271–76, 277–78, 281–83

shorthand transcription of, 125, 150–51, 246, 249
True magazine story, 267–68
Trumbo, Dalton, 129, 212
Tully, Red, 59, 158
Turner, Delos A., 325

U

U.S. State Department, xxiii, 307, 336
U.S. Supreme Court, 215, 241, 247, 271, 303, 323
U-2 incident, 351–52
Uruguay, support for Chessman in, xxiii, 307, 336

V

Valentino, Rudolph, 7–8
Vallejo, Mariano Guadalupe, 43
Victoria (aunt), 2, 13
Villon, François, 140, 376, 381
Virginia (girlfriend), 23–27
"A Voice from Death Row" (Chessman), 160

W

Wabau (prison ship), 43, 44, 45
Wade, Lawrence, 316
Wald, Jerry, 197, 198
Walker, Herbert V., 272, 316
Wallace, Henry A., 128
Wampler, William, 370–71
Wanger, Walter, 81–82, 145–46, 280
Want Ad Rapist, 311–13

Warden's Wife (G. Duffy), 52
Warren, Earl, 114
Wayne, John, 6
Webb, Jack, 73
Web site on Chessman, 92
Weeks, Paul, 191
Wein, Edward Simon, 311–13
Weissich, William O., 299–301, 314
Wells, Wesley, 183–84
"What I Would Do with My Life" (Chessman), 206–7, 216, 227–32
Whittier, John Greenleaf, 4
The Wild One (film), 199
Williams, Stanley "Tookie," 332
Wirin, Abraham Lincoln "Al," 276, 282, 298
Woodfield, William Read, 35, 77, 85, 88–89, 92
World War II, 63–64
writing ban for prisoners, 234–35, 241, 244, 256
writing classes at San Quentin, 109–11

Y

"Young Man with a Right Hand" (Chessman), 232

Z

Ziferstein, Dan, 6, 23, 211–12, 356, 369–70
Ziferstein, Gail, 356, 369